DISSERTATIONS IN NINETEENTH-CENTURY AMERICAN POLITICAL AND SOCIAL HISTORY

Editor
RONALD P. FORMISANO
Clark University

A Garland Series

The Culture of the Press in the Early Republic

Cincinnati, 1793–1848

JOHN NERONE

GARLAND PUBLISHING, INC.
NEW YORK & LONDON 1989

Library of Congress Cataloging-in-Publication Data

Nerone, John C.
[Press and popular culture in the early republic—Cincinnati,
1793–1848]
The culture of the press in the early republic—Cincinnati, 1793–1848/
John Nerone.
p. cm.—(Dissertations in nineteenth-century American political and
social history)
Reprint of the author's thesis (Ph.D.—University of Notre Dame, 1982)
Originally presented under title: The press and popular culture in the
early republic—Cincinnati, 1793–1848.
Includes bibliographical references.
ISBN 0–8240–4070–8 (alk. paper)
1. Press—Ohio—Cincinnati—History—18th century.   2. American
newspapers—Ohio—Cincinnati—History—18th century.
3. Journalism—Social aspects—Ohio—Cincinnati—History—
18th century.   4. Cincinnati (Ohio)—Intellectual life—History—
18th century.   I. Title.   II. Series.
PN4899.C53N47   1989
071'.7178—dc20   89–36552

Printed on acid-free, 250-year-life paper
Manufactured in the United States of America

ACKNOWLEDGMENTS

This study began as a doctoral dissertation in U.S. history at the University of Notre Dame. It has been greatly revised since then, though in the main the findings remain the same. Much of the revision is the result of thoughtful comments from readers, especially Nathan Hatch, Robert Schmuhl, Robert Kerby, Michael Schudson, and William Gilmore. Thanks are also due to colleagues in the College of Communications at the University of Illinois, especially Kevin Barnhurst, Ellen Wartella, and Chuck Whitney, and to the staffs of the Cincinnati Public Library and libraries at the Cincinnati Historical Society, the University of Notre Dame, the University of Cincinnati, the University of Illinois, and the University of Nebraska. Invaluable assistance in the preparation of several drafts came from Jon Bekken, Anita Specht, and Diane Tipps.

CONTENTS

Introduction   1

I: The Cincinnati Press Establishment, 1793–1848   23

II: The Transformation of the Press, 1820–1848   63

III: The Press and Political Culture, 1793–1820   99

IV: The Press and Political Culture, 1820–1848   131

V: Religious and Literary Periodicals   179

VI: The Press, Science, and the Professions   228

VII: The Press, Individualism, and Reform   257

Conclusion   283

Bibliography   290

Introduction

Only by the most brutal surgery, therefore, can social communication be separated from society, and when the operation is complete, both parts of the organism are dead. For the facilities of communication are part of the living structure of society, and the act of communication is part of the living function of society. Communication grows and changes with society because it is something society does. It is a way society lives.
—Wilbur Schramm[1]

A society is possible in the last analysis because the individuals in it carry around in their heads some sort of picture of that society.
—Louis Wirth[2]

Ways of communicating are fundamental to any society. The patterns and practices of transmitting and presenting ideas, information, and all kinds of messages are inseparable parts of the constitution of any society, and are crucial to that society's self-definition. This is especially true of the early national period of U.S. history, when an essentially artificial polity placed unprecedented emphasis on achieving social and political coherence through the development of transportation and communications systems. Indeed, understanding communications is central to explaining culture, politics, or society in the early Republic.

[1]Wilbur Schramm, "Communication Development and the Development Process," in Lucian W. Pye, ed., *Communication and Political Development* (Princeton: Princeton University Press, 1963), p. 35.
[2]Louis Wirth, "Preface," in Karl Mannheim, *Ideology and Utopia: An Introduction to the Sociology of Knowledge* (New York: Harcourt, Brace & World, 1936), xxiii.

1

This book is an attempt to study print communication in the early Republic in terms of its role in the development of distinctive modes of social, cultural, and political activity. Before beginning this specific study, though, it is appropriate to try to place it within a scholarly context.

The Historiography of U.S. Culture and Communications

Traditionally, histories of U.S. communications have fallen into several genres that together comprise a "field" called journalism history. The main genres of journalism history are comprehensive histories, biographies of individual newspapers and newspaper conductors, issue-oriented studies, and sociological studies. The first two genres are mainly concerned with the development of modern journalism; the third is concerned with political history; the final one is concerned with the function of the newspaper in society.

Comprehensive histories in general seek to record the background and development of U.S. daily newspapers.[3] Often written by career journalists, these treatments might best be described as textbooks for the standard history courses that are taught in colleges of journalism.

On a narrower level, the most common type of journalism history is the biography. The great newspapers and the most famous editors and journalists have proven to be congenial topics for biographical treatments.[4]

---

[3]The most important of these comprehensive histories are: Frederic Hudson, *Journalism in the United States: From 1690 to 1872* (New York, 1873); S.N.D. North, *History and Present Condition of the Newspaper and Periodical Press of the United States* (Washington, D.C., 1884); Willard G. Bleyer, *Main Currents in the History of American Journalism* (Boston: Houghton-Mifflin, 1927); Frank Luther Mott, *American Journalism: A History* 3rd ed. (New York: MacMillan, 1962; first published in 1940); Edwin Emery and Michael B. Emery, *The Press and America: An Interpretive History of the Mass Media*, 5th ed. (Englewood Cliffs NJ: Prentice-Hall, 1984; first published in 1954).

[4]Some of the better biographical treatments are Glyndon Van Deusen, *Horace Greeley: Nineteenth-Century Reformer* (Philadelphia: University of Pennsylvania Press, 1953); W.A. Swanberg, *Pulitzer* (New York: Scribner's, 1967); Norval Neil Luxon, *Niles' Weekly Register* (Baton Rouge: Louisiana State University Press, 1947); William Ames, *A History of the National Intelligencer* (Chapel Hill: University of North Carolina Press, 1972).

These treatments are the bricks, as it were, of which the house of journalism history has been built.

Through comprehensive and biographical studies, a paradigm of journalism history was constructed. This paradigm emphasized the role that the great men of American journalism played in the development of the independent objective newspaper, and highlighted the contributions that the American newspaper made in the achievement of personal liberty and political democracy. This paradigm has been described as a "Whig" or "Progressive" history.[5]

This sort of history has been recognized as having several shortcomings.[6] First, it tends to introduce several biases into our record of the past. It is frankly concerned with the lineage of contemporary newspaper practices, and thus concentrates on successful innovation, ignoring much of what must have been common newspaper practice in the past. It concentrates on the exceptional—especially those relatively few newspapers and newspaper conductors who can receive extended biographical treatment—so that the average newspaper never really emerges from the shadows of the "great men." It imposes contemporary genres on the past, so that genres that have no contemporary equivalent are ignored or distorted—a good example of this is the slighting of the weekly newspaper as a serious news medium. At its worst, Whig or Progressive journalism history became an anecdotal treatment of a series of famous editors and their papers, especially the New York dailies—Bennett's *Herald*, Greeley's *Tribune*, Pulitzer's *World*, Ochs' *Times*, Hearst's *Journal*.

Even at its best, though, journalism history of this sort has had to wrestle with a serious conceptual problem precisely because it seeks to describe the history of journalism as though journalism were a thing in itself, an independent actor on the stage of history. Inevitably, a tendency arises to

[5]James W. Carey, "The Problem of Journalism History," *Journalism History* 1 (1974), pp. 3–5, 27; Joseph McKerns, "The Limits of Progressive Journalism History," *Journalism History* 4 (1977), pp. 88–92.

[6]A brief list of historiographical criticism of this sort, which has flourished since the 1970s, would include Carey, "Problem"; McKerns, "Limit"; Garth S. Jowett, "Toward a History of Communication," *Journalism History* 2(1975), pp. 34–7; J. Herbert Altschull, "Journalism History: Mediacentric or . . . . ," *Mass Communication Review* 5(1978), pp. 2–8; and Hazel Dicken Garcia's chapters in Dicken Garcia and John D. Stevens, *Communication History* (Beverly Hills: Sage, 1980).

discuss the newspaper *in vacuo*: isolated from other forms of communication and isolated from a larger social and cultural context.[7]

The third main genre of journalism history is the issue-oriented study.[8] Issue-oriented studies focus on a specific cotroversy and recount the contributions of newspapers to the development of opinion in that controversy. It is clear that these studies are less present-minded than other types of journalism history. This genre also implies that the real object of study is not the newspaper or medium itself but public opinion. Such studies are not necessarily then "mediacentric." But they still tend to present a skewed view of the medium in the past, because the medium is treated as though it consisted essentially of editorial opinion, and because this editorial opinion is seen as having a direct and unambiguous effect upon public opinion. Again, the tendency is to look upon the newspaper as an independent political and intellectual agent, something that influences (and may be influenced by) public opinion, but something that is removed from a larger social and cultural environment.

The fourth main genre of journalism history, the sociological study, achieved its first major expression in the works of Robert Ezra Park and Alfred McClung Lee. Park called for a "Natural History of the Newspaper" and Lee sought to describe the evolution of the newspaper as a "social instrument.[9] This sociological history is more pertinent to the present study.

The crucial insight of Park and Lee is that the newspaper is a creature of its environment. They incorporated a Darwinian evolutionism in their work, depicting newspaper history as the natural selection of mutations in editorial policy through a competition for means of support. In the case of the daily newspaper, the crucial means of support was circulation.

---

[7]Altschull, "Mediacentric," argues that this is the central tendency of conventional journalism history.

[8]Typical issue–oriented studies include Arthur M. Schlesinger, Sr., *Prelude to Independence: The Newspaper War on Britain, 1764–1776* (New York: Knopf, 1957); Donald E Reynolds, *Editors Make War: Southern Newspapers in the Secession Crisis* (Nashville: Vanderbilt University Press, 1970); and Jeffery A. Smith, *Printers and Press Freedom: The Ideology of Early American Journalism* (New York: Oxford University Press, 1988)

[9]Robert E. Park, "The Natural History of the Newspaper," *American Journal of Sociology* (1923), pp. 80–98; Alfred McClung Lee, *The Daily Newspaper in America: The Evolution of a Social Instrument* (New York: MacMillan, 1937).

This Darwinian outlook had both good and bad results. It forced the historian to focus on the environment, hence broadening the perspective of journalism history. But it also encouraged a bias toward innovation, and hence the exceptional, and it emphasized the competitive aspects of journalism history.

I have described—some might say caricatured—the main genres of journalism history in order to clarify the need for new approaches to the history of communication.[10] We can conclude from this brief treatment that new approaches should contain three key ingredients:

An environmental approach. Communication developed in terms of a social and cultural environment that encompassed and informed it.

An awareness of the functional nature of the media. A medium is essentially *a relationship or a combination of relationships,* it is not a thing in itself. The history of any medium is a history of changing relationships, and that history will always be in part a function of the elements that the medium "connects." If for instance we use the biological metaphor of communications as the nervous system of society, as is common, then we must keep in mind that the nervous system can exist only within and as a part of a larger living organism.

A cultural approach. Any medium of communication operates through the transmission of information and opinions, which in turn derive whatever meaning or impact they have from cultural values. Media are by their nature cultural or intellectual; no understanding of the media in the past can be

---

[10]Some of the more notable recent works that take new approaches to the history of communication are Allan Pred, *Urban Growth and the Circulation of Information: The United States System of Cities, 1790–1840* (Cambridge: Harvard University Press, 1973), which studies the geography of information diffusion; Michael Schudson, *Discovering the News: A Social History of American Newspapers* (New York: Harper, 1978), which discusses, among other things, the relationships between social and economic development and newspaper styles; Daniel Czitrom, *Media and the American Mind: From Morse to McLuhan* (Chapel Hill: University of North Carolina Press, 1981), which examines both popular and academic ideas concerning the media; Dan Schiller, *Objectivity and the News: The Public and the Rise of Commercial Journalism* (Philadelphia: University of Pennsylvania Press, 1981), which discusses the connection between the rise of a commercial press in the U.S. and the rise of objectivity; and Thomas C. Leonard, *The Power of the Press: The Birth of American Political Reporting* (New York: Oxford University Press, 1986) which discusses key moments in the development of styles of reporting in U.S. daily newspapers.

achieved apart from the cultural milieu that gave them meaning. (It should be noted that, just as a study of the media should include a study of ideas and values, so should any study of ideas and values include a study of the media through which they are expressed.)

An appropriate genre for such an approach to the history of communications is the local study. Intensive local study will permit attention to environment, both social and cultural, and an analysis of the way means of communication functioned in terms of social, political, and cultural activities. Moreover, a local study permits treatment of a much wider variety of media. It is not possible to study every newspaper and periodical published in the United States over any considerable period of time, but it is possible to study every newspaper and periodical published in a single city.

This work is also intended to be an attempt to come to terms with the problems of writing U.S. cultural history in general. It was begun as a study primarily in cultural history; my interest in the media was a result of a desire to find some concrete grounding for discussion of U.S. culture. Some elaboration here would be useful.

Up until a few decades ago, scholars in the U.S. generalized confidently about the nation's culture. Terms like "the American character" were employed to explain the apparently unique course of U.S. development, and intellectual or cultural history held more prestige and seemed more timely to historians—especially following World War II. This confidence has not survived.

In recent years, historians of U.S. culture have had to deal with a number of challenges.[11] Most important have been the challenges rooted in social history, which are various. Social history's emphasis on dense description of the local and concrete has contradicted cultural history's earlier tendency to generalize on a national level. Social history's emphasis on daily life and studying society from the bottom up has contradicted cultural history's

---

[11]For good accounts of and comments on the state of cultural or intellectual history, see Paul K. Conkin and John Higham, eds., *New Directions in American Intellectual History* (Baltimore: Johns Hopkins University Press, 1979); Robert Darnton, "Intellectual and Cultural History," in Michael Kammen, ed., *The Past Before Us: Contemporary Historical Writing in the United States* (Ithaca NY: Cornell University Press, 1980), pp. 327–54; and John E. Toews, "Intellectual History After the Linguistic Turn," *American Historical Review* 92 (1987) pp. 879–907.

earlier tendency to dwell on persistent themes, timeless issues, and the formulations of elite figures. Social history's emphasis on matters like fertility, family structure, property-holding, and social and occupational mobility has implied that the bases of historical change are material and not cultural, whereas the implication of cultural history has traditionally been the opposite. Thus the success of social history in the 1960s and 1970s called into question the value of doing cultural history.

But the problems of cultural history ran deeper than competition from other styles and interests. In fact, the challenge of social history demonstrated that cultural historians had been reluctant to articulate the theory behind their work. What, after all, did one mean by the term "American culture?"[12] Were appeals to the American character simply mythical? Or could this style of writing be shown to make sense to a more demanding scholarly world?

It is clear that two distinct problems were posed here. The first was one of definition. Cultural historians had to clarify what it is they claim to study and construct coherent theories to justify their methods and practices. The second problem was one of demonstration. Cultural historians had to find ways to show cultures (however defined) in action, changing over time and informing lived experience.

Several strategies have been employed in response. By way of definition, cultural historians have been attracted to recent trends in anthropology, especially as presented in the work of Clifford Geertz;[13] or to concepts like ideology;[14] hegemony,[15] or *mentalité*;[16] or to theories of literary criticism;[17]

---

[12]Though this issue had been addressed from time to time: see especially Caroline Ware, ed., *The Cultural Approach to History* (New York: Columbia University Press, 1940).

[13]Clifford Geertz, *The Interpretation of Cultures: Selected Essays* (New York: Basic Books, 1973).

[14]Bernard Bailyn, *The Ideological Origins of the American Revolution* (Cambridge: Harvard University Press, 1967); Gordon Wood, *The Creation of the American Republic, 1776–1787* (Chapel Hill: University of North Carolina Press, 1969); Lance Banning, *The Jeffersonian Persuasion: Evolution of a Party Ideology* (Ithaca NY: Cornell University Press, 1978).

[15]T.J. Jackson Lears, "The Concept of Cultural Hegemony: Problems and Possibilities," *American Historical Review* 90 (1985), pp. 567–93. For a concrete application, see Lears, "From Salvation to Self Realization: Advertising and the Roots of the Consumer Culture, 1880–1930," in Lears and Richard Wrightman Fox, eds., *The*

or to the study of language (especially political language),[18] or to psychology.[19] As a result, cultural history seems to be developing a vocabulary of its own, an amalgam of Marx and Gramsci, Roland Barthes and Michel Foucault, Weber and Veblen. To skeptics it will seem that what this attention to theory has led to is the substitution for vague terms like "democracy" and "American character" of still vague but more arcane terms like "discourse," "*mentalité*," and "intertextuality." After all, theoretical sophistication was only part of the problem.

The other part was demonstration. And here cultural historians have shown great ingenuity, uncovering novel source material,[20] grounding

Culture of Consumption: Critical Essays in American History, 1880–1980 (New York: Pantheon, 1983), pp. 1–38. A well–known but problematical application of Gramscian hegemony theory is in Eugene D. Genovese, *Roll Jordan Roll: The World the Slaves Made* (New York: Pantheon, 1974). Genovese has been taken to task by John Patrick Diggins in "Comrades and Citizens: New Mythologies in American Historiography," *American Historical Review* 90 (1985), pp. 619–23.

[16]On *mentalite*, see Patrick H. Hutton, "The History of Mentalities: The New Map of Cultural History," *History and Theory* 20 (1981), pp. 237–59.

[17]A relevant example is David R. Papke, *Framing the Criminal: Crime, Cultural Work, and the Loss of Critical Perspective, 1830–1900* (Hamden CT: Archon Books, 1987).

[18]J.G.A. Pocock, *Politics, Language, and Time: Essays on Political Thought and History* (New York: Atheneum, 1971); Quentin Skinner, "Meaning and Understanding in the History of Ideas," *History and Theory* 8 (1969), pp. 3–53; Bailyn, *Ideological Origins*; Wood, *Creation*.

[19]Peter Gay discusses psychohistory in *Freud for Historians* (New York: Oxford University Press, 1985). See also Thomas Kohut, "Psychohistory as History," *American Historical Review* 91 (1986), pp. 336–54. A good example of the promises and perils of cultural history is Philip Greven, *The Protestant Temperament: Patterns of Child-Rearing, Religious Experience, and the Self in Early America* (New York: Knopf, 1977). A more tempered but no less sweeping application of psychology to cultural history is Ronald T. Takaki, *Iron Cages: Race and Culture in Nineteenth-Century America* (New York: Knopf, 1979).

[20]For instance, Lawrence Levine's use of hymns and popular music in *Black Culture and Black Consciousness: Afro-American Folk Thought from Slavery to Freedom* (New York: Oxford University Press, 1977) and Lewis Saum's study of diaries and letters of undistinguished people in *The Popular Mood of Pre-Civil War America* (Westport CT: Greenwood Press, 1980).

studies in local society,[21] or in specific classes within society,[22] or—most pertinent to this particular work—discussing ideas within the context of the media of idea-transmission.[23] The overall effect of these studies is to underscore how culture is embedded, whether in everyday life or in local society or in specific media.

The work that follows is intended to be very much within this new tradition of cultural history. It seeks to discuss a culture—what the title identifies as the "culture of the press"—by grounding it in a particular society and a particular set of media. It might thus be read in the context of current trends in both cultural history and journalism history.

This study will focus on print communication in Cincinnati from 1793 to 1848. It will examine American culture at a time when newspapers and periodicals were irreplaceable media for the transmission of social ideas. The significance of the press in this period is underscored by Alexis de Tocqueville, who, in noting the breakdown of traditional forms of associational cohesion in the fluid society of the early Republic, remarked that "the more equal men become and the more individualism becomes a menace, the more necessary are newspapers. We should underrate their importance if we thought they just guaranteed liberty; they maintain civilization."[24]

U.S. society was most attenuated in the new communities of the trans-Appalachian west. Here settlers faced the task of creating a polity *de novo*, and reliance on print communication was more notable. Historian Richard Wade referred to the press in the early west as "the most important unifying

[21]The most notable example being Rhys Isaac, *The Transformation of Virginia: Community, Religion, and Authority, 1740–1790* (Chapel Hill: University of North Carolina Press, 1982).

[22]For example, Eric Foner, *Tom Paine and Revolutionary America* (New York: Oxford University Press, 1976); Sean Wilentz, *Chants Democratic: New York City and the Rise of the American Working Class, 1788–1850* (New York: Oxford University Press, 1984).

[23]For example, Harry Stout, *The New England Soul: Preaching and Religious Culture in Colonial New England* (New York: Oxford University Press, 1986); Susan Davis, *Parades and Power: Street Theatre in Nineteenth-Century Philadelphia* (Philadelphia: Temple University Press, 1986).

[24]Alexis de Tocqueville, *Democracy in America*, George Lawrence, tr., (New York: Doubleday, 1969), p. 517.

element of urban culture, . . . a plumb line which touched all levels of society."[25] A rigorous study of early western press could be very revealing.

The Centrality of the Early Western Press

The early western newspaper was much more than a newspaper. Mrs. Trollope, who (for good or ill) based many of her opinions concerning U.S. society on her experiences in Cincinnati, considered the "universal reading of newspapers" the only exception to an otherwise complete absence of popular literary culture. It was because of its lonely status, she inferred, "that every *American newspaper* is more or less a magazine . . . ."[26]

Until the development of specialized literary periodicals in the 1820s, Cincinnati's newspapers were its only regular outlets for creative literature. Obligingly, most newspapers carried a column of poetry and *belles lettres*, often with pretentious titles like "Parnassiad" or "Seat of the Muses." The surprising frequency with which attempts at literature are found in these papers attests to their significance as literary organs.[27]

The newspaper office in a young community was the center of all publication ventures. Proprietors of newspapers issued almanacs and published books; they also served as retailers of books and magazines. The early newspaper office was the conduit for virtually all print communications.[28]

From this position of influence, the newspaper figured prominently in the larger life of the community. The newspapers in the west campaigned vigorously and unanimously for improvements in transportation, helping to usher in the canal era. They were also effective in encouraging extension and improvement of the postal system, a cause of no little interest to enterprises which relied on the mails for a steady supply of information through exchange papers.

[25]Richard C. Wade, *The Urban Frontier: The Rise of Western Cities, 1790–1830* (Cambridge: Harvard University Press, 1959), p. 130.

[26]Frances Trollope, *Domestic Manners of the Americans*, Donald Smalley, ed., (New York: Knopf, 1949), pp. 92–3.

[27]William H. Venable, *Beginnings of Literary Culture in the Ohio Valley: Historical and Biographical Sketches* (1891; repr. New York: Peter Smith, 1949), pp. 92–3.

[28]*Ibid.*, pp. 50–2.

Communication has been called "the neural system of organization."[29] In the early Republic, a society otherwise virtually invertebrate, the press played a crucial role in associational life. Organizations of every variety—religious, educational, political, reform, ethnic, literary, commercial, even historical—relied on periodicals for communication. The press was the backbone of associational life.[30]

The significance of the press was enhanced—especially in remote communities—by the absence of any rival medium of information-transmission. All national political news was disseminated through the press, and the authority consequently attributed to a newspaper item is made dramatically clear by the example of a newspaper hoax. It is not too difficult to find intentional falsehoods in early papers. A few weeks before the election of 1800, for instance, a newspaper printed a report of the death of Thomas Jefferson. Issues of this paper circulated through the mail, the story was reprinted from paper to paper, and in some areas it was weeks before the news could be definitely disproven.[31] The credibility accorded to the printed word, even the apparent stratagem of a disgruntled Federalist, would be further indicated in the controversy over slavery. Slaveowner's fears of abolitionist literature and slave literacy are also vital testimony to the perceived power of the printed word. Even in situations where actual readership was highly questionable–few slaves could have read antislavery newspapers like the *Liberator*–the power of the press was assumed to be immense.

[29]Daniel Lerner, "Notes on Communication and the Nation State," *Public Opinion Quarterly* 37 (Winter, 1973–4), p. 541.

[30]The role of the press in associational life in the early Republic is discussed in Tocqueville, *Democracy in America*, pp. 517–25.

[31]*Western Spy*, July 16, 1800.

The Ideology of the Early Press: Impartiality and Impersonality

The perceived importance of the press in the early Republic was a bequest of the eighteenth century. The role of the press in the American Revolution is well known:[32] insofar as that movement achieved widespread popular support through the diffusion of political ideas, insofar as it was a case of mobilizing and informing public opinion, its success hinged on the effective use of the press. There is an aptness to the fact that the characteristic figure of the American Enlightenment, Benjamin Franklin, was a printer, and that Thomas Jefferson, the author of the Declaration of Independence, was also America's foremost apologist for freedom of the press.

Jefferson articulated a commonly held belief in the power of public opinion. A populace enlightened by a free press could never fall victim to the duplicity or machinations of politicians.[33] Hence, in a list of principles "vitally essential to the protection of the life, liberty, property, and safety of the citizen," Jefferson included

Freedom of the press, subject only to liabilities for personal injuries. This formidable censure of public functionaries, by arraigning them at the tribunal of public opinion, produces reform peacably, which must otherwise be done by revolution. It is also the best instrument of enlightening the mind of man, and improving him as a rational, moral, and social being.[34]

To Jefferson, and to many of his contempories, the free flow of information, particularly through newspapers, was essential to informed public opinion, which was in turn essential to successful republican government. His eloquent formulation of this attitude will bear quotation at length:

[32]Schlesinger, *Prelude to Independence*; Philip Davidson, *Propaganda and the American Revolution, 1763–1783* (Chapel Hill: University of North Carolina Press, 1941); Bernard Bailyn and John B. Hench, ed., *The Press & the American Revolution* (Worcester: American Antiquarian Society, 1980); Smith, *Printers and Press Freedom*.

[33]Frank Luther Mott, *Jefferson and the Press* (Baton Rouge: Louisiana State University Press, 1947), pp. 4–8 *et passim*.

[34]Thomas Jefferson to Monsieur A. Coray, Oct. 31, 1823, in Andrew A. Lipscomb, ed., *The Writings of Thomas Jefferson* 20 vols. (Washington: Thomas Jefferson Memorial Association, 1905), XV, p. 489.

The basis of our government being the opinion of the people, the very first object should be to keep that right; and were it left to me to decide whether we should have a government without newspapers, or newspapers without a government, I would not hesitate a moment to prefer the latter. But I should mean that every man should receive these papers, and be capable of reading them. I am convinced that those societies (as the Indians) which live without government, enjoy in their mass an infinitely greater degree of happiness than those who live under the European governments. Among the former, public opinion is in the place of law . . . . Cherish, therefore, the spirit of the people, and keep alive their attention. Do not be too severe upon their errors, but reclaim them by enlightening them. If once they become inattentive to public affairs, you and I, and Congress and Assemblies, Judges and Governors, shall all become wolves.[35]

The dominant characterization of the press here is as the guardian of popular rights against the encroachments of selfish, currupt, and arbitrary power. Yet, underlying this negative definition, is a clearly implied description of the positive function of the press: it is the means of re-establishing the rule of public opinion "in the place of law," of returning to the pristine republicanism of face-to-face societies. Enlightenment of the public through the press was the key to the Garden of Eden.

The idea of the press elucidated by Jefferson, a legacy of the Enlightenment and the American Revolution, showed a sensitivity to the fundamental role of communications in the structure and operation of politics and society in general. Just as face-to-face communication was the characteristic neural system of the primitive body politic, so the press would function in the modern republic. To function effectively, however, the press would have to exercise considerable restraint.

Conductors of newspapers inherited great responsibilities in their self-assumed capacity as "the daily TEACHER"[36] and the "secular Priest."[37] Printers and editors cogently argued for the value of newspapers in a republic by proclaiming that "Intelligence is the Life of Liberty";[38] at the same time, however, they incurred the duty of reporting intelligently. The press

[35]Jefferson to Col. Edw. Carrington, Jan. 16, 1787, *Ibid.*, VI, 57–8.

[36]Rev. G. D. Abbott, *Weekly Liberty Hall and Cincinnati Gazette*, Dec. 5, 1844.

[37]Daniel Aaron, "Cincinnati, 1818–1838: A Study of Attitudes" (Unpublished doctoral dissertation, Harvard University, 1943), p. 358.

[38]*National Republican and Ohio Political Register*, Nov. 5, 1824.

was to be a public servant:[39] "the press is the prime minister" of public opinion, which is in turn "the constitutional, and the only sovereign, in every democratic or republican community."[40]

The idea of the press as public servant implied an ideal of impartiality. Benjamin Franklin argued as early as 1731 that the printer should disregard his personal views in presenting news and opinions to the public.[41] This ideal of impartial conduct was ignored regularly during the Revolution and the Federalist era,[42] but it remained a theme in the American press ideology. Its durability is apparent in the fact that Cincinnati's first newspaper, the *Centinel of the North-Western Territory*, appearing in 1793, adopted as its motto a standard formulation of this notion, "Open to all Parties, but Influenced by None." Even after Cincinnati newspapers became avowedly partisan, there was a felt need for press conductors to disavow personal interests. Thus the editors of a pro-Adams campaign monthly in 1828, in homage to the trappings of impartiality, declined "to blazon their names to the public," and insisted that "They are not '*stipendiary advocates*,' but are '*principled partizans*,'" stimulated to action solely by a sense of duty to inform the public.[43]

Impartiality in the conduct of the press implied an intelligent readership. Faced with a choice between right or wrong facts or opinions, such a public would instinctively choose the right. The public was thought to be a wise consumer in the marketplace of ideas. This belief, as Tocqueville observed, is central to the dogma of the sovereignty of the people: "When each man is given the right to rule society, clearly one must recognize his capacity to choose between different opinions debated among his contemporaries and to appreciate the various facts that may guide his judgment."[44] Neither editors

---

[39]Culver Smith, *The Press, Politics, and Patronage: The American Government's Use of Newspapers, 1789–1875* (Athens, GA: University of Georgia Press, 1977), p. 4.

[40]*Literary Cadet*, March 9, 1820.

[41]Benjamin Franklin, "An Apology for Printers" (1731), in Leonard W. Labaree, ed., *The Papers of Benjamin Franklin* (New Haven: Yale University Press, 1959), I, 194–99.

[42]Donald H. Stewart, *The Opposition Press of the Federalist Period* (Albany: State University of New York Press, 1969).

[43]"Address," *Truth's Advocate and Monthly Anti-Jackson Expositor*, I (Jan., 1828), pp. 3–4.

[44]Tocqueville, *Democracy in America*, p. 181.

nor printers, politicians nor social elites, need do the thinking for the enlightened populace of a republic.

Faith in the wisdom of the people may be held in part to blame for the erosion of scrupulous impartiality as an ideal in the conduct of the press. Thus despite repeated diatribes against "Party Spirit,"[45] the belief that "it is one of the blessings of a free press, that it corrects its own errors and licentiousness," that errors of opinion "May safely be tolerated, when the same engine can be wielded to counteract its own bad effects,"[46] clearly removed the burden of impartiality from the backs of press conductors. The ideal of public service became in effect a conditional thing, a matter subject to interpretation.

Another legacy of the eighteenth century was an ideal of impersonality. This ideal functioned on two levels. First, the personality of the printer or editor was not expected to intrude in the impartial transmission of information or opinions. Second, the press was to avoid *ad hominem* attacks. The political violence of the Revolution and the Federalist era violated this ideal of impersonality, but did not overturn it. "Personalities" in the press were still considered misconduct, and were exceptions to the rule of impersonality. Indeed, the raucous conflict of the late eighteenth century was temporary, and seems to have been concentrated among a small but highly visible class of newspapers not really representative of the American press as a whole. Regardless, it is clear that in some parts of the country remote from the urban centers of the east, the ideal of impersonality remained in force well into the nineteenth century.

In Cincinnati in the late eighteenth and early nineteenth centuries, the press was not integrated into a national party structure. Newspapers there remained non-aligned into the 1820s, and for a time thereafter refused to deal in personal abuse. The prospectus of the *Liberty Hall and Cincinnati Mercury* in 1804, while announcing that paper's openness to communications of any sort, nevertheless protested "against the admission of every low, mean, indelicate invective, and every species of vulgarism both in sentiment and expression."[47] The prospectus of the *Inquisitor and*

---

[45]See, for example, *Western Spy*, May 28, 1799, Oct 29, 1800, and Feb. 6, 1802.
[46]*Literary Cadet*, Feb. 3, 1820.
[47]*Liberty Hall and Cincinnati Mercury*, Dec. 4, 1804.

Cincinnati Advertiser in 1818 reiterated this attitude, adding that "the welfare of the country will always be better consulted by a rational and deliberate examination of public affairs.[48]

Changes in the Press

Yet the press had changed remarkably in the early decades of the nineteenth century. This transformation of the press was characterized by availability, both to readers and to would-be manipulators. By 1828, the Cincinnati press was overwhelmingly partisan, and *ad hominem* attacks among the editorial corps were quite common. The doctrine of impersonality had been breached.

The response to this new brashness in the press emphasized its wide readership and immense moral influence. The British traveler Frederick Marryat noted in his diary "that newspapers are vended at a very low price throughout the states, and that the support of a major portion of them is derived from the ignorant and lower classes. Every man in America reads his newspaper . . . ."[49] The French traveler Chevalier noted that traditional authority figures in the United States had "no greater power than is allowed to minors, women and idiots."[50] Though he undoubtedly underestimated the influence of elites and women (and perhaps idiots), Chevalier correctly described the vacuum of recognized authority in Jacksonian America. According to the evolving ideology of the press, values were left to compete in the marketplace of ideas. But some began to question the wisdom of the consumer. Marryat noted that "People are too apt to imagine that newspapers echo their own feelings, when the fact is that by taking in a paper, which upholds certain opinions, the readers are, by daily repetition, become so impressed with these opinions, that they have become slaves to them."[51] It was thus argued that the power to enlighten was also the power to enslave.

---

[48]*Inquisitor and Cincinnati Advertiser*, June 23, 1818.

[49]Frederick Marryat, *A Diary in America, with Remarks on its Institutions*, Sydney Jackman, ed., (New York: Knopf, 1962), pp. 410–11.

[50]Michel Chevalier, *Society, Manners, and Politics in the United States: Letters on North America*, John William Ward, ed., (Gloucester, Mass.: Peter Smith, 1967), p. 182.

[51]Marryat, *Diary*, pp. 410–11.

By the late 1820s, a deep ambivalence became apparent in the images of the press found in newspapers and periodicals. John P. Foote, writing in the *Cincinnati Literary Gazette* in 1825, stated this forcefully:

> The Press is an engine of immense power and influence; it controuls to a great extent, both the moral and political world, and is either productive of much good, or unlimited mischief, according to the manner in which it is conducted. Editors of newspapers occupy an important and responsible station, in which they should not act without great deliberation; nor should they consult exclusively the gratification of their readers. The enquiry should not be, what will please, but what will benefit, . . . chasten the thoughts, refine the feelings, enlighten the mind, and elevate the human character.[52]

Foote clearly thought the press capable of chastening, refining, elevating, and enlightening. He and his contempories, both critics and friends, conceded the press its great moral influence, whether for good or ill, in agreement with the lines of this poet:

> Thou fountain, at which drink the good and wise;
> Thou ever bubbling Spring of endless lies;
> Like Eden's dread probationary Tree,
> Knowledge of good and evil is from thee.[53]

If the press was the key to a republican Garden of Eden, it unlocked a door which led both into and out of paradise.

Early proponents of a free press had envisioned it an aid to reason, an impersonal and high-minded guardian of what was called "rational liberty." Contrasted to rational liberty was the excess of liberty, licentiousness, marked by a lack of concern for correct knowledge or behavior. Thinkers rigorously discriminated between liberty and licentiousness: the motto of Cincinnati's second newspaper, *Freeman's Journal*, was "Free but not Licentious." As the early press expanded along with the marketplace of ideas, and as partisanism and personalities became commonplace in newspapers, the resulting chaos was seen as licentiousness. Marryat remarked that "A due liberty allowed to the press may force a government to

[52]*Cincinnati Literary Gazette*, III (April 30, 1825), p. 142.

[53]*Saturday Evening Chronicle of General Literature, Morals, and the Arts*, March 15, 1828.

do right, but a licentiousness may compel it into error. . . . The press in the United States is licentious to the highest possible degree, and defies control . . . ."[54] Tocqueville described the tactics of the licentious journalist: "a direct and course attack, without any subtleties, on the passions of his readers; he disregards principles to seize on people, following them into their private lives, and laying bare their weaknesses and their vices." He concluded that such conduct of the means of communication was a "deplorable abuse of the powers of thought."[55]

This perversion of rational liberty, this abuse of the powers of thought, this subversion of the Republic of Letters,[56] was seen as a repudiation of the idea of freedom of the press which had come out of the Revolution. Charles Dickens, in his *American Notes*, opined that "year by year, the memory of the Great Fathers of the Revolution must be outraged more and more in the bad life of their degenerate child."[57] In Cincinnati, the *Independent Press* invoked the patron saint of printers in the following quotation from the *Albany Register*: "Spirit of Franklin! whither hast thou fled? Inspire they fellow-craftsmen, we beseech thee, with the holy flame of independence . . . ."[58] Many apparently thought that true liberty of the press had been traded away for tyranny over public opinion and vassalage to partisans and demagogues, and that the press had come to undermine that very popular intelligence that it was designed to serve.

[54]Marryat, *Diary*, p. 406.

[55]Tocqueville, *Democracy in America*, p. 185. His opinions have been confirmed by a study of the frontier press in Michigan: Jeffrey L. Hirsh, "Tocqueville and the Frontier Press," *Journalism Quarterly*, 51 (1974), pp. 116–19.

[56]The concept of a Republic of Letters is discussed in Lewis Simpson, "Federalism and The Crisis of Literary Order," *American Literature* 32 (1960), pp. 253–66.

[57]Charles Dickens, *American Notes for General Circulation* (1842), in *The Works of Charles Dickens* (New York: Bigelow, Brown, and Co., undated), XIV, pp. 320–21.

[58]*Independent Press and Freedom's Advocate*, Oct. 31, 1822.

Republicanism and Early U.S. Culture: Prospect

In the preceding discussion of the ideology of the press, several aspects of the relationship of press to society were apparent. It is clear that the role of the press in society was defined in terms of ideas pivotal to the experience of the American Revolution: ideas of independence of thought, of rational liberty, of checks upon political power, and of the efficacy of public opinion. These ideas also defined the press establishment: the independent printer, in the tradition of Franklin, would transmit, in an impartial and impersonal manner, ideas, information, and opinions for consideration by an independent, enlightened, and rational electorate, who would turn the knowledge gained into an effective check against the abuse of power. The press was the key to informed public opinion, which was in turn the key to republican government.

The American experiment in republicanism extended beyond government. The influence of the Revolution was visible in religion, literature, and social thought; the significance of the press was asserted in each of these areas, and, logically enough, the ideology of the press as an instrument of rational liberty was central to the establishment of newspapers and periodicals devoted to all kinds of causes and interests. The moral influence of the press was considered immense and not confined to politics.

This study will deal with the press as a whole, in every field. It will examine the relationship of press and society as it changed over time in the period from the Federalist era to the end of the age of Jackson, from 1793 to 1848. I shall attempt to integrate the changing structure and ideology of the press with the changes in American culture at large at that time: improvements in transportation, innovations in technology, the development of a laissez-faire market economy, the appearance of a non-ideological national party system, the rise of the idea of democracy and its cultural ramifications, the rise of literary nationalism and localism, of ethnic pluralism, of early professionalism, and of reformism. Each development shaped and was shaped by the press.

This is a local study. To discuss the relationship of press to society would be absurd unless the society under study were kept ready-to-hand: knowledge of that society must be available in minute detail. The appropriateness of this approach will become apparent in the course of the study: the local character of communications in the early Republic is not readily grasped in the age of network television.

I have chosen Cincinnati, Ohio, as the locus of this study. Cincinnati was not then and has never been in the vanguard of social and cultural innovation. Indeed, Cincinnati largely missed the political violence of the 1790s; daily papers, successfully established in the larger cities of the eastern seaboard by 1800, did not appear in Cincinnati until 1825. Cincinnati was hardly a leader in the press. But it is an all-too-common fallacy, an error of the whig theory of history, that the history of the press is the history of press innovation.

The traditional approach to press history, in bringing to light the origins of contemporary journalism, has obscured the day-to-day functioning of the great bulk of the press in the past. The spectacular career of James Gordon Bennett's *Herald*, for example, does not define the penny press, but tends to obscure its real cultural significance. That significance may be more readily perceived in a study of the aggregate penny press of a city of lesser stature than New York, a city like Cincinnati.

In addition to this negative rationale for studying the Cincinnati press, there are positive reasons. Cincinnati was founded in the year after the drafting of the federal constitution: in time and circumstance, its origins coincided with the beginning of the great experiment in republican government. Benjamin Drake and Edward Deering Mansfield, both local newspaper editors, in a guidebook to Cincinnati published in 1826, contended that "there is, perhaps, no place in the United States, more favorable for observing the influence of our Republican System upon Society at large, than in Cincinnati."[59] Similarly James Handasyd Perkins, an immigrant to Cincinnati from New England, also a local editor, asserted that in the Ohio Valley, "society was born Republican . . . ."[60] Cincinnati was characteristically American and republican.

In the years covered by this study, Cincinnati grew from a frontier settlement to "The great central mart of the West."[61] Its rise to cultural and

[59]Benjamin Drake and Edward Deering Mansfield, *Cincinnati in 1826* (Cincinnati: Morgan, Lodge, & Fisher, 1827), pp. 88–9.

[60]James Handasyd Perkins, "Agrarianism," *Western Messenger*, I (Sept., 1836), p. 600.

[61]Chevalier, *Society, Manners, and Politics*, p. 198.

economic dominance in the old Northwest in the two decades following 1830 is not a matter of pretense, despite the pretentiousness of the titles eager citizens claimed: "Athens of the West," "Tyre of the West," "Queen City of the West." The history of Cincinnati from 1793 to 1848 is the history of the early urbanization of the U.S.

Likewise, the history of the early Cincinnati press sheds light on a wide variety of press types, from the frontier press to the metropolitan press. In 1793, Cincinnati had one weekly newspaper; in 1845, it had twenty-five weeklies and six monthlies, and in 1848 thirteen dailies.[62] The census of 1850 listed Cincinnati as the nation's fourth largest publishing center, surpassed only by New York, Boston, and Philadelphia.[63]

This study is organized roughly into three parts. The first part, consisting of the first two chapters, is a treatment of the structure of the press establishment. In it I discuss press machinery, newspaper circulation, the mechanics of transpor-tation and communication, press personnel, and press finance, concentrating on Cincinnati but highlighting national trends where relevant. This opening part is meant to provide a skeleton upon which to reconstruct the muscle and tendon of communication. While the topics covered in these chapters are essential to press history, they are not of primary importance in this book.

Part two is a discussion of the relationship of the general newspaper to politics in the early Republic. Important issues in this section are the role of the press in party formation and the relationship of the press as medium to political rhetoric. These chapters will deal with the interaction between the press and its environment of ideas and values; I will discuss how the press functioned in the formulation and resolution of issues and in the acquisition and exercise of political authority.

The third part deals with the periodical press in religion, literature, science, reform, and the learned professions. These chapters examine the

---

[62]Walter Draper, "Newspapers and Periodicals in Cincinnati," undated manuscript, Cincinnati Public Library.

[63]Walter Sutton, *The Western Book Trade: Cincinnati as a Nineteenth-Century Publishing and Book Trade Center* (Columbus: Ohio State University Press, 1961), p. 67; Frank Luther Mott, *A History of American Magazines, 1741–1905*, 5 vols., (Cambridge, Mass.: Harvard University Press, 1930), I, p. 375 ftnt.

role of the press in the generation and organization of enthusiasm, both popular and elite, for knowledge, culture, and enlightenment.

This book is ultimately intended to present an account of the formation of the contours of early American culture. An implicit argument here is that the media were central to this formation in that they provided means and opportunities for participation and reception. In no small way, the history of the culture of the press in the early Republic is the history of the working out of the idea of democratic culture. This study is a contribution to that history.

CHAPTER I

The Cincinnati Press Establishment, 1793–1848

During the fifty-five years covered by this study, Cincinnati's print production grew from a single frontier weekly newspaper to an industry comparable to that of almost any other large city in North America. The growth in print accompanied the growth of Cincinnati from village to town to city to regional metropolis. In the meantime, new techniques of production and transportation were introduced, making possible more efficient production and distribution of newspapers and periodicals.

The growth of Cincinnati as a center of print communication took place within a national context of rapid expansion and maturation. These years witnessed what George Rogers Taylor has called the transportation revolution—a striking proliferation of improvements like roads and canals, the introduction of the steamboat, the expansion and improvement of postal service: in short, the construction of the vital arteries of commerce and communication.[1] The growth of the Cincinnati press is both a creature and an example of this national growth.

This chapter examines the origins and development of the press in Cincinnati.

---

[1]George Rogers Taylor, *The Transportation Revolution: Industry, 1815-1860,* Economic History of the United States, Henry David *et al.*, ed. (New York: Holt, Rinehart, & Winston, 1954).

The Establishment of the Press, 1793–1820

Cincinnati was founded in 1788, and chartered as a town in 1802. In the intervening years it was a frontier village, consisting mostly of log cabins, with a few more substantial buildings dotting the river-side basin that would later contain a thriving city. This village's great distinction was the fact that it was host to the garrison at Fort Washington. This military presence turned Cincinnati into something of a regional financial center, since specie was scarce in the old Northwest, and the chits the military issued for purchases served as currency. It also meant that the village would have a disproportionate number of trading posts and taverns. Indeed, the garrison set the tone for the life-style of the settlement: citizens imitated soldiers' idleness, drinking, and gambling, pursuits that would occupy local worthies long after Cincinnati's incorporation as a city in 1819.[2]

This rude village was also the site of the territorial government (Ohio did not become a state until 1803). It is likely that the prospect of income from printing the territorial laws lured William Maxwell to Cincinnati in 1793. In that same year, he set up his type and print in a garret on Front Street and issued, on November 9, 1793, the first number of the first newspaper ever published in the old Northwest, the *Centinel of the North-Western Territory*.[3]

The *Centinel* was a small, four-page weekly. Over half of its material was advertising, with the remainder divided among "Foreign Intelligence" and "American Affairs" (both copied verbatim from other

[2]Jacob Burnet, *Notes on the Early Settlement of the Northwestern Territory* (Cincinnati: Derby, Bradley, & Co., 1847), pp. 31, 36-7; Charles Cist, *Cincinnati in 1841: Its Early Annals and Future Prospects* (Cincinnati: Charles Cist, 1848), pp. 38-9; Andrew R.L. Cayton, *The Frontier Republic: Ideology and Politics in the Ohio Country, 1780-1825* (Kent, OH: Kent State University Press, 1986), p. 64.

[3]The initiation of the *Centinel* is recounted in William H. Venable, *Beginnings of Literary Culture in the Ohio Valley: Historical and Biographical Sketches* (1891; repr. New York: Peter Smith, 1949), pp. 40 *et seq.*; Osman Castle Hooper, *History of Ohio Journalism, 1793-1933* (Columbus: Spahr and Glenn, 1933), pp. 13-4; and Reuben Gold Thwaites, "The Ohio Valley Press before the War of 1812," *Proceedings of the American Antiquarian Society*, n. s. XIX (April 1909), pp. 337-38.

papers), transcribed speeches and minutes of legislatures, occasional letters from subscribers, or rare editorial remarks. In his prospectus, Maxwell had also promised "a thousand particulars . . . of a philosophical, political, or moral nature."[4] Poetry, literary anecdotes, and essays were indeed printed when lack of paid advertising left space. While political commentary in the form of letters from readers was apparent from the first,[5] Maxwell himself neither endorsed nor closed his paper to either side of a debate, living up to his motto, "Open to all Parties, but Influenced by None."[6]

William Maxwell was a characteristic pioneer printer. He was an independent proprietor who later became a man of considerable influence in the community, a sophisticated tradesman who moved to a new and promising settlement in hope of financial reward in an unchallenged market. His "printing establishment" consisted of a wooden hand-press, much like the one Franklin had used decades earlier, and a few cases of type, altogether no more than could be moved in one load with a wheelbarrow. His "employees" were his wife, the former Nancy Robins, and an apprentice named Benjamin Stokes, who ran away in 1795.[7]

Maxwell was born in New York in 1755. He apparently learned printing in the east. After service in the Revolutionary Army and a sojourn in New Jersey, he came west in the early 1790s, set up a print shop in Lexington, Kentucky, then moved to Cincinnati in 1793. As the only practitioner of his craft there, he became printer of the laws for the territory; he was also appointed postmaster for Cincinnati in 1795. His newspaper enterprise made him a public figure: he would later hold

[4]*Centinel*, Nov. 9, 1793.

[5]See, for example, letters of Manlius and Plebius, *Centinel*, Nov. 9, 23, 30, 1793.

[6]On the conduct of the *Centinel*, see Charles B. Galbreath, "The First Newspaper of the Northwestern Territory (The Editor and His Wife)," *Ohio Archaeological and Historical Society Publications*, XIII (Fall, 1904), P. 335; for a sampling of news and advertising of local interest, see Robert C. Wheeler, "Selective Index to the Centinel of the North Western Territory," *Ohio State Archaeological and Historical Quarterly*, LII (Summer, 1943), pp. 217-47.

[7]William C. Robinson, "The Pioneer Printer in the United States," *Journal of Library History*, IV (July, 1969), pp. 207-12; Hooper, *Ohio Journalism*, p. 4; Galbreath, "First Newspaper," pp. 332, 345. Maxwell offered a .10 reward for the return of his runaway apprentice, a satirically low figure, perhaps attesting to the worthlessness of an apprentice in so small a firm. *Centinel*, June 27, 1795.

public office as a state representative, associate judge, sheriff, and officer in the state militia before his death in 1809.[8]

In 1796, Maxwell sold the *Centinel* to Samuel Freeman and his son Edmund, who changed its name to *Freeman's Journal*. In 1800, Edmund Freeman moved to Chillicothe, the new territorial capital, and took the paper with him.[9] By that time, however, a rival weekly had been established in Cincinnati.

The *Western Spy and Hamilton Gazette*[10] was founded in 1799 by Joseph Carpenter, an immigrant from Massachusetts, one of the first New Englanders to move to Cincinnati. He edited the *Spy* until 1809, meanwhile serving in many local public offices. In 1809 he sold the original *Spy*, but founded another newspaper of the same name in the next year. This second *Spy* survived until 1823. Carpenter himself did not live so long. After earning the rank of Captain in the War of 1812, he died in the field. Meanwhile, the paper he had sold became in turn the *Whig* and the *Advertizer*, then passed out of existence in 1811. In 1814, the *Spy* came under the control of Ephraim Morgan and Micajah T. Williams. Morgan, a Quaker from New England who had served an appprenticeship in the *Spy* office, would become one of the most important printers in the west as proprietor of the *Daily Gazette* and printer of Truman and Smith's Eclectic School Books, including McGuffey's Readers. Williams would, as a state legislator, be the most important proponent of internal improvements in Ohio. This sort of managerial partnership between a political hopeful and a knowledgable printer would become characteristic of newspapers in the early nineteenth century.[11]

---

[8]Galbreath, "First Newspaper," pp. 346-47; Douglas C. McMurtrie, "Antecedent Experience of William Maxwell, Ohio's First Printer," *Ohio Archaeological and Historical Publications*, XLI (Spring, 1932), pp. 98-103; Rollo G. Silver, *The American Printer, 1787-1825* (Charlottesville: University Press of Virginia, 1967), pp. 123-24.

[9]Venable, *Literary Culture*, p. 40.

[10]Title varies: *Western Spy and Hamilton Gazette*, 1799-1805; *Western Spy and Miami Gazette*, 1805-1809; *Western Spy*, 1810-1819; *Western Spy and Cincinnati General Advertiser*, 1819-1820; *Western Spy and Literary Cadet*, 1820-1822.

[11]Hooper, *Ohio Journalism*, pp. 15-6, 18; Thwaites, "Ohio Valley Press," pp. 338-39; Venable, *Literary Culture*, pp. 410-11; Charles Theodore Greve, *Centennial History of Cincinnati and Representative Citizens* (Chicago: Biographical Publishing Company, 1904), p. 474.

After the removal of *Freeman's Journal* in 1800, the *Western Spy* enjoyed a brief monopoly on the Cincinnati news market. In August, 1804, however, a challenger appeared in the form of the *Liberty Hall*,[12] a weekly paper conducted by John W. Browne. At first, according to Browne, it seemed that "the *Spy* and *Liberty Hall* will be competitiors and *one must fall*."[13] But it soon became apparent that the market for news and advertising in Cincinnati and the surrounding countryside was large enough to support both papers.

John W. Browne was a minister, publisher, bookseller, and retailer of medicines. A native of England, he did not come to Cincinnati until 1798, but quickly earned enough respect to be elected to Ohio's constitutional convention in 1802. He served as recorder of courts for Hamilton County from 1803 to 1810, as commissioner for leasing school lands in 1804, and as a fund-raising agent for Miami University in 1811 and 1812, until his death by drowning.[14]

For almost a decade and a half after 1804, the Cincinnati press was dominated by these two papers, the *Western Spy* and the *Liberty Hall*. Other papers were either run out of business or absorbed. A proprietor of a local coffee house began a paper called the *Cincinnati Observer*, which quickly failed. In 1814, a paper called the *Spirit of the West* made its appearance, but did not survive the year. In 1815, Thomas Palmer bought the equipment of the *Spirit* and issued the *Cincinnati Gazette*, a paper which did survive, but only by merging with the successful *Liberty Hall*.[15]

In June of 1818 the *Inquisitor and Cincinnati Advertiser* was founded by the firm of Cooke, Powers, and Penney. A well-executed paper, with a fairly strong editorial voice and well-chosen material, the *Inquisitor* would join the *Spy* and the *Liberty Hall* to form a triumvirate that would

---

[12]Title varies: *Liberty Hall and Cincinnati Mercury*, 1804-1809; *Liberty Hall*, 1809-1815; *Liberty Hall and Cincinnati Gazette*, 1815-1857. The establishment also included the *Tri-Weekly Cincinnati Gazette* and the *Cincinnati Daily Gazette*.

[13]*Western Spy*, Aug. 22, 1804.

[14]William Turner Coggeshall, *The Newspaper Record* . . . (Philadelphia: Lay and Brother, 1856), pp. 164-65; Beverly W. Bond, Jr., *The Civilization of the Old Northwest* (New York: MacMillan, 1934), p. 441; Hooper, *Ohio Journalism*, pp. 25-6.

[15]Bond, *Civilization*, p. 438; Venable, *Literary Culture*, p. 41; *Western Spy*, June 16, 1815; Coggeshall, *Newspaper Record*, p. 165.

effectively control the Cincinnati press until the advent of overt partisan political controversy. When, for example, Joseph R. Buchanan challenged this group by establishing in 1819 a paper called the *Literary Cadet and Cheap City Advertiser* (featuring advertising at 20% below the going rate), it was absorbed into the *Western Spy*.

In 1820, then, there were three established newspapers: the *Liberty Hall*, whose editor was Isaac G. Burnet, then Cincinnati's mayor; the *Inquisitor*, whose chief editor was Benjamin F. Powers, brother of sculptor Hiram Powers, and later a member of the Ohio Legislature; and the *Western Spy*, then under the guidance of James M. Mason and Thomas Palmer.[16] The upstart *Literary Cadet* would not survive the year.

Throughout this period, the weekly newspaper dominated the periodical press. Specialized publications, like religious, literary, and technical journals, made their appearance in Cincinnati only in the 1820s, as did biweekly, tri-weekly, and daily newspapers. Although newspaper offices issued almanacs, printed the laws, and published books and pamphlets, the characteristic printing venture was the four-page weekly newspaper. Diversification in format, production, and market appeal would begin later.

Press conductors during this period were of two sorts: editors with influence in the community, and publishers or printers with technical expertise or entrepreneurial talent. In the case of the *Liberty Hall*, which generally had the highest circulation of any Cincinnati paper, the editor was Isaac G. Burnet, a lawyer by training, member of a prominent local family, and Cincinnati's mayor. Burnet decided what would be printed in the paper and wrote the editorials. He also owned a large share of the printing establishment. But the actual printing was done by Ephraim Morgan and James Lodge, also proprietors, with the help of journeymen and apprentices. Differentiation in function had increased since the days when William Maxwell and his wife or Samuel and Edmund Freeman personally composed, printed and distributed their newspapers.

The Cincinnati press before 1820 displayed certain characteristics. It was uniform in format, consisting almost exclusively of four-page weeklies. It was stable, in that newspaper starts were rare and usually unsuccessful.

---

[16]*Literary Cadet*, Feb. 24, 1820.

Established papers did not compete vigorously among themselves. They also tended to avoid overt political controversies, observing the twin rules of impartiality and impersonality. Throughout the period, functional differentiation in the press establishment gradually increased, along with the editor's prestige in the community.

After 1820, this stable press establishment would erode. Newspapers and periodicals devoted to special causes would proliferate; partisanism would come to characterize the political newspaper, which would increase in frequency from weekly to daily; a separate German press would appear; and the aggregate number of publications would skyrocket, from three or four weeklies in 1820 to twelve dailies and a total of forty periodicals in 1845.[17] The press would undergo a great transformation in the years from 1820 to 1848. Before discussing this transformation, however, it will be necessary to detail the development of press technology, finance, and distribution in the whole period, 1793-1848.

Improvements in Printing, Transportation, and Communication

Printing equipment in the eighteenth century was simple. A standard outfit for a printer like Maxwell consisted of a wooden hand-press, using hand-set type and hand-spread ink, powered by human muscle. The operation of such a press required time and skill. Impressions were made one at a time, and it was a rare printer who could turn out more than seventy-five impressions an hour.[18] Paper was manufactured in the east and shipped west. The supply lines remained capricious throughout the first decade of the nineteenth century, however, and newspapers commonly carried apologies for being forced to delay publication or use paper of substandard quality.[19]

The state of the art did not permit massive circulations or instant communications. On the other hand, printing was a craft: printers like Maxwell and Freeman were independent; they needed at most a few hundred dollars to establish a business; and they employed only an

[17]Charles Cist, "Cincinnati Periodical Press," *Cincinnati Miscellany*, I (Jan. 1845), pp. 107-8.
[18]Hooper, *Ohio Journalism*, p. 3; Thwaites, "Ohio Valley Press," p. 351.
[19]See, for example, *Centinel*, Dec. 20, 1794.

occasional apprentice, a printer's devil, and a delivery boy.[20] Increasing sophistication in press technology, coupled with changes in long-distance communications and the rise of a mass audience, wrought drastic changes in the typical print establishment.[21] (The mechanics of the print shop will be discussed more fully below.)

The format of the newspaper remained the same throughout the period. It consisted of a single sheet, folded in the middle to form four pages. The outside pages carried mostly advertising and filler material— all matter that could be printed in advance. The inside pages carried news items, editorials, letters from correspondents, and commercial information, material which would be considered timely.

While format changed little, size, frequency, and aggregate circulation increased steadily. Maxwell's *Centinel*, with its large type and small pages, contained little more than 2500 words of non-advertising material weekly. In 1841, each daily issue of the *Enquirer* carried 8000 words. In 1835, the *Daily Gazette* printed the entire first issue of the *Centinel*—including advertisements—in four and a half columns. The *Gazette* carried twenty-eight such columns in each daily issue. In 1845 a typical edition of the *Weekly Liberty Hall and Cincinnati Gazette* ran to 50,000 words of non-advertising material, twenty times the *Centinel*'s original tally.[22]

The expansion of the press proceeded step by step with the introduction of new technology. In Cincinnati this process began with the establishment of local paper mills and a type foundry.

The unreliability of the paper supply up to 1810 has already been noted. In 1810, Christian Waldsmith built a paper mill on the Little Miami River, just north of Cincinnati. In the same year, John Cross and C. Earenfight opened a competing mill nearby. The *Western Spy* began printing on paper from the Waldsmith Mill as early as January 26, 1811.[23] From the

---

[20]Silver, *American Printer*, pp. 64-6; Stephen Botein, "Printers and the American Revolution," in Bernard Bailyn and John B. Hench, ed., *The Press & the American Revolution* (Worcester, Mass.: American Antiquarian Society, 1980).

[21]Silver, *American Printer*, p. 40.

[22]In arriving at these figures, I have examined issues of the *Centinel*, 1793-4, the *Enquirer*, 1841, and the *Weekly Gazette*, 1845. The first issue of the *Centinel* was reprinted in the *Daily Gazette*, Dec. 3, 1835. Coggeshall, *Newspaper Record*, p. 163.

[23]Bond, *Civilization*, pp. 411-12; Marie Dickore, "The Waldsmith Paper Mill,"

From the 1810s, then, printers were no longer hindered by the unpredictability of the paper supply. In 1820s John P. Foote established the Cincinnati Type Foundry, making Cincinnati self-sufficient in the production of type.[24]

Beginning in the 1820s new presses were introduced in Cincinnati. In 1826, the *Liberty Hall* began printing with "the first Iron Press used in the West," capable of turning out over 250 impressions per hour, a great advance over the old wooden press.[25] The manually-powered iron press was to be made obsolete, however, by the application of steam power and the substitution of cylinders for plates.

The first successful use of steam power on a press was the accomplishment of a Saxon journeyman named Frederick Koenig in 1810. By 1813, the Koenig press also featured a cylinder and automatic inking, and was capable of printing 2000 impressions an hour. The first steam press used in the United States was designed by Daniel Treadwell; it used plates and was capable of 1000 impressions an hour. Steam cylinder presses capable of 2000 impressions per hour were designed by David Napier in England and Robert Hoe in New York in 1824 and 1830 respectively. Such presses cost between four and five thousand dollars. The substitution of a cylinder for plates incidentally made an increase in the size of paper used to print on practical. A revolution in surface area was the result.[26]

The steam cylinder press did much to cheapen printing. It has often been credited with democratizing print culture by making possible wide circulation of cheap publications. Ironically, the press that did so much to cheapen printing was so expensive as to be affordable only to well-to-do

Bulletin of the Historical and Philosophical Society of Ohio, V (March, 1947), pp. 6-24; *Western Spy*, Jan. 26, 1811.

[24]Walter Sutton, *The Western Book Trade: Cincinnati as a Nineteenth-Century Publishing and Book Trade Center* (Columbus: Ohio State University Press, 1961), p. 13.

[25]*Weekly Liberty Hall and Cincinnati Gazette*, Dec. 12, 1844.

[26]Alfred McClung Lee, *The Daily Newspaper in America: The Evolution of a Social Instrument* (New York: MacMillan, 1937), pp. 113-17; Frank Luther Mott, *American Journalism: A History, 1690-1960*, third edition, (New York: MacMillan, 1962), pp. 203, 294; Edwin and Michael Emery, *The Press and America: An Interpretive History of the Mass Media* (5th ed., Englewood Cliffs, NJ: Prentice-Hall, 1984) pp. 133-5.

individuals or well-established firms.

The *Gazette* acquired Cincinnati's first power press in 1834. Designed by Isaac Adams in 1830, this press tripled the *Gazette's* per-hour capacity to 750 impressions. It cost $750. By 1841 there were five power presses in Cincinnati.[27] In 1843, the *Gazette* bought a Hoe cylinder press, capable of printing over 15,000 newspapers in a single day, work that would have taken at least ten days on an old-fashioned hand-press.[28]

This staggering increase in capacity reflected other changes in press-related fields. There was a steady speeding-up of communications, part of what historian George Rogers Taylor has called the "transportation revolution." Improvements in mail service and river navigation made information transmission reliable and reasonably quick; the invention of the telegraph promised instantaneous communication. Improvement in long-distance communication was an integral part of the ongoing sophistication of the press.[29]

In the early Republic, newspapers relied on the postal system for information. The symbiosis of post and press was recognized by the Federal Government in the Postal Act of 1792, which provided for free postage on papers exchanged among press conductors, exchange papers being the primary source of news for all but the elite eastern newspapers. This provision also indicates recognition of an intimate relationship between press and government. Newspapers were entitled to special privileges in government services because they were thought to be essential to the life of the Republic, both in informing the public and in encouraging citizens to participate in the affairs of an otherwise invertebrate nation.[30]

[27]Sutton, *Book Trade,* p. 74; Hooper, *Ohio Journalism,* p. 7.
[28]*Weekly Gazette,* May 11, 1843; Dec. 12, 1844.
[29]Taylor, *Transportation Revolution.*
[30]Julian P. Bretz, "Some Aspects of Postal Expansion into the West," *Annual Report of the American Historical Association,* 1909 (Washington: 1911), pp. 141-49; Culver Smith, *The Press, Politics, and Patronage: The American Government's Use of Newspapers, 1789-1875* (Athens: University of Georgia Press, 1977), p. 7. When the federal government began running postal expresses in 1825, it also built privileges for newspapers into the rate structure: Richard Kielbowicz, "Speeding the News by Postal Express, 1825-1861: The Public Policy of Privileges for the Press," *Social Science Journal* 22 (1985), pp. 49-63. Postal policy encouraged circulation of rural weeklies over urban

The introduction of press and post in Cincinnati were virtually simultaneous. The second issue of the *Centinel* announced the formation of a line of packet boats between Cincinnati and Pittsburgh, providing the first regular transportation line between these two cities.[31] In June of the next year, the *Centinel* noted the establishment of a regular mail route to Pittsburgh. After this initial step more routes were added, and arrivals came more and more frequently, though progress was slow and complaints common.[32]

Meanwhile, Cincinnatians began campaigning for increased navigation of western waters. The Miami Exporting Company was formed to develop the New Orleans trade in 1803, by which time newspapers had been promoting free navigation of the Mississippi for a decade.[33] This early clamor for improvements in commerce and navigation, climaxing in the Louisiana Purchase, foreshadowed the arrival of the steamboat age.

The steamboat first appeared on the Ohio River in 1811.[34] The press greeted this invention with enthusiasm, noting especially its speed, as

dailies, partly because it was thought that this would promote local cultural development, partly because carrying local weeklies was cheaper, and partly because it was felt that rural weeklies did not engage in "the rage of party": Kielbowicz, "The Press, Post Office, and Flow of News in the Early Republic," *Journal of the Early Republic* 3 (1983), 269-70. The dependence of newspapers on the post was staggering: "Of the roughly 22.5 million newspaper copies printed in 1810, nearly 4 million or one in six were distributed by the post office." Kielbowicz, "Press, Post Office," p. 270. See also Kielbowicz, "Newsgathering by Printers' Exchanges Before the Telegraph," *Journalism History* 9 (1982), 42-8.

[31]This was a round trip of four weeks; the line operated four boats, providing for one arrival a week. *Centinel*, Nov. 16, 1793; Sutton, *Book Trade*, p. 4; Charles Henry Ambler, *History of Transportation in the Ohio Valley* (Glendale, Ca.: Arthur H. Clarke Co., 1932), pp. 44 *et seq.*; Leland D. Baldwin, *The Keelboat Age on Western Waters* (Pittsburgh: University of Pittsburgh Press, 1941), p. 176.

[32]*Centinel*, June 28, 1794; Bond, *Civilization*, pp. 378-81.

[33]Sutton, *Book Trade*, pp. 4-5; *Centinel*, Feb. 4, 1794; *Western Spy*, Feb. 16, 1803 *et passim* records in full debates in Congress on free navigation of the Mississippi. Ambler, *Transportation*, pp. 71-2. See Baldwin, *Keelboat Age*, for a general treatment of river transportation in the west before the introduction of the steamboat. See Vernon David Keeler, "The Commercial Development of Cincinnati to the Year 1860" (Unpublished doctoral dissertation, University of Chicago, 1935), pp. 78-9, on western demand for transportation improvement.

[34]Louis C. Hunter, *Steamboats on the Western Rivers: An Economic and Technological History* (Cambridge: Harvard University Press, 1949), pp. 3-43.

well as its promise for increased commerce and economic independence from the east. A mania for transportation improvement appeared and grew with the building of canals and railroads.[35]

The canal movement in Ohio dates from the 1820s. In 1825, the Ohio legislature authorized construction of the Miami and Erie Canal from Cincinnati to Toledo, a scheme which was eventually to open a water route from the Great Lakes to the Ohio River. By the 1840s, this trip the length of the state took but two and a half days. Also in 1840s, the Little Miami Railroad was completed from Cincinnati to Sandusky, making it Ohio's first trans-state railroad.[36]

Neither canal nor railroad would play a major role in improving long-distance communication before 1848. Canals came too late to supplant well-established land routes and did not match in speed their great advantage in cost of transportation. The railroad reached Cincinnati at roughly the same time as the telegraph. Canals and railroads reflected, however, simultaneous improvements in the postal system.

Mail routes to and from Cincinnati improved gradually. In 1818, the National Road was completed from the Potomac to the Ohio River, permitting mail coaches to travel conveniently over the Appalachians.[37] Meanwhile, the steamboat had become established on the Ohio River. Steamboat packet lines were routinely awarded mail contracts throughout

[35]*Western Spy*, June 16, July 21, Sept. 15, 1815. On the economic impact of the steamboat in the west, see James Hall, *The West: Its Commerce and Navigation* (1848; repr. New York: Burt Franklin, 1970); Ambler, *Transportation*, pp. 107-31; Eric F. Haites, James Mak, and Gary M. Walton, *Western River Transportation: The Era of Early Internal Development, 1810-1860*, Johns Hopkins University Studies in Historical and Political Science, 93 ser. no. 2, (Baltimore: Johns Hopkins University Press, 1975). All of these books are disappointing in their failure to deal with communications.

[36]Ambler, *Transportation*, pp. 141-45; John H. White, Jr., "The Steam Railroad comes to Cincinnati," *Bulletin of the Cincinnati Historical Society*, 32 (1974), pp. 177-79; Sutton, *Book Trade*, pp. 63-6. Harry N. Scheiber, *Ohio Canal Era: A Case Study of Government and the Economy, 1820-1861* (Athens: Ohio University Press, 1969), and Carl W. Condit, *The Railroad and the City: A Technological and Urbanistic History of Cincinnati* (Columbus: Ohio State University Press, 1977) are sound treatments. Scheiber concentrates on governmental efforts, while Condit examines the effect of the railroad on urban topography. Neither deals with communication.

[37]Haites *et al.*, *Western River Transportation*, p. 5; Ambler, *Transportation*, pp. 134-37.

the antebellum period, being the swiftest and most reliable means of transportation between points on the river. While the improvements effected in the postal system by the steamboat may have been minor, an informal communications network sprang up around the river traffic, and steamboat captains regularly "favored" newspaper editors with copies of the latest papers from river cities.[38] Cincinnati, for example, had a thrice-weekly mail route from Louisville in 1831. But boats ran daily between those two cities,[39] permitting more frequent newspaper exchanges.

The press was clearly aware of its reliance on the postal system. It associated itself with movements for postal expansion, greeted enthusiastically any steps in that direction, and campaigned vigorously for exemption from postal charges.[40] By 1831, newspapers and pamphlets accounted for 14/15 of all postage carried by weight; at the same time, they provided only 1/9 of all postal revenue.[41] The government continued to favor the press, and in 1845 a law went into effect, providing free delivery of all newspapers to any post office within thirty miles of the printing office. The *Enquirer* noted that this would permit delivery of its paper to ten countries in Ohio, Kentucky, and Indiana.[42] The postal system provided both source and outlet for the early press, and the expansion of the press was directly tied to the expansion of the postal system.

The culmination of improvement in communication in the early Republic was the invention of the telegraph. The telegraph promised to end the quest for quicker communication by making communication

[38]Ambler, *Transportation*, p. 163 *et passim*; Hunter, *Steamboats*, pp. 336-42. See *Daily Commercial*, April 4, Nov. 28, Dec. 2, 1843, for examples of a newspaper editor thanking steamboat captains for recent papers from cities like St. Louis and New Orleans.

[39]Allan K. Pred, *Urban Growth and the Circulation of Information: The United States System of Cities, 1790-1840* (Cambridge: Harvard University Press, 1973), pp. 91, 132-33.

[40]For examples of campaigning for improvement, see *Liberty Hall*, Nov. 22, 1814; *Western Spy*, Nov. 5-Dec. 3, 1814; *National Republican and Ohio Political Register*, April 9, 1824. For announcements of postal improvements, see *National Republican*, May 5, June 16, 1826.

[41]Smith, *Patronage*, p. 7.

[42]*Daily Enquirer*, June 17, 1845.

instantaneous. The impact of this technological innovation has therefore generally been considered revolutionary. Was it so?

The first telegraphic message was sent and received on May 1, 1844. The first newspaper use of a telegraphic message occurred on the 24th of the same month.[43] Hence the initial application of telegraphic communication to news reporting was almost immediate. Yet it would be incorrect to assume from this that newspapers suddenly converted wholesale from use of exchange papers to wires. Rather, daily newsgathering continued to rely on "traditional" methods. Telegraph operation was too expensive to permit its use for "routine" news.[44] Also it must be kept in mind that telegraph messages were carried by wire; that wires were built gradually, not instantaneously; that they were expensive to maintain and frequently broke down; and that a telegraph line could connect only two points at a time on the vast plane of a country that stretched from ocean to ocean. If the telegraph wrought a revolution in journalism, it was a piecemeal one.

I contend that the telegraph should be considered as one part of an ongoing process of improvement in communication rather than as a revolutionary departure from previous efforts. In the newspaper, for example, it was incorporated into the regular format: a column headed "By the Electric Telegraph" was added next to the one headed "By the Latest Mails." This was augmentation, not transformation. Telegraphic communication was viewed within the context of postal improvement: thus the *Weekly Liberty Hall and Cincinnati Gazette* argued that the telegraph "should be a *Government* affair, . . . a branch of the Post Office Department."[45]

Most early telegraphic communication came from a traditional source, either a newspaper or Congressional report or something of that nature.

[43]Mott, *American Journalism,* p. 247. On the history of the telegraph, see also Brooke Hindle, *Emulation and Invention* (New York: New York University Press, 1981); Hindle, "From Art to Technology and Science," *Proceedings of the American Antiquarian Society* 96 (1986), pp. 25-37; and James Carey, "Technology and Ideology: The Case of the Telegraph," *Prospects* 8 (1983), pp. 303-25.

[44]Victor Rosewater, *History of Cooperative Newsgathering in the United States* (New York: D. Appleton, 1930), p. 34.

[45]*Weekly Gazette,* Dec. 5, 1844.

News from outside North America arrived by ship, was printed in a port city newspaper, then was transmitted to other points in the nation by telegraph. News from Liverpool, for example, took about three weeks to reach New York by steamer in 1840.[46] By 1848, the establishment of the Cunard Line had cut this time lapse to just two weeks. Meanwhile, the telegraph had cut the time lapse from New York to Cincinnati from about six days to an instant. But remarkable as telegraphic communication may have been, it was steamship communication which did more to hasten news transmission from Europe to Cincinnati.

TABLE I

Time-Lapse in News Transmission to Cincinnati
from Key Cities, 1793–1848

City of Origin	1793-4	1805	1825	1845	1848
London	107	72	37	21	19
Paris	114	81	42	23	21
Havana	–	32	–	19	–
New York	49	26	10	6	1*
Philadelphia	47	28	9	5	1*
Boston	44	34	14	7	1*
Baltimore	39	26	8	4	1*
Washington	–	23	9	5	1*
Lexington	10	8	5	2	1*
New Orleans	–	55	16	11	9
Columbus/Chillicothe	–	9	6	2	1*

*Denotes telegraphic, or next-day reportage.
Source: Centinel, 1793-4; Liberty Hall, Western Spy, 1805; National Republican, 1825; Daily Enquirer, 1845, 1848. Samples for 1793-4 and 1805 were from weeklies; the sample for 1825 was from a bi-weekly. A subjective element is involved: items which looked to have been inefficiently communicated were discounted. The goal was to come up with a standard minimum time-lapse, like I. K. Steele's "colonial instant": "Time, Communications, and Society: The English Atlantic, 1702," Journal of American Studies, 8 (April, 1974), pp. 1-21.

46Mott, American Journalism, pp. 244-45.

European news was only one example of the way in which traditional and electronic means worked together to enhance speed of communication. News from Mexico during the Mexican War was delivered by a combination of express rider and steamer to New Orleans and other southern ports, then transmitted by a variety of means—including the telegraph—to other points within the Union. Similarly, news from California during the gold rush of 1848-1849 traveled east to the Mississippi by a variety of conventional means. On a more local level, Cincinnati papers could get news from Columbus, Lexington, Louisville, and other nearby places more cheaply by post rider and express than by telegraph, and in virtually the same time, since a newspaper was published only once a day.

A quick glance at time-lapse figures for the entire period 1793-1848 from key cities reveals a smooth curve of improvement. (See Table I.) Between 1793 and 1805, regular postal lines to the east were established; between 1805 and 1825, the steamboat was introduced and the National Road completed between 1825 and 1845, steam lines to Europe were set up and regular means of communication refined; and by 1848 telegraph lines were in place between Cincinnati and the major cities of the east. Improvement seemed to generate enthusiasm for even more rapid communication. A growing sense of urgency became associated with the news, a cultural phenomenon just as significant in communication improvement as technology. Speed itself became a value, therefore speed was sought.[47]

Items of special urgency were relayed with maximum speed. (See Table II.) Communication improved constantly between Cincinnati and regular sources of important news, like Washington, D. C., but lengthy delays remained common, even after the introduction of the telegraph, in

[47]Throughout the nineteenth century, however, time-lags in news reporting remained considerable, diminishing most notably in domestic (as opposed to foreign or local) news in the years 1859-1874--the years in which wire service reporting became a significant feature of the news environment, and significantly *not* the years in which the telegraph was deployed as a technology. Susan Brooker-Gross concludes that "timeliness varied in value according to the origin of news, such that technological improvements alone do not explain the decrease in time lag during the 19th century." "Timeliness: Interpretations from a Sample of 19th-Century Newspapers," *Journalism Quarterly* 58 (1981), p. 594.

transmitting information from unlikely sources. A telling example was Zachary Taylor's acceptance of the Whig Party's nomination for the Presidency in 1848. Acceptance was sent in the form of a letter, posted at Baton Rouge, Louisiana, on July 15, 1848, in response to a communication sent from Philadelphia on July 10. The *Enquirer* reported Taylor's acceptance on July 30, having received word from Louisville by telegraph the day before. The telegraph's role in hastening this information was negligible.

TABLE II

Time-Lapse in Transmission of Urgent News
to Cincinnati, 1799–1848

Year	Event	Source	Days
1799	Death of Washington, Va.	*Western Spy*, 1/7/1800	24
1811	Battle of Tippecanoe	*Western Spy Extra*,11/21/1811	13
		Liberty Hall Extra,11/21/1811	13
1815	Battle of New Orleans	*Western Spy*, 1/21/1815	13
1845	Death of Jackson,Nashville	*Enquirer*, 6/12/1845	4
1848	Taylor accepts nom., La.	*Enquirer*, 7/30/1848	15

Urgent News from Washington, D. C.

Year	Event	Source	Days
1801	Jefferson's election	*Western Spy*, 3/11/1801	24
1807	Passage of the Embargo	*Liberty Hall*, 1/18/1808	27
1813	Madison's inaugural	*Western Spy Extra*, 3/24/1813	21
1815	Madison's annual address	*Western Spy Extra*, 12/18/1815	14
1824	Monroe's annual address	*National Crisis Extra*, 12/16	9
1833	Jackson's inaugural	*Advertiser*, 3/13/1833	9
1841	Tyler's inaugural	*Enquirer*, 6/4/1841	3
1845	Polk's inaugural	*Weekly Gazette*, 4/13/1845	2
1847	Polk's annual address	(telegraphic)	1

The telegraph has been credited with more than speeding up information transmission. It has been claimed that this technological innovation ushered in the age of cooperative newsgathering, and that it thereby generated a "modern" style of reporting, characterized by impersonality, objectivity, and uniformity.[48]

It is beyond the scope of this book to evaluate the long-term effects of the telegraph upon cooperative newsgathering (the Associated Press, for example, was not founded until later). It is not true, however, that cooperative newsgathering began with the telegraph. News from Europe was cooperatively prepared, and generally presented in the form of an impersonal summary or digest. Congressional debates were likewise presented in impersonal form, either copied verbatim or printed in digest. The style of reporting changed gradually throughout the first half of the nineteenth century: third person reporting became more common. But this movement preceded the telegraph, and was more closely associated with local news. And, if an ideal of objectivity was associated with telegraphic reporting,[49] this ideology was not novel. Rather, it was a restatement of the ideal of impersonality commonly found in the newspapers of the early Republic. I will deal with the question of style more fully in the next chapter. It should be noted here, however, that changes in style were gradual, and that no revolution in style was wrought by any single innovation, not even the telegraph.[50]

Careful study of the period 1793-1848 reveals a continuous process of improvement in communication. In Cincinnati, this process began in 1793 with the establishment of a regular packet line to Pittsburgh; it gathered momentum with the introduction of the steamboat, the building of railroads and canals, and the expansion of the postal system; and it culminated in 1847 with the completion of a telegraph line to Cincinnati.

[48]See, for example, Gunther Barth, *City People: The Rise of Modern City Culture in Nineteenth-Century America* (New York: Oxford University Press, 1980), pp. 94-5; Fred Siebert, in Siebert, Theodore Peterson, and Wilbur Schramm, *Four Theories of the Press* (Urbana: University of Illinois Press, 1956) p. 60.

[49]See, for example, *Daily Enquirer*, May 10, 1848: telegraph operators "should lay aside their party feelings in their despatches."

[50]Donald L. Shaw has argued that a significant turn away from biased reporting did result from use of the telegraph. His conclusions are based on quantitative analysis of political news in newspapers in one state during presidential elections over a long period of time. But his statistics reveal the massive shift taking place only in the 1880s, far after the telegraph had been successfully introduced, and attributable to the non-technological innovation of wire service reporting. Even so, Shaw does not argue for the novelty of the idea of news objectivity. "News Bias and the Telegraph: A Study of Historical Change," *Journalism Quarterly*, 44 (Spring, 1967), pp. 3-12.

Improvements in communication coincided with improvements in print technology and were in part responsible for the expansion of the press.

Readership and Circulation

So far this treatment of the press establishment has dealt with the materials of production—presses, postal services, and so forth—what might be called the supply side of newspaper history. But it is crucially important that we make an attempt to understand not only how newspapers were put forth but also how they were taken in. Who read newspapers?

As a cultural institution, the importance of the press is in the public creation and transmission of meaning, and thus the involvement of the press is mediated by two processes. One is the interaction of press and reader in terms of the transmission of texts; the second is the interaction of reader and text. It is very difficult to recover this second process, but it is clear that it cannot take place without the first—readers cannot read texts they do not see. Robert Ezra Park states this cogently in his seminal essay, "The Natural History of the Newspaper":

> A newspaper is not merely printed. It is circulated and read. Otherwise it is not a newspaper. The struggle for existence, in the case of a newspaper, has been a struggle for circulation. The newspaper that is not read ceases to be an influence in the community. The power of the press may be roughly measured by the number of people who read it.[51]

While it may not necessarily be true that the number of people who read a newspaper correlates with its "power" (since readers may choose to read a paper in diverse and possible perverse ways, and the newspaper's text cannot control the readers' uses of it), still it must be acknowledged that the press must be read as a precondition for its having influence on its readers. How wide was newspaper readership, then, in the early Republic?

[51]Robert Ezra Park, "Natural History of the Newspaper" (1923), in Everett Charrington Hughes *et al.*, ed., *Society: Collective Behavior, News and Opinion, and Modern Society*, Collected Papers of Robert Ezra Park, (Glencoe, Ill.: The Free Press, 1955), p. 90.

And how did readership change over time?

Impressionistic evidence suggests that readership was wide indeed. A letter to the *National Republican*, for instance, expressed outrage that a man would call himself an American and not take a newspaper: "I should respect him more, and pity him less, if I saw him with a newspaper, altho' destitute of a coat and a breakfast."[52] Mrs. Trollope commented on the amount of time the average American spent in reading the newspaper, to the sad neglect of other pursuits, and to the great profit of the liquor stores and coffee houses which subscribed to such papers for the perusal of their patrons.[53]

Early newspapers were circulated by subscription only. The cash system of buying individual papers was not successfully introduced in Cincinnati until the 1840s. Hence we can be certain that early newspapers printed very few extra copies, since the printer always knew in advance how many copies of his paper would be paid for. The number of papers printed was the rough equivalent of the number of papers circulated.

The number of newspapers circulated was probably much smaller than the number of readers, however. Papers were available at public houses and at reading rooms, for example, and subscribers frequently complained that their non-subscribing neighbors enjoyed fuller use of their papers.[54]

[52]*National Republican*, Nov. 5, 1824.

[53]Frances Trollope, *Domestic Manners of the Americans*, Donald Smalley, ed., (New York: Knopf, 1949), pp. 102-3. Literacy rates do not seem to have significantly limited readership. Illiteracy rates for adult whites in 1840 in Ohio were around 6%, according to the U.S. census for that year: Lee Soltow and Edward Stevens, *The Rise of Literacy and the Common School in the United States: A Socioeconomic Analysis to 1870* (Chicago: University of Chicago Press, 1981), p. 159. While no specific figures for Cincinnati are available, it seems likely that its illiteracy level was lower than the state average, since population density usually correlates negatively with illiteracy. Illiteracy declined gradually over the period covered here, but it doesn't seem likely that the market for print was limited at any point to a restricted class, or that declines in illiteracy were sufficient to change the shape of the reading population. Edward Stevens' study of book ownership in Ohio shows that the percentage of estates that included books remained roughly stable (between 40% and 50%) throughout the period, and that, while families above the median wealth line were more likely to own books, a large percentage (25% to 47%) of book owners came from below that line. Stevens, "Books and Wealth on the Frontier: Athens County and Washington County, Ohio 1790-1859," *Social Science History* 5 (1981), pp. 417-43.

[54]See, for example, the letter of Fair Play in the *Independent Press*, April 11, 1822. It

Newspaper sharing or borrowing was undoubtedly common practice, especially in the days of the weekly paper.

Though hard evidence is not readily available, there are good reasons to believe that a single copy of an early weekly paper might reach as many as twenty readers.[55] Such papers were printed on durable paper, unlike later newspapers. And, as the only media of news communication outside of personal sources, these papers would remain compelling past their date of publication. The latest news stayed fresh for a longer time than it would later. And these papers were expensive: they weren't as disposable, as it were, as today's papers.

Besides these intrinsic reasons why multiple readership could be expected in the age of the weekly paper, there also seem to be cultural reasons that we can only speculate about. For instance, we know that during the Revolutionary period it was common for newspapers and broadsides to be read aloud in public—that is, to be included in a broader arena of social communication beyond the limited group of people who bought or subscribed to newspapers. These papers are characterized by a tone of seriousness that seems to indicate an awareness of a large secondary audience, a readership greatly in excess of a paper's subscription list. This tone persisted through the early National period.

While much of this line of argument is conjecture, nevertheless it is apparent that early newspaper *readership* was much larger than *circulation* figures would suggest. The ratio of readership to circulation for the period of the weekly newspaper may safely be estimated at ten to one, and it seems that this ratio fell gradually with the introduction of new formats: the daily newspaper and the penny paper, which tended to enhance the ephemerality and disposability of papers. As late as 1842, however, the *Daily Microscope* felt justified in claiming 25,000 readers, though it was a penny daily that circulated fewer than 2500 copies.[56] The *Microscope* no doubt artificially magnified its readership, but did not seem

is significant that the author of this letter was a storekeeper.

[55]Lawrence Cremin suggests a figure of 20 readers for each paper. See *American Education: The National Experience, 1783-1876* (New York: Harper & Row, 1980) pp. 188-9.

[56]*Daily Microscope*, July 12, 1842.

ridiculous in assuming it to be several times the size of its circulation.[57]

The simplest measurement of the penetration of newspaper circulation into the population as a whole is the ratio of papers sold to population. Thus, in 1815, the two existing newspapers, the *Western Spy* and the *Liberty Hall*, had circulations of 1200 and 1400 respectively. This gives a total of 2600 copies per week when the city's population was 6000.[58] In 1826, Cincinnati papers printed a total of 7200 copies per week, and in the meantime the city's population had increased to 16,230.[59] In both years, the ratio of copies:person was roughly 1:2. We might also say that the ratio of copies:adults was 1:1, assuming that half the population was adult. This figure is surprisingly high, because it would indicate that every household in Cincinnati subscribed to at least one newspaper.

Yet this simple measurement is deceiving. These early papers circulated widely throughout the countryside, not primarily within the cities, like the later dailies. And many people subscribed to more than one paper, so that the total number of subscribers was probably significantly lower than aggregate circulation. James Gazlay, editor of the *Western Tiller*, in 1826, estimated that there were only some 1500 subscribers in Hamilton County. Figuring the total population of the county to number 35,000, he concluded that there was only "one newspaper reader for every 22 inhabitants; that is provided there be no borrowing."[60] Since Gazlay cited this figure to encourage people to subscribe to his own paper, we can assume it to be the lowest figure he could contrive.

What was the actual readership of Cincinnati's early newspapers? One

---

[57]Today's readership figures usually are about three times circulation. It should be kept in mind, though, that today's circulation figures are based on audits and reflect fairly accurately the number of papers that are actually bought. The circulation figures that are handed down from the nineteenth-century penny papers are based on publishers claims and tend to reflect the number of newspapers that were printed--a larger number than the number that were bought. It would not be appropriate to multiply a penny paper's claimed circulation by three, even assuming that those papers were used in the same fashion as a modern daily paper, because this might still give an inflated picture of penny daily readership.

[58]Daniel Drake, *Natural and Statistical View or Picture of Cincinnati* (Cincinnati: 1815), p. 152; *Cist*, 1841, p. 38.

[59]Benjamin Drake and Edward Deering Mansfield, *Cincinnati in 1826* (Cincinnati: Morgan, Lodge, and Fisher, 1827), p. 57.

[60]*Western Tiller*, Sept. 8, 1826.

in two? One in twenty-two? Keeping in mind that households tended to be large, that the median age of the population tended to be low—around seventeen in 1810—implying a large number of children,[61] and that readership tended to exceed circulation, I would contend that even before 1826 virtually every literate adult in Cincinnati had access to a newspaper on a regular basis, whether by subscription, borrowing, or perusal at a public house or reading room.

Ultimately, questions of readership and circulation are important only insofar as they provide some indication as to how widely ideas, information, and opinions contained in newspapers circulated among the overall population. It is not possible to make conclusive statements regarding newspaper circulation without examining subscription lists, and even then it is not possible to make conclusive statements regarding readership. But the numbers that are available, coupled with recorded observations and other impressionistic evidence, tend to indicate that newspaper readership was not confined to a social or economic elite in Cincinnati before 1825, when the first daily newspaper in Cincinnati was issued. On the contrary, I have found no evidence to indicate that either readership or familiarity with the information and opinions contained in newspapers was limited. The early weekly newspaper seems to have been a truly popular medium.

After 1825 readership becomes more difficult to estimate. Daily papers appeared, along with bi- and tri-weeklies and weeklies, monthlies, and quarterlies; the number of separate publications was far greater in the decades following 1825. Census figures for 1850 show thirty-nine publications with a total of 8,753,200 copies issued.[62] For an urban population of around 115,000, this amounts to about 1.5 copies per person per week. Yet it is uncertain, for reasons implied above, that this increase in circulation translated into an increase in readership. Quarterlies and monthlies were distributed regionally, and did not necessarily enhance local readership. And the introduction of the daily newspaper had an

[61]Daniel Drake, *Notices Concerning Cincinnati* (1810), in Henry D. Shapiro and Zane L. Miller, ed., *Physican to the West: Selected Writings of Daniel Drake on Science and Society* (Lexington: University Press of Kentucky, 1970), p. 28.

[62]Frank Luther Mott, *A History of American Magazines, 1741-1905*, 5 vols., (Cambridge: Harvard University Press, 1930), I, 375 ftnt.

ambivalent effect. While it increased aggregate circulation, it may not have increased readership significantly, since a daily paper loses currency much more quickly than a weekly, and hence is less often re-read. Daily newspapers probably accounted for nearly two-thirds of all publications in Cincinnati in 1850. If we allow, then, a proportional drop in the ratio of readership to circulation, it is likely that newspaper readership did not rise sharply from 1825 to 1850.

The effect of press expansion, then, was not a simple increase in the number of newspaper readers. Its effect, rather, was to add a class of daily newspaper readers, and another class of magazine and journal readers. What emerges from the welter of statistics is not a linear quantitative growth in readership, but a qualitative shift, a differentiation in kinds of readers, a phenomenon that matched the growth and diversification of the urban setting. The increase in circulation, as distinct from any increase in readership, cannot be interpreted as a simple increase in some single element called the power of the press. Rather, it more likely means that what we may call the power of the press slowly changed with the evolution and expansion of the press establishment.

The Business of the Press

The financial structure of the press displayed a mixture of continuity and drastic change. The price of a newspaper subscription remained relatively stable, but at the same time the cost of running a newspaper establishment increased exponentially, causing great changes in the print workplace, while advertising moved toward maturity as a source of revenue, peripheral sources of income were developed, and different methods of distribution introduced.

Annual subscriptions changed little in price. Maxwell charged between $1.50 and $2.50 for his *Centinel*, and the *Weekly Liberty Hall and Cincinnati Gazette* charged $2.00 in 1844. All the bi-weeklies I examined cost $4.00 in advance, and all the tri-weeklies $5.00. When the *Mercantile Daily Advertiser* began publication in 1826, it charged $8.00 *per annum* in advance, the same price as the *Daily Gazette* would ask throughout the 1840s. Within these classes of newspapers, then, price stability prevailed.

The most telling change in the price structure was the introduction of the penny paper. The *Daily Microscope* charged $5.00 *per annum* in advance for its paper, a significantly lower price than competing conventional dailies. A penny paper sold a single copy for one or two cents; conventional dailies stuck mostly to their subscription lists, and when condescending to sell single issues, usually charged five cents or more.

The introduction of penny papers marked a downward trend in prices that spread throughout the press establishment. Both penny papers and conventional papers began issuing "dollar" weeklies in the 1840s, so-called because a year's subscription cost one dollar. This downward trend was mitigated, however, by the gradual deflation of the dollar in the antebellum period.

Subscriptions were a capricious source of income. In the early nineteenth century, specie was scarce enough that editors regularly accepted payment in agricultural produce.[63] Payment was not always demanded in advance on papers, and non-payment was common. Even in the event of non-payment, subscriptions would be continued, lest the newspaper be forced to forfeit all hope of back-payment; frequently a subscriber would default on several years' payment. More important sources of income were job printing, patronage, and advertising.

Commissions for book printing figured in a printer's income from the start. William Maxwell was hired to print the laws of the territory in book form in 1795; the result was the first book ever published in the Northwest Territory.[64] John Browne published almanacs. By 1815, both the *Liberty Hall* and the *Western Spy* owned an extra press for job printing.[65] It was not uncommon for an early paper to print proposals for publishing a certain work, then circulate a subscription list, meanwhile enticing potential customers by excerpting a key chapter or two in the paper.[66] Eventually book publishing came to be dominated by the larger publishing houses, but independent print shops continued to derive a

[63]See, for example, *Liberty Hall*, Jan. 15, 1805.
[64]Venable, *Literary Culture*, pp. 49–50; Burnet, *Notes*, p. 41.
[65]Sutton, *Book Trade*, p. 10.
[66]See, for example, *Liberty Hall*, Jan. 19, 26, 1815, for proposals to publish Matthew Carey's *The Olive Branch*.

large part of their profit from similar enterprises, like printing pamphlets and other political tracts.[67]

Another source of income for a newspaper was government printing. The federal government always tended to favor newspapers. Regulations granted postal privileges to newspapers. Publication of the laws was another way in which public money nourished the press. Throughout the period 1793-1848, the Secretary of State was authorized to choose local newspapers in each Congressional district to publish the laws "by authority," paying advertising rates for the space consumed. Designation as "Printers of the Laws of the United States" assured a newspaper office of a steady source of income. For a time rival newspapers complained that this practice encouraged servility in the press by favoring pro-administration papers, but complaints ceased when editors contemplated the prospect of a change of administrations.[68] In addition to federal patronage, loyal partisan newspapers could occasionally expect a cash transfusion from party coffers.[69]

Nevertheless, the most important source of income for a newspaper was advertising. Solomon Smith, editor and proprietor of the *Independent Press and Freedom's Advocate*, called advertising "the only source of PROFIT in a newspaper."[70] The importance of advertising revenue increased with the coming of the daily press and, with the rising costs of printing and communications technology, advertising costs increased in proportion.

In the first decade of the nineteenth century, the going price of advertising was $1.00 for four insertions of one square (ten to twelve lines), with .25 charged for each additional insertion. In the 1810s, $1.00 bought only three insertions; and by the 1840s it bought just one insertion

[67]The *National Crisis and Cincinnati Emporium*, Aug. 6, 1827, boasts of printing up 2000 copies of a speech by Henry Clay for distribution at a penny a copy.

[68]*Literary Cadet*, Feb. 24, April 20, 1820; *Advertiser and Phoenix*, April 9, 1825. For a general treatment of state department patronage, see Smith, *Patronage*.

[69]For a description of Daniel Webster's and Henry Clay's funding of party organs in the campaign of 1828, see Robert V. Remini, *The Election of Andrew Jackson*, Critical Periods in History, Robert D. Cross, ed., (Philadelphia and New York: J. B. Lippincott, 1963), pp. 127 *et passim*.

[70]*Independent Press*, Sept. 26, 1822.

in a weekly paper, with .37 charged for each additional insertion.[71] Meanwhile, as columns became narrower and papers larger, the number of squares per issue increased as well. These figures suggest an exponential increase for advertising revenue for weeklies throughout the period, while subscription revenues increased only with circulation expansion.

Table III shows estimates of the corresponding increases in subscription and advertising income for the office of the *Liberty Hall*. The increasing importance of advertising revenue indicates a new reliance on the marketplace. The press became a business, selling a service to other businesses by printing prices current and bank note exchange rates, and offering a product to consumers. It is in the context of market expansion that we should interpret the expansion of the press after 1820.

TABLE III

Comparison of Advertising and Subscription Income for
Liberty Hall and Gazette, 1815-1841

Year	Subscriptions	Advertising	Advertising as percentage of Income
1815	$3500	$1560	31%
1841	$14,800	$21,190	59%
Net Change	$11,300	$19,630	
Percent Change	323%	1258%	

Source: *Liberty Hall*, 1815, and *Cincinnati Daily Gazette*, *Tri-Weekly Cincinnati Gazette*, and *Weekly Liberty Hall and Cincinnati Gazette*, 1841. A subjective element is involved in estimating the number of new and repeat insertions. These figures presume that all subscription and advertising charges were paid.

Advertising, as a business, was kept separate from the news and opinions offered in the press. Competing papers quickly learned not to let philosophical differences interfere with money-making, and agreed on uniform prices for advertising as early as 1814.[72] Similar agreements appeared from time to time. It is clear that, after 1814, lowering advertising

[71]Prices derived from *Western Spy*, *Liberty Hall*, and *Weekly Liberty Hall and Cincinnati Gazette*.

[72]"Terms of Advertising in Cincinnati Newspapers," *Liberty Hall*, Dec. 13, 1814.

rates was seen as unfair competition, a violation of accepted procedures attempted only by upstarts like Joseph Buchanan's *Literary Cadet*, which offered rates *"twenty percent cheaper* than the customary prices." The *Literary Cadet* quickly failed.

TABLE IV

Comparison of Advertising Rates
for the *Enquirer* and *Microscope*, 1842

Description	*Enquirer*	*Microscope*
1 square, 1 insertion	.75	.50
2 insertions	1.00	.75
1 week	2.00	1.50
1 month	5.00	4.00
6 months	15.00	15.00
1 year	20.00	30.00

Source: *Enquirer* and *Microscope*, 1842.

Competition on advertising rates was forestalled by concerted action on the part of press conductors until around 1840. It was at this time that penny papers were successfully introduced. Table IV is a comparison of advertising rates for the penny *Daily Microscope* and the *Daily Enquirer*, a conventional political daily. Each paper is representative of its genre. It is clear that the *Microscope* generally offered lower rates. More significant is the way its rates were especially designed to favor short-term advertisements. This bias in advertising prices corresponds to the cash system of distribution, which appealed to occasional purchasers rather than year-long subscribers. The *Enquirer*, on the other hand, with a long subscription list, appealed to long-term advertisers. This kind of competition could occur only in a market diverse enough to support not only different classes of readers but different classes of advertisers as well.

Cincinnati's growth as an urban market thus was crucial to the expansion and differenetiation of its press establishment. The key phase occurred during the recovery from the Panic of 1819, which had seriously weakened the area's economy on all levels. In the 1820s, the city became increasingly involved in regional and national networks of trade and commerce, especially after the completion of the Miami Canal in 1828, linking the city to the Great Lakes. The city's growth was again interrupted, even more severely, by the Panic of 1837, which caused hardship especially for the working class and brought forth class tensions that had been less apparent earlier.[73]

This cycle of boom and bust coincided with changes in print technology and newspaper formats to produce vast changes in the structure of the print workplace.

The amount of capital invested in a newspaper rose steadily. Early printers required no more than a few hundred dollars; but in 1845 Eliphalet Case paid $13,000 for the *Enquirer*.[74] Twenty-five years later, the *Cincinnati Times* was appraised at $200,000.[75] The press was a big business.

Market expansion in printing centered in the decade of the 1830s. It was then that the combination of technological innovation and urban growth permitted the introduction of new types of printed materials. It was then that dailies flourished and penny papers appeared. It was then that viable audiences were found for technical, religious, literary, and reform periodicals. By 1840, Cincinnati could boast of a mature publishing industry, with twenty-five book, newspaper, and job printing firms employing 362 men, with a gross product of over half a million dollars a year. One of every twenty workers in Cincinnati was employed in some print-related field. Printing was an integral part of the city's economy.[76]

As the press matured as an industry, the people involved in producing papers found specialized roles in the workplace. The independent printer gave way to a combination of entrepreneurial publisher, political editor, and hired laborers. By the late 1840s, Cincinnati papers regularly employed reporters. Indeed, the increasing division of labor in the press establishment was apparent in many of the changes in style and content

---

[73]Cayton, *Frontier Republic*, pp. 126-7; Steven J. Ross, *Workers on the Edge: Work, Leisure, and Politics in Industrializing Cincinnati, 1788-1890* (New York: Columbia University Press, 1985), pp. 26, 32-3.

[74]*Daily Enquirer*, Nov. 24, 1846.

[75]Hooper, *Ohio Journalism*, pp. 92-3.

[76]*Cist*, 1841, p. 56.

that we will discuss below.[77]

Meanwhile, rising costs affected different sectors of the press establishment. It remained relatively cheap to buy a hand press, which cost $150 in the early 1840s, compared with the $3000 price of the sort of steam press used for urban dailies. But papers printed on hand presses could not compete with the products of more advanced print shops, and nationally small weeklies began to disappear from the cities. At the same time, surviving print shops sought more secure specialized markets, concentrating on book publishing or job printing rather than newspaper work. In Cincinnati, the first print shop to specialize in book and job printing was opened in 1828 by Ephraim Morgan and John Sanxay.[78]

Master printers were forced to keep pace with this rapid change. In many cases, lack of available capital to finance new equipment purchases forced print shops out of business. As a result, printers resorted to new financial arrangements. Carolyn Dyer's study of press ownership in Wisconsin, 1833-1860, though dealing with an area more rural and less developed than Cincinnati in those years, reveals that the typical weekly paper required equipment and office space costing $1,500 and had annual expenses totalling $1,700, but could expect an annual profit of only $314. She concludes that financial independence was not the norm for Wisconsin printers. Instead, they resorted to mortgages, joint-stock ownership, sponsorship of various sorts, and primitive forms of group ownership.[79]   Workers were even more troubled than owners by market and technological change. Traditionally organized as a craft enterprise, the print shop had taken in youths as apprentices, and graduated them as journeymen with marketable skills, providing young men with geographic if not economic mobility, and certainly with some expectation of economic security. Proprietors of press establishments had themselves worked through the ranks and shared with their workers a craft culture, though this shared mentality became more problematical as

[77]A want ad for reporters appeared in the *Daily Microscope*, August 12, 1842. Undoubtedly reporters had been employed occasionally before then.

[78]William J. Rorabaugh, *The Craft Apprentice: From Franklin to the Machine Age in America* (New York: Oxford University Press, 1986), p. 146; Ross, *Workers*, 38-9.

[79]Carolyn Dyer, "Economic Dependence and Concentration of Ownership among Antebellum Wisconsin Newspapers," *Journalism History* 7 (1980), pp. 42-6.

print shops grew.[80]

The work in a print shop can be broken down into three categories. Most elementary was the unskilled work of breaking down type and inking, tasks generally left to apprentices or printer's devils. More demanding was press work, which required some skill in handling equipment, but primarily called for physical strength and endurance in repeating the same movements in lever-pulling (resulting, incidentally, in a visible over-development of the right half of the body). The most skill was required in composing or setting type. The compositor held a stick in one hand and placed type from a typecase in order into the stick with the other while reading copy, all of which demanded an instinctive knowledge of the typecase and a degree of manual dexterity that came only with long experience.[81]

The 1820s and especially the 1830s saw the work of the print shop transformed, however. New presses made physically demanding presswork obsolete. As a result, proprietors began hiring unskilled labor at low wages (often including women, who had never entered the craft through apprenticeship) to replace overqualified journeymen, who in turn were left to compete in growing numbers for work as compositors (composing would not be mechanized until the end of the century). In Cincinnati, the first proprietors to recognize the division of labor between compositors and pressmen and to hire lower-payed workers to do unskilled work were Stephen L'Hommedieu and Charles Starbuck around the year 1830. In 1835, L'Hommedieu, who owned the *Gazette*'s printing office, bought the city's first steam press over the objections of his journeymen. The average number of workers in Cincinnati's print shops rose from 6.3 in 1826 to 11.6 in 1841, while the largest shops became virtual factories.[82] In response, workers turned to unions.

Printers had begun to organize early. In 1824, Cincinnati's printers had

---

[80]On the craft culture of printers and related issues, see William S. Pretzer, "'The British, Duff Green, The Rats and the Devil': Custom, Capitalism, and Conflict in the Washington Printing Trade, 1834-1836," *Labor History* 27 (1985-6), pp. 5-30; and Pretzer, "The Quest for Autonomy and Discipline: Labor and Technology in the Book Trades," *Proceedings of the American Antiquarian Society* 96 (1986), pp. 85-131.

[81]Rorabaugh, *Craft Apprentice*, pp. 11-14.

[82]Rorabaugh, *Craft Apprentice*, ch. 4; Ross, *Workers*, pp. 38-9.

met separately to celebrate the Fourth of July.[83] In the 1830s, printers joined with other artisans in forming the Trades' Union Society.[84] In 1835, Cincinnati's Franklin Typographical Society issued a circular calling for a national meeting of printers; this move resulted in the formation of the short-lived National Typographical Society. Journeymen printers called strikes with some success in 1834 and 1836 to protest declining living standards and encroachments in traditional workplace customs and organization. These early attempts at organization fell victim to the Panic of 1837, but by 1845 a new Cincinnati Typographical Society had formed, one which would be instrumental in the launching of the National (later International) Typographical Union, which held its first convention in Cincinnati in 1852.[85] In 1848, an "association of journeymen printers" got together to issue the *Daily Nonpareil*, a cooperative move that indicates dissatisfaction with what was by then virtually complete separation of labor from ownership.[86]

This change in the structure of the press establishment had already begun by 1820. The "independent printer" still existed, but he was a maverick, and rarely economically viable. Solomon Smith, in 1822, owned and operated the *Independent Press and Freedom's Advocate*. He was a colorful figure, a Swedenborgian, a preacher and an actor, and he was so personally attached to his paper that he wept openly when forced to sell it. But his small weekly was unable to compete with the larger bi- and tri-weeklies, and, even while circulation rose, advertising income remained so low that Smith suspected a conspiracy against him among business interests.[87] The sad truth was that the independent printer could not compete in the marketplace for readers and advertisers.

Most newspaper proprietors still came from a background in printing.

---

[83]*Advertiser*, July 10, 1842.

[84]Discussed in Walter Stix Glazer, "Cincinnati in 1840: A Community Profile" (Unpublished doctoral dissertation, University of Michigan, 1968), p. 114; Daniel Aaron, Cincinnati, 1818-1838: A Study of Attitudes" (Unpublished doctoral dissertation, Harvard University, 1943), pp. 91-8.

[85]Lee, *Daily Newspaper*, pp. 135-39; *Daily Enquirer*, Jan. 4, 1845. Mott discusses professionalization in journalism in *American Journalism*, pp. 311-14. Ross, *Workers*, pp. 46-8.

[86]*Daily Enquirer*, Sept. 29, 1848.

[87]Hooper, *Ohio Journalism*, p. 91; *Independent Press*, Sept. 26, 1822.

But, starting in the 1820s, employees were laborers, and employers no longer needed to be craftsmen. A proprietor needed capital, not expertise. Printing was an industry, not a craft, and a gap had opened between the men who owned printing plants and presses and the men who operated them.[88] Proprietors concentrated on business, and left control of news and opinion content to professional editors. These men usually boasted more knowledge of politics or law than printing.[89] In terms of practical arrangements, the message had become independent of the medium.

The economic history of the newspaper indicates growth and diversification. Production rose, in terms of both number of publications and dollar value, and publications began to appeal to specific groups of people or to specialize in specific fields. Meanwhile, the number of men engaged in printing grew, and functions were divided among diverse occupations in what was becoming a complex industry. This economic growth was associated with the maturing marketplace in Cincinnati: the press became a business like other businesses.

The Press and Geography

If Cincinnati matured as an urban setting in the first half of the nineteenth century, this development should be manifest in the press in a number of ways. As the city grew, face-to-face communication would become inadequate for the purpose of transmitting local news, and newspapers would consequently begin to carry more local news.[90] At the

[88]Hooper records that "thirteen of the line of proprietors of the *Gazette* up to 1839 had served an apprecticeship at the printer's trade." *Ohio Journalism*, pp. 82-3. That the status of printers as independent craftmen was deteriorating is argued by William Pretzer in "Quest for Autonomy."

[89]Aaron, "Cincinnati," p. 76, noted the predominance of lawyers in the editorial corps in the 1820s and 1830s. James Wickes Taylor, a young lawyer in Cincinnati in the 1840s, when pressed for cash, found it natural to seek some kind of editorial employment. Taylor, *A Choice Nook of Memory: The Diary of a Cincinnati Law Clerk, 1842-1844*, James Taylor Dunn, ed., (Columbus: Ohio State Archaeological and Historical Society, 1950), p. 9.

[90]Historian Richard Wade contends that this did take place. *The Urban Frontier: The Rise of Western Cities, 1790-1830* (Cambridge: Harvard University Press, 1959), pp. 252-53.

same time, distinctly urban newspapers should have appeared. Did these developments in fact take place? Evidence suggests that such a pattern of localization occurred.

Before discussing localization, it is necessary to point out that printed material other than local newspapers was available. Federal laws were designed to facilitate mailing of newspapers between cities. In 1815, in Cincinnati, a yearly subscription to *Niles' Weekly Register* was advertised at $5.00, surely an affordable price for many.[91] Urban maturity seemed to mean increasing availability of out-of-town periodicals and newspapers. In 1845, Robinson & Jones of Cincinnati sold 26,828 magazines from outside Cincinnati, including 7785 copies of *Graham's Magazine* alone. Similarly, the firm sold 4500 copies of Bennett's *Weekly Herald* from New York, an average of around 90 per weekly issue, among sales of 25,390 out-of-town papers sold during the year, averaging some 490 copies per week. These figures represent only one bookstore, and do not include papers delivered directly to subscribers by mail.[92]

Cincinnati's libraries and reading rooms also carried out-of-town papers. A "Circulating Library" was begun as early as 1814.[93] In the 1820s, the Western Museum maintained a reading room "furnished with a great variety of papers, prices current, etc.," from various parts of the Union, and Elam P. Langdon operated a similar reading room attached to the post offce.[94] The Young Men's Mercantile Library, which survives to this day, kept subscriptions to the most important newspapers of the 1830s and 1840s, including the *National Intelligencer*, the *United States Gazette*, the *Boston Courier*, and the *New York American*.[95] Since Cincinnatians showed such interest in newspapers from other cities, the significance of readership of out-of-town newspapers warrants some discussion.

Four factors limit the significance of out-of-town papers. First, they

[91]*Liberty Hall*, Oct. 16, 1815.

[92]Charles Cist, *Cincinnati Miscellany*, II (March, 1846), p. 331.

[93]Haynes McMullen, "The Use of Books in the Ohio Valley Before 1850," *Journal of Library History*, I (Jan., 1966), pp. 43-56, 73; *Western Spy*, March 12, 1814.

[94]*Cincinnati Literary Gazette*, II (Sept. 18, 1824), p. 94; (Oct. 16, 1824), p. 127; Drake and Mansfield, *1826*, p. 44.

[95]Young Men's Mercantile Library, "Bound Newspapers," undated manuscript, Cincinnati Public Library.

tended to be weeklies or monthlies. Mail service was never so efficient as to encourage subscription to an out-of-town daily. Moreover, most out-of-town papers were probably religious, literary, or technical; few were relied on for general news, and those were probably favored for a unique political perspective, or detailed coverage of matters like Congressional debates, covered in more cursory form in local papers. But the news function of the press remained primarily in local hands.

TABLE V

Geographical Origin of News
in Cincinnati Papers, 1795–1845

Location	1795	1805	1815	1825	1835	1845
Europe	41	27	22	21	14	9
South America	2	5	4	8	3	.3
Other Foreign	-	4	4	4	3	2
Total Foreign	43	36	30	33	20	14
Eastern U. S.	12	13	15	17	20	20
Southern U. S.	1	11	21	8	14	13
Western U. S.	28	29	15	14	20	24
Cincinnati	16	8	9	18	16	19
U. S. General	-	3	10	10	10	10
Total Western	43	37	24	32	36	43
Total U. S.	57	64	70	67	80	86

Source: These figures were drawn from a sampling of two newspapers for each year, except 1795, when only one was published, and 1845, when three were consulted. Papers used were the *Centinel* (1795); the *Western Spy* and *Liberty Hall* (1805 and 1815); the *National Republican* and *Advertiser* (both bi-weekly 1825); the *Daily Gazette* and *Daily Republican* (1835); and the *Daily Commercial, Daily Enquirer,* and *Weekly Liberty Hall and Cincinnati Gazette* (1845). Samplings are designed to be representative of the entire conventional newspaper establishment in each year. Samplings covered the entire year, thus accounting for seasonal variations. The basic sampling unit was one item, with additional weight for lengthy items. Percentages for individual papers for each year were averaged together then rounded off to whole numbers to yield the figures presented.

Second, out-of-town newspapers were expensive. Even libraries and reading rooms charged dues high enough to discourage casual membership. Because of their cost and comparative rarity, out-of-town papers were probably not passed from hand to hand: subscribers would be more jealous of their rights as owners. Hence readership probably was not high.

Third, local newspapers used exchange copies of out-of-town papers as their primary news source. Non-local news and newspapers were thus co-opted under the aegis of local editorial authority.

Fourth, and finally, circulation of out-of-town newspapers was minuscule compared to that of local papers. Robinson & Jones reported sales of around 50,000 in 1845, and, as the largest such retailer in Cincinnati, probably accounted for more than a fourth of the total number of out-of-town papers purchased in any manner that year. The annual figure of 200,000 is very small compared to the 8,753,200 copies put out by the Cincinnati press in 1850. In contrast to the media today, the antebellum newspaper was local: papers were read and printed locally.

Still, people read newspapers to learn of goings-on outside their locality. If most newspapers were local, most news was not. Geographical origin of the news is easily quantified.

Table V shows place of origin of news items at ten-year intervals from 1795 to 1845. Of special interest are the subtotals for foreign, domestic, and western news. Graph I shows the decline of foreign news to the benefit of domestic news. The most dramatic change here occurred in the years between 1825 and 1845, roughly coinciding with the great expansion of market and press. Domestic news, we may infer, was part of a conscious or semi-conscious appeal to news consumers' tastes. We may also conclude that, as the nation had grown, more important things tended to occur within its boundaries. Graph II shows regional (western plus Cincinnati) broken down into local (Cincinnati) and non-local components. Several significant details appear.

GRAPH I

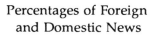

Percentages of Foreign
and Domestic News

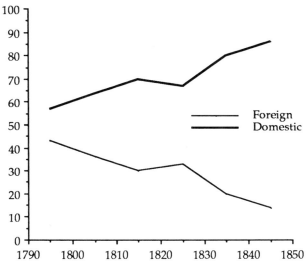

With the exceptions of 1795 and 1835, Cincinnati's share of the news rose steadily. But there are good reasons to revise the sample for 1795. In that year the territorial government was located in Cincinnati, so that news that would later be non-local, coming from Chillicothe or Columbus, future sites of territorial and state governments, is marked local. Hence the local figure for 1795 could be lower. The drop in 1835 is relatively minor, and of no significance.

One may conclude that local news became steadily more important. This rising importance is associated with Cincinnati's spectacular growth as a city, and with the rise of an urban audience or market for news.

The figures for total regional and non-local regional news require some explanation. They seem to start high, dip low, then rise again. I attribute this odd behavior to the interplay of two discrete processes: the rise of the region and the rise of competition for a regional audience or market. This latter process explains the early fall in regional news.

GRAPH II

Percentages of Regional and Local News

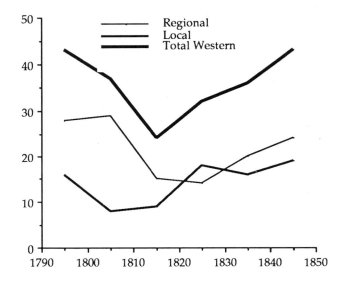

In 1795, the *Centinel of the North-Western Territory* was the only newspaper in the entire Northwest. It therefore had to serve a geographically vast market. In addition, located at the seat of government, it was relied on to provide news of all regional governmental matters. Hence the early preponderance of regional material: the root cause was an unchallenged regional market.

During the next two decades, Cincinnati's unchallenged control over the newspaper market in the Northwest disappeared. The seat of government was removed. And, until the 1820s, the west developed but gradually, with significant gains derived from the introduction of the steamboat and the end of the War of 1812 wiped out by the Panic of 1819. Regional news dropped to a low of 24 percent in 1815.

In the 1820s, regional news became more important. This came about as a local market arose to replace the lost regional one, and as a western economic boom began on the wave of schemes for internal improvements. The most important factor, though, was the local market, and it is no accident that the expansion of regional news coincided with expansion of the region.

The figures listed above concern only newspapers. By the 1830s, however, there was a new regional market in non-news publications, namely religious, literary, and technical periodicals. Cincinnati became a center for such publications. Though circulation of these papers abroad is difficult to gauge without subscription lists, impressionistic evidence suggests a wide regional audience. And occasional hard evidence is available. A postmaster's log book from Jacksonville, Illinois, lists out-of-town publications received for the years 1831-1832. Included are twenty-eight subscriptions to ten different Cincinnati periodicals. Of these, six are religious in nature, one literary, one agricultural, and two political; and in one year these twenty-eight subscriptions would have entailed the mailing of about 1500 individual copies.[96] There is no reason to believe that other regional towns subscribed to fewer Cincinnati publications, or that Cincinnati's share of the regional market declined after 1832. On the contrary, I suspect—judging from local production figures—that Cincinnati's share rose with time, and was larger in areas less remote than Illinois. In 1840, for example, Cincinnati, with a population of 46,382, printed 4,005,768 copies of periodical literature, for an average of 86.3 copies per person per year. The national average for that year was 8.6. Part of this imbalance is due to Cincinnati's large urban daily newspaper market, but this uncommonly large ratio of urban population to press product also implies a sizable ex-urban readership. It is likely that this readership consumed largely non-news publications.

Non-news publications first appeared in Cincinnati in the 1820s. Their appearance seems linked to the genesis of a regional market for such publications, created by population growth and improvements in intraregional transportation. A tentative economic independence from the east was achieved. Simultaneously, a sense of cultural identity

[96]Frank J. Heinl, "Newspapers and Periodicals in the Lincoln-Douglas Country, 1831-1832," *Journal of the Illinois State Historical Society*, XXIII (Oct., 1930), pp. 371-438.

appeared, and attempts were made to create and refine a western literature and a western spirit in religion, as is clearly illustrated by the names of the new periodicals: the *Western Christian Advocate*, the *Western Messenger*, the *Western Monthly Magazine*, the *Sentinel and Star in the West*, the *Ladies' Repository and Gatherings of the West*, and the *Western Academician*, to name a few. These periodicals entered into vigorous competition with their eastern counterparts, often similar in name (with the exception of the adjective western) and superior in content and execution.

Geographical interests as they changed over time betray several developments: local news drew a larger share of newspaper space, indicating a new urban news market, while non-local regional news generally declined, indicating increased competition for the regional news market. Meanwhile, a new regional market for non-news publications appeared, and attempts were made to exploit it. The watershed years for these developments were the 1820s, the years of economic revival following the Panic of 1819. The changes in the Cincinnati press reflect changes in the Cincinnati and western economy, and seem to indicate a growing integration of the press into regional and local markets.

Press technology, finance, and distribution changed dramatically in the early nineteenth century. But these are external factors, perhaps superficial, perhaps having little effect on the quality or content of information transmission. Were there corresponding changes in the social function of the press? Did the periodical acquire new meaning in the minds of its readers? These questions require a more in-depth examination of the transformation of the press in the years from 1820 to 1848.

CHAPTER II

The Transformation of the Press, 1820–1848

Antebellum Cincinnati is best known through Mrs. Trollope's description. Entertaining though her *Domestic Manners of the Americans* may be, its portrayal of early Cincinnati's society and culture seemed to later travelers an unfair caricature.[1] Indeed, the city was more mature and substantial than Mrs. Trollope was willing to concede.

As early as 1830, Cincinnati had taken the lead in midwestern economic life. Eight times larger than any other midwestern city, it controlled the meat-packing industry and was the marketplace for much of the agricultural produce of the Ohio Valley. By 1850, the "pork-shop of the Union" would also be the world's largest distilling center.[2]

Cincinnati's population was young, energetic, and diverse. There were relatively few older citizens, as most were newcomers to the rapidly growing city. As late as 1840, less than half of the residents of Cincinnati

---

[1]Frederick Marryat, *A Diary in America, with Remarks on its Institutions*, Sydney Jackman, ed., (New York: Knopf, 1962), pp. 224-25; William R. Seat, Jr., "A Rebuttal to Mrs. Trollope: Harriet Martineau in Cincinnati," *Ohio Historical Quarterly* LXVIII (July, 1959), pp. 276-89.

[2]Marryat, *Diary*, p. 222; Francis P. Weisenburger, "The Urbanization of the Middle West: Town and Village in the Pioneer Period," *Indiana Magazine of History* XLI (March, 1945), pp. 29-30.

had lived there as long as ten years. In that same year, less than 10% of the adult males listed their state of birth as Ohio: surely fewer than one in ten were native Cincinnatians. Over half in that year were foreign-born; 28% were German-born, up from 2.5% in 1825; and 33% came from eastern states, down from 58% in 1825.[3]

As the population grew and diversified, discrete social and occupational classes appeared. Social cleavages along economic lines had long been apparent in associational activities, but in the 1820s an elite class of merchants and professionals emerged. This was a distinctly urban class, alien to the surrounding agricultural region. The elite was mirrored by another distinctly urban class, propertyless workers, who by 1840 constituted a majority of Cincinnati's householders. There was a tightening of social lines. As the village became a city, it lost a sense of community; there were new tensions between groups, and new reasons for associational activity within each group. These developments would all affect communications.[4]

The context of urban change was explosive urban growth. Table VI illustrates expansion from 1795 to 1840. Again in the decade 1840-1850 the population would more than double in size.[5] Population growth was matched by economic growth, slowed only by the Panics of 1819 and 1837, and a constant shortage of sound currency.

Demographic and economic growth was matched by growth in printing. In 1826, Cincinnati boasted two daily, three semi-weekly, and two weekly papers, in addition to a weekly literary paper and a professional

[3]Walter Stix Glazer, "Cincinnati in 1840: A Community Profile" (Unpublished doctoral dissertation, University of Michigan, 1968), pp. 212, 213; Charles Cist, *Cincinnati in 1841: Its Early Annals and Future Prospects* (Cincinnati: Charles Cist, 1841), p. 39; Glazer, "1840," p. 102.

[4]On early social class, see Richard C. Wade, *The Urban Frontier: The Rise of Western Cities, 1790-1830* (Cambridge: Harvard University Press, 1959), pp. 105-6; for rural nostalgia and alienation, see *Western Tiller*, Dec. 1, 1826. Glazer, "1840," pp. 120-23, discusses urban stratification; Wade, *Urban Frontier*, p. 204 discusses early social stratification after 1820. Also see Steven J. Ross, *Workers on the Edge: Work, Leisure, and Politics in Industrializing Cincinnati, 1788-1890* (New York: Columbia University Press, 1985).

[5]Figures drawn from Cist, *1841*, pp. 28-38 *et passim*; Cist, "Population of Cincinnati," *Cincinnati Miscellany*, I (Oct., 1844), p. 19.

professional journal which appeared twice a month. At the beginning of 1845, there were twelve daily papers, many with subsidiary weeklies, along with fourteen weeklies devoted to religion, business, or reform, and another fourteen technical, religious, or literary monthlies. Nine printing plants grossed $52,000 and employed 23 hands in 1826, compared to 25 plants employing 362 and grossing $518,500 in 1840.[6] In the years from 1815 to 1850, the office of the *Liberty Hall and Gazette* increased in value from $1000 to $100,000; the number of hands it employed increased from 6 to 90; and the number of copies issued per year rose from 21,190 to 2,475,200.[7]

TABLE VI

Population Growth
in Cincinnati, 1795–1840

Year	Population	Number change	Percent change
1795	500		
1800	750	250	50
1805	960	210	31
1810	2540	1580	162
1815	6000	3460	136
1820	9602	3602	60
1825	15,000	5398	56
1830	24,831	9831	66
1835	33,624	8793	36
1840	46,382	12,758	38

Source: Cist, *1841*, pp. 28-38 *et passim.*

[6]In the same years, the city's gross product increased from $1,800,000 to $17,432,670. *Mercantile Daily Advertiser*, Sept. 18, 1826; Charles Cist, "Cincinnati Periodical Press," *Cincinnati Miscellany*, I (Jan., 1845), pp. 107-8; Benjamin Drake and Edward Deering Mansfield, *Cincinnati in 1826* (Cincinnati: Morgan, Lodge, & Fisher, 1827), pp. 64-6; Cist, *1841*, pp. 56, 58.

[7]William Turner Coggeshall, "History of the Cincinnati Press and its Conductors" (Unpublished manuscript, Cincinnati Historical Society), p. 14.

Newspaper Content and News Ideology, 1795–1845

Press growth occurred in a context of changing content. I have quantified newspaper content under eight discrete substantive headings and eight discrete stylistic headings at ten-year intervals from 1795 to 1845. Results are listed in Table VII and Table VIII.

Substantive changes reflect newspaper growth. For example, filler material—religious and moral items and essays, poetry, reviews of literature and performances, anecdotes and short stories—and scientific and agricultural items increased with frequency of publication. Likewise, decrease in publication of minutes and laws is in part due to an increase in available space: the production of laws did not increase commensurately. Other changes in content reflected social and cultural trends. Greater attention was paid to commercial and economic news as the market grew and commercial information became more timely and urgent. Military and diplomatic information, which generally dealt with European affairs, became less popular as cultural nationalism grew after the War of 1812.

There was a steady increase in the number of items printed of the sort which I have simply labeled News. This category includes reports of deaths and weddings, fires, crimes, and other events which fall outside the areas of affairs of state or of the markets. What caused this increase?

TABLE VII

Substantive Content Analysis
of Cincinnati Newspapers, 1795–1845

Category	1795	1805	1815	1825	1835	1845
Political/Judicial	33	24	22	32	25	25
Military/Diplomatic	21	21	32	9	10	6
Indian/Slave	6	2	4	2	2	1
Minutes/Laws	31	17	14	7	6	3
Commercial/Economic	2	8	9	15	17	18
News	–	6	5	10	17	23
Filler	7	17	7	19	16	18
Scientific/Agricultural	–	5	7	6	7	6

Source: Sources and sampling technique same as geographical content analysis. See Chapter I, Table V.

Speed of communication was essential for the reporting of out-of-town fires or crimes. Such events had no news interest unless they were quickly reported, and there is a clear connection between reportage of this kind and improvements in long-distance communications.

Yet much if not most of what I have called News was local. Improvements in long-distance communications would have no effect upon local reporting, which must have received greater emphasis for some other reason. I contend that there were two other reasons, one social, and one cultural or ideological.

As Cincinnati grew, face-to-face communication was less effective in handling an increasing amount of local information. The process of urban growth itself entailed increased emphasis on local non-political and non-economic news. The appearance of the daily press made this practical.

TABLE VIII

Stylistic Content Analysis
of Cincinnati Newspapers, 1795–1845

Category	1795	1805	1815	1825	1835	1845
Editorial Reportage	20	13	7	9	8	12
Editorial Comment	1	1	1	7	10	7
Third Person	15	14	21	20	13	32
Copy from Another Paper	8	23	40	35	43	25
Copy from Nonpaper Source	43	32	24	14	14	13
Letter to the Editor	7	3	5	6	5	3
Belletristic	6	13	2	8	4	4
"Correspondent"	-	1	-	1	3	4

Source: Sources and sampling technique same as geographical content analysis. See Chapter I, Table V.

At the same time, the ideology of the press was undergoing changes. Items which would once have been considered trivial were often printed, while information once considered important—reports of battles abroad, or details of laws or treaties, or verbatim transcripts of key political speeches—occupied an ever-smaller percentage of news space. News was reported simply because it happened. It had no public significance, unlike the rest of a newspaper's content.

What is implied in these changes of substance is a subtle alteration in the ideology of the press. The press was no longer seen as the bastion of rational liberty, but as a servant of the market—hence attention to the economy—and as a neutral purveyor of processed news—hence attention to News. Further evidence of this shift is visible in stylistic trends.

While certainly less clear-cut, the stylistic statistics also reveal a subtle shift in attitudes. (See Table VIII.) Third-person reportage replaced publication of primary materials (copy from non-paper source), for example. This shift seems to indicate a change from an ideal of the press as an impartial carrier of news for independent and intelligent citizens to an ideal of the press as a processor of news. This change is reflected by a qualitative strengthening of the editorial voice.

GRAPH III

Change over Time In Percentages
of Selected Substantive Categories, 1795–1845

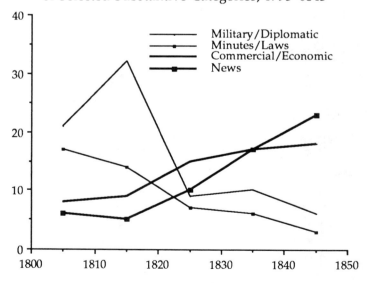

Graph IV shows the developing role of the editor in quantitative terms. As is readily apparent, the total percentage of editorial material did not increase dramatically: the editor usually wrote one column under the paper's masthead and the heading "Cincinnati," and this space did not expand. But there was a great change in style. Graph V illustrates this by charting the ratio of editorial comment to editorial reportage. It is clear that the editor had become more assertive, less impartial, less impersonal: as we shall see, the press was no longer "Open to all Parties, but Influenced by None."

GRAPH IV

Change over Time in Editorial Style, 1795–1845

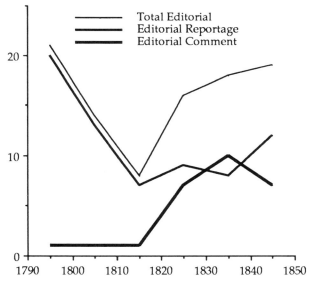

The crucial decade for the shift from a passive to an active editorial role was the 1820s. Before 1820, editorial comment never accounted for more than one-fifth of all editorial content. For the years 1795, 1805, and 1815, comment averaged 7% of an editor's output. As partisan contests became more overt and passionate, this figure rose, so that in 1825, 1835, and 1845 it measured 45%—just under half of all editorial output. This was obviously an opinionated press.

GRAPH V

Ratio of Editorial Comment to Editorial Reportage, 1795–1845

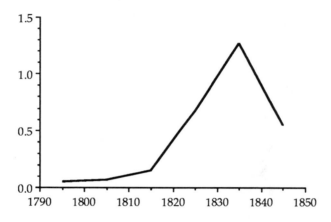

The statistics suggest a cyclical rather than a linear movement, however. In the 1840s, it seems that editorial pronouncements became less common. This does not necessarily imply a slackening-off of political interest, for the figures on political content remain high in the 1840s. Rather it suggests, I think, a dissatisfaction with partisanism in its more extreme form, and reflects the channeling of political dogmatizing into specialized periodicals. The drop in political comment also hinged upon the passing away of the heroic generation of political editors, led by Charles Hammond of the *Gazette* and Moses Dawson of the *Advertiser*.

The lasting legacy of the 1820s was the strengthening of the editorial voice. The editor became an oracle on a wide range of public issues. He spoke with a new authority, claimed a wider field of action than hitherto allowed.

As the editor put himself forward as an authority, however, he departed from the old ideal of impersonality—the tradition of the weak editorial voice which newspapers had honored before 1820. The press no longer expected an independent, intelligent electorate to interpret facts, to digest information, to constitute public opinion in an atmosphere of rational liberty; rather, the press sought to manipulate facts, to mould public opinion. This was an ideological innovation of the partisan press.

The press as partisan instrument was not new in the United States. Newspapers had divided along party lines in the struggle between Federalists and Jeffersonians, and most newspapers from 1790 on claimed some party allegiance. But such allegiance did not entail any strong editorial partisanism. The 1820s witnessed the rise of a new kind of partisan journalism, a genuine departure from the press ideology that informed the political papers of the Revolution and the early Republic. The precise contours of this partisanism I shall leave for later discussion. Two points concerning it are relevant now, however.

First, this partisanism involved a claim to positive authority on the part of newspapers. In other words, papers sought an active role in leading public opinion. Second, this authority was exerted in the context of a rapidly expanding press industry. This meant competition among editors, among the leaders of public opinion, in a manner analogous to the competition among products in the marketplace.

If seeking active authority made editors dogmatic, then being forced to compete for favor in the marketplace of public opinion transferred this dogmatism to public opinion itself. The omnipotent majority could exercise a tyranny over political discourse. The press ideology of the early Republic, the belief in rational liberty, was not equipped to handle this excess of democracy. New restraints would have to come into play.

The moderation of the editorial voice in the 1840s was a conservative reaction to a period of hyperbolic politics. In Cincinnati this reaction sprang from several sources. One factor was a general dampening of journalism after the Panic of 1837. Economic hardship tempered enthusiasm for political extremes on the one hand and, by making it more difficult to establish a successful newspaper, lessened competition for public favor. The late 1830s also saw a tremendous increase in the cost of adequate printing equipment. This tended to enhance the status of established papers and hinder the sort of political extremism or dogmatism that thrived in an atmosphere of open competition. Paradoxically, then, the moderation of the editorial voice seemed to signal a transfer of authority back from public opinion to the press conductor.

In the 1840s, a new cohort of partisan press conductors appeared, replacing the fallen generation of Hammond and Dawson. At the same time, however, a strong challenge was presented to political journalism by the appearance of the non-partisan penny press. Eschewing partisan politics as "humbug," the penny press was another factor in the moderation of the editorial voice. Its acceptance signals a shift in popular attitudes toward the intended role of the press in politics.

A necessary precondition for a successful non-partisan press was a disaffection with partisan journalism. This disaffection coincided in time with technological and economic innovations that encouraged production and distribution of newspapers on the cash basis. Hence the appearance of a politically neutral penny press. But popular sentiment concerning partisan journalism was distinct from the commercial and mechanical devices employed by the penny press. In the proper cultural context, a political penny press was possible, and in fact, partisan newspapers like the Democratic *Daily Enquirer* soon adopted the cash system of distribution, wedding it to a political program promoted by a strong editorial voice. Thus, while the penny press was a participant in the moderating of the editorial voice, it did not cause that moderation and that moderation was not the result of the adoption by either the penny press or the political press of the cash system of distribution.

One final factor in the moderation of political rhetoric in the 1840s was the proliferation of periodicals devoted to special causes. These journals ranged in topic from nativism to phonetic spelling, and appealed to an audience discrete from the general public. They therefore provided an outlet for extreme sentiments outside the general political press.

The establishment of reform journals indicates another change in press ideology. This change may be identified as a shift from a utopian to a business press. The attitudes associated with the press in the early Republic attributed to it a unique power toward the creation of a republic of rational liberty. Reformers still recognized that power, but, by the 1840s, conventional press conductors had become more business-minded. As statistics on press conduct indicate, they were ever more concerned with commercial information and ever more aware of the function of the press in facilitating market transactions. And, as the discussion of press technology indicated, the increasing sophistication of the typical print establishment effected a structural assimilation of the press to the business concerns that appeared with the coming of the industrial revolution. In terms of production and management, the press changed from a craft to an industry.

Press industrialization, urbanization, and improvements in long-distance communications all contributed to a new emphasis on News. In concrete terms, we see in the 1840s the simultaneous introduction of the reporter and the local news column, as well as a significant increase in the use of third-person reporting.[8] These developments coincided with changes in attitudes toward the press.

Before elaborating on the transformation of attitudes toward the press, it is appropriate to discuss the changes in structure alluded to above. This will mean a detailed treatment of the daily paper, the German press, and the penny paper.

The Daily Newspaper

The newspaper increased frequency of publication gradually. The first step in this process was for different weeklies to publish on different days, rendering effective bi-weekly coverage. In 1814, for example, the *Liberty Hall* was published on Tuesday, and the *Western Spy* on Saturday. The days of publication depended on mail arrivals. Beginning in the 1820s, more frequent mail arrivals permitted individual papers to become bi- or tri- weeklies.

Switching to bi- or tri-weekly publication entailed expansion of the print establishment. The independent printer, like Solomon Smith, could not make this transition: "If we were able, and could conveniently, hire an editor, &c. &c. &c. as the other papers do, there is no telling what change might take place in our paper...."[9] The expansion of printing space per week, however, required the full-time efforts of an editor. As the editor's

---

[8]The *Enquirer* began a local column in 1841--the first Cincinnati paper to do so.
[9]*Independent Press*, Jan. 9, 1823.

work load expanded, as he devoted more time to his newspaper work (as opposed to some other occupation, like a law practise), he seemed to develop a stronger voice, to become a more prominent personality.

In late 1825, Samuel S. Brooks issued the first daily newspaper in Cincinnati. The *Cincinnati Commercial Register* was only a half-sheet, or two pages in length, and lasted but six months before lack of support and managerial squabbles killed it.[10] But its appearance testified to an increasingly reliable flow of news—especially commercial news—and an increasingly apparent daily news market—especially among mercantile interests. The subsequent history of Cincinnati's daily press would confirm this testimony.

In late 1826, Samuel J. Browne (son of John W. Browne, founder of the *Liberty Hall*) and Hooper J. Warren issued proposals for a *Mercantile Daily Advertiser*. Their prospectus appealed directly to the "disposition always manifested by the mercantile and trading classes to foster the undertaking of such objects as are calculated to promote their interests . . . ." The *Mercantile Advertiser* announced its intention "to promote the interests of COMMERCE and MANUFACTURES" by giving prices current and currency exchange rates for New York, Philadelphia, Boston, Baltimore, and New Orleans, announcing steamboat arrivals and departures, and giving accounts of exports, imports, and the foreign markets. The *Mercantile Advertiser* also promised full news coverage, including "interesting local occurrences, important law cases, as well as all necessary discussion of political subjects." In politics, Browne and Warren promised to avoid all "editorial contentions, as tiresome and unedifying," and asserted that "their columns shall be open at all times for a fair and candid investigation of the merits of candidates for public offices, to whatever party they may be attached."[11]

These proposals illustrate several themes touched on above. First, and most obvious, is the importance of business interests: daily news was primarily business news. Second, specific mention was made of local

---

[10]Samuel S. Brooks, "To the Public," *National Crisis and Cincinnati Emporium*, June 11, 1827; William Turner Coggeshall, *The Newspaper Record . . .* (Philadelphia: Lay and Brother, 1856), p. 165; Osman Castle Hooper, *History of Ohio Journalism, 1793-1933* (Columbus: Spahr and Glenn, 1933), p. 71.

[11]*Mercantile Daily Advertiser*, Sept. 4, 1826.

news, underscoring a new interest in local occurrences or a new need to convey local information by means of the press. Third, the promise to avoid editorial contentions illustrates dissatisfaction with partisan conduct of newspapers, this in the midst of Andrew Jackson's presidential "campaign by continuation." Finally it is noteworthy that the profession of political neutrality echoed the sentiment embodied in the old formula, "Open to all Parties, but Influenced by None."

The *Mercantile Daily Advertiser* could not sustain itself as a daily, and returned instead to bi-weekly publication as the *National Crisis and Cincinnati Emporium*. The first newspaper to successfully introduce daily publication was the *Liberty Hall*, then Cincinnati's oldest continuous paper. The *Liberty Hall* began publishing the *Daily Cincinnati Gazette*, under the editorship of prominent lawyer and former Federalist Charles Hammond, at the request of a group of local businessmen in 1827. The *Gazette*'s original subscription list numbered 164, and almost all of the addresses on it were on the lower side of town, in the business district. The *Gazette* too initially called for the support of all political factions. Later it was to be the primary mouthpiece of Cincinnati's Whiggery.[12]

The *Gazette* was to have a long and distinguished career as a political daily. Charles Hammond himself would be the model of the political editor in Cincinnati, would publish Cincinnati's first campaign paper in 1828, and would become famous as one of Andrew Jackson's bitterest detractors.

The first successful dailies did become partisan. On the other hand, their associations with commercial and mercantile interests encouraged a political neutrality, at least initially, before direct competition became the norm for daily papers as well as weeklies. And the reporting of economic information tended to be factual or objective in style. These characteristics should be kept in mind during our discussion of the penny press.

---

[12]Hooper, *Ohio Journalism*, pp. 71-2; Coggeshall, *Newspaper Record*, pp. 165-66; Robert C. Wheeler, *Ohio Newspapers: A Living Record* (Columbus: Ohio History Press; Ohio Archaeological and Historical Society, 1950), p. 196; *Daily Gazette*, June 25, 1827.

The German-Language Press

At the same time as the first dailies appeared, appealing directly to mercantile interests, a foreign-language press appeared, with a specific readership of German immigrants. The early German press in Cincinnati has already been the topic of a scholarly dissertation.[13] Hence we need not recount in detail the founding of the various German papers or chronicle in depth the lives of their founders. But certain questions must be addressed: What was the role of the press in the German community? Did that role change over time? And how does the German press fit into the context of the Cincinnati press as a whole?

The first local German paper was the *Ohio Chronik*, a weekly, established in 1826. I was able to identify twenty-five German periodicals published in Cincinnati between 1826 and 1848. Of these, twenty-one endured less than five years, and sixteen less than a single year. Sixteen of the twenty-six were devoted to politics and general news, seven to religion or philosophy, and one each to literature and reform. Of the four papers that survived five years or more, two were political and two religious. The German press, like the press at large in the 1830s and 1840s, was topically diverse.

Charles Cist's *Cincinnati in 1841* gives useful statistics on the German population and its press. Cist numbers the Germans at 14,163, including some second-generation Germans. Ethnic Germans, then, accounted for 31% of the total population. Of these, adult males numbered 3440, 28% in a total adult male population of 12,292.[14] The German community was numerically large. It was also articulate.

Cist lists three religious and three political papers. The political papers circulated 312 daily, 250 tri-weekly, and 1900 weekly copies. This meant one daily or tri-weekly copy for each six adult male Germans, compared to one English-language daily or tri-weekly copy for every 2.7 non-Germans, not counting penny papers. Considering many Germans could also read English, then, it is likely that the German political press was just as

---

[13]Henry J. Groen, "A History of the German-American Newspapers of Cincinnati Before 1860" (Unpublished doctoral dissertation, Ohio State University, 1945).

[14]Cist, *1841*, p. 39.

effective for Germans as the English-language press was for others.[15] But the German press was effective with a difference, as it appealed to a select audience.

What was the role of the German-language press in the lives of those Cincinnatians literate in German? We can put this question several ways. Did the press facilitate the maintenance of a particularistic community? As Robert Park remarked, "How far the foreign-language press enables the immigrant to *participate* in the national life is the question raised . . . . For it is participation rather than submission or uniformity that makes Americans out of foreign-born peoples."[16] Did the German-language press enable Germans to participate in politics, in civic life? And how did its functioning compare to the English-language press? The easiest way to deal with these questions is to examine the most influential of the German papers in Cincinnati before 1848, the *Volksblatt*.

The establishment of the *Volksblatt* was an assertion of political maturity on the part of local Germans. It was the undertaking of a group of German Democrats, claiming to represent the majority of local Germans, and was begun in direct response to the defection of the *Deutsche Franklin* to the Whig camp in return for a reported cash gift of $600.[17] Karl Rümelin later recalled these events:

Boffinger [editor of the *Franklin*] sold out to the Whigs, who thought, that any German paper, provided it was printed in "Dutch," could carry the German vote. This idea might have proved true, if we emigrated Germans, had not interposed, in 1836, and rallied the more intelligent Germans of Cincinnati in favor of starting a new paper, the "Volksblatt," which spoiled the whole game of the Whigs, in buying out Boffinger.[18]

[15]*Ibid.*, pp. 93-4.

[16]Robert Ezra Park, *The Immigrant Press and Its Control* (New York: Harper, 1922), pp. 87-8.

[17]Karl Rümelin, "Geschichte des Gründung des Volksblatts," *Deutsche Pionier*, I (May, 1869), p. 81; Max Burgheim, *Cincinnati in Wort und Bild* (Cincinnati: M. and R. Burgheim, 1888), pp. 118-19. Emil Klauprecht, *Deutsche Chronik in der Geschichte des Ohio-Thales und seiner Haupstadt Cincinnati in's Besondere* (Cincinnati: 1864), pp 171 *et seq.*; Carl F. Wittke, *The German-Language Press in America* (Lexington: University of Kentucky Press, 1957), p. 32.

[18]Karl Rümelin, *Life of Charles Reemelin, in German: Carl Gustav Rümelin, from 1814-1892* (Cincinnati: Weier and Daiker, 1892), p. 46.

The *Volksblatt*, then, was essentially a German paper, founded by Germans, owned by a joint-stock company of Germans, edited, written, printed, and read by Germans. Its popularity among local Germans is indicated by its rapid rise in circulation, from an initial 300 to over 1000 within a single year, "for that time an unheard of number."[19] In November, 1838, the *Volksblatt* issued a daily paper, taking its place among the leading political dailies of Cincinnati.[20]

The *Tägliches Volksblatt* did not differ in format from other Cincinnati dailies. Pages one, three, and four were primarily advertising; page two featured an editorial head, followed by national news, then foreign news, then a column headed "Stadt Cincinnati," then an excerpt from a serialized literary piece.[21] It tended to pay more attention to foreign news, but not at the expense of domestic news. It followed politics closely: in 1841, it carried digests of the proceedings of the Ohio legislature, sent by Heinrich Röcter, then a state representative,[22] and one of the prime movers in the founding of the *Volksblatt*. By the mid-1840s, it regularly printed "Skizzen von Washington" (Sketches from Washington), written by a correspondent under the pseudonym Cincinnatus. In terms of issues, the *Volksblatt* was Democratic, but opposed slavery and paid particularly close attention to "Nativismus."

The *Volksblatt* boasted of its political influence among local Germans. We may tend to doubt these editorial puffings, as well as the memoirs of people associated with the paper, like Karl Rümelin, but the English-speaking Whig press also expressed concern over the monopoly that the *Volksblatt* seemed to hold over German public opinion.[23] We may conclude that the *Volksblatt*, as the leading representative of an autonomous German press, had great symbolic importance for local Germans.

---

[19]Burgheim, *Wort und Bild*, p. 119, my translation.

[20]Groen, "German American Newspapers," pp. 33-75, recounts the founding, early expansion, and political significance of the *Volksblatt*.

[21]This description is based on an examination of the files of the *Volksblatt* for the mid-1840s.

[22]Groen, "German American Newspapers," p. 107.

[23]*Weekly Liberty Hall and Cincinnati Gazette*, Feb. 8, 1844.

What kind of people were involved in the writing and printing of German papers? It would seem that for the most part they were highly respected men, generally members of the learned professions. It also seems that few had any press experience before coming to the United States.

Karl Gustav Rümelin was born in Heilbronn in 1814, and worked as a clerk in his father's business and in a commercial house before deciding to come to America in 1832. As a youthful devotee of the Greek independence movement, he found Jacksonian politics much to his liking. He began making speeches on behalf of Jacksonian candidates as early as 1837, at about the same time as he became involved in the publication of the *Volksblatt*. He was to be a successful politician, winning election as state representative in 1844, and state senator in 1846. Rümelin also found the American business climate to his liking. He began as a grocery-store clerk in 1833, and by 1839 was sole owner of the business.[24]

Heinrich Rödter was another of the founders of the *Volksblatt*. He was born in Neustadt in 1805, and, after serving in the army, studying law, and working in his family's paper mill, was caught up in the republican fervor surrounding the French Revolution of 1830 and decided to come to America. He originally came to Cincinnati in 1832, and found his knowledge of paper-making useful both as a source of income and as a bridge into the field of journalism. He too became a staunch Democrat, a well-to-do businessman, and a successful politician. He was a leading figure in the Deutsche demokratische Verein von Hamilton County, and served as director of the Cincinnati poorhouse, as state representative, and as Justice of the Peace before his early death in 1857.[25]

Another leading figure in the operation of both the *Volksblatt* and the demokratische Verein was Stephan Molitor. Molitor was born in Cheslitz, Bavaria, and, upon graduating from the University of Würzburg, practiced law in Munich. But he found the bureaucratic lifestyle of the

[24]Rümelin, *Life of Reemelin*, pp. 1-45; Armin Tenner, *Cincinnati Sonst und Jetzt: Eine Geschichte Cincinnati's* . . . (Cincinnati: Mecklenburg & Rosenthal, 1878), pp. 324-30; Burgheim, *Wort und Bild*, p. 87; Max Burgheim, *Cincinnati und sein Deutschtum: Eine Geschichte der Entwickelung Cincinnati's* . . . (Cincinnati: 1901), p. 79.

[25]*Deutsche Pionier*, I (July, 1869), pp. 129 *et seq.*; Burgheim, *Wort und Bild*, pp. 86-7, 130.

German lawyer intolerable, and came to America in 1830. After supporting himself as a teacher of German and Greek, Molitor became involved in journalism, and edited the New York *Staatszeitung*, the Philadelphia *Demokrat*, and the Buffalo *Weltbürger* before coming to Cincinnati in 1837. There he found work as a foreman in the office of the *Apologete*, a religious paper, and later as editor and proprietor of the *Volksblatt*. His political influence in this last position was felt throughout the entire state of Ohio.[26]

The editor of the *Republikaner*, the *Volksblatt*'s Whig rival, was Emil Klauprecht. Klauprecht was born in Mainz in 1815, but, unlike Rümelin, Rödter, and Molitor, came to America as a child and was raised on a farm in Kentucky. He began his career in the press as a lithographer, and assisted in the publication of the *Cincinnati Fliegende Blätter*, an illustrated literary weekly. As a Whig and later a Republican editor, Klauprecht became an influential politician, and received an appointment to the United States consulate in Stuttgart in 1864 from Abraham Lincoln.[27]

Klauprecht was an irascible journalist in his day: on one occasion, he actually shot a rival editor, Dr. Wilhelm Albers, and would have gone to jail had he not received a pardon from Governor Medill. Albers had been born in Westphalen in 1813, and during his editorial career was involved with the Cincinnati *Demokrat*, the *Locofoco*, the *Alte Hickory*, and the *Volksblatt*. After his shooting, Albers returned to the practice of medicine, where he remained until his death in 1860.[28]

Albers was assisted in the publication of *Der Locofoco* by one of the most colorful of the early editors, Georg Walker. Walker was both a theological and a political radical, and was involved in the publication of *Der Deutsche Amerikaner*, the *Volksbühne*, *Locofoco*, and *Volksblatt*. His last venture was a rationalist philosophical newspaper, the *Hochwächter*, a paper which was revived some years later by Friedrich Hassaurek, the

[26]Burgheim, *Wort und Bild*, pp. 86-7; Tenner, *Sonst und Jetzt*, pp. 25-6; Burgheim, *Wort und Bild*, p. 125.

[27]Burgheim, *Wort und Bild*, p. 123.

[28]Wittke, *German Language Press*, p. 53; Burgheim, *Wort und Bild*, p. 122; Groen, "German American Newspapers," pp. 144-45.

most famous of the Cincinnati Forty-Eighters. Walker was a failure as a journalist. He died in the cholera epidemic of 1849.[29]

The conductors of the German press were motivated in a fundamental way by their contact with the U.S. Those who came as adults seemed to become intoxicated by the heady wine of U.S. political institutions, and all were smitten by an intense love for freedom of the press. None had any experience in the conduct of newspapers before coming to the U.S.; all seemed to encounter journalism as a fundamental feature of their contact with U.S. culture.

These men were mostly successful in private and public life. Most were either well-to-do businessmen or members of the learned professions. Most were involved to some degree in German associational activities.

Perhaps the most important form of early German associational activity was the militia. The German companies, with fanciful names like the Jackson Garde, the Steuben Garde, and the Deutsche Scharfschützen, were a vital element in German social life, a link between Germans and U.S. politics, and a vehicle for participation in national life, especially in the celebration of U.S. national holidays. The importance of the German militia is illustrated by their pivotal role in restoring order after the anti-abolitionist riots of 1841-1842. Hence it is significant that editors like Heinrich Rödter and Karl Rümelin were also captains of militia companies.[30]

It is clear that the conductors of German newspapers were influential men in the German community. Generally German-born, they were key figures in business, politics, and associational life. Yet, even in their symbolic affirmation of German autonomy, and even in their enthusiastic campaigns against nativism and for German language instruction in the public schools, their habit of frequently expressing devotion to U.S. political institutions and ideals is most notable. And their devotion to freedom of the press was expressed in terms of an affirmation of the traditional U.S. ideal of the role of the press in politics and society. The

[29]Groen, "German American Newspapers," pp. 144-45; Burgheim, *Wort und Bild*, p. 120.

[30]Burgheim, *Wort und Bild*, pp. 57-65; Groen, "German American Newspapers," p. 148.

press as they conducted it was American in format and ideals, although German in language.[31]

German papers devoted to non-political topics followed the same pattern of autonomous adoption of American forms and usages. These range from the literary *Fliegende Blätter* to the abolitionist *Freisinnige* and the numerous religious papers: the Catholic *Wahreitsfreund*, the rationalist *Protestant*, the Methodist *Apologete*, and the free-thinking *Licht Freund*. These will be discussed in later chapters.

After 1848, the nature of the Cincinnati German press would change. A relatively small but very vocal contingent of political refugees from the German Revolution of 1848 would arrive, and bring about a sudden efflorescence of radical and free-thinking newspapers and periodicals. This transfusion of German nationalism was fundamentally different in nature from the earlier German press.[32] Chronologically, it is beyond the scope of this study.

The German press before 1848 was not unlike the U.S. press as a whole. It covered the same range of issues, appeared in the same format, and offered no ideological innovations. In its appeal to a specialized market, it is perhaps best considered along with the other results of press diversification, like the daily paper or the reform journal. A more difficult challenge to this schema of press development was the penny press.

The Penny Press

Most historians of the penny press limit their treatment to the more spectacular and successful penny-dailies of the eastern seaboard, particularly the Baltimore and New York papers. Such treatments tend to rely on self-interested sources for information—the penny papers themselves are frequently quoted, along with the memoirs of their owners and editors, and for contrast the equally suspect indictments of

[31]Wittke, *German Language Press*, contends that the German press "has been essentially an American press in a foreign tongue." p. 6.

[32]Joseph White, "Religion and Community: Cincinnati Germans, 1814-1870" (Unpublished doctoral dissertation, University of Notre Dame, 1980), pp. 45-6.

penny press detractors are cited.[33] This use of a narrow range of source materials in studying what has been described as a broad social phenomenon betrays, I think, a dangerously uncritical approach, and this concentration on the east, and particularly New York, undermines any claim to genuinely historical treatment of American journalism as a whole.

Treatments of the penny press are also marred by an intrusive present-mindedness. Concern with the origins of contemporary journalism has led to an over-emphasis on press innovations, and on the few spectacularly successful penny papers. But any real attempt to deal with the social or cultural historical significance of the penny press will have to consider the press as it was, not in terms of what it would become; it will have to deal with the press as it was read, not with the most influential papers as they were later imitated.

Cincinnati's penny press has generally been ignored in standard journalism histories. Yet the penny press of a smaller urban center, more remote from the eastern network of communication, should offer a revealing perspective on the penny press as it appeared to a large body of Americans. The following discussion, then, could be seen as both a critique and a comparative analysis of the standard interpretations of the penny press in light of Cincinnati's penny papers.

The first successful penny daily was Benjamin H. Day's *New York Sun*, founded in 1833. The *Sun* was a small sheet, established to promote a job-printing business, selling for a penny a copy, and available on a day-to-day basis—the cash system of distribution—rather than by subscription alone. The *Sun*'s circulation increased phenomenally. Imitators appeared in other large cities, and soon a substantial number of penny dailies were in operation.

[33]Michael Schudson, in his influential *Discovering the News*, quotes only papers from Boston, New York, and Baltimore in dealing with the penny press, and relies for additional information on Philip Hone's *Diary*, James Gordon Bennett's *Memoirs*, P. T. Barnum's *Recollections*, and other secondary works based on the same material, like Willard G. Bleyer's and Frederic Hudson's general histories of American journalism. Schudson, *Discovering the News: A Social History of American Newspapers* (NY: Harper, 1980). The historiography of the penny press is discussed and criticized more fully in my article, "The Mythology of the Penny Press," *Critical Studies in Mass Communication* 4(1987), pp. 376-404.

Journalism histories commonly treat spectacularly successful penny papers, like the *Sun* in New York and Baltimore, the New York *Herald*, *Tribune*, or *Transcript*, and similar papers in Boston and Philadelphia. The general impression given by such treat-ments is that the penny press as a whole was phenomenally successful. Such was not the case in Cincinnati.

I have been able to identify thirty-three papers published in Cincinnati which can certainly be called penny papers. Undoubtedly there were more. The earliest of these was the *Western World*, founded by William A. Harper, formerly of the staff of the Whig *Republican*, in 1836. This paper lasted only twenty-five issues, or about a month, before it failed due to lack of revenue.[34] The fate of the *Western World* would be the norm for Cincinnati's penny papers. Of the thirty-three I have identified, twenty-three lasted less than a year, most of these only a few weeks. Only a very few of the ten "successful" penny papers are represented by more than a few scattered issues today. The paucity of extant sources leads me to believe that there were even more unsuccessful penny papers. I also suspect that surviving copies of penny papers may be unrepresentative of the penny press as a whole, that readership was much lower than circulation, that reporting was whimsical and uninteresting, that printing was poorly executed. These suspicions cannot be confirmed, of course, but we must keep in mind that the bulk of penny dailies in Cincinnati—and perhaps elsewhere—are irretrievably lost, and that our picture of their importance must remain dark and vague. We can say with some assurance, though, that if it was characteristic of penny papers, as historian Dan Schiller has argued, to take "business success as their most fundamental goal,"[35] then Cincinnati's penny papers were almost all failures.

Nationally, the penny press is credited with greatly boosting the circulation of newspapers. Frank Luther Mott credits it with the "addition

[34]Charles Theodore Greve, *Centennial History of Cincinnati and Representative Citizens* (Chicago: Biographical Publishing Co., 1904), p. 797.

[35]Dan Schiller, "An Historical Approach to Objectivity and Professionalism in American News Reporting," *Journal of Communication*, 29 (Autumn, 1979), p. 46.

of a new economic level of the population to the newspaper audience."[36] Edwin Emery contends that, prior to penny papers, the masses had been all but ignored by journalism.[37] Michael Schudson maintains that, before the penny press, "Newspaper readership was confined to mercantile and political elites . . . ." As opposed to conventional papers, he concludes, "the circulation of penny dailies was correspondingly enormous."[38] This much-accepted notion of expanded circulation requires some qualification.

First, statistics describing circulation of penny dailies are probably misleading. Schudson draws his statistics from Willard G. Bleyer's 1927 book, *Main Currents in the History of American Journalism*, but adds in a footnote, "Bleyer's information comes from the newspapers' own claims of their circulation, and so surely overestimates the actual circulation."[39] More reliable statistics, however, are generally not available.

Second, such statistics are usually quoted only from extremely successful dailies. We have no real reason to suspect that these statistics are representative of all penny papers, even moderately successful ones, and we have no reason to believe that extremely successful penny papers in cities outside the east had such high circulations. It is unsafe to generalize about the significance of penny papers from such statistics.

Third, statistics on penny dailies are generally compared to statistics on political or commercial dailies. Such comparison is meaningful only in a limited context, that is, in a circumscribed discussion of the daily newspaper, or in a context where daily readership is the only meaningful readership. A present-minded treatment would tend to overlook conventional antebellum weekly papers, as they have no real counterpart today. But we must not read too much of the present into the past.

The most reliable statistics on Cincinnati's press are found in Charles Cist's *Cincinnati in 1841*. The census of 1840 lists Cincinnati's population as 46,382. For 1841, Cist lists seven daily papers and their circulations.[40]

[36]Mott, *American Journalism*, p. 215.

[37]Edwin Emery and Michael B. Emery, *The Press and America: An Interpretive History of the Mass Media* (Englewood Cliffs, NJ: Prentice Hall, 1984), p. 143.

[38]Schudson, pp. 15, 17.

[39]*Ibid.,*p. 196, ftnt. 11.

[40]Cist, *1841*, pp. 35, 93.

Of five conventional dailies—including the German *Volksblatt*—the average daily circulation was 542. Two penny papers, the *Public Ledger* and the *Daily Times*, listed circulations of 1400 and 1500 respectively for an average of 1450 a day, almost three times that of the average conventional daily. Care must be taken not to exaggerate the importance of this difference in circulation, however. There were mitigating circumstances.

First, conventional dailies as a whole had a circulation roughly equal to that of penny dailies. Taking into account the fact that virtually every paper printed by a conventional daily was bought and read, it is reasonable to maintain that in 1841 more Cincinnatians read conventional than penny dailies. Still, figures for daily papers alone imply that the introduction of the penny press virtually doubled newspaper circulation.

It must be remembered, then, second, that conventional dailies also circulated weeklies. The five conventional papers in Cincinnati in 1841 circulated an average of 1550 weekly copies, almost three times their daily circulation. Many of these papers were mailed to subscribers in the countryside, but many also circulated among the less well-to-do in the city (a subscription cost no more than two dollars a year). Weekly readership, it seems, was more important than is generally acknowledged.

Third, impressionistic evidence suggests that conventional papers were passed from hand to hand and re-read several times. Editors complained frequently of newspaper borrowing, since it cut into circulation figures; Mrs. Trollope maintained in 1830 that every man read a paper. There is, however, no evidence that penny papers were re-read. Indeed, their cheapness suggests that they were disposable, and the fact that so few issues survive implies that they were considered so by their purchasers. Hence we should probably revise conventional readership upwards, and penny readership downwards.

Fourth, virtually all penny papers in Cincinnati failed, and failed quickly. These failures do not make sense if we believe circulation figures to be honest and meaningful. The *Public Ledger*, for instance, claimed a rise from 1400 to 2000 readers over its five-month existence,[41] but it failed anyway. One wonders how illusory circulation figures were.

[41] *Ibid.*, p. 93; Greve, *Centennial History*, p. 797.

One final consideration about the circulation of penny dailies involves the social status of their readers. The only thing we know for sure is that penny papers were low-priced. It has been assumed, therefore, that they appealed to working-class readers. Yet a more important consideration is that they were available on a non-subscription day-to-day basis. Can we assume that day-to-day readers were working-class readers? Is there any rule of social or economic class to govern occasional readership? It is uncertain whether the purchasers of Cincinnati's penny papers were predominantly working-class, although such papers often made explicit appeals to laborers. The *Daily Times* maintained that "it is by the intelligent and industrious mechanics and working men, the 'bone and sinew,' that our small sheet is principally read."[42] To what extent this readership actually differed from that of conventional papers is not clear.

We may conclude that penny papers did boost circulation, and that they did appeal to new groups of readers. Yet neither development was as dramatic or clearcut as historians have portrayed them elsewhere,[43] and Cincinnati's experience shows no sign of being unrepresentative of a large· part of the nation. The standard interpretation of penny daily circulation is probably misleading.

The penny press is usually acknowledged to have been politically neutral. Mott lists as a key part of its creed the belief that "the newspaper's first duty is to give its readers the news, and not to support a party . . . ."[44] Schudson is even more explicit:

No less original than the economic organization of the new journalism was its political position. Most of the penny papers, including all of the pioneers in the field, claimed political independence, something the earlier papers rarely pretended to.[45]

[42]"Our Anniversary," *Daily Times*, April 26, 1841.

[43]Emery, p. 141, links the appearance of the penny press to the rise of the common man in politics. The connection between working-class politicoes and the penny press has been argued in more detail in Dan Schiller's *Objectivity and the News: The Public and the Rise of Commercial Journalism* (Philadelphia: University of Pennsylvania Press, 1981), especially in regard to New York City. Likewise, see James L. Crouthamel, "The Newspaper Revolution in New York, 1830-1860," *New York History* XLV (April, 1964), pp. 91-113.

[44]Mott, *American Journalism*, pp. 242-43.

[45]Schudson, *Discovering the News*, p. 21.

Schudson credits the penny press with inventing political neutrality, a stance that he considers novel in U.S. journalism.

But professions of political neutrality were traditional in the United States. In Cincinnati, these ranged from William Maxwell's motto, "Open to all Parties, but Influenced by None," to the *Mercantile Daily Advertiser*'s pledge to give an equal hearing to all sides. Declarations of party interest were themselves novel in Cincinnati, first appearing regularly only in the 1820s. The penny paper's allegiance to political neutrality should be seen more as a reaffirmation of this tradition than as a revolution in news consciousness.[46]

The Cincinnati penny press regularly reiterated its pledge to political neutrality. The *Daily Times* asserted that

Our columns have never been under the exclusive control of a party, or ruled by a local clique. We have never been solicitous of 'small favors' from the General Government, the State, County, or City, which are within the bestowal of the functionaries belonging to each, but our small paper draws its support from the unbought and unsolicited patronage of the people who sustain it.[47]

The editorial policy of the *Times* was rooted in a disaffection with partisan journalism. It was the violence and irresponsible blackening of personal reputation that the conductors of the *Times* objected to in partisan papers—hence their promise to exclude from their columns "all articles of a personal nature, and to endeavor to render it worthy of the patronage of the reading public."[48] The goal then was the impersonality of the traditional press ideology, and the penny press adopted the rhetoric of the neutral press and its influence on public opinion from traditional ideas. Hence the penny press was in fact conservative:

[46]Schiller, *Objectivity and the News*, identifies the ideology of the penny press as artisanal republicanism, but does not connect this republicanism with earlier attitudes associated with the American press. He therefore tends, incorrectly I believe, to see this press ideology as an innovation associated with the appearance of an urban working-class mentality in New York.

[47]"Our Anniversary," *Daily Times*, April 26, 1841.

[48]*Spirit of the Times*, April 25, 1840.

It is capable of wielding a greater and wider influence. In consequence of its neutral character, it finds its way into the midst of all parties. In times of great party excitement, when passion is inflamed, prejudice sharpened, and dogmatic adhesion to party demanded;—then the Press, free from party trammels, hope, and fears, and influence, and character, can exercise a conservative power greater than any other.[49]

Political neutrality was conservative. It was not a radically new philosophy of journalism, but one that by the 1830s was well-rooted in republican tradition.

The timing of these assertions of political neutrality in Cincinnati was important. In national politics, the 1820s saw the appearance of the second party system, with its innovations in campaign techniques and its debasement of issue-oriented political rhetoric. As the party system became more entrenched, the respectability of party organs became more suspect. It is no accident, then, that in Cincinnati the first truly successful penny papers were founded in 1840, in the midst of the most fervent and ill-reasoned presidential campaign the nation had experienced.[50] In Cincinnati, the political neutrality of the penny press was a conservative reaction against a fit of political epilepsy.

Political neutrality was neither an innovation nor an inherent characteristic of the penny press, nor of its system of finance and distribution. The cash system of distribution was perhaps more conducive to neutrality in freeing papers from bondage to subscribers' opinions, but partisan papers later adopted the cash system without neutrality. And a lessening of emphasis on subscriptions could lead as easily to dependence on advertising and bondage to advertisers' opinions. Rather, political neutrality stemmed not from the cash system of distribution but from disaffection with party politics among the readers of newspapers, a root cause which operated equally in moderating the tone of editorial comment in conventional papers in the 1840s.

The penny press is often considered to have pioneered new press technology. Rather than being in the vanguard of technological

[49]James D. Taylor, "Salutatory," Daily Times, August 2, 1841.

[50]On the widespread dismay with the rowdiness of the 1840 campaign, see Malcolm J. Rohrbough, The Trans-Appalachian Frontier: People, Societies, and Institutions, 1775-1850 (New York: Oxford University Press, 1978), pp. 393-4. Such electioneering will be discussed below in Chapter IV.

innovation, however, Cincinnati's penny press was actually reactionary. In means of production it initially resembled the pioneer printer rather than the sophisticated equipment of the conventional press establishment. The Cincinnati *Times* for instance, began publication on an old Dickinson press, which it rented from the *Republican* office at five dollars a month. For several years, virtually all the work of the press establishment—editing, reporting, bookkeeping, and transaction of business—was done by two men, the editor and the proprietor.[51] Conventional papers were far more advanced in technology and management. It was they who introduced the first modern presses in Cincinnati and supported the project to construct a telegraph line to the Queen City.

The penny press is often credited with having invented news. The word news used in this sense carries a cluster of related meanings. Dan Schiller refers to news objectivity: "Although not so-called until the twentieth century, news objectivity was the fundamental contribution of a thoroughly commercial press arising in the middle decades of the nineteenth century."[52] Schudson is more forceful:

> The penny press was novel, not only in economic organization and political stance, but in its content. The character of this originality is simply put: the penny press invented the modern concept of 'news.' For the first time the American newspaper made it a regular practice to print political news, not just foreign but domestic, and not just national but local; for the first time it printed reports from the police, from the courts, and from private households. One might say that, for the first time, the newspaper reflected not just commerce and politics but social life. To be more precise, in the 1830s the newspapers began to reflect, not the affairs of an elite in a small trading society, but the activities of an increasingly varied, urban, and middle class society of trade, transportation, and manufacturing.[53]

Other scholars follow a similar line in describing the penny paper's invention of human interest stories, sensationalist reporting, and gossip.[54]

[51]Coggeshall, "Cincinnati Press and its Conductors," pp. 46 *et passim*.
[52]Schiller, "Objectivity," p. 47.
[53]Schudson, *Discovering the News*, pp. 22-3.
[54]Mott, *American Journalism*, pp. 242-43; Emery, *Press and America*, pp. 143-46; Calder M. Pickett, "Technology and the New York Press in the Nineteenth Century," *Journalism Quarterly*, XXXVII (Summer, 1960), pp. 400-2; Crouthamel, "Newspaper

Did the penny press invent either objective news or human interest stories?

Objectivity in reporting, in its most basic sense, means the separation of the reporter from the thing reported. Objectivity is the belief in the independent existence of the thing reported—it exists as an object outside the reporter's experience of it. This belief is inherently related to reporting in the third-person style. The third-person style implies first that the thing reported exists independently of its artifacts and can be talked about—otherwise one would simply copy its artifacts—and second that the thing reported exists independently of the reporter, so that the personality of the reporter can be excised from the report. Objectivity in the news is an idea with its own style: its rise is inherently related to the rise of third-person reporting.

Content analysis of conventional newspapers shows the third-person style to have risen at a fairly steady pace throughout the first half of the nineteenth century, in inverse proportion to copy from non-newspaper sources. In the conventional press, objective reporting replaced the simple reprinting of an artifact of an event. This is a subtle shift in the idea of newspaper impartiality or impersonality, from a passive to an active mode, through the interjection of an actor, the reporter. Objectivity evolved from impartiality.

But then objectivity was not a revolutionary or radically innovative concept. Rather, it was rooted in traditional press ideology, had the same practical function as impartiality, and was more an adjustment of traditional values to new realities than a rejection of traditional ideals.[55]

Revolution"; Helen M. Hughes, *News and the Human Interest Story* (Chicago: University of Chicago Press, 1940). These studies tend to ignore factors outside of editorial policy that might have caused a change in style and content of news reporting. For instance, Schudson, in the passage quoted above, notes that "police" reporting was an innovation in American newspapers. He does not, however, explore the possible relationship between the development of professional policing in the early nineteenth century and the new style of crime reporting. It is likely that the connection is more than casual, and that crime-reporting styles changed more in response to changes in news sources than to change in editorial policy. The same might be said for theatrical and commercial news—the reports from Broadway and Wall Street that Bennett's *Herald* pioneered.

[55]Schudson, pp. 3-11, argues that objectivity in the modern sense of the word did not

Objectivity in the conventional press did not differ from objectivity in the penny press. But the penny press appears more objective because editorial partisanism is excised. But editorial partisanism was being moderated in the conventional press at same time.

The penny press was more aggressively objective in some respects. Protestations of political neutrality encouraged third-person reporting of political events rather than editorial notice. Penny papers, even in Cincinnati, were more ready to employ reporters, although the bulk of the daily news was clipped from other papers. And, as cost dictated a smaller sheet, reduced space encouraged a terseness of style which precluded editorial or reportorial intrusions.

Objectivity, then, was neither a radically new idea, nor one associated strictly with the penny press. Like the ideal of political neutrality, its introduction preceded the penny press and was not antithetical to traditional press ideology. The same is true of human interest stories.

Examples of early human interest stories abound. Eighteenth-century newspapers generally carried such items under a heading like "Melancholy" or "Tragic Occurrence!" Such stories were meant to appeal to the reader's affections, his or her tragic sensibility of the inherently human quality of single events.[56] Human interest was news from the start.

But the penny press is supposed to have been different. It pioneered in personalities, in gossip, in rude sensationalism, much to the horror of the established press. Is this true?

The penny press in Cincinnati was shaped by a reaction against personalities in political journalism. It was never gossip-oriented and never practiced the kind of character assassination employed by the staid Whig *Gazette*, whose editor, Charles Hammond, was the first to try to make political capital out of rumors of Rachel Jackson's marital infidelity.

---

become a pressing concern in journalism until the intellectual currents of the late nineteenth and early twentieth centuries made journalists aware of the problem of subjectivity. While this twentieth-century notion of objectivity is more refined than the more vulgar "objectivity" referred to above, the distinctions are not important in terms of the style of news reporting in the early penny press.

[56]See, for example, "Unexempled [sic] Cruelty: A Fragment of the Reign of Robespiere [sic]," *Freeman's Journal*, July 9, 1796.

Nor did the editors of penny dailies in Cincinnati make a habit of hurling derogatory epithets at rival editors. It was the conventional press that pioneered in personal journalism. Cincinnati's first gossip sheet was the *True Blue and Castigator*, a four page weekly subscription paper which claimed a circulation of 800 and was destroyed by a mob in 1832.[57] The penny press in Cincinnati was, if anything, less lively than its conventional counterpart.

"Sensationalism" is harder to gauge than personality. Sensationalist reporting aims to arouse the emotions, to appeal to the primitive instincts of the reader. The best example of sensationalist reporting I found in my reading of Cincinnati's papers was an account of the struggle for survival of three starving men in a boat:

> They... agreed to cast lots to see who should die for the benefit of the other two. The lot fell on Van Clief, who was killed by blows on the head with a stone. They then cut off his arm and throat and drank his blood; after which they cut a piece from his right arm and ate it.

This story deals with a sensational incident in a detailed and graphic manner, but without comment from the author or reporter. Rather, facts are recorded, and the reader is expected to react according to primitive instinct. The intent is quaintly ethical: the reader is expected to feel moral revulsion. The example is from the *Weekly Liberty Hall and Cincinnati Gazette* of November 28, 1844. The local penny press was no more prone to print such stories than the local conventional press.

The proclivity of the penny press toward scandal is usually adduced from the policy of James Gordon Bennett's *New York Herald* and the tenor of its opposition in the conventional press. Granting the *Herald* its individual historical significance, one must yet wonder whether it represented or was supported by the penny press as a whole. In the case of Cincinnati, the answer is emphatically negative.

Cincinnati's papers did not support Bennett's *Herald*. The most influential of the penny dailies, the *Times*, called Bennett a blackmailer and his paper a "scandal-rag," and sympathized with those elements of the

[57]See Chapter VII for a discussion of the *Castigator*.

the New York press then trying to run him out of business.[58] The *Times* tried to avoid rather than follow Bennett's example:

We have ever endeavored to avoid the evil which is falsely charged upon the class of papers to which this belongs by some of the large political sheets of the Eastern cities, the conductors of which, although daily outraging public morals and decency in political slang and party vituperation, fearing the inroads which the small, yet more ably and industriously conducted independent press is making upon what they call their exclusive rights, and privileges, to divert public opinion from themselves, and enlist public sympathy by warning the people to beware of the 'immoral tendency' of what they term the 'penny press,' the sentiments inculcated by which, they contend, are not 'wholesome, or necessary for the public good.'[59]

The *Times* apparently believed its course more typical of the penny press as a whole. Further, it located opposition to the penny press as well as the abuses identified in the conduct of the penny press in the metropolitan east. It mentioned no such opposition in the west, and thanked the local conventional newspapers for their favorable notices.[60] Western penny papers were not scandal-rags.

It is ironic that papers distributed on the cash system should be identified as ushering in "a new order, a shared universe in which 'public' and 'private' would be redefined."[61] Exposés of private character are generally considered one of the standard abuses of the conventional partisan press. And gossip columns made far more sense in the context of a regular subscription readership than a fluctuating and unreliable daily readership. Indeed, local news became more important and more personal as the penny paper was introduced. But, at least in Cincinnati, this development was more closely associated with the conventional press. It was, after all, the *Enquirer*, the regular Democratic paper, which pioneered the local column in Cincinnati.

Cincinnati's penny press eventually became a part of the press establishment. I have argued that it was never so radical a departure from the practices and attitudes of the mainstream or conventional press in the

[58]*Spirit of the Times*, June 12, 1840.
[59]*Daily Times*, April 26, 1841.
[60]*Ibid.*
[61]Schudson, *Discovering the News*, p. 30.

first place. Its assimilation is typified by the career of the *Cincinnati Daily Commercial*.

I have not identified the *Commercial* as a penny paper. This is because the *Commercial*, established in 1843, sold for a penny for only a matter of weeks before the price was raised to two cents on the issue. But the *Commercial* was edited by Lucius Greeley Curtiss, a veteran of such penny dailies as the *Post*, the *Microscope*, and the *Sun*, and shared many of the characteristics of the penny press.

The *Commercial* was non-partisan. It deplored the fact that "the masses may occasionally be led into error by the arts of the intriguer and demagogue." But it espoused a faith in the intelligence of the people: "We have the most abiding confidence in the controlling and permanent influence of the democratic principle."[62] This non-partisan democracy was typical of the neutral penny press.

Likewise, the *Commercial* invoked impersonality: "All personalities will be excluded . . . . No person of fine taste desires to take a daily paper filled with personal warfare . . . ."[63] In line with this philosophy, the *Commercial* deplored the behavior of the "vile and slanderous sheets that, engendered by the low and vulgar avarice of petty larceny knaves, pander to the sympathizing taste of scoundrels and harlots in the purlieus of our large cities. It is to be regretted that the 'art preservative' should be thus prostituted."[64] The *Commercial*'s attitude was conservative, then, and its intent—like that of Cincinnati's penny press in general—was to return to a pure press, free from party corruption: "the press is the guarding spirit of our liberties; and with its purity and freedom they will be sustained and cherished, as surely as with its corruption and prostitution they will become a scorn and a bye word to the tyrant and demagogue."[65]

The motto of the *Commercial* was "Commerce, News, and Literature." It featured belletristic selections on the first page, and included prices

---

[62]*Daily Commercial*, Oct 6, 1843.
[63]*Ibid.*, Oct. 2, 1843.
[64]*Ibid.*, Oct. 19, 1843.
[65]*Ibid.*

current, commercial news, and a bank note and exchange list. In addition, it printed columns headed "City News," "Police," and "Criminal Court." It featured a strong editorial voice and third-person reporting.

In terms of style and content, then, the *Commercial* embodied all of the elements of change in the press establishment identified in the content analysis presented above. As a cross of sorts between a conventional paper and a penny paper, it was perhaps ahead of its rivals in printing third-person news, but it was moving in the same direction, not moving to reverse the direction of change.

The *Commercial* is important for two reasons. The first is its adoption of aspects of the penny press. The second is its longevity. The *Commercial* did not fail until the great depression of the twentieth century.

The reason for the *Commercial*'s success was its commercial viability. It appealed to middle and upper class readers through its reporting of commercial and economic news, as well as through its affirmation of conventional press morality. And because of its established readership, it was able to attract a substantial amount of advertising revenue.

The *Commercial*'s success was significant, then, not because it was similar in format to a penny paper, but because it was similar in readership and social function to a conventional paper. It had co-opted the innovations of the penny press—the cash system of distribution and political neutrality—to the interests of conventional newsmanship.

The career of the *Commercial* shows that the innovations of the penny press were not revolutionary. Penny papers accentuated certain trends in style and content. These trends were shared by the conventional press, which in turn adopted the cash system of distribution—the most distinctive feature of the penny press. The innovations of the penny press ultimately served to enhance rather than overturn the authority of the conventional press.

I have argued throughout this section that the penny press was not what it has been made to seem. It was not essentially a radical departure from traditional American journalism, either in expanded circulation, political neutrality, or style of reporting. Nor was it essentially radically more objective, or more attached to human interest stories, local news, or sensationalist reporting than established papers. Rather, I have argued, all of the innovations credited to the penny press can be found in the mainstream press, though sometimes in lower profile. But I have elsewhere argued for a genuine transformation of the press in the years 1820-1848. What, then, was the nature of this transformation?

The Transformation of the Press

We have identified characteristics of the transformation of the press. There was a strengthening of the editorial voice and an increase in third-person or objective reporting, indicating a shift from a passive to an active press. There was an increase in circulation, but this was matched by a drop in price and a probable decline in multiple readership, indicating not so much *more* newspaper readers as *more individualistic* readers. There was an increase in frequency of publication, in speed of communication, and in the relative importance of local news, indicating an increase in the importance of the newspaper in local society. We have noted the industrialization of the press in management, personnel, production, and distribution. And we have noted a process of politicization and urbanization in the press. We have remarked on the intrusion of the periodical press into the fields of religion, literature, reform, and the professions.

This transformation of the press meant nothing less than the genesis of a popular culture in print. The transformation of the press was in essence its introduction as a medium into every aspect of culture. The result was the propagation of a culture in every region of the nation that was popular, literate, predominantly middle-class, characteristically city-oriented, and rooted in the metaphor of the marketplace.

I have declined to use the word "revolution" to describe any aspect of this transformation. There was no revolution within journalism of the sort that Schudson describes, because at every step of the development a traditional press ideology was invoked and traditional goals were set. And journalism did not effect a revolution in society at large, but was introduced successively as a buttress of commercial, economic, and moral structures that had been brought into existence independently of the press. The transformation of the press was at every point somehow conservative. This will become dramatically clear when we discuss the fate of reform journalism. Editors of reform newspapers tanded to share a strong disdain for the mainstream press of their day, and viewed their brethren in the partisan and commercial papers as guardians of a social order in need of change.

Culture in its broadest sense is communication. In the early Republic, communication was carried on increasingly through print. If there was a transformation of the press, the cause lay deep in antebellum culture, in the values applied to the conduct of the press, in the meaning assigned to press-conveyed information and opinions. In the remainder of this study I shall examine in depth the theories and practices associated with the conduct of the press in politics, religion, literature, the professions, and reform. It may be possible thereby to arrive at a clearer understanding of how deep changes in the press were related to deep changes in American culture.

CHAPTER III

The Press and Political Culture, 1793–1820

The extent to which news circulates, within a political unit or a political society, determines the extent to which the members of such a society may be said to participate, not in its collective life—which is the more inclusive term—but in its political acts. Political action and political power, as one ordinarily understands these terms, are obviously based not merely on such concert or consensus as may exist in a herd or in a crowd.

-Robert Ezra Park[1]

The next two chapters examine the political culture of the press. Political culture here means something other than politics—it refers to the set of ideas, values, attitudes, and practices informing political discourse. Our aim will be to recover not arguments, then, but styles of argument.

Historians have found the political culture of the Revolution and early Republic to be a fertile field for research in recent years. Of their rich harvest, two areas of inquiry are important to note. The first is ideology; the second, the rise of the two-party system.

The study of Revolutionary ideology by U.S. historians has a venerable history, but can fairly be said to have begun anew with a series of works in

---

[1]Robert E. Park, "News as a Form of Knowledge," in *Society: Collective Behavior, News and Opinion, and Modern Society*, The Collected Papers of Robert Park, E. C. Hughes *et al.*, ed., (Glencoe Park: The Free Press, 1955), p. 79.

the 1960s, especially seminal studies by Bernard Bailyn and Gordon Wood.[2] These scholars and others[3] reconstructed a political vocabulary, dubbed republicanism, which was shared by eighteenth-century Anglo-Americans and which formed an ideological filter, slanting both elite and popular perceptions of, among other things, British imperial policies, and thereby also shaping the course of events. This language of politics—for these studies see ideas embedded in their forms of expression—was rooted in seventeenth-century British politics, or perhaps was even older, extending back to Italian political philosophy of the age of Machiavelli. And it differed in fundamental ways from what had traditionally been thought of as the characteristic philosophy of the American Revolution, that is, the political philosophy of Locke and the Enlightenment.[4]

Republicanism differed from Lockean liberalism most notably in its emphasis on civic virtue. Eighteenth-century Anglo-Americans were intensely aware of the fragility of republics throughout history (so the analysis runs). They believed that republics fell when their citizens lost a public-spirited commitment to the common good, instead pursuing private interest. One particular source of this loss of civic virtue was the corruption that inevitably followed when power was closely held by a narrow set of individuals: the classic Whig notion that power tends to

[2]Bernard Bailyn, *The Ideological Origins of the American Revolution* (Cambridge: Harvard University Press, 1967); Gordon S. Wood, *The Creation of the American Republic, 1776-1787* (Chapel Hill: University of North Carolina Press, 1969).

[3]Key works in the republican synthesis include J.G.A. Pocock, *The Machiavellian Moment: Florentine Political Thought and the Atlantic Republican Tradition* (Princeton: Princeton University Press, 1975); Lance Banning, *The Jeffersonian Persuasion: Evolution of a Party Ideology* (Ithaca: Cornell University Press, 1978); and John M. Murrin, "The Great Inversion, or Court versus Country: A Comparison of the Revolution Settlements in England (1688-1721) and America (1776-1816)," in J.G.A. Pocock, ed., *Three British Revolutions: 1641, 1688, 1776* (Princeton: Princeton University Press, 1980), to name a few.

[4]A classic exposition of the Lockean philosophy of the Revolution is Carl L. Becker's analysis of Thomas Jefferson's thought in *The Declaration of Independence: A Study in the History of Political Ideas* (New York: Knopf, 1922). A controversial rebuttal is Garry Wills, *Inventing America: Jefferson's Declaration of Independence* (Garden City NY: Doubleday, 1978). Wills draws on Douglass Adair's famous essay "'That Politics May Be Reduced to a Science': David Hume, James Madison, and the Tenth Federalist," *Huntington Library Quarterly* XX(1957), pp. 343-60, in attributing to the Scottish common sense philosophers the main influence on Jefferson's thought.

corrupt. Those in power were prone to conspire against the liberties of citizens. The great bulwark of liberty or independence for citizens was property—the freehold. A conspiracy against liberty would thus naturally take the form of an attack against property, and republicans would thus be prone to view "unconstitutional" new taxes—such as the duties levied on the colonies in the 1760s and 1770s—as attacks on property signifying a conspiracy against liberty designed to enslave the colonists. Because of their republican ideological filter, they reacted to such legislation in an exaggerated fashion.

This republican synthesis has been a compelling explanation of the origins of the American Revolution. It has had its critics, however, the most noteworthy being Joyce Appleby, who has argued forcibly that the characteristic style of thought of the Revolutionaries was indeed liberalism.[5] In her reconstruction, the republican opposition of interest versus virtue, licentiousness versus liberty, and private interest versus public good miscasts especially attitudes toward economic activity, attitudes that were at root informed by American experience, not European traditions. Liberal critics of the republican synthesis maintain that the Revolutionary generation did not consider the pursuit of private interest to be a necessary threat to the republic; rather, they sought to free private energies from burdensome restrictions. They had a positive attitude toward commerce and capital, and did not view them as subversive of the commonwealth.

[5]Relevant works by Appleby include "Commercial Farming and the 'Agrarian Myth' in the Early Republic," *Journal of American History* 68(1982), pp. 833-49; "What is Still American in the Political Philosophy of Thomas Jefferson?" *William and Mary Quarterly* 3rd ser. 39(1982), pp. 287-309; *Capitalism and a New Social Order: The Republican Vision of the 1790s* (New York: New York University Press, 1984); and a special issue of *American Quarterly* (37, 1985) which she edited on "Republicanism in the History and Historiography of the United States." Similarly, but with somewhat more heat, see John Patrick Diggins, *The Lost Soul of American Politics: Virtue, Self-Interest, and the Foundations of Liberalism* (New York: Basic Books, 1984) and "Comrades and Citizens: New Mythologies in American Historiography," *American Historical Review* 90(1985), pp. 614-43. A nice summary of the controversy over republicanism is presented in two articles in the *William and Mary Quarterly*: Lance Banning, "Jeffersonian Ideology Revisited: Liberal and Classical Ideas in the New American Republic," 3rd ser. 43(1986), pp. 3-19, and Joyce Appleby, "Republicanism in Old and New Contexts," *ibid.*, pp. 20-34.

The debate between the republican synthesis and liberalism continues, and probably will not be resolved. But it is safe to draw some conclusions significant for our discussion of the political culture of the press.

The language of politics at the seedtime of the Republic incorporated a hostility toward political activity of a self-interested nature. The pervasiveness of anti-party rhetoric in the Revolutionary period is undeniable. Insofar as parties necessarily represented class or party or factional interests, supposedly at the expense of the public good, they constituted an evil, though perhaps an unavoidable one. This is part of the argument of Madison's famous tenth Federalist, wherein he remarks that liberty will always nurture factions. Madison goes on to argue that factions and parties may safely be tolerated in an extensive federal republic where the multiplicity of parties would prevent the predominance of any single party. His thinking was characteristic: parties were not good, but could not be prevented without depriving politics of the very liberty that it is designed to protect.

It may be argued that this anti-party rhetoric was simply for public consumption, and represented neither genuine attitudes nor actual behavior. There may be truth to this objection. It remains significant, however, that political rhetoric was restrained by suspicions of partisan promotion. The thinkers of the Revolutionary generation, no matter what their attitudes toward the marketplace, considered it inappropriate to treat the political arena as if it were one.

A second useful conclusion is that this language of politics— republicanism—survived the Revolution and remained potent throughout the early national period. It constituted a unitary rhetorical legacy that the first generations of U.S. citizens grew up with. The language was a common inheritance, though it seems far from likely that all groups in society used it in the same way. Sean Wilentz, for one, has shown how New York City's artisans used the language of republicanism to construct a political mentality quite distinct from those of other social groups.[6] The existence of a unified political language must not be taken to indicate wide political consensus, then.

[6]Sean Wilentz, *Chants Democratic: New York City and the Rise of the American Working Class, 1788-1850* (New York: Oxford University Press, 1984).

Here it might be appropriate to distinguish between some different aspects of political culture. We might call these language, consciousness, and practice. So far we have been discussing language primarily. But in noting that language can mean different things to different people, or that groups and individuals can use the same language for different purposes, we imply that, beyond the language, there is a mentality or consciousness that uses it. Furthermore, we seem to suggest that this mentality is collective.

This leads us to the question of whether political language reflects or perhaps even forms political consciousness. On the one hand, it seems that the available language limits the range of ideas and policies that can be publicly formulated and promoted. But common sense tells us that rhetoric is often disingenuous. Throughout the discussion that follows, then, we should be wary about drawing conclusions about what people thought from political language alone.

In addition, there is the question of the relationship of political language and consciousness to behavior. Not only can it be true that people think and speak differently, but they may also speak and act differently, or act and think differently. The language of politics can consciously or unconsciously misrepresent behavior.[7] We should also be alert to this possible disjuncture.

To bring this discussion concretely to bear upon our subject matter, consider what republicanism as a language means to press ideology and conduct. In terms of ideology, it dictates a disciplined and self-possessed attitude—called "rational liberty" by contemporaries—as well as a belief in neutrality and the dispassionate presentation of information and opinion—our twin ideals of impartiality and impersonality. In terms of practice, it encourages rational and serious inquiry—continuously, not just at election time—into political affairs, and allegiance to "measures,

[7]It should be noted that throughout this study I use the term ideology to refer to the body of ideas that specific people consciously held. Ideology can, of course, be used in other senses. Most important is the usage which describes ideology as that system of ideas spontaneously produced by a particular social praxis. In this latter sense it is not necessary to an ideology that the actual people involved in that praxis have an actual conscious allegiance to that ideology. In this study, however, it will be essential to demonstrate that the ideologies discussed were consciously held.

not men"—loyalty to ideals rather than organizations, especially partisan ones.

Republicanism should thus have discouraged the rise of a partisan press. Whether it did so is part of the subject matter of the chapters that follow. As background to that discussion, the body of literature concerning the rise of U.S. political parties is significant.

The traditional narrative of U.S. national political history presents this sequence of events: a first party system arose from disputes in Congress between Federalists and Republicans; when the Republicans captured the Presidency in 1800, the Federalist Party withered away; a non-partisan "era of good feelings" ensued; it was terminated by Andrew Jackson's campaigns against the nominee of the Congressional caucus in 1824 and 1828, ending the monopoly of the Republican Party and creating the second party system. Disagreements appear in recent scholarship concerning this history that have import for our discussion.

First is the issue of whether the first party system was a true party system. Several scholars have argued that it was not: the parties are said to have lacked either national organizations or Congressional voting blocs or consistent voter loyalty or an ideology of legitimate opposition.[8] Others have maintained that the parties were indeed organized and run as modern parties in terms of Congressional action, electioneering, and voter loyalty.[9]

Was the first party system a true party system? While it seems clear from recent studies that Federalists and Republicans behaved like modern partisans in many regards, still it is not clear that they thought like

[8]Richard Hofstadter, *The Idea of a Party System: The Rise of Legitimate Opposition in the United States, 1780-1840* (Berkeley: University of California Press, 1972); James Sterling Young, *The Washington Community, 1800-1828* (New York: Columbia University Press, 1966); Ronald P. Formisano, "Deferential-Participant Politics: The Early Republic's Political Culture, 1789-1840," *American Political Science Review* 68(1974), pp. 473-87; Formisano, "Federalists and Republicans: Parties, Yes--System, No," in Paul Kleppner, ed., *The Evolution of American Electoral Systems* (Westport CT: Greenwood Press, 1981), pp. 33-76; and Ralph Ketcham, *Presidents Above Party: The First American Presidency, 1789-1829* (Chapel Hill: University of North Carolina Press, 1984).

[9]Most notably and recently John F. Hoadley, *Origins of American Political Parties, 1789-1803* (Lexington: The University Press of Kentucky, 1984).

partisans. Most importantly, it does not seem that they regarded political opposition as a normal or healthy state of affairs. This meant that attitudes toward and behavior in the presentation of political information—especially in the press—would hew to nonpartisanism or impartiality as a value.

What, then of the Era of Good Feelings? If the first party system did not produce a partisan ideology, we should not expect to find one in the years when partisan competition dwindled. But perhaps this narrative is too simple. David Hackett Fischer's important book, *The Revolution of American Conservatism*,[10] argues forcefully that, as the Republicans came into power nationally, older anti-party Federalists began to yield leadership positions to younger party activists with more positive attitudes toward electioneering. The result was a period—lasting through the War of 1812—of intense party competition that produced, among other things, increased popular participation in elections. Partisan competition survived the election of Thomas Jefferson, especially on a state and local level.

Nor did competition end with the War of 1812, though that war certainly did end the viability of Federalism as a party. Rather, local and state factions and parties continued to vie with each other, often within the ranks of the Republican Party, even as harmony seemed the rule in presidential politics.[11]

In the Ohio country, Republicans outnumbered Federalists from the early years. Political competition tended to center around intraparty struggles or charismatic leaders.[12] As a result, partisanism was not consistently meaningful as a way of thinking about politics. Whether this was true of the nation as a whole is not certain. But, perhaps as a result of Ohio's Republican ascendancy, the press tended to remain impartial in

[10]David Hackett Fischer, *The Revolution of American Conservatism: The Federalist Party in the Era of Jeffersonian Democracy* (New York: Harper, 1965).

[11]For a state by state account of partisan and factional disputes leading up to the formation of the second party system, see Richard P. McCormick, *The Second American Party System: Party Formation in the Jacksonian Era* (Chapel Hill: University of North Carolina Press, 1966).

[12]Andrew R. L. Cayton, *The Frontier Republic: Ideology and Politics in the Ohio Country, 1780-1825* (Kent OH: Kent State University Press, 1986), preface *et passim*.

conduct until the rise of the second party system. It is possible to identify a particular newspaper with a particular leader or faction, and to discern patterns in content in news and opinion resulting from such an identification, but before the 1820s no newspaper in Cincinnati applied party affiliation habitually as a test to all editorial material, the practice that would become common during the second party system. And newspapers tended to adhere to a set of conventions—the use of pseudonyms, the printing of transcripts of legislation and imnportant speeches, the absence of an editorial voice—that disappeared quickly once the second party system established itself.

It should be clear by now that I find the second party system to have been fundamentally different from the first in language, consciousness, and behavior. This is definitely true in Ohio, but Ohio did not become a state until after Jefferson's election to the presidency. As a political entity, it did not participate fully in the contests of the late 1790s. And Federalism did not have a powerful organizational presence there. The findings of the pages that follow, then, may not accurately represent the experience of the nation as a whole. Still, a strong case can be made that, nationally, there was a basic change in political culture with the rise of the second party system, along much the same lines as what I will describe.

The Political Importance of the Press

The political institutions of the American Republic are said to derive their legitimacy from public opinion, which in turn depends on intelligent and reliable information. The leading statesmen of the early Republic saw the newspaper as the chief medium for informing public opinion. In a new and experimental national polity, a great deal of attention was devoted to the appropriate role of the press in politics, as for example in the controversy over the Sedition Act. Questions raised then about newspaper conduct remain current today: To what extent is personal abuse an acceptable rhetorical technique? To what extent is exclusive devotion to the interests of a single party desirable or tolerable?

Debate over conduct of the press ultimately focused on the manipulation of public opinion. It was feared that the public could be led astray by political rhetoric designed to confuse the reason and arouse the passions of a naive or licentious electorate. Information was essential to rational liberty, but false opinion could destroy it, and both were conveyed by the press.

It is not clear whether the press was an efficient means of shaping public opinion in the early Republic. Ralph L. Rusk, referring specifically to the midwest, asserted that it was a rare man who "could rival the editor of a weekly gazette in power to shape the popular will. The editor and printer, by his knowledge of language and of the mysteries of his craft, rose to the dignity of an oracle."[13] Edwin Emery, however, has pointed out that, at the time of Jefferson's election, the majority of political papers claimed allegiance to the Federalist Party. He concludes that "the power of the press is not in its persuasion by opinion, but in its dissemination of information and its arousal of interest in important issues hitherto submerged in popular apathy."[14] We are left to wonder whether the press could persuade as well as inform.

In the next two chapters I mean to analyze the relationship between the press and political rhetoric. Rhetoric may be loosely defined as the art of persuasion. As such, a rhetoric includes both a set of ideas and a strategy for propagating these ideas: hence the importance of studying medium and message together.

In studying political rhetoric, I will also attempt to evaluate the early press as a source of political information. Did newspaper conductors attempt to present information sufficient for a rational public to make intelligent decisions? Did newspapers seek to inform as well as persuade?

Press behavior changed over time. But an ideology of the press and press behavior in politics persisted, though with modifications, and was invoked constantly throughout the early national period. This ideology was an integral part of the rationale of the American Republic. It was generated by the revolutionary movement that gave birth to the political institutions the press was intended to preserve.

[13]Ralph Leslie Rusk, *The Literature of the Middle Western Frontier*, 2 vols, (New York: Columbia University Press, 1925), I, p. 132.

[14]Edwin Emery, *The Press and America: An Interpretive History of the Mass Media*, third edition, (Englewood Cliffs, N. J.: Prentice-Hall, 1972), p. 126.

Press Ideology

When Americans of the early national period spoke or wrote of their political institutions in the abstract, their tone was adulatory. The birth of the United States was epoch-making, and the great experiment in self-government was of import to all mankind. An age of enlightenment had begun; the rule of reason had been initiated. An unsigned letter to Cincinnati's *Liberty Hall* crowed that "the march of the human mind in the United States of America, has met with no obstruction whatever; but every encouragement that our republican institutions offered to free enquiry, and liberal discussion . . . ."[15] The times demanded access to information of every variety. The prospectus of one proposed paper linked the proliferation of popular journals to the uniqueness of the moment in history.

An age like the present, portentous beyond any parallel to be found in the History of Mankind, will offer the best apology for the multiplication of periodical publications—whose object is, lst. the diffusion of literature and science in the most enlightened and scientific Epoch known within the pale of human knowledge, and 2dly. an early communication of great political events, both Foreign and Domestic, which are now agitating every corner of the Globe.[16]

The movement of world history had made necessary the multiplication of newspapers.

The epoch of reason dawned with the American Revolution. The establishment of the Republic of rational liberty was the central moment of recent history. Mankind entered the age of reason en bloc for the first tine in America.

As the new order of the ages took form, means of communicating political knowledge to the people were extended, especially newspapers. The *Inquisitor and Cincinnati Advertiser* expressed the rationale behind this expansion:

[15]"American Institutions," *Liberty Hall*, July 24, 1815.
[16]Prospectus of the *Miami Gazette*, published in the *Western Spy*, April 17, 1813.

The superiority which newspapers seem to possess over other methods of diffusing political or practical knowledge among the people, has occasioned an extraordinary multiplication of them in this country over the last twenty-five years. From their uncommon cheapness, their pages are made accessible to every individual, however humble and indigent: thousands of worthy freemen are consequently instructed and benefitted by this means, who would otherwise be doomed to a life of perpetual ignorance. Indeed,there is no country in existence, where the common people are so well acquainted with their laws and the administration of their government, as ours. This is chiefly done through the medium of our newspapers.[17]

The importance which early federal leaders attributed to the press is clear. Special postal privileges acknowledge their role in preserving republican government. The fact that newspapers were awarded contracts to publish the laws also affirms their quasi-official status.

This strain of press ideology emphasizes information. The political implications of the free flow of information are clear and simple: the more men know, the wiser their decisions will be. The informational role of the press was unchallenged in the press ideology insofar as the correctness of the information conveyed remained unchallenged in the abstract. The press in a republic should always be encouraged to publish such information, and when newspapers printed lists of Fourth of July toasts around the turn of the century, there were sure to be several like the following:

"The Press: Free as air, beneficial as light, and as congenial to liberty as sun-beams to vegetation."[18]

"Liberty of the Press—may no man be imprisoned for publishing the truth."[19]

"The press—may it remain forever unshack[l]ed, and serve to destroy all delusion."[20]

To describe the function of information diffusion, the ancient metaphor of the light of the sun was used. In later years, *Sun* would become one of the most popular newspaper names, partly because the sun sheds light, partly because it shines on rich and poor alike.

[17]*Inquisitor and Cincinnati Advertiser*, June 23, 1818.
[18]*Liberty Hall*, July 7, 1807.
[19]*Ibid.*, July 14, 1807.
[20]*Ibid.*, July 9, 1808.

Freedom of the press also implied the availability of a newspaper for the public expression of opinions. A letter to the *Western Spy* written over the venerable pseudonym A Constant Reader claimed that "the propriety of communicating our remarks thro' the medium of the press, is obvious . . . ."[21] But the press was to be used as a medium for expressing useful opinion, and one open to its readers; it was not to be used as the instrument of propagating the opinions of its conductors. It was not to be closed to readers opposed to its political philosophy.

Press ideology demanded truthful and impartial conduct of newspapers in expressing political opinions and conveying political information. The prospectus of virtually every paper published before 1820 which I examined confirmed this. The prospectus of the *Liberty Hall and Cincinnati Mercury* was typical, and will bear quotation at length:

When a newspaper is about to be ushered into existence, the public is in general enquiring, what are the political sentiments of its Editor? Suffice it therefore to say that he considers a Republican Government as the only one grounded on rational principles, and from a general view of the system pursued by those who, at the present, hold the reigns of government, he is convinced of the judiciousness and propriety of it. Yet, consonant with these principles, he dares to judge for himself: and, that he and others may be able to exercise their reason thereon, he means to set Truth, in its simple dress, before his readers; he will never become the dupe of any party, nor degrade himself, by putting a false glare on what appears unwarrantable in any party or body of men whatever.

To encourage the investigation of Truth, LIBERTY HALL will be open for the reception of any communications, from any and every party regulated by the rules of propriety and decorum; but the editor protests against the admission of every low, mean, indelicate invective, and every species of vulgarism both in sentiment and expression.[22]

The press ideology expressed here demands the press be free from dogmatic partisanism or impropriety in language and sentiment. These twin ideals may be designated impartiality and impersonality.

The ideal of impersonality is most apparent in repeated assertions by printers that they will not enter into personal disputes or print personal abuse. These assertions were characteristically phrased in line with a

[21] *Western Spy*, Sept. 17, 1800.
[22] *Liberty Hall*, Dec. 4, 1804.

republican ideology of rational liberty as voluntary restraints on liberty necessary to prevent licentiousness:

> A free press has been justly considered by all wise men as the great bulwark of liberty . . . . (As) . . . this freedom should have certain bounds and limits, to render it salutary, the conductors of the Inquisitor shall be ever so slow to enter into personal controversy or to engage in violent or passionate discussion, because they consider that the welfare of the country will always be better consulted by a rational and deliberate examination of public affairs.[23]

Of course, the frequency of these protestations might be taken to mean that personal abuse was a common feature of the journalism of the early Republic. Indeed, it was not uncommon for an editor to cry foul, as John Browne of the *Liberty Hall* did during the early competition between his paper and the *Western Spy*:

> When this editor published his proposals for LIBERTY HALL, he protested against the admission of any personal invectives or abuse—he has noticed the many sarcasms which have been flung personally at him in the Spy with silent contempt, and he still quietly wipes the dirt without a word . . . .[24]

Browne's complaint is curious. He surely exaggerated the amount of abuse in the *Spy*, which was small indeed compared to the kind of personal journalism that would flourish in Cincinnati two decades later. He also exaggerated its scurrility. And it is significant that, even in what must have been a fierce competition for subscribers in a previously uncontested market, the *Spy* would itself publish a letter from Browne.[25] Indeed it must have considered itself open to all parties. Early accusations of personal journalism mean simply that standards were high, since by later standards conduct was not "licentious."

Impersonality extended beyond this negative rationale of rejecting personal abuse. On the positive side, it meant a rational examination of measures, an appeal to the independent man's reason, not his passions or

---

[23]Prospectus of the *Inquisitor and Cincinnati Advertiser*, June 23, 1818; similarly, see letter of John Bigger to the *Western Spy*, August 22, 1804.

[24]*Liberty Hall*, Feb. 26 (28), 1805.

[25]*Western Spy*, August 22, 1804.

affections. The presentation of political opinions must be impersonal, then. Hence the significance of pseudonymous letters.

Virtually all political opinions in Cincinnati's papers on concrete issues before 1820 were presented in the form of letters over a pseudonym. Very little overtly political rhetoric appeared under an editorial head or in a letter with a true signature. What this meant in practice will be considered later. In theory it meant that the opinions expressed should be judged in and of themselves, not as the production of a known person. Ideas were impersonal, and were to be evaluated on no authority beyond themselves.

Impersonality was also the guiding idea behind verbatim transcripts of laws, debates, and public documents. These items of information were to be presented without first being run through an editor's or reporter's ideological laundry. It was considered an essential part of a newspaper's function to present raw political information for the public to use in independently forming opinion.

Allied to impersonality was impartiality. Impartiality meant both an openness to both sides of any argument—a newspaper should be "Open to all Parties, but Influenced by None"—and freedom from party allegiance. Joseph Carpenter's initial address "To the public" is to the point:

> It would be useless in him [the editor] to expatiate on the usefulness of a well-conducted and impartial Newspaper to the enlightened citizens of this country, and the public are equally sensitive of the disadvantages of a Newspaper devoted to party spirit: however improper it may be, it is believed that nearly three-fourths of the Printers in the United States (since party spirit has unfortunately been very prevalent) have attached themselves to the one party or the other, and their papers have been devoted to justifying their own and ridiculing the other; and their opponents would [not] get liberty to say a single syllable in justification of their opinions though ever so just—the grand object which makes a newspaper so valuable and useful to society, is entirely destroyed, and deprives a part of the community of privileges to which they are all equally entitled. He is therefore determined as far as his abilities will enable him, to be strictly impartial.[26]

Carpenter would continue to criticize "Violent party printers, who embargo the truth on one side and have recourse to fabrication on the

[26]*Ibid.*, May 28, 1799.

other"; he would attribute their editorial policies to selfish office seeking.[27] This latter criticism is particularly important: it was counter to press ideology for a newspaper to promote the candidacy of any particular man for any particular office. Newspapers were supposed to facilitate popular participation in political discourse, rather than focusing attention on elections, particularly in promoting the interests of a single man or party. Their purpose was to inform citizens, not to persuade voters.

Carpenter's criticisms of party spirit were echoed throughout the early nineteenth century.[28] This might be taken to indicate that party spirit did in fact prevail in newspapers. Such was not the case in Cincinnati, and would not be until after 1820, when practices would change dramatically and ideology would make the necessary adjustments.[29]

Criticism of party spirit attests to the vitality of the press ideology outlined above. Editors and writers repeated these criticisms because of a commitment to this ideology, because of a belief in the role of a free press in a republican society, and because of an intuition that such criticism struck a responsive chord in the minds of their readers. This press ideology provided a coherent theory for a political press. We must now determine whether it was applied in practice.

Territorial Politics and the Press in Cincinnati

The administration of the Northwest Territory under Governor Arthur St. Clair was filled with controversy. St. Clair was a Federalist, a strong-willed military man, an appointee, unpopular for the most part with the settlers of the early west, who were generally Republican, young, male, and single, and often veterans of the Revolutionary War. Political conflict was inevitable.

Political controversy appeared in the newspapers of the Territory from the first. It was commonly acknowledged that a newspaper should carry

---

[27]*Ibid.*, Oct. 29, 1800; Jan. 16, 1803.

[28]See, for example, *Ibid.*, Sept. 3, 1814.

[29]Cayton, in *Frontier Republic*, argues that a notion of discipline and virtue dominated political attitudes in Ohio in this period, the most famous negative role model being Aaron Burr: pp. 86-92.

"judicious remarks, and suitable animadversions upon the laws and administration of government," as submitted by "men of talent": the "champions of public virtue."[30] Early newspapers did not shun political conflict.

Early newspapers, however, did not explicitly endorse either side of a controversy. They were a medium for discussion, ideally, rather than an instrument of persuasion. Hence political rhetoric appeared in the form of anonymous letters and transcribed speeches, not as editorial pronouncements.

The appearance of a newspaper in Cincinnati was welcomed by would-be luminaries, who eagerly seized the opportunity to make their views known. Grievances over taxation were argued in an exchange of letters among Manlius, Plebius, and Vitruvius.[31] The argument heated up in the fall of 1794. Criticisms of taxation voiced by Vitruvius[32] were answered by Judge Rufus Putnam's charge to the Grand Jury, reprinted in the Centinel, in which Vitruvius is referred to as an "anonymous scribler [sic] who libelled the ordinance for the government of the territory, and in a billingsgate dialect abuses the principle officers of it."[33] Philo Vitruvius and Dorastus replied, and the debate wore on into 1795. In spring of that year, a rebuttal to Vitruvius appeared, an ad hominem attack, stating that Vitruvius, Philo Vitruvius, and Dorastus were one and the same man, and that he was a sycophant, a hypocrite, and an associate of women of bad fame.[34]

Several important characteristics of political controversy in print are evident in this exchange. First, the press itself was neutral. The Centinel carried letters from both sides, endorsing neither, and printing no editorial comment on the issues involved. Second, almost all comment was either anonymous or pseudonymous. The implication is that the ideas presented need rely on no authority beyond themselves, that

[30]Letter of Hospes, Centinel, July 4, 1794.
[31]Beverly W. Bond, Jr., The Civilization of the Old Northwest (New York: MacMillan, 1934), pp. 411-12.
[32]Centinel, Sept. 20, 27, 1794.
[33]Ibid., Oct. 18, 1794.
[34]Ibid., April 4, 1794.

independent readers would evaluate these ideas without reference to their sources.

A third feature of political controversy in print is attention to form. By this I mean that contributions were criticized not merely on the basis of logic, argument, and evidence, but also on literary quality. For example, Plebius criticized a letter from Manlius minutely for grammatical errors that seem minor, if not illusory.[35] Putnam ridiculed Vitruvius' literary ability by calling him a scribbler.[36] The Farmer's Friend asserted the superiority of a "masculine stile [sic] and plain sense" to "metaphorical jargon and bombastical rant."[37] Felicity of expression seems to have been an acknowledged criterion of political argument.

A fourth characteristic of this early political controversy was the endorsement of such exchanges as an appropriate use of the medium in a republic. Dorastus, for example, affirmed that free men "have an undoubted right to animadvert on the proceedings of government . . . ."[38] Free discussion in the press was a positive good.

Another significant feature of this early political controversy was the image of the American Revolution. The metaphor and rhetoric of the Revolution were pervasive. For example, an anonymous writer referred to the territorial government as "rulers of their own appointment . . . who . . . tax us without our consent."[39] Vitruvius compared the administration of the territories to that of the colonies under Great Britain:

> . . . are not the people in this territory in a much worse situation, than the United States were, before the late revolution?—Are we not obliged to pay taxes without our consent?— Are not judges of inferior courts, and others in commission, dependant [sic] on the will of the governour for the tenure of their offices?—Or, have we a representative in any legislature?— And will not the excise law shortly be inforced [sic] in this territory?—And, above all, is it not a fact that, (in direct opposition to every maxim in politics) the legislative, judicial, and executive powers in this government are blended together?[40]

[35]*Ibid.*, Nov. 19, 1793.
[36]*Ibid.*, Oct. 18, 1794.
[37]"The Farmer's Friend," *Western Spy,* Oct. 1, 1800.
[38]*Centinel,* Jan. 24, 1794.
[39]*Ibid.*, August 23, 1794.
[40]*Ibid.*, Oct. 4, 1794.

Dorastus referred to the separation from Great Britain as "one of the most happy events transmitted to this age, in the page of antient [sic] or modern history"; he went on to criticize in contrast the system of government established in the territory as "oppressive, impolitical, and altogether improper, and in its leading principles intirely [sic] opposite to those rights and priviledges [sic] belonging to free men."[41] The rhetoric employed here was the rhetoric of the Revolution; the symbol most effectively invoked was the symbol of the Revolution.

The memory of the Revolution was often celebrated in the early Cincinnati press. Long lists of toasts drunk on the Fourth of July were reprinted in the *Centinel, Freeman's Journal, Western Spy,* and *Liberty Hall.* These eulogized the achievements of the founding fathers in winning independence and establishing a republican government, cheered elected officials, boasted of the progress of liberty and enlightenment in the world, and urged encouragement of agriculture, industry, and commerce. Fourth of July toasts were an exercise, as it were, in republican ideology.

It was routine for early papers to annually print these lists of Independence Day toasts. Indeed, the formula of the Independence Day toast was adopted for the final shot fired in the controversy over taxation described above. An anonymous writer submitted a list of proposed Fourth of July resolutions which included a salute to

An universal land tax, proportioned to the local intrinsic value, exclusive of the improvements of industry: the most just, simple, productive, and permanent source of all revenue—May it be substituted instead of these partial impositions, iniquitous projects of finance, which have been devised solely for the purpose of enslaving nations.[42]

In language and formula, then, the Revolution was a potent element in political rhetoric.

Letters to newspapers and verbatim accounts of patriotic celebrations were forms of persuasion. Letters argued for a point of view; Fourth of

[41]*Ibid.*, Jan. 24, 1795.
[42]*Ibid.*, July 18, 1795.

July toasts endorsed political ideas, and later became an instrument for advocating positions in political (and later electoral) controversies. There were other methods of political persuasion in the territorial papers.

The *Centinel, Freeman's Journal,* and *Western Spy* copied out choice items from other papers. The *Centinel,* for instance, printed a sympathetic account of a burning in effigy of John Jay which had appeared in the *Kentucky Gazette,* and the protest of the Democratic Society of Pennsylvania against his appointment as special envoy to Great Britain.[43] The *Centinel* even printed the complete text of Jay's Treaty, although it took two installments.[44] *Freeman's Journal* also reprinted articles criticizing Jay.

But these reprints were presented without specific endorsement by the paper, printer, or editor, and often opposing pieces were printed in the same issue. The press conductor realized that the purpose of the piece was to persuade, but, by printing it as copy from another paper, separated the opinions expressed from their author, and lent the item the same impersonality afforded a pseudonymous letter.

The impersonal presentation of opinions in the territorial newspapers constituted an act of information more than an act of persuasion. The newspaper conductor remained passive: he was not himself an avowed advocate of the opinions he presented. By presenting persuasion as information, the press conductor remained in line with the ideology of the press as public servant.

The territorial press was also conscientious in supplying other sorts of political information. Digests of the sessions of the territorial legislature, as well as important judicial decisions and major speeches, were printed regularly. At times the devotion with which a newspaper would print verbatim transcripts of political documents was remarkable. In 1795, for example, the *Centinel* devoted a large part of five consecutive issues to the publication of a plan proposed for a French constitution.[45] Whether readers were as concerned about French politics is unkowable, though unlikely.

---

[43]*Ibid.,* June 21, 28, 1795.
[44]*Ibid.,* August 8, 15, 1795.
[45]*Ibid.,* Oct. 3-31, 1795.

Territorial Elections and the Press

When we think of characteristic political processes in the United States, the first that come to mind are popular elections. And when we think of elections, the first that come to mind are presidential elections. But it is doubtful that elections dominated the political consciousness of the early Republic, and it is a fact that fewer people voted in presidential than in state or local elections. (National and state-local elections were always held on different days.)[46]

The political role of the press was seen as one of informing the populace about the proceedings of government. The theory was that informed public opinion would steer government aright. Public opinion was to assert its authority continually; it was not to be felt only at election time.

The press was not assigned a specific role in electioneering in its capacity of public servant. It would acquire such a role later in the capacity of partisan organ. But in Cincinnati throughout the territorial period and well into statehood the press was never used to advocate a candidacy of a particular man or the election of a particular ticket.

National elections received less attention in the press than local elections, and congressional elections more than presidential. Even in the hotly contested presidential election of 1800, when the issue of the Sedition Act would seem to imply a great deal of press involvement, there was virtually nothing printed in the Cincinnati papers that could be considered election-oriented. John Adams' speeches were published verbatim in the *Western Spy*, but because of his office as president, not because of his capacity as presidential candidate.

The single clear example of an election tactic in Cincinnati aimed at the presidential contest in a newspaper was in the form of a pair of Fourth of July toasts. These were the third and fourth in a list of over a dozen such toasts drunk written "at the house of Major Ziegler, joined by a number of real republicans," and read

[46]Donald J. Ratcliffe, "Voter Turnout in Early Ohio," *Journal of the Early Republic* 7(1987), pp. 223-51.

"3. The president of the United States, may he soon enjoy the benefits of retirement without interruption.

"4. The vice-president of the United States, may his merits be awarded by the approbation of his fellow citizens."[47]

This gathering of "real republicans" was ridiculed some weeks later by Plain Truth:

Amongst the 'real republicans' mentioned by the Major, there was not a man of good character, except Mr. Rutter, a journeyman sadler [sic], Henry Smith, soldier, and waiter to capt. Vance, and two or three Kentucky slaves (who are good men in their way); they were negroes, servants, and idle fellows, straggling about the streets.[48]

This incident hardly comprised a campaign effort; it certainly did not indicate an intelligible press strategy in the presidential campaign. And, of course, the same medium was available to both opposing sides. As a territory, however, Ohio did not vote in the 1800 presidential election.

A territorial legislature was elected in 1800. The newspaper had a particular role to play in this election, but as public servant, not as political advocate. In early September, An ELECTOR submitted a list of nominations, remarking that "it is generally allowed that the best way of selecting proper characters on an occasion like this, is through the medium of the press . . . ."[49] There followed eleven more tickets in the next five weeks, all sent in under pseudonyms—A Citizen, A Well-Wisher to the Country, Constant Reader, A Subscriber, Tom Thumb, and A Voter. The twelve tickets named a total of over forty candidates for eight positions. Some men were nominated only once, some as many as five times. The intention of this press behavior was to provide a public service, although it is doubtful whether it served more to confuse or inform. The *Western Spy* itself did not advocate a ticket. Likewise, the tickets it presented overlapped crazily, so no unified nomination or ticket was presented for public scrutiny.

[47] *Western Spy*, July 16, 1800.
[48] *Ibid.*, Aug. 13, 1800.
[49] *Ibid.*, Sept. 3, 1800.

It is clear that such early territorial elections were not oriented toward national political issues or organizations. Nominations were not carefully orchestrated. One nominee refused to stand for office;[50] the names of several others were spelled differently on different tickets, implying that their nominations had not been authorized, much less orchestrated. New nominations were made in the last issue of the *Spy* before election day.

Such careless electioneering is indicative of two facts. First, territorial campaigning was not partisan. Second, the press was not assigned a specific role either as a forum of opinion or as an instrument of persuasion in early campaigns in Cincinnati. This does not mean readers were not interested: the large number of nominees is evidence of popular attention. It does mean that readers did not expect electioneering in the press.

The debate over statehood was even more chaotic. A special convention was called in 1802 to respond to an offer of statehood for Ohio from the federal Congress. Heated debate arose between those anxious for full status in the Union and those suspicious of the partition of the Northwest Territory. These sides fell into line with the national parties, in that the offer of statehood had been passed by a Jeffersonian Congress over the objections of a Federalist minority.[51]

Nominations for the state convention began appearing in the *Western Spy* on September 25, 1802. They proceeded in the same chaotic fashion as nominations in 1800, but for one added dimension: local Republican societies had formed in Hamilton County, and these put forward their own tickets, unified by an opposition to territorial governor St. Clair. Of the ten delegates elected from Hamilton County, eight had been nominated by a Republican Society.[52]

The Republican victory at the polls could not have been predicted by reading the *Western Spy*. That journal listed ninety-nine nominees for

[50]He claimed that his nomination had not been authorized. *Ibid.*, Oct. 1, 1800.

[51]Jacob Burnet, *Notes on the Early Settlement of the Northwestern Territory* (Cincinnati: Derby, Bradley, & Co., 1847), pp. 347-48.

[52] William T. Utter, *The Frontier State: 1803-1825*, The History of the State of Ohio, Carl Wittke, ed., (Columbus: Ohio State Archaeological and Historical Society, 1942), pp. 7-9; John D. Barnhart, *Valley of Democracy: The Frontier versus the Plantation in the Ohio Valley, 1775-1810* (Bloomington: Indiana University Press, 1953), p. 150.

the ten positions, put forth on a welter of tickets that once more overlapped crazily. Of these ninety-nine, all received votes; twenty-six of them received more than 121 votes, with the highest receiving only 1635.[53] It would seem that virtually every man of any reputation in the county was considered by someone to be a suitable representative.

Statehood was an immensely popular cause in Hamilton County, as the voting shows. That candidates favoring statehood were elected is no surprise; that these candidates had been nominated by Republican societies testifies more to the popularity of the candidates than to the power of the Republican organization.

Debate on statehood had preceded the election by almost a year. The *Western Spy* printed a letter from A Hamilton Farmer on the issue as early as November 21, 1801. In May of 1802 it published a call for statehood submitted by the Republican Corresponding Committee of Cincinnati.[54] For the next few months, letters debating the merits of statehood were common: attention to the issue preceded the election process.

As was customary, this debate was anonymous. It was unconnected with any candidacy. As usual, the key symbol was the American Revolution. A satire of the anti-statehood position was submitted, for example, by Peter Squib, Knight, Nimbletongue Hornet, Marquis of Cincinnati, and Bruin Eitherside, Duke of Hamilton, which read in part "that these revolutionary times in this territory, do with dread and horror, remind us of the diabolical spirit of revolt which pervaded the British colonies in 1775 . . . ."[55]

Arguments from both sides were printed in the *Spy*. Attention was paid to the tone and style of debate. A writer under the pseudonym Impartial begged both parties to "cease to render yourselves contemptable [*sic*] by an ill-timed exposure of your vulgarity."[56] The editor refused to publish "personal disputes."[57] The debate over statehood, then, was wholly characteristic of territorial political controversy in the press.

---

[53]*Western Spy*, Oct. 20, 1802.
[54]*Ibid.*, May 1, 1802.
[55]*Ibid.*, May 15, 1802.
[56]*Ibid.*, May 22, 1802.
[57]*Ibid.*, July 17, 1802.

Immediately after the state convention was elected, it voted in favor of statehood. A state constitution was drafted, and preparations were made to hold Ohio's first election for Governor and United States Representative. Nominations for these positions began appearing in the *Western Spy* on December 29, 1802, anonymously submitted, and at first with no apparent party affiliation. On January 5, 1803, the *Spy* published a slate of nominations by delegates from the Republican societies of Hamilton County. Many of these men were named on other tickets.[58]

Especially interesting was the Republican nominee for coroner—Joseph Carpenter, owner and editor of the *Western Spy*. This is the first real evidence in the file of the *Spy* of Carpenter's political affiliation. He was elected coroner by a wide margin, although sixteen other candidates received votes.[59]

As the territorial period came to a close in Cincinnati, political papers remained impartial and impersonal, geared more toward information than persuasion, more toward public affairs than elections. The press was still ideally a public servant, not a partisan advocate. Practice remained in line with the theory of the press that had emerged from the American Revolution and the Enlightenment.

Several factors contributed to the impartiality of the press. Most obviously, Cincinnati remained a one-newspaper town, and that one newspaper would necessarily be expected to remain open to all parties. Also, since the single paper was under contract to print the laws of the territory, it could hardly be expected to jeopardize a source of revenue by identifying itself with outspoken criticism of the territorial government. Furthermore, politics in the region was still in an embryonic state.

But attitudes toward the press were important. Popular expectations were influential, and the quality of political rhetoric and information found in Cincinnati's territorial papers indicate wide acceptance of a press ideology that forbade partiality and demanded impersonality. Hence the

[58]William Utter claims that this was a political ploy on the part of Federalists to divide the Republican vote among various tickets. If this was the case, it is evidence that the party structure was weak indeed, and that partisan tickets were designed more to co-opt the popularity of prominent men, rather than to mobilize loyalty to a partisan program. *Frontier State*, p. 26.

[59]*Western Spy*, Jan. 5, 19, 1803.

anonymity of political contributions, and, for the most part, of nominations. Hence the limited attention to electioneering. Hence the dearth of editorial pronouncements. These traits would continue to characterize the press in the early years of statehood.

The Politics of Early Statehood

In 1804, the complexion of Cincinnati's press establishment changed with the introduction of a second newspaper, the *Liberty Hall and Cincinnati Mercury*. The editor of the *Liberty Hall* was the Rev. John W. Browne, a relative newcomer, but one who had already established his reputation by election to the state convention of 1802. Browne was a Republican, like Carpenter, and was involved with the local Republican organization as secretary of the Republican Society.[60]

Although the *Liberty Hall* and *Western Spy* competed for advertising and subscriptions, they did not represent opposing political views. The two papers clashed on occasion, for example on the issue of the formation of a Democratic Society in Philadelphia in 1805,[61] but such occasions were more the exception than the rule. Cincinnati became a two-newspaper town without abandoning the rule of impartiality.

The politics of early statehood differed from territorial politics. For constitutional reasons, elections occurred much more often after 1803, and national issues had more direct bearing on such elections. Party lines became much more clearly drawn, and tended to focus attention on campaigns for office. Improved communications facilitated the alignment of local factions into statewide organizations, like the Tammany societies.

Despite the gradual development of a more modern political system, however, the press did not become openly involved as a political advocate in Cincinnati until the late 1820s.

It will not be possible to trace in detail the political developments of early statehood. Instead, I will concentrate on key themes, like elections, political information, and anonymity in communications, trying to characterize them over the whole period 1803-1820. In addition, I will

[60]Obituary of J. W. Browne, *Liberty Hall*, Jan. 7, *Western Spy*, Jan. 9, 1813.
[61]*Liberty Hall*, April 30, 1805.

touch upon press advocacy of causes like internal improvements and the War of 1812, and press involvement in factional disputes, especially the controversy over the Tammany Society.

The duty to inform was apparently strongly felt. Raw information was regularly presented throughout the period. The Secretary of the Treasury's annual report was reprinted in its entirety, Congressional debates were copied from the *National Intelligencer*, and digests of "Foreign Intelligence" were reprinted from a number of sources. Local information was also presented in this unprocessed form: in 1811, for example, the *Western Spy* printed complete transcripts of two city ordinances involving the establishment and regulation of markets. The fact that these were published in the form of an "Extra" is further testimony to the seriousness with which press conductors perceived their duty to inform the public.[62]

Controversial events were dealt with in the same way. In 1807 and 1808, during Aaron Burr's trial, the *Liberty Hall* reprinted without comment or abridgment entire letters and affidavits submitted as evidence, along with transcripts of speeches to the court. This undigested material was the raw stuff of controversy, presented unadorned for public scrutiny and consideration. Likewise, in 1812, as hostility toward Britain flared up, the *Liberty Hall* reprinted at great length a diplomatic exchange between James Monroe, then American Secretary of State, and his British counterparts.[63]

The press gradually became more involved in elections. Contributions were more direct in advocating candidates, and although a paper would not endorse a candidate and accepted contributions from all parties, it became more and more clear that people expected to find electioneering in the press.[64]

Nominating gradually became less chaotic. In the fall elections of 1805, for instance, several Republican tickets were printed, each claiming legitimacy. A letter from Long Bow warned that "The federalists will no

[62] *Western Spy . . . Extra*, Nov. 30, 1811.

[63] *Liberty Hall*, Feb. 12, April 4, *Extra* April 4, June 9, 1812.

[64] In 1806, debate on candidates became so heated that both the *Spy* and *Liberty Hall* were forced to print extras to catch up on communications. *Western Spy Supplement*, *Liberty Hall Hand-Bill Extra*, Oct. 7, 1806.

doubt endeavor to disconcert us by publishing a number of tickets with Republican names . . . so that we may vote several tickets while they vote only one . . . ."[65]

Long Bow's complaint underscores the haphazard nature of the nominating process: it had not yet been completely co-opted by political organizations. In the same election, for example, a reader wrote as follows: "The election is drawing on apace, and so every Hodge and Bumpkin is starting his ticket, and as I am opposed to all of them, I will try my hand at an heat, and see whether the production of a Blacksmith will meet the attention and approbation of the public."[66] The openness of the nominating process implies continuing weakness in party structure.

Gradually a formula emerged for nominations. A meeting, usually self-styled as "large and respectable," of the voters or citizens or republicans of a certain township or city or county, would submit a list of candidates to a newspaper. These would be more easily identified as the product of a party or faction than an anonymous ticket. Often these would be signed by a secretary or presiding officer. Still, in most elections, it is impossible to group all candidates under two opposing parties until after 1820.[67]

Regularization of the nominating process is one indication that factions within the state or county were solidifying. But no faction had yet captured a newspaper in Cincinnati, and no paper emerged as the advocate of a particular candidate.

News of strictly local elections was rare in the press. Apparently other means of communication were employed to convey information about candidates and issues. After 1820, however, face-to-face communication became insufficient for local elections, and news and opinions for races for city council and so forth would become more common.

The majority of the electorate in early Ohio was Republican. But the Republican Party was divided, with liberal and conservative factions complicated by local variations. Party organization was never complete, and party unity was never the norm.

[65]*Liberty Hall*, Sept. 10, 1805.

[66]*Ibid.*, Oct. 1, 1805.

[67]Caucus nominations on a state level were never really accepted. See editorial in *Western Spy*, Feb. 23, 1816.

One strategy to achieve partisan unity was the creation of Tammany societies. A branch of the famous New York organization, the Tammany movement in Ohio began with the establishment of a "Wigwam" in Chillicothe in 1811. Cincinnati's wigwam was organized in January of the next year.

The Tammany organizations were semi-secret. Membership was strictly controlled. Activities were political in purpose, but centered around an elaborate ritual based on American Indian legends. The Ohio Tammany movement had an organ in the Chillicothe *Scioto Gazette*, and a leader in gubernatorial candidate Thomas Worthington.

Tammany encountered strong opposition statewide, not only from anti-Republicans (led by Charles Hammond's *Ohio Federalist*), but also from elements within the Republican Party. This opposition took the form of factional disputes within the state legislature and the multiplication of Republican electoral tickets. The controversy was short-lived, however: after 1812, the war effort brought harmony to Republican ranks.[68]

Reaction to the Tammany controversy in the Cincinnati press was characteristic of early political rhetoric in most respects. Both sides invoked the image of the Revolution. Tammany and anti-Tammany factions held separate Independence Day celebrations.[69] Letters written over pseudonyms like A Watchman and An Elector were submitted.[70]

Several features of the controversy were novel, however, and prefigured later politics. Letters were submitted under real names by people involved And candidates for state office in Cincinnati were presented on opposing Tammany and anti-Tammany tickets, with the earlier customary nominating chaos little apparent.[71]

---

[68]The history of Ohio's Tammany societies is recounted in William T. Utter, *Frontier State*, pp. 55-9; Utter, "Saint Tammany in Ohio: A Study in Frontier Politics," *Mississippi Valley Historical Review*, XV (1928), pp. 321-40; and Samuel W. Williams, "The Tammany Society in Ohio," *Ohio Archeological and Historical Society Publications*, XXII (Summer, 1913), pp. 349-70.

[69]*Western Spy*, July 6, 1811.

[70]*Liberty Hall*, August 28, Sept.

[71]See letters of James Heaton and J. Clark, *Western Spy*, May 25, 1811; of Francis McCormick and Jacob Felter, *Liberty Hall*, Sept. 25, 1811; and of Daniel Hosbrook, *Liberty Hall*, Oct. 2, 1811.

Nominating procedures were a matter of controversy. Anti-Tammanyites contrasted unannounced Tammany nominating meetings with "the open & Republican course pursued by the citizens who were called together in the several townships by <u>public advertizement</u>.."[72] Tammany members accused their opponents of being "Burrlike" and "disorganizers."[73] In Cincinnati, the overwhelming support for non-Tammany Republicans left little doubt as to the ineffectiveness of "closed" nominations.[74]

The Tammany movement in Ohio was in part an attempt to depart from established political procedures. It was an attempt to organize elements of the political process by a political cadre. It is significant that this attempt failed. It is testimony to the strength of attitudes in favor of open nominations and opposed to organizations perceived as elitist.[75]

There were, however, intimations of things to come. More attention was focused on elections. Tickets were printed, with candidates identified by allegiance to opposing factions. Contributors to newspapers, particularly candidates, addressed the public under their own names.

These developments imply some modification of the press ideology, but in a limited sense. The rule of impersonality was temporarily ignored. But both the *Spy* and the *Liberty Hall* remained impartial, and printed letters from both sides. There was no acknowledged Tammany organ in Cincinnati.

Press conduct in Cincinnati during the War of 1812 implied another departure from accepted procedure. William Turner Coggeshall, among other things an historian of the press, characterized Cincinnati's papers during the War thus:

The *Liberty Hall* and *Western Spy* were patriotic papers . . . . Week after week appeared the most heroic songs; and many a patriotic individual gave vent to long-smothered indignation, in high sounding sentences and rhetorically sounded periods, against British aggression, tyranny, and oppression; while repeated energetic essays on

[72]"An Elector," *Liberty Hall*, Sept. 18, 1811.

[73]*Ibid.*, May 25, 1811

[74]*Ibid.*, Oct. 9, 1811.

[75]A letter to the *Western Spy*, April 27, 1811, accused the Tammany Society of promoting "Despotism, Monarchy, and Aristocracy."

Columbia's great power and might, evinced, in the "glorious Revolution of 1776," were furnished as solid, after-dinner reading for the men of leisure, who loved to dwell upon what their forefathers had done in the ever-to-be-remembered eight-years' struggle.[76]

Both Cincinnati papers were strong advocates of the war effort, and their advocacy amounted to a full-fledged propaganda effort, with information presented in a manner intended to persuade. Before the War, for example the *Liberty Hall* repeatedly printed reports of British depredations[77] and Indian uprisings,[78] catering to western anti-British sentiment. During the War itself the *Liberty Hall* offered a steady diet of propaganda, including articles belittling the British through satire,[79] hortatory essays,[80] poetry,[81] and accounts of gallant exploits in the field.[82] Reports of troop movements and battles were often exhaustive, though usually out-of-date. A particularly effective rhetorical device was the invocation of the heroes of the Revolution.[83]

Cincinnati's newspapers were typical of the western press, which stood wholeheartedly behind the War. The key exception to this unanimity was Charles Hammond's *Ohio Federalist*, published in St. Clairsville. Hammond was unique not only in his opposition to the War but in the force with which his views were presented and the clearly editorial style in which he wrote.[84]

Cincinnati's press advocated the War, but in an impersonal way. Opinions were not conveyed through editorials, but were copied as songs or essays. Attitudes were reinforced through information presented in undigested form. The *Spy* and *Liberty Hall* were passive propagandists.

[76]William Turner Coggeshall, "History of the Cincinnati Press and Its Conductors" (Unpublished manuscript, Cincinnati Historical Society), p. 9.

[77]*Liberty Hall*, Oct. 9, 30, Nov. 13, 27, 1811.

[78]*Ibid.*, Sept. 25, Oct. 9, Nov. 20, 27, 1811.

[79]"Extract from the Diverting History of John Bull and Brother Jonathon," *Ibid.*, July 26, 1814, *et passim*.

[80]Amicus Patriae, *Ibid.*, Aug. 9, 1814.

[81]"The Field of Battle," *Ibid.*

[82]"Gallant Exploit," *Ibid.*, Sept. 13, 1814.

[83]"Franklin's Opinion of England," *Ibid.*, July 12, 1814.

[84]Utter, *Frontier State*, pp. 98-100.

Such a course of persuasion was common in regard to issues with virtually unanimous support in the west. The War of 1812 was one of these. Another was internal improvements. All of Cincinnati's papers supported the building of roads and canals by printing letters from groups or individuals[85] and minutes of governmental bodies dealing with such issues.[86] Western papers were also unanimous in supporting postal expansion and navigation of western waterways.[87]

Advocacy of causes like the War and internal improvements did not violate impartiality. Such causes were held to have the support of the entire people, not just a part; hence support did not cater to a party. Such behavior was in line with the ideology of the press as public servant.

Throughout the 1810s in Cincinnati the press remained committed to this ideology. But late in the decade cracks began to appear in this consensus. In December 1819 the editors of the *Liberty Hall and Gazette* and the *Inquisitor* exchanged insults over which was more "abusive" or "intemperate," over whether either indulged in "personal invective" or "deliberate malice."[88] In August 1818 the editors of the *Inquisitor* entered into a controversy with the Reverend Joshua Lacy Wilson on the morality of a public theater in Cincinnati.[89] In 1815, the same issue had been debated in the press, but in the form of mostly anonymous letters between Wilson, Theatricus, Philanthropos, and Y.[90] The conduct of the press, it would seem, was becoming less impartial and impersonal.

Politics in Cincinnati became heated in the late 1810s. There were a number of closely contested elections, especially a Congressional election in 1819 between William Henry Harrison, a veteran Indian fighter and long-time resident of southern Ohio, and James Gazlay, a lawyer and newcomer to the Cincinnati area who had achieved notoriety as a friend of the common man.[91] Bitter electoral struggles of this sort ushered in a

---

[85]*Inquisitor and Cincinnati Advertiser*, Nov. 16, 1819; A., "Roads and Canals," *Liberty Hall*, June 6-10, July 24, 1815.

[86]*Western Spy*, Dec. 13, 1816.

[87]See Chapter I.

[88]*Liberty Hall*, Dec. 14, 1819; *Inquisitor*, Dec. 21, 1819.

[89]*Inquisitor*, August 18-25, 1818.

[90]*Western Spy*, Jan., 1815, *passim*; *Liberty Hall*, Jan. 11, 23, Feb. 18, 1815.

[91]Utter, *Frontier State*, pp. 309-10.

new kind of political rhetoric. Consequently, after 1820, the press would assume a new role in political affairs.

Conclusion

Before 1820, the press proclaimed an ideology that drew its support from an image of the press as public servant. In this ideology, the press was to be impartial and impersonal, a medium for information transmission rather than persuasion. Under this ideology, less attention was to be paid to elections, and newspapers were not to back candidates or serve as the exclusive instruments of a party.

In Cincinnati, newspaper behavior mostly stayed true to this press ideology. Adherence was made easier by the absence of powerful political organizations and the smallness of the press establishment. Ultimately, however, the role of the press in politics would change, and press ideology would change with it.

CHAPTER IV

The Press and Political Culture, 1820–1848

But as our cities expanded and life grew more complicated, it turned out that political parties, in order to survive, must have a permanent organization. Eventually party morale became a greater value than the issues for the determination of which the parties are supposed to exist. The effect upon the party press was to reduce it to the position of a sort of house organ of the party organization. It no longer knew from day to day just what its opinions were. The editor was no longer a free agent. It was of this subjugated *Tribune* that Walt Whitman was thinking when he coined the phrase, "the kept editor."

-Robert Ezra Park[1]

American politics before 1820 was chaotic. If it was discordant, that was because of the confusing disarray of geographical, ideological, and economic interests that sought expression in the political forum. It was not because of organized, well-defined opposition.

The 1820s saw the organization of the first truly modern political party in the United States. The next two decades witnessed the establishment of a mature national two-party system. It is with the role of the press as it developed with the emergence of stable two-party politics that this chapter is concerned.

[1]Robert E. Park, "Natural History of the Newspaper," *Society: Collective Behavior, News and Opinion, and Modern Society, The Collected Papers of Robert E. Park,* Everett C. Hughes *et al.*, ed., (Glencoe, 1L: The Free Press, 1955), p. 98.

Partisanism and Press Ideology

Historians have commented on the partisan violence of the 1790s.[2] Party spirit was indeed vocal, and involved much of the press (although Cincinnati's was unaffected). But this partisanism was issue-oriented; it was ideological more than organizational; it was a partisanism that denied the legitimacy of parties.

I have argued that an ideology of the press as public servant survived this partisan warfare. In fact, because the so-called "first party system" tended to deny its own legitimacy, the ideology of the impersonal and impartial press thrived on disavowals of partisanism and invocations of the public good.

Parties during the Jacksonian era, however, were radically different. Acceptance of a notion of institutionalized opposition legitimized political organizations geared toward electioneering.[3] This new partisanism deeply influenced attitudes toward press behavior.

Democrats justified the formation of a political organization in terms of service to the public good and devotion to principle. One of the earliest Jacksonians in Ohio, James Gazlay, wrote to this effect:

The great mass seldom or ever see more than one political object at a time, and that not very distinctly. They are enlisted from accident or promises of favor, on the side of some one of the office-hunters; and as it is much easier and indeed safer in some instances to support the man than his real principles, and as this course saves one the

[2]Marshall Smelser, "The Jacobin Phrenzy: Federalism and the Menace of Liberty, Equality, and Fraternity," Review of Politics, XIII (Fall, 1951), pp. 457-82; Smelser, "The Federalist Period as an Age of Passion," American Quarterly, X (Fall, 1958), pp. 391-419; Donald H. Stewart, The Opposition Press of the Federalist Period (Albany: SUNY Press, 1969); Walter Francis Brown, Jr., "John Adams and the American Press: The First Full-Scale Confrontation between the Executive and the Media" (Unpublished doctoral dissertation, University of Notre Dame, 1974).

[3]On the novelty of the second party system in these respects, see Richard Hofstadter, The Idea of a Party System: The Rise of Legitimate Opposition in the United States, 1780-1840 (Berkeley: University of California Press, 1969); and Richard P. McCormick, The Second American Party System: Party Formation in the Jacksonian Era (Chapel Hill: University of North Carolina Press, 1966).

trouble of much thinking, people are apt to become the zealous advocates of men, at the very time when they suppose they are advocating principle: But if it be principle alone at which they aim, there must be strict organization, or they will become the humble tools of men in power, when they least expect it.[4]

This rationale of party organization hinged on principle and opposed itself to deference in politics.

The press would have a key role to play in such a partisan organization. The press would be the organ by which principles would be advocated. Such a press would not be passive or neutral. Yet it would have to be justified in terms of the public good. Scire Facias summed up the role of the party organ as public servant thus:

The use of an organ is to keep the people constantly advised of their opinions, to acquaint them with the newest changes in the same—of a merely apparent kind—and to inform them concerning the course which they are anxious to pursue. In this way it becomes, what it was designed to be, the voice and exponent of the people. As it is in the very nature of an organ to be freely devoted to the interests of the people, so does it contain all the apparatus of sound necessary to the people's use. By this the people declare their conventions, and in their sovereign way nominate their candidates . . . . But an organ is also devoted to the purposes of general illumination. It advises the people of all the nefarious schemes and schemers which are abroad against their good, warns them against the insidious designs of unpatriotic parties . . . . It serves, moreover, to record with wonderful accuracy the defeats of the "enemy," and its own particular triumphs.[5]

The party and the press would serve the people by telling them what they wanted and how to get it.

This rationale of party relies on the popular will, but it is a will expressed as consent to political action. Partisan machinery proposes an agenda, and voters subsequently express their approval or disapproval at the polls. Parties thus competed for support from political consumers. Newspapers "advertised" a political program. Moses Dawson, Jacksonian editor of the *Inquisitor and Advertiser*, summed up this philosophy when he wrote "It is, we conceive, in government, as in commerce—where

---

[4]James Gazlay, "State of Parties," *Western Tiller*, Sept. 29, 1826.
[5]Scire Facias, "Politics--Parties," *Herald of Truth*, II (Dec., 1847), pp. 442-43.

there is no competition, there can be but little success."[6] The political system was conceived of as a marketplace.

So the metaphor of the free market characterized partisan politics. And apologists for the partisan press claimed that whatever untruths were published in one paper would be exposed by a competing paper: "The errors and licentiousness of the press, which are to some extent inseparable from its efficient independence, may safely be tolerated, when the same engine can be wielded to counteract its own bad effects."[7] This argument in turn hinged on the wisdom and virtue of the voter, the political consumer. It assumed that he would be able to recognize truth and would reward bona fide efforts to advance the public good.

This new wrinkle in press ideology granted newspaper conductors great license. They were now permitted to gear their efforts to persuasion rather than information, to openly advocate candidates, to attempt to manipulate public opinion in favor of men or programs. And the great occasion for exercising public opinion would be election day; hence, a greatly enhanced emphasis on electioneering appeared in partisan rhetoric.

This new emphasis on elections would be effective in a number of ways. First, there would be increased voter participation in elections, with a greater percentage of eligible voters voting. Second, there would be a shifting of attention to national elections, especially presidential elections. For example, in Ohio in 1820, five times as many voters voted in the gubernatorial than in the presidential election.[8] By 1828, local and national elections had achieved rough parity in voter participation.

Third, nominations would be co-opted almost completely by the party organization. And fourth, political information, under the control of the party organ, would be geared almost exclusively toward persuasion during elections. Processed information and nomination by convention would replace the raw and unstructured fare offered by the early press.

---

[6]Moses Dawson, "Party Spirit," *Advertiser*, Feb. 25, 1824.

[7]*Literary Cadet*, Feb. 25, 1820.

[8]Harry R. Stevens, *Early Jackson Party in Ohio* (Durham, NC: Duke University Press, 1957), p. 34. See also Donald J. Ratcliffe, "Voter Turnout in Early Ohio," *Journal of the Early Republic* 7(1987), pp. 223-51.

Changes in the role of the press in politics coincided with an overall expansion in print. As the number of papers increased, the variety of positions espoused and the force with which each was advocated also increased. The result was that, as the press expanded, the single newspaper lost influence. As Tocqueville pointed out, "Each individual American newspaper has little power, but after the people, the press is nonetheless the first of powers."[9]

The power of the press lay in its pervasiveness. The medium of print lent itself to all programs, political, professional, cultural, or religious. Its power also lay in its power to inform—the press could manipulate public opinion by informing it. But these powers did not lend themselves to centralized control. And the conduct of the press, liberated by the analogy of the free market, caused alarm among many.

The behavior of the partisan press was criticized in terms of the venerable distinction between liberty and licentiousness. An article entitled "Independence" in one Cincinnati periodical stated the case thus:

> That spurning of all moral restraint and obligation which is evident in many of the intrigues of our political parties, may be considered rather as a dereliction of principle than as a manifestation of the liberty and independence of which they boast, for that liberty is prophaned, which allows the individuals of a party the privilege of traducing and blackening the character of other individuals of opposite political opinions, but perhaps of unspotted fame, and it is an unmanly and unfreeman-like use of this precious right, which should call forth the indignation of all honest minds.[10]

James H. Perkins asserted that "our periodicals reek with lying praise and yet falser blame";[11] another writer claimed that "there is nothing better calculated to make narrow minded, intolerant bigots, either in politicks or religion, than the limiting one's reading to writers of his own party."[12] Thus it was claimed that partisanism would lead to ignorance, falsehood, and licentiousness, the very opposite of the utopia of rational liberty once dreamed of by press advocates:

[9]Alexis de Tocqueville, *Democracy in America*, George Lawrence, tr., (New York: Doubleday, 1969), pp. 182-84.

[10]N., "Independence," *Cincinnati Literary Gazette*, I (Sept. 25, 1824), p. 99.

[11]James H. Perkins, "Agrarianism," *Western Messenger*, I (April, 1836), p. 590.

[12]*Cincinnati Literary Gazette*, I (Jan. 17, 1824), p. 17.

It is this adherence to party under all circumstances and upon all occasions, that has degraded the public presses of our country, and made them the instruments of faction, rather than the vehicles for the dissemination of useful information and sound political truths. Properly conducted, the press is a mighty instrument—in wise and judicious hands it is the preservative of public liberty; in the hands of the vicious and unprincipled, it degenerates into licentiousness, and becomes a curse instead of a blessing.[13]

Critics also accused partisan activists of power-seeking. The analogy here was to the acquisitiveness of the marketplace: "Party spirit is the madness of the many for the gain of the few," Timothy Flint opined.[14] Parties specialized in arousing the passions of a naive populace for the mere purpose of placing men in office.

These criticisms had a certain basis in fact. The new party system was election-oriented, and its invocation of the popular will did entail a strategy of manipulating public opinion. To place these innovations within a context of the changing role of the press in politics it will be necessary to treat in some detail the political history of Cincinnati from 1820 to 1848.

Early Electoral Contests

The 1820s in Cincinnati began in political and economic turmoil. At the root of the crisis was the Panic of 1819 and the ensuing depression; at the root of the Panic in Cincinnati was the foreclosure of the local branch of the Bank of the United States. Severe economic dislocation engendered hostility toward the Bank, and toward the merchants and land speculators associated with it.

The anti-Bank movement had immediate political implications. Opponents of the Bank organized, and after 1818 authorized political tickets.[15] The economic movement also had class implications. In 1819, a

---

[13]"Autobiography of an Ex-Editor," *Western Literary Journal and Monthly Review*, I (Nov., 1836), pp. 399-400.

[14]"Party Spirit," *Western Monthly Review*, III (April, 1830), p. 517.

[15]Stephen C. Fox, "The Bank Wars, the Idea of Party, and the Division of the Electorate in Jacksonian Ohio," *Ohio History*, 88 (Summer, 1979), p. 263.

Fourth of July parade was held, with mechanics marching in groups by trade. The climax of the gathering was when a radical cabinet-maker addressed the crowd, bitterly denouncing the Bank.[16] On Independence Day in 1820, a mob formed at one of the celebrations and attacked the local Bank office.[17]

The economic crisis threatened to polarize politics into rich versus poor, or Bank versus anti-Bank parties. Such was the tone of the electoral battle between William Henry Harrison and James Gazlay in 1819. But Harrison successfully disassociated himself from the Bank, and won election to Congress.[18]

Party organizations did not at first polarize, however. They multiplied chaotically. In local elections in 1820, so many tickets were announced that there was one candidate for every ten voters:

Tickets of candidates were presented in every possible permutation: every interest was represented, every aspiring individual, every frustrated banking group, every industrial concern and mechanic element, every trade, rival religious factions, rivals in age and family kinship, the merchants of the lower market against those of the upper, friends and opponents of lawyers, doctors, clergymen . . . .[19]

The political situation was indeed volatile.

At this time the press establishment also became volatile. In 1819, Joseph Buchanan, a newcomer from Louisville, began the *Literary Cadet and Cheap City Advertiser*. This weekly was smaller than the other Cincinnati papers, and was intended, apparently, for readers dissatisfied with the established papers.

Buchanan quickly entered into controversy. He first earned the enmity of the local establishment when he proposed that Elijah Slack be replaced as the head of the Cincinnati College by a more charismatic figure. Slack was a prominent member of the community, and the conductors of the established newspapers expressed their resentment at recommendation, coming as it did from an outsider. Buchanan's claimed in response that he

[16]Stevens, *Jackson Party*, p. 27.
[17]*Ibid.*
[18]*Ibid.*, pp. 20-2.
[19]*Ibid.*, pp. 25-6.

had been unfairly denied the right to express an opinion by "*these good old citizens—patres conscripti* of ten or twenty years standing—lords of the city . . . ."[20]

Friction between the lords of the city and the *Literary Cadet* led to personal abuse in the press. The *Inquisitor* ran an editorial insinuating that Buchanan was a quack physician given to dalliance with "Africa's FAIR damsels." His retort contrasted "that sort of <u>indefinite, vulgar, personal abuse, and slander</u>" to his own "decent ridicule," and claimed that "We shall never be so unprincipled, when criticizing the conduct of a <u>public print</u>, as to wander into the <u>private character</u> of its Editor."[21]

Buchanan's attack on the Cincinnati press establishment was short-lived. But it was significant for several reasons: it was directed specifically against a press elite, and it appealed specifically to recently-arrived Cincinnatians and other outsiders. And it was associated directly with an individual personality.

If Buchanan's *Cadet* heralded the arrival of personal journalism, it did not survive long enough to become involved in partisan politics. It was bought out by the *Western Spy* in 1820.

The established papers at this time were associated with powerful individuals. The *Liberty Hall and Cincinnati Gazette*, for instance, was edited and partly owned by Isaac G. Burnet, a lawyer, board member of many of Cincinnati's business enterprises, and Mayor from 1819 to 1831.[22] The *Advertiser* too was edited by a lawyer, Benjamin F. Powers (brother of sculptor Hiram Powers) who moved on to succeed Burnet as chief editor of the *Gazette* in 1823.[23] Cincinnati's papers were operated by an elite, then, and hence had an implicit political interest. But they had not yet been used as instruments in a political campaign, or for a partisan program. The first real use of a newspaper as a political advocate in Cincinnati occurred in 1822. The newspaper involved was Solomon Smith's

[20]*Literary Cadet*, Jan. 20, 27, 1820.

[21]*Ibid.*, March 23, 1820.

[22]Robert Herron, *Cincinnati's Mayors* (Cincinnati: Young & Klein, 1957), pp. 10-11.

[23]A. G. W. Carter, *The Old Courthouse: Reminiscences and Anecdotes of the Courts and Bar of Cincinnati* (Cincinnati: Peter E. Thompson, 1880), p. 95; Ophia D. Smith, "Adam Hurdus and the Swedenborgians in Early Cincinnati," *Ohio State Archaeological and Historical Quarterly*, LIII (Spring, 1944), p. 128.

Independent Press and Freedom's Advocate. The occasion was James Gazlay's second campaign for Congress against William Henry Harrison.

James Gazlay was raised in upstate New York. He studied law in Poughkeepsie, was admitted to the bar in 1809, and moved to Cincinnati in 1813, where he quickly earned a reputation as an agrarian and an opponent of banking interests.[24] Gazlay's notoriety resulted in particular from a spectacular case in law. It seems that a drayman was whipped by a group of merchants with whom he had gotten into an argument after he had removed some planks from the muddy road in front of their business establishments because he had found it impossible to drive over the planks. The drayman decided to appeal for redress through the courts. Gazlay was the only lawyer who would take his case. Meanwhile, the community became very excited, took sides in the question, and eventually Gazlay was awarded with great personal popularity after winning the drayman a very large settlement from the merchants.[25]

Gazlay was a powerful speaker and a republican ideologue. As an individualist, he refused to become a member of any organization, religious or secular. As a believer in science and reason, however, he did promote groups like the Society for Mutual Instruction in Natural Science, and began the *Western Tiller*, a weekly paper devoted to the dissemination of agricultural science and the promotion of Jacksonian democracy.[26]

Gazlay's candidacy in 1822 was backed by Solomon Smith's *Independent Press.* Smith was organist and choirmaster at the Swedenborgian Temple, secretary of the Haydn Society, and manager of the Globe Theater in Cincinnati. He was a colorful and enthusiastic character, and edited the *Independent Press* with "a bit more zeal than

---

[24]*Biographical Directory of the American Congress, 1774-1961,* compiled by Clifford P. Reynolds, (Washington: United States Government Printing Office, 1961), p. 992; *Independent Press,* Sept. 5, 1822.

[25]Maurice Joblin, *Cincinnati Past and Present* (Cincinnati: Elm Street Printing, 1872), pp. 26-7.

[26]Joblin, *Past and Present,* p. 28; Daniel Aaron, "Cincinnati, 1818-1838:. A Study of Attitudes" (Unpublished doctoral dissertation, Harvard University, 1943), pp. 175 *et seq.; Western Tiller,* April 27, 1827.

[27]Smith, "Hurdus," pp. 118-19.

Smith's paper differed from its contemporaries in a number of ways. It was associated strictly with the personality of its editor, who singlehandedly composed the paper. It was concerned largely with local affairs.[28] For example, in March, 1823, it began printing digests of the sessions of City Council. It had trouble obtaining advertising, indicating both the disapprobation of the business community and a relatively narrow readership. It was fond of baiting dandies. It printed far more letters from subscribers than established papers. It was a chatty paper which referred to local notables by nickname or initial. As a self-appointed gadfly, Smith aroused the anger of many elements within the city, and referred regularly to threats of personal violence.[29]

The *Independent Press* entered the Congressional campaign in August, 1822. The first shot in this battle was an editorial ridiculing Harrison, satirizing his social pretensions, referring to him facetiously as "Excellency."[30] Opposition to aristocracy was to be a persistent theme in the campaign. The next week an electoral ticket was presented, signed by A Freeman, which named Gazlay as candidate for United States Representative, and Benjamin Powers, like Smith a Swedenborgian, as candidate for Ohio State Representative. These nominations were seconded by letters from MANY CITIZENS, Hundreds, A Farmer and Mechanic, a large and respectable meeting of the mechanics, and a meeting of a respectable number of the electors of Millcreek township.[31] The nominating process was chaotic, but attention was focused on Gazlay's candidacy, and the result was a fairly unified movement.

The rhetoric of the campaign pointed to the sorry state of the economy and resulting class tensions as the main forces behind Gazlay's victory. Hundreds complained about federal debt, the pretensions of rulers, and "public servants rioting in luxury";[32] No Sycophant referred to Harrison's backers as the "Old Hive" and characterized them as "fraudulent land

---

[28]*Independent Press*, Oct. 24, 1822.
[29]*Ibid.*, Nov. 11, 18, 1822.
[30]*Ibid.*, Aug. 8, 1822.
[31]*Ibid.*, Aug. 15, 29, Sept. 5, 12, 1822.
[32]*Ibid.*, Sept. 5, 1822.

speculators, and swindling bank oppressors";[33] Reformation dubbed Harrison the candidate of the "speculators and aristocrats";[34] and editorial comments criticized Harrison's disposition as "too despotic," citing for example his support of slavery in Missouri.[35] The pages of the *Independent Press* echoed and reinforced popular attitudes of fear of the Bank, and of resentment of the bankers and land speculators held responsible for economic depression.

This was a violent campaign the likes of which Cincinnati had never seen. After the election, Gazlay was personally attacked and beaten by the son of a prominent local family.[36] For the first time the press establishment had openly divided in supporting candidates, with the *Western Spy* supporting Gazlay, and the *Advertiser*, under new editor Moses Dawson, backing Harrison. Dawson, ironically, would be Harrison's chief local antagonist in the presidential campaign of 1840.[37]

Reminiscing decades later, Edward Deering Mansfield, a veteran editor, would write simply, "Some questions arose about aristocracy, and Gazlay represented the plebeian interests and was elected to Congress."[38] For our purposes, though, the election was much more significant. It marked the beginning of a new age in political journalism in Cincinnati, with the press seen as a crucial means of advocating a candidacy, and with the columns of local papers wide open to editorials and contributions of a pointed sort. This was just a step away from outright partisan journalism: all that was lacking was a party system.

After the campaign, Solomon Smith was pressed to answer criticisms of his unorthodox conduct. He responded "false" to charges that the *Independent Press* was owned or operated or had been established by or to support James Gazlay. Apparently there was widespread suspicion regarding Gazlay's connection with the paper, so novel had its open

---

[33]*Ibid.*

[34]*Ibid.*, Sept. 19, 1822.

[35]*Ibid.*, Sept. 12, 1822.

[36]*Ibid.*, Nov. 18, 1822.

[37]Stevens, *Jackson Party*, pp. 44-7.

[38]Edward Deering Mansfield, *Personal Memories, Social, Political, and Literary, with Sketches of Many Noted People, 1803-1843* (Cincinnati: Robert Clarke & Co., 1879), pp. 162-63.

support been. To the accusation that he had refused to print material favorable to Harrison, Smith replied simply that none had been submitted.[39]

Party formation began with the presidential election of 1824, especially crystallizing around the candidacy of Andrew Jackson. In Cincinnati, Jackson's following would come largely from Gazlay's supporters.[40] The national parties in Cincinnati would thus be instruments for organizing political sentiment generated locally, and directing this sentiment toward national issues and elections. One essential medium through which organization was effected was the press.

The Presidential Election of 1824

As a concentrated process of spreading values and ideas, attitudes and beliefs, propaganda is particularly likely to expand and proliferate in times of political confusion. When values are in flux, when competing parties and factions and interests offer their distinctive ideological goods in the market place of opinion, when a unity of moral outlook has been suddenly shattered or has slowly decomposed into shapeless disagreements, the propagandist has his hey day.
                                                        –Robert K. Merton[41]

Attention must now be turned to presidential elections. It was in the presidential election of 1824 that Cincinnati first witnessed overt partisan advocacy in its newspapers. But it should be kept in mind that party organization began with the contest for the Presidency and spread downwards: Andrew Jackson's political henchmen constructed a network of Jackson corresponding committees and Hickory Clubs throughout the nation. Thus organization moved from a center outward by accretion. In Cincinnati, this Jackson party was unique, not identified strictly with any earlier faction.[42]

[39]*Independent Press*, Oct. 17, 1822.

[40]The *Independent Press* printed a pro-Jackson letter as early as June 26, 1823--the first evidence of a pro-Jackson movement in Cincinnati. Stevens, *Jackson Party*, pp. 63-4.

[41]Robert K. Merton, *Mass Persuasion: The Social Psychology of a War Bond Drive* (New York: Harper, 1946), xi.

[42]Stevens, *Jackson Party*, x, 111.

Partisan behavior, however, preceded partisan organization. As was obvious in the case of the Congressional election of 1822, popular attitudes toward elections had changed significantly, most notably in terms of press behavior. The press was permitted, perhaps even expected, to take sides after that campaign. For the next two decades, impartiality would be exceptional, and calm campaigns would be unheard of.

Party organization spread gradually to local elections. In 1824, the *National Republican*, a Jackson paper, printed up the traditional non-partisan and anonymous nominations and tickets for local offices.[43] In 1825, Jacksonian attempts to employ a county convention for nominations to county offices were frustrated, although the same technique had been very successful in selecting pro-Jackson electors in 1824.[44] Nomination by convention would become more frequent on all levels, however and by 1832 would be the customary method for selecting candidates for local, state, and national offices.[45] The municipal election of 1828 was the first local election where convention nominations were the norm. But even in that election, it is all too obvious that local concerns were not perceived within a matrix of national politics. Twelve of fifteen candidates elected were pro-Administration, although in the fall election the vote would go overwhelmingly for Jackson.[46]   Cincinnatians were primarily concerned with two national issues. First was the Bank. Anti-Bank sentiment fueled the Jackson movement, and was primarily directed against Henry Clay, strongly associated in the region with the Bank of the United States.[47] Equally significant was an interest in internal improvements. All candidates tried to capitalize on this sentiment, with Jackson's men harping on "Western interests" and invoking the image of a "united

[43]See, for example, *National Republican*, March 26, 1824.

[44] *Advertiser*, Sept. 23, 1825. Eventually nominations were put forward by a county convention in which representatives from only a single ward participated. Sept. 14, 1825.

[45]Homer J. Webster, "History of the Democratic Party Organization in the Northwest, 1824-1840," *Ohio Archaeological and Historical Society Publications*, XXIV (Winter, 1915), pp. 13-17, 19.

[46]Mary Baker Furness, "The Cincinnati Municipal Election of 1828," *Ohio Archaeological and Historical Society Publications*, XX (Summer, 1911), pp. 255-68.

[47]Donald J. Ratcliffe, "The Role of Voters and Issues in Party Formation: Ohio, 1824," *Journal of American History*, LIX (Fall, 1972), pp. 857-60.

a "united west."[48] But these programmatic issues were too ill-defined to function as the basis of a campaign. No candidate would oppose internal improvements in Ohio, and none would endorse the foreclosure of the Bank in Cincinnati. Issues did not divide the electorate—indeed, the social composition of each candidate's following was remarkably similar in terms of occupation, age, class, and place of origin.[49] The battle would be organizational. The winner would be the candidate who could most effectively rally support around images and an organizational structure.

The most important tools in this battle would be newspapers. The press would be instrumental in conveying information essential for organizational activities—announcing meetings, reporting results of conventions, and so forth—and in providing a vehicle for regular reinforcement of attitudes and images associated with a campaign. Political organization coalesced around newspapers.

The *Independent Press* and the *Advertiser* led the Jacksonian movement. Especially significant here was Moses Dawson, Irish-born editor of the *Advertiser*, and a Jacksonian stalwart until his death in 1844. The *National Republican* would also come to support Jackson after the demise of DeWitt Clinton's candidacy. The *Gazette* supported Henry Clay. And Adams supporters founded two newspapers, the *National Crisis* and the *Cincinnati Emporium* (the two later merged). The *Emporium* was edited by Samuel J. Browne, son of John W. Browne, early editor of the *Liberty Hall*.

Jackson's campaign in Cincinnati began with the failure of Clinton's.[50] Dawson's *Advertiser* called for a meeting to nominate Jackson, and such a meeting convened on April 17, 1824. Later that week, notices appeared in the pro-Jackson press that he had been nominated by "a large and respectable meeting" in Hamilton County.[51] Subsequent to the county nomination, a state convention was held, and a unified state-wide ticket of pro-Jackson electors was announced. Also, a state committee of

---

[48]Eugene H. Roseboom, "Ohio in the Presidential Election of 1824," *Ohio Archeological and Historical Society Publications*, XXVI (Winter, 1917), pp. 163-66.

[49]Stevens, *Jackson Party*, pp. 148-49.

[50]Roseboom, "1824," pp. 172-73, 176-77.

[51]*Ibid.*, p. 181; *Advertiser*, April 10, 17, 21, 1824; *National Republican*, April 23, 1824.

correspondence was formed, chaired by Elijah Hayward of Cincinnati's *National Republican*.[52]

This nominating process was anything but spontaneous. Supporters of Jackson called meetings of men friendly to Jackson to nominate Jackson, and it was unthinkable that a Jackson nominating convention would do anything but nominate Jackson. Nevertheless, Jacksonians were fond of contrasting this process to King Caucus: "It is impossible to produce a stranger instance of the undue influence which power and patronage gives [sic] to the members of the executive government than this vile attempt at over awing the republicans of this great nation."[53]

Newspapers were used most effectively by Jackson's partisans. They were employed to convey information and campaign rhetoric and to facilitate organization; they further amplified the effect of the material they presented by generating the impression of a spontaneous and rapidly growing Jackson movement.[54] The *National Republican*, for instance, carried a column headed "Public Sentiment" which was devoted exclusively to presenting toasts, resolutions, and speeches from Jackson meetings around the country. The intended effect was to present a specific image of public opinion at large, to awe the voter with reports of the strength of Jackson's following.

The upshot of Jackson's campaign was to convince the people that Jackson represented the people. This was achieved not by addressing issues or presenting a program, but by pointed criticisms of opponents as corrupt intriguers seeking to circumvent the public will. Seventy-Six, writing to the *National Republican*, cried out against "the machinations of profligate politicians . . . the most tyrannous usurpation . . . the most flagrant contempt for the voice of the people . . . ."[55] An editorial in the same paper struck out against "legislative intrigue and caucusing" by a "corrupt and aristocratic faction."[56] Again it claimed that Jackson's nomination by convention took the presidential election "from the

[52]Webster, "Democratic Party Organization," pp. 8-11.
[53]*Advertiser*, Feb. 28, 1824.
[54]Stevens, *Jackson Party*, pp. 71, 155.
[55]*National Republican*, Sept. 24, 1824.
[56]*Ibid.*, April 2, 1824.

leading demagogues of the country, and place[d it] where the constitution always intended it, <u>in the hands of the independent citizens</u>. Intrigue and secret management have lost their effect upon an intelligent community . . . ."[57] The great theme of the election was the electoral process itself. Thus Moses Dawson's response to John Quincy Adams' election by the House of Representatives: "Thus continues the chain of succession which we and every other true republican must deprecate as the greatest possible evil which can be apprehended in a republic."[58] And thus the stage was set for the election of 1828.

The Presidential Election of 1828

The election of 1828 differed markedly from that of 1824. There were only two candidates instead of half a dozen, and those two had been acknowledged opponents for four years. Whereas in 1824 no one knew what the contest would be like until the election itself, in 1828 the candidacies of Adams and Jackson had long been apparent. In 1828, opposing organizations faced each other on a battleground already tested with weapons already proven.

Again the most significant feature of the campaign was the use of newspapers. Among Jackson's supporters, a Central Committee monitored the press around the country, issuing rebuttals to anti-Jackson stories and circulating pro-Jackson propaganda. Local committees corresponded with this Central Committee in Nashville. Cincinnati's Jackson Committee had been set up in 1826; Elijah Hayward was again a member.[59]

The Jackson organization co-opted sympathetic political leaders in all areas of government. A nationwide party leadership, composed of state, local, and federal officials, was the result. Historian Robert Remini evaluates the work of this cadre thus:

[57] *Ibid.*, May 7, 1824.

[58] *Advertiser*, Feb. 19, 1825.

[59] Robert V. Remini, *The Election of Andrew Jackson*, Critical Periods in American History, Robert D. Cross, ed., (Philadelphia and New York: Lippincott, 1963), pp. 63-5, 89-90; Culver Smith, *The Press, Politics, and Patronage: The American Government's Use of Newspapers, 1789-1875* (Athens, GA: University of Georgia Press, 1977), p. 68.

Perhaps the single most important accomplishment of the Democrats in Congress and in the states was the creation of a vast, nationwide newspaper system. The initiative and drive for this enterprise came from Congressmen, but the work was aided by governors, state legislators, county leaders, and politicians of every rank.[60]

Newspapers were set up for the purpose of promoting Jackson, and existing newspapers were taken over. This "top-down" expansion of the press was evident in Ohio, where the number of pro-Jackson newspapers increased from five to twenty-three in the three-year period from 1824 to 1827. These papers were often funded in part by the national political organization or the local chapter.[61]

This information network may have been more effective in confusing than in informing. Jackson's position on issues like patronage, the tariff, and internal improvements, already ambiguous, were "reshaped to accord with varying sectional opinions."[62] This was one of the weaknesses (or strengths) of a communication system as local in character as the newspaper.

The Adams organization did its best to imitate Jackson's strategy. Daniel Webster and Henry Clay constituted the driving force, raising funds for distribution to selected newspapers. The difference was that Adams' men failed to "rivet their high-powered newspapers to the emerging state organizations as the Jacksonians had done."[63] Political rhetoric was best in mobilizing voters when aligned with a partisan organization.

In Cincinnati, Jackson and Adams men established opposing papers devoted exclusively to the presidential campaign. Both journals were monthlies, and both were connected with conventional partisan newspapers. The Jackson campaign paper was the *Friend of Reform and Corruption's Adversary*, edited by Moses Dawson and aligned with the *Advertiser*. The Adams paper was entitled *Truth's Advocate and Monthly Anti-Jackson Expositor* and was edited mostly by Charles Hammond of the

[60]Remini, *Election*, p. 76.
[61]Webster, "Democratic Party Organization," pp. 30-1; Remini, *Election*, pp. 77, 80.
[62]Remini, *Election*, p. 75.
[63]*Ibid.*, pp. 128-29.

Gazette.

Hammond's *Truth's Advocate* was of national significance. Historian Culver Smith testifies that it "printed some of the cruelest and most extreme charges against Jackson."[64] Most notable among these were the allegations of marital irregularities: it was Hammond who first accused Rachel Robards Jackson of adultery.[65]

Anti-Jackson arguments in *Truth's Advocate* took two forms: *ad hominem* attacks against Jackson, and attacks on Jackson's campaign strategy. The latter approach is exemplified by the opening address to the public:

In proportion as efforts are made to mislead and abuse the public mind, counteracting efforts become necessary to diffuse correct information. The torrents of misrepresentation and falsehood that flood the country, through the channels of the opposition presses, must be met, and rolled back to overwhelm their authors.[66]

Truth's Advocate contended that Jackson's campaign strategy was designed to produce "an excitement of the animal spirits. . . . to render the subject of its influences reckless of thought and reflection, and empower the senses to shake off the controul and silence the admonitions of reason."[67] It was a dangerous mistake to suppose that the people had "arrived to such a degree of intelligence as to be proof against designs on their credibility, or to such a degree of moral power, as to place them beyond the possibility of an improper and wayward indulgence of their passions."[68] To demonstrate the irrationality of the Jackson movement, *Truth's Advocate* set out to expose it as an amalgamation of "discordant and heterogeneous materials."[69] Evidence of this was the attempt in the west to portray Jackson as a champion of internal improvements, a portrayal considered

---

[64]Smith, *Patronage*, p. 104.

[65]"Address," *Truth's Advocate*, I (Jan., 1828), pp. 4-20; Francis P. Weisenburger, "Charles Hammond: The First Great Journalist of the Old Northwest," *Ohio State Archaeological and Historical Quarterly*, XLII (Fall, 1934), pp. 383-5.

[66]"Address," *Truth's Advocate*, I (Jan. 1828), p. 1.

[67]"Administration Convention," *Ibid.*, pp. 31-2.

[68]G., "General Reflections," *Ibid.*, (Feb., 1828), pp. 70-3.

[69]X.Y., "The Opposition," *Ibid.*, (March, 1828), p. 94.

ludicrous by Adams men.[70] This heterogeneity was contrasted to the eminent consistency of Adams.[71]

Truth's Advocate was most adept at personal criticism of Jackson. He was characterized as an adulterer, a dictator, a military despot, a military incompetent, a "Military Chieftain," an "exterminator of Indians," a "Negro Trader," "a man of violent and ungovernable temper," a land speculator, "illiterate, vulgar, and violent.[72] In short, claimed the *Advocate*,

No doubt can remain, upon the impartial and intelligent mind, that General Jackson is, and ever has been, a rash, vain, and presumptuous ignoramus: that it is to a good portion of animal courage, and to an uncommon share of vindictive fury, united with an impetuous temper, that he has made an impression on those around him.[73]

The campaign as waged by Adams men and as typified by the *Advocate* was on the whole a campaign of men, not measures. The press was used to present and amplify an image of Andrew Jackson as an anti-republican demagogue, a genuine threat to rational liberty, and Jackson's campaign strategy was criticized as an abuse of rational liberty, an excess of democracy, an example of the licentiousness which the Revolutionary fathers had so feared.

The *Friend of Reform* struck back effectively at these charges. Moses Dawson derided the *Advocate's* low estimate of the intelligence of the people: "He treats the American people as if they were the disembodied troops of a military conqueror, who had no judgment in political affairs, but were carried away by the glare of military achievements . . . ."[74] Dawson argued for the wisdom of the populace: the Jackson movement

---

[70]"General Jackson and the American System," *Ibid.*, (Jan. 1828), pp. 20-24.

[71]"Vindication of the Political Consistency of John Quincy Adams," *Ibid.*, (Sept., 1828), pp. 321-30.

[72]"General Jackson's Violence," *Ibid.*, (May, 1828), pp. 161 *et seq.*; Charles Hammond, "General Jackson's Land Speculations Reviewed," *Ibid.*, (July, 1828), pp. 241-50; "General Jackson's Land Speculations: Murder, Adultery, Treason, Swindling!" *Ibid.*, pp. 250-6.

[73]"Further Illustrations of General Jackson's True Character," *Ibid.* (Oct. 1828), pp. 389-90.

[74]"Truth's Advocate," *Friend of Reform*, I (March 22, 1828), p. 36.

was guided by firm principles, not hero worship.

Dawson characterized the Adams campaign as one of "the most scurrilous abuse, and unjust vituperation."[75] So thorough was its reliance on calumny that Jackson had been charged with "the breach of almost every law, human and divine."[76] This was an honest criticism: the Adams campaign was in fact fiercely personal.

But Jackson's men were not above personal abuse. Adams was in turn characterized as profligate, an addict of luxury, and an abuser of patronage.[77] He was depicted as an aristocrat who had gained office through an abuse of democratic processes, a corrupt bargain.[78] And his followers were so morally bankrupt as to resort to slandering female reputation to gain their ends.[79] Adams himself was an incompetent who had lost an opportunity to gain important concessions in the French colonial trade through diplomatic bungling.[80]

In contrast, Jackson was a paragon of integrity and devotion to democratic principles. He was a true champion of internal improvements and western interests.[81] And he deserved comparison to Washington as an unselfish patriot.[82] His followers tried to convey the image of Jackson as a virtuous farmer, a nineteenth-century Cincinnatus:

Now we have closed the campaign, we show them the gallant warrior on his spacious and well-cultivated farm. A straw hat covers those white locks bleached by the midnight dews in the tented field—a coat of plain homespun made on the farm is substituted for the uniform . . . . [After overseeing the work in the field] he repairs to his fireside, and is surrounded by his friends and neighbors, and the evening closes in rational and improving converse. This is the picture of the Tennessee Farmer. It is the picture of Andrew Jackson as he is now. Such a man who can follow the plough, or follow the enemy as occasion may require, who has plain practical sense and sound experience in affairs of government, who has honesty as his land mark, and decision

[75]*Ibid.*, p. 37.

[76]*Ibid.*, p. 18.

[77]*Ibid.*, pp. 42-4; letter of Western, pp. 45-7; "Official Profligacy," pp. 47-8.

[78]"The Investigation," *Ibid.*, pp. 2-4; "Speech of Mr. Maupin," pp. 25-30; "The Bargain," pp. 30-2; "The Bargain—More Proof," (May 22, 1828), pp. 82-4.

[79]"Female Reputation," *Ibid.*, (April 22, 1828), pp. 71-2.

[80]"French West India Trade," *Ibid.*, (March 22, 1828), pp. 44-5.

[81]"General Jackson and the American System," *Ibid.*, pp. 11-15.

[82]"Truth's Advocate," *Ibid.*, pp. 39 *et seq.*

as his guide, even such a man will the people take from his farm, and make him president of the United States.[83]

So Jacksonians placed the image of the virtuous farmer in opposition to the image of the slaveowning dictator; so they portrayed the characteristic of common sense in opposition to the accusation of licentious unreason. The campaign was, in large part, a battle to construct favorable or unfavorable images of the candidates.

Such open attempts to manipulate public opinion by shaping popular attitudes were novel in the Cincinnati press. The establishment of papers devoted exclusively to campaigning was also novel. And with these new modes of press behavior, there appeared a new sort of editor.

The Partisan Editor

Cincinnati's editors before 1820 were not highly visible in their papers. They were well-known in the community, but generally through activities outside journalism. John Browne was a minister, Isaac Burnet was Mayor, and other editors devoted most of their time to law or some similar pursuit. The "professional" editor did not emerge until the 1820s, and then appeared as a creature of partisan politics.

The champions of the Jackson and anti-Jackson parties in Cincinnati in the 1820s and 1830s were the editors of the *Advertiser* and *Gazette*, Moses Dawson and Charles Hammond. Both became important figures in party formation. And both took leading roles in the introduction of partisan rhetoric into Cincinnati's papers.

Charles Hammond was born near Baltimore in 1779, one of sixteen children. Although his formal education was sparse, he studied literature and read law, preparing himself for an eminent career in the press and at the bar. During the 1790s, he wrote a series of letters to newspapers over the pseudonym The Ploughboy, exhibiting the conservative political temper that he had inherited from his loyalist father. In 1801 he moved to the Northwest Territory, was admitted to the bar, and began practicing

---

[83]"The Tennessee Farmer," *Ibid.*, (Aug. 22, 1828), p. 285.

law.[84]

Hammond had been involved in political journalism from his teens. In 1813 he undertook editorial duties for the first time when he founded the *Ohio Federalist* at St. Clairsville. This paper would gain notoriety through its opposition to the War of 1812. The paper survived until 1817, a remarkably long life-span in light of the near-complete dissolution of Federalism in Ohio by that time. Meanwhile, Hammond's personal political star rose with election to the state legislature. He would continue to derive an income from public office until 1838 as Reporter of the Ohio Supreme Court, a position to which he was appointed in 1823.[85]

Hammond became one of Ohio's first promoters of Henry Clay's presidential candidacy when he wrote and published a sixteen-page pamphlet advocating Clay in 1822.[86] During the campaign he contributed a number of items to Cincinnati papers, especially the *Gazette*, partly owned by his son-in-law, Stephen S. L'Hommedieu. Few were surprised when in 1825 Hammond succeeded Benjamin F. Powers as editor of that paper.[87] Although he devoted a great deal of time and effort to the conduct of the paper, Hammond received no salary until 1830, when he demanded and was granted the substantial sum of $1000 a year.[88]

Contemporaries praised Hammond for his independence of mind and devotion to political principles.[89] Historians have complimented his moral courage in supporting freedom of the press and opposing anti-

---

[84]William Henry Smith, *Charles Hammond and His Relations to Henry Clay and John Quincy Adams on Constitutional Limitation and the Contest for Freedom of Speech in the Press* (Chicago: Chicago Historical Society, 1885), pp. 12-4; William Henry Venable, *Beginnings of Literary Culture in the Ohio Valley: Historical and Biographical Sketches* (1891; reprint New York: Peter Smith, 1949), pp. 393-94; Roswell Marsh, *The Life of Charles Hammond of Cincinnati, Ohio* (Steubenville: 1863), *passim*; Weisenburger, "Hammond," pp. 340-43.

[85]Osman Castle Hooper, *History of Ohio Journalism, 1793-1933* (Columbus: Spahr and Glenn, 1933), pp. 70-1; Weisenburger, "Hammond," pp. 344-52, 364.

[86]Stevens, *Jackson Party*, pp. 54-5.

[87]Smith, *Hammond*, pp. 32 *et seq.*; Weisenburger, "Hammond," pp. 415, 424-25, 372-73.

[88]Weisenburger, "Hammond," p. 393.

[89]"Charles Hammond," *Western Messenger*, VIII (May, 1840), p. 30.

abolitionist riots in 1836.[90] Others have noted that he was a spendthrift who ruined his health by excessive drinking.[91]

Whatever his personal characteristics may have been, Hammond was a consummate politico. He used his position as editor of Cincinnati's leading newspaper to advantage, spearheading the Adams campaign in 1828, the Clay campaign in 1832, and the Harrison campaign in 1836. His *Truth's Advocate* was the first campaign paper ever published in Ohio. Together with Moses Dawson, he pioneered personal political journalism in Cincinnati.

Moses Dawson was born in Belfast in 1768. By 1790 he had affiliated himself with the revolutionary movement there, and had begun organizing societies of United Irishmen. Within a decade, he was arrested for sedition twice and for high treason once—apparently he escaped hanging through an oversight. Subsequently he left Ireland and moved to Glasgow, where he earned a living as a teacher in a Lancasterian Seminary.

In Glasgow Dawson remained politically active. He contributed a series of articles to a paper called the *Magic Lantern*, acquiring a reputation for scandal. Finally he was forced to leave Scotland, and in 1817 came to Cincinnati to teach in the newly established Lancaster Seminary. By 1822 he had purchased the *Inquisitor and Cincinnati Advertiser*. Apparently he felt more at home in the press than in the classroom.

Dawson continued to edit the *Advertiser* until 1841, when he sold it to John and Charles Brough, who changed its name to the *Enquirer*. Under that name it survives to this day. The paper remained loyal to the Democratic Party long after Dawson's death in 1844.[92]

Dawson was among Jackson's earliest supporters in Ohio in 1824. After Jackson's election in 1828, Dawson was rewarded for his fidelity by being named Receiver of Public Monies in the Land Office at Cincinnati. His nomination was rejected, however, after evidence was presented that his

---

[90]Weisenburger, "Hammond," pp. 416-20; Smith, *Hammond*, pp. 59-64 *et passim*.

[91]Weisenburger, "Hammond," p. 425.

[92]Virginius C. Hall, "Moses Dawson, Chronic Belligerent," *Bulletin of the Historical and Philosophical Society of Ohio*, XV (Summer, 1957), pp. 175-77; Stevens, *Jackson Party*, pp. 3-7; *Independent Press*, Jan. 30, 1823.

naturalization papers were not in order. That evidence had been gathered by Charles Hammond.[93]

After the *Gazette* and the *Advertiser*, the most important political paper in Cincinnati was the *National Republican*. This newspaper had been set up in 1823, superseding the *Western Spy*. The *Spy* had been bought out by Elijah Hayward, who then became editor of the *National Republican*.

Hayward was born in Bridgewater, Massachusetts, in 1786. While a resident of New England, he studied law under Judge Theophilus Parsons, voted Federalist, and sought election to the Hartford Convention. His political outlook changed after he came to Cincinnati in 1819.

The *National Republican* became a solid Jacksonian paper under Hayward's editorship. He himself served as chairman of both the Cincinnati and Ohio Jackson corresponding committees during the presidential campaign of 1824. Following that campaign, and perhaps as a result of notoriety gained during it, Hayward was elected to four consecutive terms as state representative.

After the Jacksonians came to power in 1828, Hayward had every reason to expect recognition from the men he had helped gain office. He was not disappointed. In 1830 he was appointed Commissioner of the General Land Office in Washington, D.C., at a healthy salary of $3500 a year. The heavy drinking that a government office seemed to entail drove him to a sickbed, however, and he was obliged to resign in 1835.

Hayward's final years were spent quietly. He served as state librarian, and edited a small newspaper, the *Muskingum Valley Democrat*. Sometime before his death he embraced Roman Catholicism.[94]

Not all partisan papers were associated with a single man. The *National Crisis and Cincinnati Emporium*, for example, was nominally edited by Samuel J. Browne. In fact, it was common knowledge that that paper was mostly written and composed by a group of some two dozen pro-Adams lawyers known as the axe-handle club.[95] The *Crisis and*

[93]Weisenburger, "Hammond," pp. 393-94.

[94]Francis P. Weisenburger, "The 'Atlas' of the Jacksonian Movement in Ohio," *Bulletin of the Historical and Philosophical Society of Ohio*, XIV (Fall, 1956), pp. 283-311; Carter, *Old Courthouse*, p. 94.

[95]Mansfield, *Personal Memories*, p. 163; Charles Theodore Greve, *Centennial History of Cincinnati and Representative Citizens* (Chicago: Biographical Publishing

the exception to personal journalism that proved the rule. The scorn with which its anonymous editorials were greeted by men like Moses Dawson indicates that impersonal journalism was no longer common practice in Cincinnati.

Just as the rise of partisan journalism marked the demise of impartiality in the press, so did the rise of the professional editor mark the demise of impersonality. The hgihly personal editorial running battle between Hammond and Dawson would set the tone for the political press for years to come. Beneath the sound and fury lay a profound change in press behavior.

Beginning on the presidential level and filtering downwards, the newspaper came to be seen as a vital instrument of electoral persuasion. After his election, Andrew Jackson and his men acknowledged the significance of the newspaper campaign by appointing men like Dawson and Hayward to lucrative offices. This unprecedented patronage was a cause of concern to ideologues who maintained the necessity of "purity" in the press. No one questioned whether newspapers had actually been effective in bringing about Jackson's election. Newsmen had acquired the aura of leaders of public opinion.[96]

As newspapers became more effective in promoting party interests, they began to close their pages to other parties. In 1833, A Stranger wrote to Dawson's *Advertiser*, complaining that "communication after communication on the subject of the bank . . . has been laid aside" by Hammond's *Gazette*.[97] Another stranger of opposite political persuasion could very well have taken Dawson to task for similar offenses. A decade earlier Solomon Smith had felt obliged to make excuses for the lack of opposition material in his *Independent Press*. But by the 1830s, newspapers were not expected to be "Open to all Parties."

Newspapers now endorsed a ticket by printing it under the masthead at election time. They were active participants in the nominating process, announcing conventions, reporting their proceedings, and endorsing their nominees. Before 1820, the ease with which any voter could submit

Co., 1904), p. 791; *Advertiser*, July 10, 1824.

[96]Smith, *Patronage*, pp. 90-9, 90.

[97]A Stranger, "To the Editor of the Cincinnati Gazette," *Advertiser*, Jan. 19, 1833.

nominations to a newspaper had made the press an implicit supporter of chaotic nominations. In contrast, Moses Dawson's motto was "The Ticket, the Whole Ticket, and Nothing but the Ticket."[98]

Office seekers took advantage of the press to address the electorate directly. In hotly contested state elections in 1825, for example, Elijah Hayward, Nathaniel G. Pendleton, and Abel Wolverton wrote to the *Advertiser*, openly advocating their candidacies.[99] All this is evidence that the press was no longer seen as a passive instrument of rational liberty, but as an active advocate of political and partisan interests.

Meanwhile, battles between editors became more and more personal. Dawson and Hammond squared off, and other papers took sides, with the *Mercantile Daily Advertiser*, for example, cheering on Hammond, "Whose superiority of intellect and refinement over vulgar epithets and cant phrases, showed an Ajax to a pigmy."[100] Hammond meanwhile was ridiculed and belittled by Dawson as "Slander Master General for the State of Ohio, and Conscience Keeper to the Vindictive Demagogue";[101] "Our windy neighbor in the Hammond Gazette";[102] "The sapient editor of Liberty's Grave, alias the Windy Gazette, . . . this mouthpiece of the corruptionists, . . . our man of puff";[103] "a violator of truth, . . . a base calumniator," "This contemptible creature";[104] "Signor Puffando, with his usual knack of misrepresentation . . . ."[105] This editorial battle of personalities mirrored that of the politicians. It is anyone's guess whether Dawson coined more epithets for Hammond than Hammond coined for Andrew Jackson.

As the press became more politically active, it also became a more effective instrument for political persuasion. Historian Harry Stevens has described how "partisan stories, news, and editorials were more carefully

[98]Fox, "Bank Wars," p. 266.

[99]*Advertiser*. Oct. 1, 5, 1825.

[100]*Mercantile Daily Advertiser*, Nov. 23, 1826.

[101]"The Last Will and Testament of the Late Charles Hammond," *Friend of Reform*, I (Sept. 22, 1828), p. 338.

[102]*Advertiser*, June 4, 1825.

[103]*Ibid.*, Dec. 31, 1825.

[104]*Ibid.*, April 6, 1825.

[105]*Ibid.*, May 7, 1825.

distinguished, and each was handled with great skill in working toward the desired result."[106] This was a departure from the pre-1820 press, where political items were presented in the guise of contributions, letters from readers, or copy from other papers, and the newspaper itself remained at least nominally impartial. Editors had become skilled propagandists.

Elsewhere I have argued that the ideology of the press as public servant was a legacy of the independence movement. The heritage of the free press was intimately linked in the minds of early Americans with the Revolution, and the image of the Revolution was invoked regularly in the press. But in the 1820s, a change in attitudes toward the Revolution occurred.

The 1820s saw the passing away of the Revolutionary generation. In 1826, the *National Republican*, which customarily printed the obituary of any veteran of the Revolutionary War who had died anywhere in the country, noted that "The brave and patriotic men who achieved our Independence are rapidly passing from this stage of action—they are dropping like withered leaves before autumnal blasts—and in a short time not a single individual will be left, who partook in that memorable struggle."[107] Only a few months later, the *Republican* would carry news of the simultaneous deaths of John Adams and Thomas Jefferson on Independence Day.[108]

There was a clear perception of generational change. A heroic generation was passing away, and the next decade would see its children feud over the inheritance. This post-heroic generation was found sadly lacking by anti-Jacksonians when compared to its predecessor:

Are we, as they were, emulous only how we may be most useful to the public? Do we individually, as they did, regard ourselves as nothing, our country as all? . . . The contrast is a humiliating one—and there is too much reason to fear, that a succeeding generation, and not a distant one, may remember the fourth of July with the deepest shame, as a reproach upon their degradation, their fallen estate and character, in contrast with the conduct and character of their ancestors.[109]

[106]Stevens, *Jackson Party*, p. 156.
[107]"Revolutionary Heroes," *National Republican*, March 31, 1826.
[108] *National Republican*, July 21, 28, 1826.
[109]*Gazette*, July 4, 1826.

These men deplored what they saw as the abandonment of rational liberty in favor of licentious demagoguery. An anonymous writer in the *Cincinnati Literary Gazette* described "with great regret, the ominous march of this unqualified and unguarded devotion to individuals, since the glorious year in which this fair land was devoted to freedom."[110] *Truth's Advocate* urged that such "servile adulation" be "regarded as censurable self-abasement, and a reprehensible dereliction from correct republican principles." Such behavior would hardly have been found in the founding fathers, those "stern, self-devoted Republicans, abhorring all attachment to men, and concentrating their judgments and their affections upon the public weal alone."[111]

Even as opponents invoked the founding fathers to censure their political behavior, so also did Jacksonians use the image of the Revolution to dramatize and legitimize their campaign. Junius in Cincinnati, writing to the *Friend of Reform*, described the election of 1828 in these terms:

> . . . this struggle is a far more serious matter. It may emphatically be called our second struggle for independence. The great parties which divided these states have become amalgamated; and in fact, numerous individuals of both parties have thrown off the mask, and come out in their true characters; they must, therefore, from this period, be designated as Republicans and Aristocrats. At the head of the latter is our present incumbent, John Quincy Adams . . . .[112]

This idea of a second struggle for independence was amplified by repeated accusations of a corrupt bargain in arranging an "official succession"; and it underscored criticisms of Adams' supposed luxurious self-indulgence. This rhetoric was, not accidentally, reminiscent of colonial and Revolutionary arguments against placemen in a corrupt bureaucracy.

The elements of this Revolutionary rhetoric remained commonly understood, and the symbols used in the Independence movement were still highly charged in the Jacksonian era. In 1833, for example, Jonathan

[110]Y., "Lafayette: An Apologue," *Cincinnati Literary Gazette*, II (Nov. 6, 1824), p. 145.

[111]"Man Worship," *Truth's Advocate*, I (Feb., 1828), p. 49.

[112]Junius in Cincinnati, "No. V: To the Citizens of the State of Ohio," *Friend of Reform*, I (Aug. 22, 1828), p. 296.

described the effects of Moses Dawson's opposition to a new city charter in these terms:

You have played the Devil. The Johny Bulls who made the new would-be City Charter, begin to lash their sides like enraged lions. Keep cool, gentlemen, your charter is too highly charged with Kingly notions, I guess, to please the Jonathans of this city.[113]

Jacksonians and their opponents continued to invoke the Revolution, but continually invoked different aspects of its legacy, and did so for explicitly partisan reasons.

Political Participation

Voter participation increased dramatically in the 1820s. This increase was nationwide, and seems linked to specifically national elections, especially presidential elections. Increased electoral participation points to a new idea of public opinion and of political participation.

Nationwide, between 1824 and 1828, there was an increase of more than 300% in the number of votes cast for the presidency. Historian Culver Smith concludes that credit for this increase should go "not only to the political managers of the 1828 campaign, and to some increase in voting population, but also to a more effective press."[114] The example of Cincinnati seems to bear out this conclusion.

[113] *Advertiser*, April 7, 1833.

[114] Smith, *Patronage*, p. 72. There is some disagreement over just how much the average citizen cared about politics. The evidence on voting is clear, but how much did ordinary folk think about politics between elections? Malcolm Rohrbough thinks not much: "Of those few accounts of frontier people that have survived, few mention politics. Fewer still display more than passing notice of national political affairs." (*The Transappalachian Frontier*, New York: Oxford University Press, 1978, pp. 394-5.) Lewis Saum agrees, arguing that the period's florid rhetoric was mostly for show, and did not indicate any real "public opinion": "Politics provided diversion. Evidently, the sound and fury often signified very little." (*Popular Mood of Pre-Civil War America*, Westport CT: Greenwood Press, 1980, p. 152.) The absence of political meditations in private journals and letters that these authors note, however, may be attributable simply to a common-sense distinction between public and private. There is no denying the importance of raucous politics in public life.

In Ohio, 50,024 people voted for President in 1824. In that same year, 76,634 Ohioans voted in a much less controversial gubernatorial election.[115] In all, less than half of Ohio's voters participated in the 1824 election.[116]

By contrast, in 1828, 90% of Ohio's eligible voters turned out for the presidential election, more than voted in state and local elections.[117] It is clear that national politics had quickly assumed more importance than local politics at the polls. And as national elections drew more interest, national political organizations became more effective in co-opting local factions.

The root cause seemed to be a fundamental change in attitudes. Political organizations became more aggressive in focusing attention on national elections, especially presidential campaigns. The electorate responded with increased voter participation in these political contests. This change in political attitudes was the essential precondition for truly effective political organization.

But changes in voter behavior signaled changes in attitudes toward public opinion and its servant, the press. The authority of public opinion was now to be exerted specifically at the polls, and was to be guided, indeed manipulated, by the press. Political participation came to mean electoral participation. And political information came to mean arguments in favor of or against a partisan ticket.

The Second Party System

Party organization in a modern sense was an invention of the Jacksonians. Anti-Jacksonians continued to deny the propriety of partisanism, to deplore party spirit, even after they, too, had become organized as a national party. But by the 1840s there was very little difference between the two party presses.[118]

[115]Roseboom, "1824," p. 214.

[116]William T. Utter, The Frontier State: 1803-1825, The History of the State of Ohio, Carl Wittke, ed., 6 vols (Columbus: Ohio State Archaelogical and Historical Society, 1942), pp. 334-35.

[117]Ratcliffe, "Voters and Issues," p. 865.

[118]Fox, "Bank Wars ," contends that the Whigs in Ohio never really accepted the

The ethnocultural composition of the two parties differed somewhat. In Ohio, Whigs were more likely to be evangelical and from the Northeast, especially New England and the Burned-Over District of New York. Democrats tended to be Catholic, with a geographical bias toward the mid-Atlantic states, the South, and Germany.[119] Specifically in Cincinnati, Whigs tended to be "better established, more successful, and more deeply involved in community affairs than the Democrats."[120] In addition, Whigs tended to control elections in the city throughout the 1840s, until the rise of anti-slavery political organizations.

In terms of political rhetoric in the press, differences between parties in composition and strength were evident in a difference of tone rather than of substance. The *Gazette*, for example, would assume a tone of moral outrage at the language used by the Democratic *Enquirer*: "Honest men, who live by honest toil, . . . are blackened by the vilest epithets—are called charlatan dupes! braggart vassals! dolts of coward masters!" Earlier in the same editorial, however, the *Gazette* had applied these epithets to the *Enquirer*: "Coarse, vituperative, virulent, untruthful, having no respect for age or character, intolerant in feeling, and tyrannical in its actions";[121] it also indulged in a personal attack on Charles Brough, then editor-in-chief of the *Enquirer*.[122] It is clear that both parties were prone to personalities in the press, but it is also clear that the Whig press in Cincinnati was also more likely to disparage this practice.[123] This is a difference of tone rooted in the cultural predisposition of Whig voters, one surmises, but it is a cosmetic difference: Whig rhetoric was no more elevated in practice.

After party organizations had been set up, newspapers played a less crucial role in partisan functions. But partisan papers were still an

---

idea of partisan politics. If such was the case, then it is certainly not implied in the behavior of the Whig press, which was every bit as partisan in exactly the same way as the Democratic press.

[119]Fox, "Bank Wars," pp. 256-57.

[120]Walter Stix Glazer, "Cincinnati in 1840: A Community Profile" (Unpublished doctoral dissertation, University of Michigan, 1968), pp. 175-76.

[121]*Weekly Gazette*, Oct. 12, 1843.

[122]*Ibid.*

[123]*Ibid.*, March 14, 1844.

important source of organizational information. Nominations, for example, still submitted to newspapers prior to being submitted to a convention. These announcements followed a simple formula:

Please announce the name of Judge Henry Morse, to the consideration of the Whig convention, to be held on the 13th prox., as a candidate to represent this district in Congress . . . .

A VOTER

Or again,

Please say that R. A. Madison, Esq., has consented to let his name go before the Democratic Whig Convention for the office of Sheriff of Hamilton County.[124]

In addition to announcing candidates, the press was important in announcing meetings and reporting the results of conventions and rallies. The press thus amplified the rhetoric generated by the party organization.

Just as a partisan paper would amplify its own party's activities, it would attempt to diminish those of the opposition party. Take for example this Whig report of a Democratic meeting:

The "great mass meeting" of the Democracy assembled here yesterday, numbering, all told, forty souls, including some six or ten Whigs of this place, five or six fine looking tallow fingered lawyers of your city, and a band of music, leaving to the party, just a full score and one—no more nor less . . . .[125]

Derogation of the opposing party's support was typical of both parties. In an age of popular politics, the chief argument for a party's program could easily become its popularity. Only the support of the populace justified the support of the populace, to state what may seem a paradox. Nevertheless, the most common form of electioneering, that is of promoting a program or candidate for public approval, was to present evidence of its popularity by printing resolutions from mass meetings from all over the country, by predicting success at the polls, and by depicting the opponent's support as a conspiratorial clique, a social elite or sub-class, or a chimerical coalition of

[124]*Ibid.*, June 10, 1844.
[125]*Ibid.*, July 11, 1844.

warring factions.

In contrast, a newspaper would try to present its own party as a unified body of opinion. Whigs, for instance, constantly found themselves denying "that the Whig party pursues one course at the South and another at the North."[126] And the Whig press constantly urged unity at the polls: "We want perfect organization, and a full vote."[127] Political persuasion was geared toward political organization.

In the early 1840s, the leading partisan editors of the 1820s and 1830s retired. Charles Hammond died, leaving his chair to Judge John C. Wright, and Moses Dawson sold the *Advertiser* to John and Charles Brough, who changed its name to the *Enquirer*. This new generation of political editors brought with it a great deal of experience in partisan politics.

John C. Wright was a member of the legal profession who had lived in and around Cincinnati since about 1830. He was described by contemporaries as eloquent and popular, "charming, abounding in anecdote, and all on fire with vivacity . . . ."[128] He had secured himself a place in Cincinnati's legal elite long before becoming editor of the *Gazette*: he was a partner of Cincinnati's leading lawyer, Timothy Walker, and his son was editor Hammond's law partner; he was related by marriage to Benjamin Tappan; and he had been appointed Justice of the Ohio Supreme Court. Judge Wright was a political associate of Hammond and an early backer of William Henry Harrison for the Presidency, serving as Harrison's closest political adviser in 1840. That he become editor of the *Gazette* was Hammond's deathbed request.[129]

John and Charles Brough were born at Marietta, Ohio, sons of the local sheriff and Justice of the Peace. John, the older of the two, was apprenticed to a printer, and at age 20, in 1831, began his own newspaper, the *Weekly Republican*, at Marietta. Before coming to Cincinnati, he held office as Clerk of the Ohio Senate, Auditor of State, and state representative,

[126]*Ibid.*, Sept. 19, 1844.

[127]*Ibid.*, Oct. 3, 1844.

[128]Isaac Appleton Jewett to Joseph Willard, Cincinnati, May 8, 1831, in James Taylor Dunn, ed., "'Cincinnati is a Delightful Place': Letters of a Law Clerk, 1831-4," *Bulletin of the Historical and Philosophical Society of Ohio*, X (July, 1952), p. 260.

[129]Carter, *Old Courthouse*, pp. 164-72.

chairing the important committee on banks and currency. Meanwhile he collaborated with his brother Charles in editing the *Lancaster Eagle*, a strict Democratic paper.[130]

John and Charles Brough moved to Cincinnati following the massive Democratic defeat of 1840. Together they purchased the *Advertiser* and began issuing it as the *Enquirer*, which remained Cincinnati's chief Democratic organ throughout the 1840s.[131] Charles would later be prominent as a Colonel in the Mexican War and presiding Judge of the Court of Common Pleas, but would die of cholera in the epidemic of 1849. John would become a railroad magnate, and remain politically active, being elected Governor of Ohio over Clement Vallandigham in 1863, only to die in office.[132]

The number of political newspapers continued to increase. For brevity's sake, I have dealt with only the most prominent political editors, and it is arguable that others, like Charles S. Todd of the *Republican*, James F. Conover of the *Whig*, and Edward Deering Mansfield of the *Chronicle*, *Gazette*, and *Atlas* also deserve extended treatment. But my purpose here is to identify common characteristics of political editors, not to chronicle the lives of individual editors.

It is significant that so many editors were lawyers. As a result, argument on issues in the press tended to be legalistic, with the editors presenting evidence for the consideration of the electorate as jury. Editors were expected to act only in the best interests of their clients, which were political parties and candidates. Legalistic argument was not specifically literary. So editorials tended to be patterned on oral models. Editors preferred Ciceronian periods and extended metaphors, characteristic of oral argument in a florid age. It is significant that editors were often also noted for their oratorical prowess.

By the 1840s, chief editors of local newspapers had usually already achieved prominence before assuming editorial duties. Editors like Wright or the Broughs, or, for that matter, Todd or Mansfield or Conover,

---

[130]Osman Castle Hooper, "John Brough," *Ohio Archaeological and Historical Society Publications*, XIII (Winter, 1904), pp. 41-50.

[131]*Ibid.*, pp. 54-5.

[132]Carter, *Old Courthouse*, pp. 242-51; Hooper, "Brough," pp. 63-4, 68.

had already acquired some stature in the public eye and in the party organization.

But editors had also become, in a sense, figureheads. The editor-in-chief did not personally write all editorials, and no longer personally composed the entire newspaper. Rather, one man was assigned the task of "scissors and paste editor," choosing copy from other papers; another was local editor, composing the column on local affairs; another was assigned the task of compiling commercial and economic information; and so forth with all the various departments of the newspaper. As functional organization within the newspaper establishment became more articulate, the functional importance of the editor declined, although his symbolic importance increased.

I have intimated an ongoing process of organizational differentiation in the press. This process was evident in the structure of the press establishment and in the nature of political rhetoric as found in the press. It remains for us to examine the functioning of the political press in practice in the 1840.

The election of 1840 is significant as a display of the maturity of the new two-party system in the United States. By 1840, opponents to Jacksonian Democracy had solidified into a national organization equal in strength and temperament to their antagonists. Thesis and antithesis clashed to generate a remarkable similarity in rhetoric, in terms of both style and medium of persuasion.

The Whig campaign of 1840 was a campaign by continuation. William Henry Harrison's candidacy had been promoted steadily since 1835. Just as in 1828, in 1840 the stage had been set four years earlier, this time for a contest between Harrison and incumbent President Martin Van Buren. Harrison was a long-time resident of Hamilton County. Thus the impetus behind his campaign came from the Ohio Whig organization, led especially by John C. Wright and Charles Hammond. Harrison was nominated by a convention of Ohio Whigs as early as May, 1838—over two years before the actual election.[133]

Harrison's campaign was managed by a small clique of political savants.

[133]Robert Gray Gunderson, *The Log Cabin Campaign* (Lexington: University of Kentucky Press, 1957), p. 50.

At the center of this elite was a so-called "conscience-keeping committee," three men who were in charge of handling all communications and queries addressed to the candidate, and who carefully edited and orchestrated all of Harrison's public letters and speeches. Two of the three were Cincinnati newspaper editors—Todd of the *Republican* and Wright of the *Gazette*.[134]

With the nation in the throes of economic dislocation following the Panic of 1837, political dissatisfaction with the incumbent Democrats was widespread. Whig strategists concluded that a strictly negative campaign promised the greatest success. Hence the Whig national convention nominated Harrison but did not endorse any kind of platform, and Harrison's political managers worked to keep his lips "hermetically sealed," as one politico quipped. Harrison was dubbed General Mum, in honor of his successful silence on issues.[135]

Prior to the election, three pressing issues had been broached: the tariff, the Bank, and abolition. Democratic strategists tried with no success to get Harrison to declare a definitive position on any of these issues. But Harrison's pronouncements were handled by his conscience-keeping committee, and responses to political questions were vague or obfuscatory, quite often nothing more than references to past speeches, or to Harrison's voting record in Congress. Democratic editors eagerly sought out contradictions in Harrison's speeches and printed them in parallel columns. But even such a graphic display of inconsistency would not counteract voters' reactions to the depressed economy.[136]

Leading the Democratic attack on Harrison in Cincinnati was the veteran editor of the *Advertiser*, Moses Dawson. Dawson ridiculed the Whig attempt to portray Harrison as a common farmer who lived in a log cabin and drank hard cider, and derided him as a minor military hero:

In the position the General now stands, all his qualifications for the president seems to consist in his gaining the battle of Tippecanoe, and the share he had in that of the Thames; with his great talents as a ploughman, who never turned a furrow in his life; and in his wielding a flail, which if he ever did attempt, it is probable his head got

[134]*Ibid.*, p. 150.
[135]*Ibid.*, pp. 65-6.
[136]*Ibid.*, pp. 22-6.

more strokes than the sheaf on the floor.[137]

The irony of this campaign is obvious. In 1828, Dawson himself had worked to portray Andrew Jackson as a common man, a virtuous farmer, and not a mere military hero. Democrats sensed that the shoe was now on the other foot:

> You said that Jackson could not write
> Or dance a polished jig
> You owned he could the British fight,
> But this don't suit a Whig.[138]

It is uncertain whether the Democrats found the similarities between Jackson's campaign and Harrison's more gratifying than embarrassing.

Dawson, like Democratic editors in general, hammered away at Harrison's effective silence on the issues. He mocked the Whig motto "Principles and not Men" by contending that "if they are determined to fight under that banner, is it not remarkable that they leave the principles to be guessed at, no explanation being given as to what these principles are?"[139] Dawson argued to no avail. This was to be his final political fight. He sold his newspaper shortly after Harrison's victory.

Historian Robert Gray Gunderson appropriately summed up the campaign when he wrote, "Generated as it was by hard times and political hatreds, the great commotion of 1840 was not subject to rational or intellectual restraints."[140] Even contemporaries sympathetic to the Whiggery deplored its tactical approach to electioneering: "No matter how praiseworthy the cause of such a movement, it unfits men for sober and calm action; it leads to constant resort to grog shops; and leaves the whole community in a state of feeling which it needs great care to counteract." The writer concluded that the Whigs had only succeeded in increasing "the spirit of political flattery," perhaps to the point of having "unfit our

[137] *Advertiser*, Feb. 28, 1840.
[138] *Ibid.*, March 4, 1840.
[139] *Ibid.*
[140] Gunderson, *Log Cabin Campaign*, p. 9.

people for self-government."[141] Neither party could claim to be a guardian of public virtue and rational freedom, as opponents of Jackson had in 1828.

The election of 1840 was not significant in terms of press innovation. No new newspaper formats or techniques were introduced, and there was no new direction taken in partisan journalism. Rather, innovations in electioneering were non-literary. The most notable and effective means of mobilizing popular support was not the press but the mass meeting. Speechmaking took on increased importance, and for the first time a presidential candidate actually went on a speaking tour.[142] Once party organization had been established, the press was no longer a moving force, but primarily an auxiliary instrument, a means of amplifying sentiments otherwise generated.

Antebellum politics was not press-dominated. Rather, the press was instrumental in effecting political organization, but that medium did not cause a revolution in political rhetoric or consciousness, which did not massively shift from oral to literary. Rather, the republic of rational liberty failed to come about, and as a result, the ideology of the press as the key to rational liberty became vestigial. Those who still believed in it were utopian.

The later campaigns of the 1840s would not match this one in sheer spirit or excitement. For the most part, however, they did little to surpass it in refinement or appeal to reason.

Party unanimity remained the chief concern of the press. In warming up for the election of 1844, the Whig *Gazette* urged its readers to "ORGANIZE WITHOUT DELAY!"[143] The *Gazette* continued to emphasize the coherence of Whig organization, and to contrast this to disagreements among Democrats, especially Democratic papers. In September, 1843, it reprinted at length a controversy between the Broughs at the *Enquirer* and their fellow Democrat Ellwood Fisher of the *Mirror*.[144] Democratic editors likewise emphasized organization and unanimity. The *Enquirer* urged

[141]*Western Messenger*, VIII (Oct., 1840), p. 285.
[142]Gunderson, *Log Cabin Campaign*, pp. 115-22, 161-72.
[143]*Weekly Gazette*, Dec. 7, 1843.
[144]*Ibid.*, Sept. 14, 1843.

that the press "be kept wholly apart from faction,"[145] and praised evidence of "unanimity of sentiment, and concert of action, among the democratic editorial corps, in advancing the great principles and permanent interests of the democratic party . . . ."[146]

Party organs continued to emphasize elections. They printed special campaign papers at special rates, like the *Campaign Gazette*.[147] Conventional papers were founded to promote specific candidates. For example, the *Daily Atlas* was established in 1843 to promote Henry Clay's campaign for the presidency. During a campaign, a political paper's columns were filled with campaign material, to the exclusion of normally important information. The May 9, 1844 issue of the *Weekly Gazette*, for instance, contained eight columns of transcribed letters from Henry Clay and Martin Van Buren, and seven columns of Whig convention reportage, along with four columns of partisan reporting of Congressional news. Only six of twenty-five columns were devoted to material unconnected with the campaign. This was not uncommon, and as election day approached, a paper's columns would become more and more dominated by campaign material. At the same time, tempers became heated, and disputes became more personal, with even editors of established papers intimating threats of physical violence.[148]

Not all elections in the 1840s were as devoid of issues as that of 1840. In 1844 the question of Texas annexation aroused great excitement in Cincinnati, with the Whig leadership in opposition. Judge Wright himself presided at a mass meeting to protest against annexation in March, 1844.[149] Whigs also openly attacked Democrats for drawing support from immigrant groups, as nativism, which would later figure very

---

[145]*Daily Enquirer*, July 17, 1845.

[146]*Ibid.*, July 11, 1845.

[147]Advertised in the *Weekly Gazette*, Feb. 22, 1844.

[148]See, for example, *Ibid.*, May 23, 1844.

[149]Norman E. Tuturow, "The Whigs of Ohio and Texas Annexation," *Northwest Ohio Quarterly*, 43 (Jan., 1971), pp. 23-33; William Birney to James G. Birney, Cincinnati, March 28, 1844, Samuel P. Chase to James G. Birney, Cincinnati, March 30, 1844, in Dwight L. Dumond, ed., *The Letters of James G. Birney*, 2 vols., (New York: D. Appleton Century, 1938), II, pp. 802-7.

prominently, first became an issue in local politics.[150]

The argument of these issues in the press was partisan and election-oriented. Opposing parties used editorials like grapeshot, firing salvo after salvo at each other. In all the commotion of battle, great care was taken not to alienate a significant constituency by advocating a sensitive position like anti-slavery. And all this rhetoric was aimed at marshalling voters in disciplined ranks behind party officers.

The climax of presidential electoral politics in the 1840s was the contest of 1848. Both parties approached this election with some reservation. There were elements of dissension over slavery and the Wilmot Proviso in the local Democracy.[151] And the Whig nomination was shaping up to be a confusing choice between two of Ohio's favorite sons, Senator Thomas Corwin and Judge John McLean, the perennial favorite Henry Clay, and two successful generals from the Mexican War, Winfield Scott and Zachary Taylor. It was Taylor who eventually received the nomination.

Taylor's nomination predictably caused some dissatisfaction in Ohio. For one thing, Taylor's refusal to endorse the Wilmot Proviso disillusioned many of Ohio's anti-slavery Whigs. Indeed, the Ohio delegation to the Whig national convention had been shouted down each time it tried to bring up the subject of slavery.[152] Ohio's first choice would have been Clay or Corwin. There was a great deal of irony in the fact that northern Whiggery, which had been so vocal in its opposition to the Mexican War, would eventually acquiesce in the nomination of that War's most prominent military hero. The Democracy also nominated a military hero in Lewis Cass. Cass was a New Englander by birth and a long-time resident of the Northwest Territory, but had remained equivocal on the subject of slavery, and would eventually come out in

[150]*Weekly Gazette*, May 16, 1844; Edgar Allen Holt, "Party Politics in Ohio, 1840-1850," *Ohio State Archaeological and Historical Quarterly*, XXXVIII (Winter, Spring, 1929), p. 100.

[151]Erwin H. Price, "The Election of 1848 in Ohio," *Ohio State Archeological and Historical Quarterly*, XXXVI (Spring, 1927), p. 100.

[152]*Ibid.*, pp. 220-22, 227. Nominations are recounted in Holt, "Party Politics," pp. 161-65.

opposition to the Wilmot Proviso.[153] Cass and Taylor were also similar in waffling on internal improvements. Taylor implied that he would not veto internal improvements legislation, and Cass referred vaguely to his voting record.[154]

In press behavior, 1848 was similar to other election years. Partisan papers concentrated positively on reporting meetings and urging unanimity. Negatively, they sought to expose the disunity of the opposing party and the inconsistency of its candidate.

Hardly a daily issue of any political paper in the final weeks of the campaign would fail to report some meeting of the electorate in some part of southwestern Ohio. These meetings were characteristically described as large and respectable. Virtually every meeting elected a chairman or secretary (usually pre-arranged, apparently) who would compile a report, complete with resolutions, and submit it to the press. In this way the party hoped to generate an image of massive popular support. In the same way, regular party papers tried to urge unanimity. The *Enquirer*, in announcing the state convention, predicted that "unity and harmony will prevail in its counsels. With unity among ourselves, we shall go into the fight with sanguine hopes of defeating our already disunited foe."[155] Leading up to the presidential nomination in May, the *Enquirer* printed no political news that would indicate a fight for the nomination. When Cass was nominated, the result was printed, along with condensed minutes of the convention. Nowhere was there any mention of internal disunity, although Cass had been nominated on the fourth ballot after putting down strong competition from factions supporting Levi Woodbury and James Buchanan. After the presidential nominee was announced, the *Enquirer* exhorted Democrats in the following terms:

One word—for we are pressed for room—as to our first duty. Another week will bring the Whig candidate upon the track. Whatever may come, let us calculate nothing now upon their dissensions or divisions. Rather let us be prepared for an open and arduous conflict. The first thing in view of this is ORGANIZATION.[156]

[153]Price, "1848," pp. 255-57.
[154]*Ibid.*, p. 260.
[155]*Daily Enquirer*, Jan. 6, 1848.
[156]*Ibid.*, May 30, 1848.

The *Enquirer* would continue to exhort its readers to "Organize! Organize!" and to "Vote the Ticket."[157]

Meanwhile, the *Enquirer* openly attacked Taylor's candidacy as inconsistent. Picking on statements often out of context Democrats sought to exaggerate Taylor's indecision on many issues. The *Enquirer*, for instance, presented an index to Taylor's opinions as embodied in his public letters:

1st. That he is a no party man.

2nd. That he is unwilling to be nominated by party, or be the candidate of party.

3rd. That he would only accept a nomination for the Presidency coming unanimously from the people.

4th. That he has not formed political opinions.

5th. That he has formed political opinions.

6th. That he would prefer Henry Clay to all other men as a candidate for the Presidency.

7th. That he will not quit the field for Henry Clay.

8th. That he is opposed to the acquisition of territory by conquest.

9th. That he is in favor of it.

10th. That he is in favor of the Wilmot Proviso.

11th. That he is against it.

12th. That he is a moderate whig.

13th. That he is a rabid whig.

14th. That he will not declare his opinions.

15th. That he does declare them.

16th. That he will not lend himself to party purposes.

17th. That he does lend himself to party purposes.[158]

It is apparent that the *Enquirer*'s list of contradictions was greatly exaggerated. Nevertheless, that this sort of argument was effective is clear. Both parties commonly resorted to it. The *Enquirer* was particularly fond of accusing Taylor's supporters of supporting slavery in the South and deploring it in the North.[159]

Both parties also played up internal dissension. In Ohio in 1848 the

---

[157]*Ibid.*, July 1, Oct. 6, 1848.

[158]*Ibid.*, Sept. 24, 1848.

[159]*Ibid.*, Aug. 23, 24, 25, Sept. 10, 20, 21, 27, 29, Oct. 4, 5, 12, 13, 18, 22, 25, 26, 29, 31, 1848.

Democratic Party could do this more effectively, as it was the Whiggery that was in more confusion. Disputes between Taylor and Clay men were reported with a certain amount of glee in the Democratic press,[160] as was conflict between "Peace" Whigs and supporters of Taylor.[161]

The 1848 campaign was less spectacular than the 1840 campaign, but it was perhaps more significant. It marked the last true national triumph of the Whig Party. And in some ways it signaled the collapse of the party system whose functioning it so well exemplified. Issues were being raised which demanded a fundamental reshuffling of partisan politics. Chief among these was the controversy over slavery. The partisan press had long warned against disunity over issues like slavery. In 1844, the *Weekly Gazette* urged its readers not to vote for Liberty Party Candidate James G. Birney, claiming that "the unselfish prompting of every man's heart" tells him to be loyal to the Whiggery.[162] And the *Enquirer* cautioned its readers that the "Abolitionist party" was a Whig trick to divide the Democratic vote.[163] Both parties feared this divisive sectional issue.

The anti-slavery *Philanthropist*, under the editorship of Dr. Gamaliel Bailey, warned its readers that "they cannot vote for either [party] and be blameless. Let them stay at home."[164] Bailey had summed up the 1840 presidential campaign in the following terms.

For the last few weeks, demagogues have been busy, parties have been abusing each other, the most grievous falsehoods have been propagated on both sides, and menacing speeches have been made, pointing to violence and bloodshed . . . . All that we have heard of these political meetings, has only served to convince us, that great questions are not required to excite great multitudes, and that Americans [*sic*] politics are fast becoming flat and contemptible for the want of the agitation of some great fundamental principles.[165]

Partisan politics must have seemed flat and contemptible to a great many individuals by the late 1840s. The two-party system by its very

[160]*Ibid.*, Jan. 14, April 30, June 7, July 25, 27, Aug. 25, Sept. 19, 29, Oct. 7, 1848.
[161]*Ibid.*, Jan. 21, July 7, Aug. 8, Sept. 22, Oct. 15, 26, 1848.
[162]*Weekly Gazette*, Dec. 19, 1844.
[163]*Daily Enquirer*, Oct. 3, 1848.
[164]*Philanthropist*, March 24, 1840.
[165] *Ibid.*, Oct. 13, 1840.

nature seemed to inhibit the agitation of great fundamental principles in its implicit self-definition, namely that a party's purpose was to appeal to as many people as possible, and that this appeal would be gauged by success at the polls. Mass appeal generated a safe vapidity—what was successful turned out to be what seemed inoffensive.

But the political system had to come to grips with slavery. As territorial regulations became more controversial and the need to organize new territories became more pressing, the issue of the extension of slavery would become more urgent in the minds of the electorate. The second party system refused to place this issue in any decisive way before the nation's voters. By its very structure, it had defined itself as incapable of handling an issue which would be internally divisive, which would engender bitter disagreements among regions, which admitted of no bland compromise and no benign neglect, which refused to be hidden under the traditional set of political symbols or obfuscated by vague references to service to the Republic. The second party system prospered during a period of substantial agreement on the tenor of political discourse. When the agitation of great principles rendered this agreement inoperable, the system fell apart.

Anti-slavery would not become prevalent until after 1848, and hence the role of the *political* press in dealing with the slavery controversy is not within the scope of this study. But there were intimations of the future debate before 1848. As early as 1840, James G. Birney, the founder of the *Philanthropist*, was nominated as presidential candidate of the Liberty Party. Dissatisfaction with the way slavery was being handled by the major parties would increase with involvement in the Mexican War and the controversy over the Wilmot Proviso. In 1848, an independent convention of Ohio voters met at Columbus. Composed of free soil elements from both parties, this convention issued a call for a national convention at Buffalo in August. This national convention nominated Martin Van Buren as a free soil candidate. In Ohio and in Hamilton County he received about 10% of the total vote.[166]

This chapter has focused on the techniques and rationale of political persuasion in the press. In so doing, I have tended to ignore the

[166]Holt, "Party Politics," pp. 287-97; Price, "1848," pp. 240, 300.

informational aspect of political newspapers, except where associated with some persuasional program. This should not be taken to imply that information transmission was ignored in the period, or that the quality of reporting deteriorated. On the contrary, newspapers were conscientious in reporting political news. Correspondents sent digests of the proceedings of state and national legislatures, meetings of city council were treated in some depth, and campaign news was presented in exhaustive detail. The significant direction of change in the presentation of political news, as I have elsewhere implied, was toward less passive press behavior. Raw information was being replaced by third-person or editorial reportage, often written with an eye toward reinforcing a partisan bias in the reader. The discerning reader could find more (and more important) information in the newspapers of the 1840s than in those of the 1810s, of course, but more of the news was presented for a political purpose.

The significant change in information was the change in attitudes toward the use of information, not improvement in information-transmission capabilities. As communications networks became more efficient, they were put to work for partisan purposes. Already by 1840 a negative reaction had set in with the founding of neutral papers devoted to the presentation of unbiased information. And—perhaps more importantly—another reaction had set in with the establishment of papers devoted to non-partisan causes like nativism, temperance, and anti-slavery.

The partisan papers of the 1820s, 1830s, and 1840s were instrumental in shaping political consciousness in the Jacksonian era. Rhetoric in the press assumed the form of legal argumentation, with an emphasis on consistency, with evidence presented to prove a point, and with the editor as attorney given full license to present only such evidence as would be in the best interest of the candidate as client. The preponderance of lawyers editing partisan papers is thus of more than coincidental significance.

The papers were instrumental in winning mass allegiance to political parties. They professed and encouraged an ideal of party discipline, applying to politics the metaphor of military organization. Indeed it is significant that martial images came to describe elections—political lieutenants waged a campaign with an army of voters—and that military heroes like Jackson, Harrison, and Taylor were such popular candidates.

The press was instrumental in effecting these changes. But the press as medium did not cause these changes. Rather, the role of the press in politics was defined by deep changes in attitudes toward politics and political opinions. Political consciousness determined the behavior of the political press.

This new political consciousness may be described by the metaphor of the market. Political candidates and programs were offered for purchase by political consumers in the marketplace of ideas. Partisan papers advertised annually a "fall line" of political products. The electorate assembled on election day as though on a market day, to select the most pleasing items. And large firms competed more and more fervently for the customers' attention, even as their output became obsolete.

This sort of political consciousness presupposed that political candidates and programs existed to please the individual voter. And it implied that the voter expressed his approval specifically at election time. Hence this political consciousness was a departure from the legacy of the Revolution, the ideology of rational freedom, which presupposed that programs and candidates should appeal impersonally to the reason of the independent intelligent citizen, who in aggregate would form an ever-effective body of public opinion.

The legacy of the Revolution was claimed by both parties as their inheritance. But in fact both parties were post-Revolutionary in political consciousness, especially in press strategy. Both viewed this vital medium as an organ rather than as an open forum, as an advocate of men and measures, rather than an impartial and impersonal means of conveying information. It is likely that the Revolutionary fathers would refer to Whig partisans and newspapers as Whigs were so fond of referring to Democrats: in a word, as licentious.

Postscript

The theme of the last two chapters has been the political ideology of the press—how it developed and what it meant in terms of practice. Implicit in this ideology was a set of models of political communications. In the primitive ideology of public service or rational liberty, the press was depicted as a neutral and transparent conveyor of information and opinions to independent rational citizens. In the ideology of the press as partisan advocate, metaphors of the courtroom, the military, and the marketplace were invoked.

In all these models, the citizen appeared as an individual with individual judgments and interests. Such an individual lacked group affiliations outside the political—he was a voter, a resident of this city and that state, and a citizen of the U.S. In press ideology, group affiliation by religion, ethnicity, or occupation or income was not acknowledged. The republican tradition did not condone political decision-making on the basis of such considerations: nativism was a natural response to a perceived interjection of ethnicity or Catholicism into politics.

But in fact political culture was deeply ethnic. Researchers like Paul Kleppner, Ronald Formisano, and Robert Kelley have argued concinvingly that ethnocultural factors (including group and religious identification) were more salient for nineteenth-century voter behavior than economic or other "rational" factors.[167] U.S. electoral politics was group politics.

Were U.S. newspapers involved in group politics? In the larger cities, like Cincinnati, numerous competing dailies were available. Is it possible to say whether their readerships were defined by ethnicity or occupation or, less precisely, mentality? Did their readerships consist of discrete ethnocultural blocs?

In some cases it is possible to guess—the *Chronicle*, for instance, seemed to appeal to transplanted New Englanders. But without subscription lists such guesses must remain unsubstantiated.

---

[167]Paul Kleppner, *The Cross of Culture: A Social Analysis of Midwestern Politics, 1850-1900* (New York, 1970); Ronald P. Formisano, *The Birth of Mass Political Parties: Michigan, 1827-1861* (Princeton: Princeton University Press, 1971); Robert Kelley, *The Cultural Pattern in American Politics: The First Century* (New York: Knopf, 1979); and see the thoughtful analysis by Richard L. McCormick in "Ethnocultural Interpretations of Nineteenth-Century Voting Behavior" in McCormick, *The Party Period and Public Policy: American Politics from the Age of Jackson to the Progressive Era* (New York: Oxford University Press, 1986), pp. 29-63.

What stands out from a reading of the newspapers is a denial of group politics. In press ideology, citizens were demographically equivalent—independent and autonomous. This attitude seems to me to be one of the lasting legacies of this period of press history, ironically so, since, I think, it is based on a fantasy.

The contemporary U.S. newspaper—unlike its counterparts in some other western countries—similarly denies that it has a group or partial readership. Because it is typically a monopoly newspaper, this is a natural stance. The result is an instinct for even-handedness that becomes actually anti-controversial. With the contemporary newspaper this extends to party politics: just as the partisan papers of the ninetennth century tended to deny ethnocultural positioning, so does the modern paper avoid explicitly partisan positioning. Just as the press of the early Republic engaged in practices that implicitly denied the salience of social and ethnocultural differences, so one might argue does the modern "objective" press deny the salience of political differences. The press of the early Republic appealed to a fictional citizen, while the modern press appeals to a fictional notion of "the news" (note the singular), a unitary version of reality untainted by considerations of interest which the public needs and deserves to know. The versions of reality presented by the press of the early Republic were obviously argumentative, as competing versions made abundantly clear. It is perhaps a cause for anxiety that competing versions of reality are rarely available in the U.S. news media today.

CHAPTER V

Religious and Literary Periodicals

The Enlightenment was not repudiated but popularized. The great democratic revolution of the period forged a new popular amalgam out of traditional folk beliefs and the literary culture of the gentry. Through newspapers, almanacs, and cheap books, lectures and other media, ordinary people increasingly acquired smatterings of knowledge about things that hitherto had been the preserves of educated elites. And at the same time they were told that their newly-acquired knowledge was just as good as that possessed by those with college degrees. . . . Under such egalitarian circumstances, truth itself became democratized, and the borders the eighteenth century had painstakingly worked out between science and superstition, naturalism and supernaturalism, were now blurred. Animal magnetism seemed as legitimate as gravity. Dowsing for hidden metals appeared as rational as the working of electricity. Scholarly studies of the origins of the Indians and the mounds of the northwest seemed no more plausible than speculations about the lost tribes of Israel. And crude folk remedies were even thought to be as scientific as the bleeding cures of enlightened medicine.

-Gordon Wood[1]

Periodicals of all sorts flourished in the United States during the Jacksonian era. Frank Luther Mott has estimated that as many as 5000 journals and magazines (not including newspapers) appeared in the years 1825–1850. The number of magazines in the Union expanded rapidly, and so did the average circulation. Before 1825, a circulation of 2000 was

[1]Gordon S. Wood, "Evangelical America and Early Mormonism," *New York History*, LXI (Oct., 1980), pp. 368-69.

considered phenomenal, but by 1849 *Godey's Lady's Book* claimed 40,000 subscribers.[2] America became a nation of magazine readers.

American periodical literature became essentially popular literature. Foreign observers like Frances Trollope sneered at this "immense exhalation of periodical trash, which penetrates into every cot and corner of the country, and which is greedily sucked in by all ranks . . . ." Mrs. Trollope believed magazines to be prohibitive of the "higher graces of composition." They forced men of talent to bow to bad taste, and rewarded less capable writers. She derided "the inflated tone of eulogy in which their insect authors are lauded."[3]

The magazines of the Jacksonian era do not, for the most part, deserve serious study as literary organs. But they are of great interest as organs of popular culture. In other words, the significance of early American periodicals lies not in the material they presented, but in their own very existence. The American periodical marked an attempt to create *de novo* a mature national democratic literature.

But magazines were not only literary. Religious journals were established to spread enlightenment or strengthen sectarian loyalty. Medical and agricultural journals were established to promote the advancement of science. Educational and reform journals were established to promote social improvements. But the stated rationale behind each periodical was to some extent democratic. Knowledge is to be made accessible to the people, and no better means is available than the periodical press.

Paradoxically, the impetus for establishing early periodicals usually came from an enthusiastic elite. This was particularly true of religious journals, which were usually edited and composed by clergymen, and journals in areas like medicine, law, and education. But it was also true of early literary periodicals, which printed mostly anonymous fiction and reviews from unpaid authors. The amateur has always been an aristocrat of sorts.

---

[2]Frank Luther Mott, *A History of American Magazines, 1741-1905*, 5 vols., (Cambridge: Harvard University Press, 1930), I, 34-42, 199-200, 514.

[3]Frances Trollope, *Domestic Manners of the Americans*, Donald Smalley, ed., (New York: Knopf, 1949), p. 311.

It would be simplistic to argue that periodicals were designed to buttress the authority of an elite. In some cases, as in the professions, this was often true. But in others, especially medicine, religion, and reform, the periodical was an attempt by one elite to depose or supersede another. In still other cases, the periodical marked an attempt to break down the barriers that protected an elite group, sometimes by the members of that very group. In any case, the boom in periodicals betrayed the state of flux in which elite groups found themselves in Jacksonian America.

Early periodicals were cooperative efforts, often utopian in outlook. Literary magazines were often based in a local literary club; other professional journals were the organ of some learned body, whether medical, educational, or legal; religious periodicals were organs of a denomination or sect. The more firmly established the organization, the more likely its journal was of success.

But as time passed viable commercial magazines appeared. These were designed to appeal to the public at large, and often featured illustrations and sensational or sentimental literature. Their aim was to be read by as many people as possible, and thereby to make as much money as possible. Their appeal was high circulation, not enlightenment: to be read was to deserve to be read.

Commercialization was an ambivalent form of democratization. The taste of the people became sovereign in literature, just as the will of the people had become sovereign in politics. But at the same time, the dream of a truly enlightened democratic polity, a dream that had come out of the American Revolution,[4] was laid aside as impractical and unprofitable.

These national cultural trends were particularly visible in Cincinnati. As a young western city, Cincinnati was anxious not merely to demonstrate cultural vitality, but to establish its cultural parity with the east. There is no elite like a provincial elite, and Cincinnati's cognoscenti enthusiastically founded periodical after periodical.[5] Each began with the

[4]Joseph J. Ellis, *After the Revolution: Profiles of Early American Culture* (New York: Norton, 1979).

[5]Cincinnati's elite, predominantly Yankee, Presbyterian or Episcopalian, and commercial or professional, really crystallized only in the 1820s, with the population increase accompanying the recovery from the Panic of 1819. See Walter Stix Glazer, "Cincinnati in 1840: A Community Profile" (Unpublished doctoral dissertation,

most high-minded intentions, each announced after the third or fourth issue that the public's approbation "has exceeded our most sanguine expectations" (or words to that effect), and most failed soon afterwards. Many others survived with a very narrow circle of readers. This would be the case as late as 1850, when Cincinnati would rank fourth among all cities in the nation in the number of periodicals published, but only eighth in average circulation.[6]

One reason why Cincinnati's periodicals fared so poorly in comparison to those of New York, Philadelphia, Boston, and Baltimore was that western readers had already become accustomed to eastern periodicals. Cincinnati editors constantly encouraged the development of a native western literature. But at the same time western periodicals in search of a mass readership came more and more to imitate their eastern rivals.[7] Paradoxically, the ultimate popular nineteenth-century literature would be the dime western, and it would be published in the east. But in the early nineteenth century, the most Victorian of "eastern" literature would be published in a west looking for cultural legitimation.

Among Cincinnati's non-news publications, several would achieve national distinction. The *Catholic Telegraph*, founded in 1831, is now the nation's oldest Catholic newspaper. The *Christliche Apologete* was the chief organ of German Methodism in the United States. Josiah Warren's *Peaceful Revolutionist* was the country's first anarchist newspaper. The *Philanthropist*, under James G. Birney and Gamaliel Bailey, was to moderate abolitionists what Garrison's *Liberator* was to radicals. The *Western Messenger* has the distinction of having been the first

University of Michigan, 1968), pp. 143-45; Richard Wade described this as a "double development . . . : one was the movement of many individuals up or down the social ladder, the other was the widening of the distance between rungs." *The Urban Frontier: The Rise of Western Cities, 1790-1830* (Cambridge: Harvard University Press, 1959), pp. 209-10. See also Cole P. Dawson, "Yankees in the Queen City: The Social and Intellectual Contributions of New Englanders in Cincinnati, 1820-1850" (Unpublished doctoral dissertation, Miami University, Oxford OH, 1977). To this new elite, Boston was "the 'hub of the Universe:'" A. G. W. Carter, *The Old Courthouse: Reminiscences of the Courts and Bar of Cincinnati* (Cincinnati: Peter G. Thompson, 1880), p. 120.

[6]Mott, *American Magazines*, I, 386.

[7]Daniel Aaron, "Cincinnati, 1818-1838: A Study of Attitudes" (Unpublished doctoral dissertation, Harvard University, 1943), pp. 363-64.

Transcendentalist periodical, and the first magazine to publish any of Emerson's poems. Other periodicals were important in promoting causes as diverse as botanic medicine, phonetic spelling, and McGuffey's Readers.

The next three chapters will treat different aspects of Cincinnati's non-news publications. Chapter V will deal with religious and literary periodicals; Chapter VI will treat the professions and science, especially medicine and education; and Chapter VII will deal with reform and non-mainstream publications. It is my belief that magazines in the west best exemplify in their very nature many of the most interesting features of early American culture. As Tocqueville noted,

> All that there is of good or bad in American society is to be found there in such strong relief, that one would be tempted to call it one of those books printed in large letters for teaching children to read; everything there is in violent contrast; nothing has fallen into its final place: society is growing more rapidly than man.[8]

Particularly in the volatile society of the west people perceived a need to promote religion, morality, and culture. Particularly in the west people perceived an opportunity to create a new democratic civilization. And although efforts to meet these ends failed, the fact that they were embarked upon is of great significance.

Cincinnati was the most important center of western publishing before 1860. Literary, religious, and professional periodicals began appearing there around 1820, and by 1848 journals of every description were printed in Cincinnati and read all over the west, competing with popular eastern magazines. The Queen City had as good a claim as any city to the title "Athens of the West."

Early Religious Periodicals: Non-Sectarianism

Religious periodicals abounded in the early west. It seems that every sect and denomination had its organ, and every persuasion found expression in the press. Some of these journals sought to reinforce eastern beliefs and patterns of behavior in the west, while others sought to sow

[8]Alexis de Tocqueville, in *Tocqueville and Beaumont in America*, George Wilson Pierson, ed., (New York: Oxford University Press, 1938), p. 566.

the seeds of a new crop in that fertile virgin soil. Some were linked with powerful organizations, while others were associated with an ambitious individual.

As in politics, the press in religion was meant to amplify and not to supersede oral presentation of information and opinion. Editors of religious papers were generally clergymen, and they viewed their papers as pulpits. There was no conflict between oral and literary religious persuasions.

But people read in private. They do not peruse newspapers as part of a congregation, as they would listen to a sermon. Nor need they be members of an exclusive organization to have access to printed religious discourse. In its universal availability, would not the press yield itself to non-sectarian use? Would not all literate people (presumable Christians) then comprise a huge non-denominational Congregation of Letters?

Some religious press conductors certainly believed that the press should be non-denominational. But even as political parties began to employ the press to promote a partisan organization, so too would denominations advocate their own particular causes in the press. The religious press promised to be non-denominational, just as the political press promised to be impartial and impersonal, but in fact religious papers came to be used most significantly for sectarian purposes. This dialectic of sectarianism and non-sectarianism will be one theme of the following discussion.

Protestants closed ranks most effectively in fighting Catholicism. Viewing the rapid rise of the Catholic Church in the Ohio Valley as an invasion of Papal forces from abroad, Baptists, Methodists, and Presbyterians in particular used print as a weapon, protecting themselves from the Roman delusion, and heaping a steady barrage of ridicule and accusation on Catholics. The Catholic Church for its part established two fairly belligerent papers in Cincinnati, the *Catholic Telegraph* and the German-language *Wahrheitsfreund*. The battle of words between Catholicism and Protestantism would erupt into physical violence in the 1850s. Between 1820 and 1848 it was a fixture in local religious journalism, and will be a second theme of our discussion.

Early nineteenth-century religion in the United States is usually characterized as revivalistic. The image called to mind is one of tribal, emotional, non-rational, and unrefined frenzy. But when we think of the printed word, the image called to mind is precisely the opposite—it is one of individual, dispassionate, rational, and educated contemplation. These images of revivalism and journalism clash, but early nineteenth-century religion was revivalistic *and* journalistic. The conflict between these two ideals will be a third theme of our discussion.

Early American religion is also characterized as utopian or millennial. Thousands in America anxiously awaited the second coming during the heyday of the Millerite excitement, and Swedenborgians believed that a new age of reason had arrived. To these extremists, the press was a servant of the millennium. But to others, the press was organ for a temporal organization that was occupied mostly with practical affairs. These different ideals of the religious press will be a fourth theme.

Religious periodicals published in Cincinnati were read throughout the west. Hence the commonness of the adjective western in the title: the Methodist *Western Christian Advocate*, the *Western Episcopal Observer*, and the Millerite *Western Midnight Cry* are the most prominent examples. So some blurring of our local focus is involved here. But still these papers were local as well as regional. Each paper was based in some organization centered in Cincinnati—the *Western Christian Advocate* was a publication of the Western Methodist Book Concern, for example—and all carried local religious news.

The first sectarian magazine published in the United States was the *Arminian Magazine*, published in Philadelphia in 1789–1790.[9] This was a full thirty years before anything of its kind would appear in Cincinnati. The use of the press for sectarian purposes was an established fact by 1820.

Nevertheless, the earliest projects for publishing religious papers in the west were non-sectarian. The first two in Cincinnati were the *Cincinnati Remembrancer* in 1822–1823[10] and the *Christian's Magazine*, proposed in 1824.[11] Their intent was to promote genuine enlightenment through rational discussion of religious matters. Argument was to be scientific, not sectarian, and through the impersonal medium of the press it was hoped

[9]Mott, *American Magazines*, I, 29.
[10]Mentioned in the *Independent Press*, Jan. 9, 1823.
[11]Mentioned in the *Cincinnati Literary Gazette*, II (July 10, 1824), p. 15.

that objectively true conclusions could be reached, ending the centuries-long history of religious strife.

Non-sectarian magazines along these lines failed, but for a long time their rationale remained appealing. Early sectarian journals invoked the same scientific ideal. The *Christian Preacher*, a publication of the Disciples of Christ, was particularly non-sectarian, seeking to "pass current among all aspirants to the name of Christian, . . . unfettered by any partisan bias . . . ."[12] Early western Universalists also hoped to transcend sect, to reach all men. Hence the prospectus of the *Star in the West*:

As the day of *free* enquiry and general toleration has arrived—a day in which many run to and fro, and knowledge is increasing: and, as some medium of communication for the free exchange of ideas and opinions, is essentially necessary, in order to combat the prejudice and superstition of a false education; and enable us to acquire useful knowledge in the principles of TRUE RELIGION and moral philosophy, we flatter ourselves that all liberal minded souls, who love to see Light, knowledge, and noble principles increase, will lend their influence and kind patronage, to support a work, the sole object of which is to support free enquiry, religious freedom, and Christian knowledge.[13]

Universalism thus tied non-sectarianism to a belief in progress in knowledge following the achievement of free enquiry.

Universalism exemplifies one syndrome in post-Revolutionary religion. Its tenets are a religious analogue to the political tenets of the early Republic: all men have an equal right to vote, and all men can equally hope to achieve salvation; there is no elect, and the belief in election is the result of superstition and ignorance; once reason has been unleashed, it will discover an objective truth in religion just as it had in politics. The data for religious enquiry are contained in the Bible. Thus the first Universalist paper in Cincinnati was named, logically, the *Rational Bible Reformer*, first published in 1825.

To Universalists, the press was to be an instrument of enlightenment. It would shed light like a sun. By 1827, then, the *Reformer* had changed its name to the *Lamp of Liberty*.[14] This paper was followed by the *Star in the*

[12]*Christian Preacher*, Jan. 1, 1836.
[13]Jonathon Kidwell, "New Prospectus," *Star in the West*, I (Dec., 1827), p. 40.
[14]Russell E. Miller, *The Larger Hope: The First Century of the Universalist Church*

West—the star being another symbol of light and enlightenment—which was to be the most important Universalist paper in the midwest throughout the middle of the nineteenth century. Its motto was originally "TRUTH has nothing to fear from investigation."[15] Two years after its founding in 1827, the word *Sentinel* was prefixed to its title, so that "the friends of civil and religious liberty should have a faithful and vigilant [*sic*] *Sentinel* to guard their sacred and unalienable rights; watch the movements of the enemies to free enquiry; expose their unfaithful works of darkness, and warn the people of the approach of danger."[16]

Universalism seemed to be a particularly journalistic religion. Between 1820 and 1850, Universalists in the United States began 138 periodicals, and although most of them failed quickly, they indicate a press instinct intimately associated with the rhetoric of free enquiry, universal availability, and the progress of human knowledge. As time passed, however, these papers tended to become less utopian and more functional.[17] In the west, Cincinnati became the center for missionary and publication efforts; the *Star in the West* would absorb a host of Universalist papers, surviving until 1880.[18] In the course of human events, it would lose the idealism of its early days.

A second ideally non-sectarian religion in the west was liberal Unitarianism, or Transcendentalism. Cincinnati was an outpost for liberal New England theology and philosophy: its Unitarian Society began meeting in 1831, and the promise of simplicity and freedom in touch with nature that the west offered lured a generation of young Yankees to the Queen City. In 1835, under the auspices of the Western Unitarian Association, these men founded the *Western Messenger*, the first Transcendentalist periodical.[19]

in America, 1770-1870 (Boston: Universalist Unitarian Association, 1979), p. 693.

[15]*Ibid.*, p. 308.

[16]"Prospectus," *Sentinel and Star in the West*, II (Feb., 1829), p. 151.

[17]Miller, *Larger Hope*, pp. 285-87.

[18]Elmo Arnold Robinson, *The Universalist Church in Ohio* (Columbus: Ohio University Press, 1923), pp. 25-6; Miller, *Larger Hope*, pp. 694-95.

[19]Dawson, "Yankees," pp. 62, 108; Elizabeth R. McKinsey, *The Western Experiment: New England Transcendentalists in the Ohio Valley* (Cambridge: Harvard University Press, 1973), pp. 8-18, 5-6. On the founding of the *Messenger*, see William H. Venable,

The *Western Messenger* was a remarkable periodical. It was Emerson's only whole-hearted champion in its early years, and it was the first journal to publish any of his poetry.[20] It also provided an outlet for such talented young men as William Henry Channing, James Freeman Clarke, Christopher Pearse Cranch, Ephraim Peabody, and James Handasyd Perkins, all of whom edited the periodical at one time or another.[21]

The *Messenger* was non-sectarian. Its prospectus called for the spread of a "rational and liberal religion," defining liberal as "only this,—opposition to all exclusiveness." It extolled "Rational Christians," asserting that "every man has a right to read with his own eyes, and to form his own creed, subject only to the judgment of God." Belief in the progress of Enlightenment was proclaimed: "A great movement is going on, although outward forms remain unaltered."[22] Among the forms unaltered but soon to be vestigial, one assumes, were religious organizations.

The *Messenger* survived until 1841. Its file makes interesting reading, as it contains some items of real literary worth. But its mission was ultimately unsuccessful, its ideal of enlightenment was never approached, its message was faithfully delivered but disregarded. In its later years its founders lost their initial enthusiasm; all but one eventually moved back to New England.

The failure of the *Western Messenger*, and of non-sectarian religious journalism in general, may be attributed to three factors: elitism, disingenuous westernism, and lack of energetic organizational support. By elitism, I mean that the conductors of the *Messenger* themselves

Beginnings of Literary Culture in the Ohio Valley: Historical and Biographical Sketches (1891, repr. New York: Peter Smith, 1949), pp. 71-3; Mott, *American Magazines*, I, 661.

[20]Mott, *American Magazines*, I, 410.

[21]Frank R. Shivers, Jr., "A Western Chapter in the History of American Transcendentalism," *Bulletin of the Historical and Philosophical Society of Ohio*, XV (1957) pp. 117-30; McKinsey, *Western Experiment*; William Henry Channing and James Handasyd Perkins, *Memoir and Writings of James Handasyd Perkins* (Cincinnati: Truman and Spofford, 1851); Francis G. and Robert Peabody, *A New England Romance: The Story of Ephraim and Mary Jane Peabody, 1807-1892* (Boston: Houghton Mifflin, 1920).

[22]"General Preface to Volume One," *Western Messenger*, I (1835), viii-xii.

cultural elite, a clique of cognoscenti, with no real contact with a broad-based readership. Unitarians in the west, and in Cincinnati in particular, were relatively few but very influential. Hence they were able to begin the magazine, and to keep it in publication for six years, with a small circle of readers. But they were never able to attract a readership outside of that circle of educated liberals with a taste for New England.

The *Messenger* claimed to be an organ of western religion and literature. But in fact, its idea of westernism was a new sort of easternism, namely the flowering of that liberal philosophy that became Transcendentalism. This natural religion would naturally flourish in the rude and unformed west, the editors thought. But westernism, as we shall see in our discussion of literary periodicals, was to be of a different sort. The *Messenger* itself was read almost exclusively by transported easterners, and had a sizable following in the east.

Finally, the *Messenger* lacked an aggressive organization to promote it. Here the contrast with Universalism is clear: Universalists were revivalistic in their aggressive promotion of their theology. The editors of the *Star in the West* engaged in public debates, and actively pursued converts to their cause. As a result, their periodical survived for half a century. This success was achieved at the expense of the rational, non-sectarian ideal, however. The *Western Messenger* remained true to that ideal, but failed.

Catholicism and Anti-Catholicism

By far the most sensational feature of religious controversy in pre-Civil War Cincinnati was anti-Catholicism. This emotional issue surfaced in the 1820s, and grew with increased immigration, the rise of the Catholic Church, the debate over the public schools, and the question of foreign aid from organizations like the Austrian Leopoldine Society. Anti-Catholicism appeared in the secular press as early as 1822. But it was in the religious press that anti-Catholic sentiment was most notable, with papers like the Presbyterian *Journal*, the Methodist *Western Christian Advocate*, and the *Cross and Baptist Journal* leading Protestant attacks. The Catholic Church responded with the establishment of the *Catholic Telegraph* in

1831. This pugnacious paper quickly entered into controversy with the *Journal* and the *Methodist Correspondent*.[23] By the 1830s, the rapid rise of the Catholic Church in the west and its great appeal to immigrants encouraged fears of a Papal plot to take over the entire Mississippi Valley. Lyman Beecher and Samuel F. B. Morse were the particular proponents of this idea. And in the 1830s, Lyman Beecher himself came to Cincinnati, accepting a call to become head of the new Lane Theological Seminary, and anxious to use his position to head off the Catholic menace.[24]

Beecher's attacks on Catholicism appeared regularly in the pages of the *Cincinnati Journal*. This weekly had been founded in 1827, and by 1836 had a subscription list of 3600—then a huge circulation—with readers throughout the west and southwest. Its editor since 1832 was Thomas Brainerd. He received the substantial salary $1000 a year. In 1836, he returned to his native New England, leaving his editorial chair to Lyman Beecher's son, Henry Ward.[25] The *Journal* failed in 1837, due to non-payment of subscriptions.

The Catholic response was presented in the columns of the *Telegraph*. This weekly was aggressive in promoting Catholicism, but met with less initial success in terms of readership and financial support than its Protestant rivals. In the early 1830s, the paper ran an annual deficit of $1000, and hence relied on organizational support to stay in print. As late as 1839, a Roman Catholic Society for the Diffusion of Knowledge was established with an eye partly toward providing financial support for the *Telegraph*, and throughout the 1830s the Catholic hierarchy was obliged to

[23]Sr. Mary M. Krummen, "Bishop Purcell–the Missionary, 1830-1860" (Unpublished master's thesis, University of Notre Dame, 1940), pp. 27-32; Aaron, "Cincinnati," p. 237; Alfred G. Stritch, "Political Nativism in Cincinnati, 1830-1860," *Records of the American Catholic Historical Society of Philadelphia*, XLVIII (Sept., 1937), pp. 228-32.

[24]Anthony Deye, "Archbishop John Baptist Purcell of Cincinnati: Pre-Civil War Years" (Unpublished doctoral dissertation, University of Notre Dame, 1959), pp. 164-65; Stritch, "Nativism," pp. 233-40.

[25]Randolph C. Randall, *James Hall: Spokesman of the New West* (Columbus: Ohio State University Press, 1964), pp. 244-49; John Baptist Purcell, "Bishop Purcell's Journal, 1833-6," Sr. Mary Agnes McCann, ed., *Catholic Historical Review*, V (July-Oct., 1919), Jan. 18, 1834, p. 247; Mary Brainerd, *Life of Rev. Thomas Brainerd, D. D., For Thirty Years Pastor of Old Pine Street Church, Philadelphia* (Philadelphia: Lippincott, 1870), pp. 79-82.

campaign for subscriptions.[26]

The climax of the early theological tension was a seven-day debate between Catholic Bishop John Baptist Purcell and the champion of united Protestantism, Alexander Campbell. The debate was peacefully conducted and well-attended, and it was covered by both the religious and the secular press. Secular papers agreed that Purcell had done much to encourage toleration of Catholicism.[27] But religious papers like the *Journal* slanted reportage to make Campbell appear the victor.

The *Journal* printed a lengthy summary of the debate in consecutive issues from January 19 to March 2, 1837. The reporting was anonymous and in the third person, but was clearly biased against the Catholic point of view. And letters from readers contrasted Campbell's strong independent reason to Purcell's reliance on prejudicial tradition.[28]

The final point of argument in the debate itself was whether Catholicism in its claim to exclusive authority was not inherently inimical to American values like freedom of religion and separation of Church and state. The response of the editor of the anti-slavery *Philanthropist* is illuminating. After comparing Catholicism to the philosophy of the slaveholder, James G. Birney concluded that

It cannot be made to consist with free political institutions, nor with mental independence. Like slavery it demands all—is content with nothing less. Its mode of warfare is, to imprison, to cramp, to crush the mind, knowing that when this is accomplished, every other triumph is easily won.

But, he goes on, the best means of dealing with this unreason is not through an equally prejudiced and irrational response:

Bad as is our opinion of it in theory and practice, there is but one way of putting it aside,—free and fair and generous discussion. . . . but give the TRUTH room, and with its naked and unshorn energies it will put this with every other error, however

---

[26]Deye, "Purcell," pp. 165-66, 106, 239; Paul F. Foik, *Pioneer Catholic Journalism* (New York: United States Catholic Historical Society, 1930), pp. 159-60, 167; Purcell, "Journal," Jan. 18, 1834, p. 246.

[27]Deye, "Purcell," pp. 168-87; Krummen, "Purcell," pp. 60-2.

[28]*Cincinnati Journal*, Jan. 19-March 2, 1837; letter of Justice, Jan. 26, 1837.

formidable and securely entrenched, to a full and everlasting flight.[29]

This early theological anti-Catholicism, then, was a curious mix of the sectarian and non-sectarian attitudes toward religious enquiry. The Campbell-Purcell debate was, in itself, an example of open and free discussion of religious issues. But the discussion was not devoid of sectarian interests, even though Campbell sought to represent a united Protestantism. And on the whole the attitude of the religious press was far from impartial, and certainly was not conducive to free and independent consideration of religious issues on the part of the reader.

Partisans on both sides of the controversy over Catholicism tried to claim the mantle of unprejudice. Purcell referred to opponents of Catholicism as "Bigots" and "Philistines,"[30] while Birney in the *Philanthropist* characterized his performance in the debate as "nothing more than a naked statement of unconnected facts (allowing them to be such)," and criticized his argument for not "laying hold of the reasoning powers of his audience . . . ."[31]

The debate over Catholicism was thus in part a debate over the nature of religious discussion in a republic. Nationwide, Protestants invoked the symbols of America's free democratic institutions to characterize their own religious institutions, and compared Catholicism by contrast to unenlightened monarchism. Free discussion and enquiry were the rationale behind anti-Catholic sentiment.

The nature of religious discussion was particularly sensitive regarding the German population. Germans were isolated from the English-language press by the language barrier, and Protestants claimed that they were helpless victims of German-speaking Papists. They thus felt that there was a need to evangelize Germans, and set about publishing German-language sectarian papers.[32]

The most prominent German sectarian paper in Cincinnati was

[29] *Philanthropist*, Feb. 3, 1837.

[30] Purcell, "Journal," Jan. 24, 1834, p. 247.

[31] *Philanthropist*, Oct. 28, 1836

[32] Carl F. Wittke, *William Nast: Patriarch of German Methodism* (Detroit: Wayne State University Press, 1959), p. 39.

Wilhelm Nast's *Christliche Apologete*. Nast was born in Germany in 1807. He attended the University of Tübingen, but became disenchanted with the Hegelianism that dominated that institution. He came to the United States in 1828, and was converted to Methodism at a camp meeting. He became a preacher, was appointed missionary to Cincinnati's German population in 1835, and succeeded in persuading the Ohio Methodist Conference to assist him in establishing a German-language Methodist newspaper. The result was the founding of the *Apologete* in January, 1839.[33]

The *Apologete* was a successful sectarian paper. Its subscription list grew from an initial 100 to 1700 subscribers in 1847 and 3500 in 1852. Yet at the end of that period it was still running an annual deficit of $800. Its success was due more to strong organizational backing—the support of the Methodist organization—than its own appeal. It was begun with a "grant" of $2400 from English-speaking Methodists, and was a publication of the Western Methodist Book Concern.[34]

The *Apologete* was national in scope. It was the organ of German Methodism, and as such was outwardly missionary, not appealing to a local constituency. Nast was fond of reporting news from "the field"—conversions, the organization of Methodist Churches throughout the states, and especially *Lagerversammlungen*, or camp meetings. The file of the *Apologete* is an invaluable source of organizational information.[35]

The *Apologete* furnished theological as well as organizational material. Sermons were reprinted, and Nast wrote and published many a lengthy disquisition—one suspects that these would have been less common in a journal not dominated by a strong-willed clergyman and not supported by non-subscribers. The *Apologete* also consciously promoted the

---

[33]Max Burgheim, *Cincinnati in Wort und Bild* (Cincinnati: M. and R. Burgheim, 1888), p. 80; Lloyd D. Easton, "German Philosophy in 19th Century Cincinnati," *Bulletin of the Historical and Philosophical Society of Ohio*, XX (Jan., 1962), p. 22; Wittke, *Nast*, pp. 5-25; Joseph White, "Religion and Community: Cincinnati Germans, 1814-1870" (Unpublished doctoral dissertation, University of Notre Dame, 1980), pp. 120-26; Karl J. R. Arndt and Mary E. Olson, *German-American Newspapers and Periodicals, 1732-1955: History and Bibliography*, 2 vols., (Heidelburg: 1961-1973), I, 436-37.

[34]Wittke, *Nast*, pp. 83-5.

[35]White, "Religion and Community," pp. 126-27; Wittke, *Nast*, p. 161.

Americanization of its readers. In line with this, it attacked Roman Catholicism as anti-American and anti-democratic.[36]

The *Apologete* was begun in part as a response to the establishment in 1837 of a German-language Catholic weekly, the *Wahrheitsfreund*. This was the first German Catholic newspaper in the United States, and as such was, like the *Apologete*, national in scope. Within a year its subscription list had grown from an initial 569 to 3300, with all but 300 being mailed to subscribers outside Cincinnati. Like the *Apologete*, it was edited by a strong-willed foreign-born clergyman, John Martin Henni, later first Bishop of Milwaukee. Henni had come to the United States in the late 1820s, and had spent several years on the frontier missionary circuit before settling with a congregation.[37]

The *Wahrheitsfreund*, like the *Apologete*, was used as an instrument of political assimilation. Henni ran translations of the Declaration of Independence, for example, and wrote didactic essays on American citizenship. Peter L. Johnson has called Henni's paper "a veritable school for citizenship."[38] The *Catholic Telegraph* also published non-partisan editorials on voter participation.[39]

Nativism was only partly theological, and was far more concerned with the assimilability of immigrants to American political institutions. Hence the attention to political instruction shown by German religious papers is significant.

After 1840, anti-Catholicism would become primarily political, not theological. Protestants, especially Whigs, would accuse Roman Catholic priests of manipulating the immigrant vote in favor of the Democratic Party, and temperance activists, also primarily Whigs, would bring to politics a deep antipathy to beer-drinking Germans, who were at the time mostly Democratic. A fundamental element in this political tension was

[36]Wittke, *Nast*, pp. 90, 82-3, 96-9.

[37]Peter L. Johnson, *Crosier on the Frontier: A Life of John Martin Henni* (Madison: State Historical Society of Wisconsin, 1959), pp. 1-57; White, "Religion and Community," pp. 162-64, 166; Burgheim, *Wort und Bild*, pp. 130-31; Emmet H. Rothan, *The German-Catholic Immigrant in the United States (1830-1860)* (Washington: The Catholic University of America Press, 1946), p. 92.

[38]Johnson, *Henni*, p. 49; White, "Religion and Community," pp. 167-68.

[39]Deye, "Purcell," p. 199.

the isolation of the German community from the mainstream of political discourse. The *Gazette*, for instance, claimed that the German press consistently printed lies, and attributed defeat at the polls to a Papal conspiracy.[40] The implication was that the presence of a large body of immigrants in the electorate was inimical to republican institutions, as non-English speaking voters did not have access to the true media of free political discourse. As far as it was political, nativism involved political communications.

The theological controversy over Catholicism had curious implications regarding religious discussion in the press. The Protestant attack on Catholicism was clothed in the rhetoric of free enquiry, implying endorsement of the idea of the religious press as an open forum for the discussion of religious issues. On the other hand, the behavior of the religious press in relating information and opinions on Catholicism was anything but impartial, with religious papers serving as propaganda sheets for denominational organizations. What was invoked in theory was rejected in practice.

Organization and Science in the Religious Press

The religious press was most effective as an instrument of religious organization, not of rational discussion. Most successful religious papers owed their success to the backing of a vigorous and aggressive organization. Sometimes this backing came in the form of direct financial assistance. More often, it took the form of the provision of a ready-made readership, a corner on a closed market, as it were. The religious organization assured a certain insulation from consumer demands.

Organizational papers are devoted to a certain kind of news. Typically, they delight in printing accounts of organizational events, replete with names of well-known members; they delight in relating items clipped from other (denominational) papers; accounts of conversions, of revivals and camp-meetings, and of victory in public debates were common.

It may seem a paradox that religious papers, supposedly the instruments of rational investigation of theological questions, were most

[40]Stritch, "Nativism," pp. 240-49; White, "Religion and Community," pp. 167-68.

successfully exploited by the more evangelical and revivalistic sects and denominations. This paradox is more apparent than real. These denominational papers were more organizational than "scientific."

The denomination most notable for its publication efforts in the early west was Methodism. We have already noted the determination of Methodists in establishing a German-language paper. Its success—the *Apologete* survived until the 1940s—is particularly remarkable in light of the small number of German Methodists in the United States.

The first Methodist class in Cincinnati was formed in 1804. By 1812, local Methodists numbered over 200, and by 1830 over 1200.[41] Four years later, a key western Methodist periodical, the *Western Christian Advocate*, was established. This weekly was published in Cincinnati, but circulated throughout the west. By 1840, it claimed 15,000 subscribers.[42]

The *Western Christian Advocate* was oriented toward aggressive promotion of Methodism, not the free rational discussion of religious issues. Its regular columns included "Revival Intelligence," "Missionary Intelligence," and "Departments" appealing to Youth, Women, and Temperance advocates. The *Advocate* contained no advertising, its revenues came solely from a $2.00 annual subscription fee. A notice under the masthead announced that "The proceeds of this paper will be divided among all the annual conferences, to be applied in spreading the gospel and in aiding distressed and superannuated preachers, and the widows and orphans of those who have died in the work."

The *Western Christian Advocate* was a publication of the Western Methodist Book Concern. The Concern had been established in 1820 as a depository for all sorts of promotional literature, and dealt wholesale with agents and circuit riders, who actively distributed this material to converts and the faithful in general. The Western Book Concern was originally subordinate to the New York Methodist Book Concern but achieved independence in 1836. By 1851, its printing office in Cincinnati employed twenty-five hands and operated five steam presses. Forty-six more men

[41]Samuel W. Williams, *Pictures of Early Methodism in Ohio* (Cincinnati; Jennings & Graham, 1909), pp. 50-67.

[42]Willian Warren Sweet, *The Methodists: A Collection of Source Materials*, vol. IV in *Religion on the Frontier: 1783-1840* (Chicago: University of Chicago Press, 1946), p. 681.

were employed at a bindery. In all, by 1851, the Western Methodist Book Concern produced $125,000 worth of books and periodicals annually.[43] By 1854, it published five periodicals: the *Sunday School Advocate* (30,000 circulation), the *Western Christian Advocate* (26,000), the *Ladies' Repository and Gatherings of the West* (18,000), the *Missionary Advocate* (6000), and the *Christliche Apologete* (5000).[44] It seems clear that at least for Methodists, religious publications had become big business.

Methodism was the most visible and successful of the denominational publishing ventures in pre-Civil War Cincinnati. But other sects and denominations also used print effectively, especially the Catholic Church. Indeed, any religious periodical with anything near a mass readership was associated with a religious organization.

Periodicals, as organs of denominations, were ancillary to other missionary efforts. Evangelical periodicals amplified the significance of camp meetings and revivals by publicizing them. The *Christian Preacher*, for example, reported revivals under the heading "Success of the Gospel."[45] And periodicals encouraged the spread of religious enthusiasm. The *Journal*, for instance, in 1837, printed an editorial "endeavoring to stir up the ministers and churches of the west, and earnestly exhorting them to pray for an outpouring of the Holy Spirit."[46] Religious periodicals thus became more commonly devoted to religious organizations, and more commonly instruments of revivalism than of "scientific" religious enquiry.

The reasons for this change in the idea of a religious press are multiple. The earliest periodicals in Cincinnati had been established by men who believed that a genuine popular enlightenment could be achieved by the free scientific investigation of religious matters. This belief entailed faith in, first, an objective discoverable religious truth; second, the efficacy of rational "scientific" investigation in discovering this truth; and third, the possibility of popularizing this enlightenment by means of a religious

[43] Walter Sutton, *The Western Book Trade: Cincinnati as a Nineteenth Century Publishing and Book Trade Center* (Columbus: Ohio State University Press, 1961), pp. 151-59.

[44] *Ibid.*, p. 160.

[45] See, for example, *Christian Preacher*, I (May, 1836), pp. 118-20.

[46] *Cincinnati Journal*, Nov. 23, 1837.

press. That such genuine religious popular enlightenment is impossible is a philosophical hypothesis, but that it did not take place is an historical fact. These "scientific" religious journals never attained a mass readership. Either the public did not believe in Baconian investigation of matters religious, or it did not care to participate in such an investigation, or perhaps it was simply unwilling to pay good money to read a periodical devoted to this kind of religious inquiry. In any case, the periodicals that thrived were organizational, not scientific.

But this is not to say that there was no support for "scientific" religion. The evident power of the rhetoric of free enquiry as applied to Catholicism betrays a widespread belief in the ability of reason to overcome prejudice and tradition. And the national popularity of movements like Mormonism and Millerism, which claimed a kind of scientific authority, is evidence of the way in which the certainty attributed to natural science was appropriated by religious faiths.

Successful "scientific" religions differed from unsuccessful attempts at scientific religious inquiry in that they proclaimed the discovery of scientifically verifiable religious truths, rather than merely calling for investigation into these matters. And they presented these truths as simple and universally accessible, rather than the end result of a long and tedious process of refinement. In the final analysis, religions like Millerism were successful in attaining a mass following because they used revivalistic techniques of religious persuasion to promote an apparently scientific truth.

Cincinnati was a regional center of the Millerite movement. The movement, centered around the prediction of an imminent second coming, began gathering momentum locally in 1843, when William Miller's close associate Joshua V. Hines began speaking at tent meetings around the city, sometimes to crowds that numbered as many as two thousand listeners. In conjunction with this revivalistic promotion, a weekly newspaper called the *Western Midnight Cry* was begun, and circulated gratuitously. This literary effort was posterior to the use of oral techniques which by that time were traditionally associates with revivalistic religion. The local movement climaxed in August, 1844, when William Miller himself came to Cincinnati, preaching daily for a week to crowds of four and five thousand people. Meanwhile, local believers had constructed a Tabernacle, and regular meetings were held there. On October 22 1844, the projected date of the announced second coming, 2500 of the faithful gathered in the Tabernacle to await the great event. As it became evident that the millennium had once again been delayed, this Millerite meeting adjourned, "as it proved *sine die.*"[47]

Millerism itself had the appearance of scientific truth. The main article of belief was that the second coming was imminent, and that this could be ascertained by a series of calculations from statements in scripture. Ultimately, belief in the second coming, then, rested on certain assumptions about the nature of the Bible.

Millerism was popular because it offered a simple belief, one universally accessible, in the guise of a scientific certainty. Miller's calculations were simple enough that virtually anyone could understand them, and virtually anyone familiar with Biblical prophecies could appreciate them. So scientific did the belief seem, that when the second coming failed to materialize, people spent years poring over Miller's conclusions and calculations, without beginning to doubt his assumptions.

But Millerism became popular not solely because of its intrinsic appeal. At the root of its popular support was a high-powered and well-managed propaganda campaign, effectively utilizing all the techniques developed by revivalists and journalists alike. Joshua V. Himes in particular was masterful at religious promotion.[48]

The success of religions like Millerism does not indicate popular enlightenment. Rather, it indicates that the rhetoric of enlightenment had become popularized, and was applied to theories that sought to claim scientific verifiability. This would be one obvious element of the spiritualism of the 1850s.[49] Nor does the success of the "scientific" religions indicate a mature religious press devoted to free religious

[47]N. Gordon Thomas, "The Millerite Movement in Ohio," *Ohio History*, 81 (Spring, 1972), pp. 98-9, 101, 103-4; Charles Cist, "Millerism–The Finale Here," *Cincinnati Miscellany*, I (Nov., 1844), p. 41.

[48]Nathan O. Hatch, "The Christian Movement and the Demand for a Theology of the People," *Journal of American History*, 67 (Dec. 1980), pp. 545-67.

[49]R. Laurence Moore, "Spiritualism and Science: Reflections on the First Decade of the Spirit Rappings," *American Quarterly*, 24 (Oct., 1972), pp. 474-500.

it indicates the coming to maturity of techniques of persuasion that involved in part the use of the press.

Women and Religious Periodicals

The religious press, as it developed over time, grew more adroit at winning over a large popular audience. Increased popularity was achieved at the expense of an elite ideal of the press as an instrument of rational enquiry, and involved a stricter alliance of press and particular movements and organizations. But the popularization of the religious press also involved an appeal to new groups in society.

Most striking among the new readers of religious periodicals were women. Religious newspapers were always "family" papers, of course; religious periodicals always, then, had by intention more appeal to women than secular periodicals. But in antebellum America, feminine religious sensibilities were to come to dominate certain kinds of religious literature.

Religious papers designed for women readers were devoted more to a sense of non-denominational morality than other religious papers. Periodicals like the Methodist *Ladies' Repository and Gatherings of the West* concentrated more on the sentiments associated with religion than on the tenets of a particular theology or the proceedings of religious bodies. In their sentimental didacticism, these papers were often more literary than religious, and constitute the chief exception to the rule of denominational or sectarian dominance of the religious press.

The *Ladies' Repository* was the most successful of the women's periodicals published in Cincinnati. Established in 1841, the *Repository* was a publication of the Western Methodist Book Concern, and was edited at first by the Rev. L. L. Hamline, a Methodist clergyman. The *Repository* was intended to be read by women, but was mostly written by men, particularly clergymen. Contributions by women were not infrequent, but tended to be sentimental poems or short fictions, while men penned the frequent didactic essays on the role of women in the home. The readers were constantly "belectured and relegated to their 'sphere.'"[50]

[50]Mott, *American Magazines*, I, 388; Venable, *Literary Culture*, pp. 97-106, 98.

Women were granted a special claim to piety and domestic virtue by writers in the *Repository*. As the noted educator Caleb Atwater remarked,

Domestic life is her proper sphere, and it is there that she is most happy and useful. Society, too, owes to her its balance and its tone. In the circle in which she moves she may correct what is wrong, moderate what is unruly, and restrain indecorum. She may prevent excess, check vice, and protect virtue.

Atwater went on to assert that "The greatest blessing attending female influence is the promotion of religious feeling."[51]

The line of reasoning here is symptomatic of the rationale behind female periodicals of this sort. Women, it was acknowledged, lacked the intellectual capabilities of men,[52] but boasted superior sensibilities. Women were capable of great piety, devotion, and charm. Hence the woman as mother and wife was to be the guardian of moral purity in the home.

The superiority of woman's affectional powers was always linked with the inferiority of her intellectual abilities. This meant that religious periodicals aimed at a female audience would naturally eschew analytical discussions of theological issues, and concentrate instead on didactic and simplistic essays outlining moral precepts and sentimental poetry and fiction designed to elevate and purify the emotions. The values embodied would be those of family and religion, but religion in general. Because women's periodicals appealed to the sensibilities, they were outstanding among successful religious periodicals in being non-denominational and non-sectarian in the material they presented.

Although women's periodicals were non-sectarian, they still aimed at promoting a specific value system. They were programmatic and persuasional, they were characteristically didactic. In these regards, they were similar to religious children's magazines.

Children's periodicals were similar to women's in their simplicity and didacticism. They differed in that they were often associated primarily with Sunday Schools and other types of denominational instruction. Children's papers would not be more theological, but would be more

[51]Caleb Atwater, "Female Education," *Ladies' Repository*, I (Jan., 1841), pp. 10-13.
[52]See, for example, Charles Elliott, "Arguing with Females," *Ibid.*, pp. 25-6.

denominational.

The Presbyterian *Child's Newspaper* has a good claim to having been the first juvenile paper in the Ohio Valley. This had a circulation of 3000, and was published semi-monthly.[53] Its wide circulation may be attributed to the fact that parents, and not children, paid for subscriptions. The Catholic Church in Cincinnati began a *Children's Magazine* in 1839,[54] and Universalists published a Sunday School paper entitled *Youth's Friend*, edited by Friend Abel.

These papers were all instructional, and all featured very little input from their readers, of course. But they were denominational, and relied on the support of religious organizations to guarantee a readership.

This discussion of religious periodicals has not been exhaustive. To deal with all the religious periodicals published in Cincinnati before 1848 would be impossible. I have mentioned only the most important ones, and discussed them in relation to key themes in religious journalism.

The real focus of this section has been the idea of religious journalism, and how this idea has changed over time. I have argued that the first religious newspapers in Cincinnati were non-sectarian, and devoted to a utopian idea of the press as an instrument of rational religious investigation. These periodicals were characteristically operated by elite figures, but were not strictly associated in ideal or intent with an exclusive organization or sect.

These periodicals failed to achieve a mass readership. The periodicals of "enlightenment" were succeeded by others, more successful, and generally more organizational. These denominational and sectarian papers often invoked the powerful symbols of science and free investigation, but were in fact devoted to the advancement of a particular organization or religious movement. The exception to this rule was the women's periodical, which was sentimental rather than organizational.

Popularization was the crucial factor in the development of religious

---

[53]Brainerd, *Brainerd*, pp. 79-82.

[54]Krummen, "Purcell," p. 96; Sr. Mary Agnes McCann, *Archbishop Purcell and the Archdiocese of Cincinnati* (Washington: Catholic University of America Press, 1918), p. 30.

journalism. The religious paper was used as a means of reaching a mass audience with an organizational program or a set of didactic values. Popularization bred sentimentalization, and served organization.

Literary Periodicals

At first glance, it may seem inappropriate to group religious and literary periodicals together. Literary periodicals printed fiction, essays, and poetry, while religious newspapers conveyed news of the workings of the spirit, along with sermons and theological disquisitions. And religious periodicals were usually associated with denominations and creeds, while literary periodicals featured individual authors and appealed to the reading public as a whole undivided by ideological adherence.

But religious and literary periodicals of the 1820s, 1830s, and 1840s shared some crucial characteristics. They were often similar in format, for example. Their historical appearance was virtually contemporary; hence it would seem that the *idea* of the literary periodical was closely akin to that of the religious periodical.

And in fact religious and literary periodicals shared a sense of mission. Both were justified by an intention to promote morality—particularly Christian morality. The nature of antebellum periodical literature was often highly didactic: art was meant to delight *and* instruct. This confluence of intention is most apparent in the ever-popular and ever more moralistic women's magazines.

Both religious and literary periodicals went through a process of popularization. In the case of religious periodicals, reaching a wide audience enhanced organizational involvement. Literary ventures, however, were not thus protected from market forces, and popularization necessitated commercialization. The history of the literary magazine in the early Republic is one of evolution from sententiousness to sentimentality and sensationalism.

I have been able to identify forty-one distinct periodicals published in Cincinnati between 1821 and 1848 which were in some way literary.[55] Only

---

[55]These forty-one include two historical magazines—the *American Pioneer* and the *Cincinnati Miscellanny*; two gossip sheets—the *Thistle* and the *True Blue and*

five lasted five years or more. These were the *Cincinnati Chronicle and Literary Gazette* (1826–1835), a weekly which also featured general news; the *Family Magazine* (1836–1841), which was actually a stereotyped re-issue of J. S. Redfield's New York publication; the *Ladies' Repository* (1841–1876), a publication of the Western Methodist Book Concern; the *Cincinnati Mirror* (1831–1836), a bi-monthly and weekly publication whose survival was due to a knack for successful mergers;[56] and the *Western Messenger* (1835–1841), supported for six years by a small but devoted non-local elite readership.[57] These periodicals all owed their success to something more than popularity and literary value.

There were several less successful literary magazines of greater artistic merit and historical interest than these. Three in particular featured high-quality prose: Timothy Flint's *Western Monthly Review* (1827–1830); James Hall's *Western Monthly Magazine* (1833–1837); and the *Western Literary Journal and Monthly Review* (1844–1845), edited by Lucius A. Hine in Cincinnati and E. Z. C. Judson (alias Ned Buntline) in Nashville. These magazines aimed at promoting serious western literature, as their titles suggest.

No less than fifteen of Cincinnati's early periodicals had some reference to the west in their titles. For the most part, this "west" meant little more than "published outside the east," as the ideal for literary periodicals remained the successful eastern prints. In the late 1840s, this imitative westernism changed, as a new generation of westerners began publishing. Typical of this later westernism was the cheap illustrated weekly the *Great West*. This was a commercial magazine; its appearance and acceptance signaled a departure from the attempt to create a refined literary westernism in the early years.

Castigator; and two which have also been discussed as religious—the *Western Messenger* and the *Ladies' Repository*.

[56] As is evident in the numerous changes of title: *Cincinnati Mirror and Ladies' Parterre Devoted to Polite Literature* (1831-3); *Cincinnati Mirror and Western Gazette of Literature and Science* (1833-4); *Cincinnati Mirror and Chronicle Devoted to Literature and Science* (1834-5); the *Buckeye and Cincinnati Mirror* (1835-6); and finally the *Cincinnati Mirror and Western Gazette of Literature, Science, and the Arts* (1836).

[57] Charles Cist, *Cincinnati in 1841: Its Early Annals and Future Prospects* (Cincinnati: Charles Cist, 1841), p. 93, reports its circulation as 1000.

Next to westernism, the most common theme in the titles of Cincinnati's early literary periodicals is the appeal to family. Grouping together all with a specific appeal to women, youth, or family, I have identified nine "family magazines." These achieved a wide readership through appeal to sentiment—the least common denominator of morality. Sentimentalization was a process enacted in imitation of eastern models, and was another departure from the quest for a serious popular western literature.

A third type of periodical common in the early west was the "general information" periodical. The aim of this was to provide "interesting and useful knowledge," be it scientific or historical. I have identified five such periodicals in early Cincinnati, though all early magazines shared some devotion to this kind of popularization of knowledge. But as time passed, knowledge came to be presented more to amuse than to instruct, more to "improve" than to enlighten. At the same time, historical knowledge became more important, as the lives of the pioneers and antiquities of the west became popular in periodical literature.

The remainder of this chapter will deal with these three types of periodical literature: western, family, and general knowledge. I will discuss each in terms of rationale for publication, popular attitudes, market influence, and the change over time in the idea of the literary press.

Westernism

The reflection in literature of the vast phenomenon of the pioneer west is to be seen properly in the great bulk of mediocre pamphleteering and journalism—and, to a much lesser extent, bookmaking—of men who wrote only incidentally to their participation in the economic, political, and religious turmoil which engaged almost their whole attention.

—Ralph L. Rusk[58]

Western literature was embedded in a social and historical context. A western elite attempted to create a western literature *de novo*, just as in

---

[58]Ralph Leslie Rusk, *The Literature of the Middle Western Frontier*, 2 vols. (New York: Columbia University Press, 1925), II, 77.

America as a whole the movement for a national literature gained momentum.[59] This attempt grew with the influx of migrants to the west during the recovery from the Panic of 1819, and the coming to maturity of a new generation of native westerners in the 1830s and 1840s.

One element of westernism was pride in the material progress of the west. Writers like Timothy Flint could point proudly to the rapid rise of the western economy, especially from the vantage point of a booming commercial town like Cincinnati.[60] Economic growth promised cultural parity with the east.

But the crucial perceived cultural difference was environmental. The western men, at least the English-speaking ones, were easterners by lineage, tradition and education. Their ideal of culture was eastern culture. Dr. Daniel Drake, for example, could propose nothing more than an ecological westernism in promoting a theory of a western cultural life. Cincinnatians did lack the theoretical and institutional sophistication of Parisians, or even Philadelphians, but could make good a claim to intellectual equality by contemplating and observing uniquely western physical phenomena, topographical, botanical, and meteorological.[61] This ideal of refinement was imitative. So too were the various attempts to use "western themes," like Indian battles or the tales of the pioneers, little more than unimaginative adoptions of eastern literary values.

On the other hand, there was a real sense of cultural rivalry with the east, and a real scorn for eastern pretensions. The editor of the *Cincinnati Mirror*, for instance, called for brevity and realism in submitted material, scorning "the sickly sentimentality so common in periodicals of a literary

[59]As is evident in the appearance of two key essays: William Ellery Channing's "The Importance and Means of a National Literature," and Ralph Waldo Emerson's "The American Scholar."

[60]Timothy Flint, "Progress of the West," *Western Monthly Review,* I (May, 1827), pp. 25-7. See also *Ibid.,* "Present Population and Future Prospects of the Western Country," I (Oct., 1827), pp. 329-34.

[61]Daniel Drake, "Anniversary Address to the School of Literature and the Arts," in Henry Shapiro and Zane L. Miller, ed., *Physician to the West: Selected Writings of Daniel Drake on Science and Society* (Lexington: University Press of Kentucky, 1970), pp. 57-65. Wade, *Urban Frontier,* pp. 314-21, describes western emulation of eastern models.

nature,"[62] referring, one surmises, to the popular eastern prints. Two years later, William Davis Gallagher published a pointed satire of reviews of eastern periodicals:

Their 'striking characteristics,' (which, by the way, it would be quite impossible to find without some assistance,) are pointed out, and commented upon; their 'splendid embellishments,' heaven save the mark! are eulogized; their monthly puff slips are copied, and the 'exquisite taste in which the whole is got up,' is sure to 'entitle Messers. Puff, Tickla-me & Co. publishers of the "Lady's Intellectual Casket of Sentiment, Shreds and Patches,"' to 'a very large slice from the big loaf of public patronage.' The 'literary enterprize of these gentlemen, is sure to be deserving of the highest praise;' and the American people are positively 'much indebted to them, for their patriotic exertions to elevate the character of American literature.'[63]

Appearing as it did in the *Cincinnati Mirror and Ladies' Parterre Devoted to Polite Literature*, this outburst seems to the modern reader like the pot calling the kettle black.

But western literati, especially Gallagher (himself an indefatigable magazinist), were extremely proud and confident of western talent.[64] Gallagher claimed that "much of the best learning of the age had migrated here, but it was idle."[65] One reason for the poverty of accomplishment in light of this wealth of talent was the absence of a respectable outlet for literary creativity: "here in the west, our choicest thoughts flow through the dingy channel of a newspaper column . . . ."[66] But by the time Gallagher published this last statement, dozens of literary periodicals had already been established in Cincinnati and had failed. He attributed this poor record to four causes: the indifference of western newspapers to western achievements; the reluctance of western writers to contribute, especially signed pieces; non-payment of subscriptions; and a dearth of "active and enterprising publishers."[67] Gallagher refused to blame a lack of

---

[62]*Cincinnati Mirror*, Oct. 1, 1831.

[63]William Davis Gallagher, "Eastern and Western Periodicals," *Ibid.*, April 27, 1833.

[64]*Ibid.*, "Sketches of the Literature of the West," *Western Literary Journal and Monthly Review*, I (August, 1836), pp. 210-14.

[65]*Ibid.*, "Editor's Budget--the East and the West," *Hesperian*, III (Nov., 1839), p. 499.

[66]*Ibid.*, "A Periodical Literature for the West: What has it been? What Ought it to Be?" *Western Literary Journal and Monthly Review*, I (Nov., 1844), p. 1.

[67]*Ibid.*, pp. 6-8.

talent, a lack of potential material, or a lack of western readership for the failure of western periodicals. All of the elements of a vital and unique western culture were there, just waiting for the proper catalyst.

There did exist in and around Cincinnati in the 1830s and 1840s a talented, concerned, and highly educated elite. And this elite congregated regularly. In the 1830s Daniel Drake customarily hosted gatherings of all the local notables, including Judge James Hall of the *Western Monthly Magazine*; Calvin E. Stowe of Lane Theological Seminary; his future wife Harriet Beecher, later author of *Uncle Tom's Cabin*; her sister Catherine Beecher, famous in her own right as a feminist and educator; and the poetess Caroline Lee Hentz.[68] A more formal gathering was the Semi-Colon Club. This literary group met from 1829 to 1847, and published a periodical called the *Semi-Colon* in 1845. It included most of the regular guests at Drake's house, plus prominent lawyers Timothy Walker, Nathan Guilford, Edward Pearse Cranch, and Benjamin Drake; clergymen and divines, like Lyman Beecher, James Handasyd Perkins, James Freeman Clarke, and Timothy Flint; editors like James Hall and Edward Deering Mansfield; and publisher and bookseller John P. Foote.[69] Thus there existed a body of men and women of talent, training and social standing sufficient to produce literary periodicals. And periodical after periodical was in fact begun.

The earliest periodical that could certainly be called literary published in Cincinnati was the *Olio*, established in 1821, but lasting less than a year.[70] In 1824, the first really significant periodical, the *Cincinnati Literary Gazette*, was set up. This weekly was conducted by a clique of local professionals, including John P. Foote and Benjamin Drake, both later members of the Semi-Colon Club, along with J. H. James, a publisher, A. N. Deming, printer, and Lewis Noble.[71] These men were well-to-do

[68]Edward Deering Mansfield, *Personal Memories, Social, Political, and Literary, with Sketches of Many Noted People, 1803-1843* (Cincinnati: Robert Clarke & Co., 1879), pp. 261-67.

[69]Louis L. Tucker, "The Semi-Colon Club of Cincinnati," *Ohio History*, 73 (Winter, 1964), pp. 13-26.

[70]Venable, *Literary Culture*, p. 66. The *Literary Cadet* was basically not a literary periodical, but a general weekly newspaper, *contra* Sutton, *Book Trade*, p. 28.

[71]Venable, *Literary Culture*, p. 66; Mansfield, *Personal Memories*, p. 180.

amateurs: "In preparing our weekly sheet, we have spent much time and labor; and in this we have not been influenced by any hope of pecuniary reward . . . ."[72] They were dedicated to establishing a western cultural identity: "It is one of the objects of this paper to notice Western Institutions, which are calculated to promote the interests of Literature and Science. . . . Next, therefore, to cherishing a national feeling, we would cherish a western feeling . . . ."[73] That the goal of the *Gazette* was primarily didactic was embodied in its first motto, "Not to display learning, but to excite a taste for it."

The *Literary Gazette* was very eclectic. Although each weekly paper was only eight pages long, each contained not only poetry (original and select) and short fiction, but also reviews, a summary of news, obituaries, scientific items, and notices of local cultural events. The *Literary Gazette* retained many of the features of the general newspaper.

The *Literary Gazette* complained constantly of a lack of support. Finally, after a year and a half, it failed. It was succeeded a few months later by the *Parthenon*, like the *Gazette* small and fairly short-lived. The *Parthenon* was in turn succeeded by the *Ladies' Parterre and Literary Gazette*. Meanwhile, a more successful and significant literary weekly had been established in 1826. This was the *Cincinnati Chronicle*, and its founder and original editor was Benjamin Drake, brother of the famous Dr. Daniel Drake, and a regular contributor to the old *Literary Gazette*. The *Chronicle*, like the *Gazette*, was something of a cross between a literary sheet and a general newspaper, but unlike the *Gazette* it survived by tending more toward the latter genre. Under the editorship of Edward Deering Mansfield, it devoted more space to political items, supported issues like temperance and anti-slavery, and eventually turned to daily publication in 1839. Finally it merged with the Whig *Atlas* and passed out of existence. During its career, it had been associated with the publication of Peabody's *Prices Current* and the *Prices Current* of the Merchant Exchange. But as a literary organ, on the other hand, it has the distinction of having published Harriet Beecher Stowe's first story, "Cousin William."[74]

[72]*Cincinnati Literary Gazette*, III (Oct. 29, 1825), p. 278.
[73]*Ibid.*, I (May 15, 1824), p. 157.
[74]Charles Theodore Greve, *Centennial History of Cincinnati and Representative*

Edward Deering Mansfield was a Yankee whose ancestors had lived in New England since the 1630s. His father was a professor at West Point who moved west to Marietta in 1803 when he was appointed surveyor-general of the United States by Thomas Jefferson. Among his employees in this position were three future governors: Thomas Worthington and Ethan Allen Brown of Ohio, and Lewis Cass of Michigan.[75]

Mansfield was born in 1801 in New Haven, Connecticut. He spent his childhood (1805–1812) in Cincinnati, where he was educated by his mother. In 1812 he went back to Connecticut for more advanced schooling, and eventually attended Princeton and West Point. Upon graduating, he went to Litchfield, Connecticut, to study law. There he lived across the street from Lyman Beecher. Mansfield returned to Cincinnati in 1825.[76] He was well-connected in local society: a cousin had married Benjamin Drake. (Another cousin was a regular contributor to the prestigious literary journal, the *PortFolio*.)[77]

But the *Chronicle* was not a purely literary organ, nor were any of the other periodicals mentioned so far. They were weeklies or bi-monthlies, no more than eight pages long, and were devoted to a wide range of matter. Due to size and frequency of publication, they were more local than regional in character. They did, however, share most of the characteristics of later periodicals in their concern with western affairs, their didactic intent, and their elite management.

The first significant monthly in Cincinnati was Timothy Flint's *Western Monthly Review*. Flint was born in North Reading, Massachusetts, in 1780. He came from old New England stock, was educated at Phillips Academy, Andover, and graduated from Harvard in 1800. By marriage to Abigail Hubbard he became a beneficiary of Joseph Peabody, wealthy Salem merchant and father of Ephraim Peabody, later an editor of the *Western Messenger*. It was at the encouragement of the elder

Citizens (Chicago: Biographical Publishing Co, 1904), pp. 791-2; Osman Castle Hooper, *History of Ohio Journalism, 1793-1933* (Columbus: Spahr and Glen, 1933), p.91; Dawson, "Yankees," p. 136; Mansfield, Personal *Memories*, pp. 291-5.

[75]Mansfield, *Personal Memories*, pp. 1-5, 18-9, 32.

[76]Venable, *Literary Culture*, pp. 409-13; Mansfield, *Personal Memories*, pp. 48-141 *passim*.

[77]Mansfield, *Personal Memories*, p. 34.

Peabody that Flint came west in 1815. He wandered throughout the Mississippi Valley for ten years, then settled in Cincinnati in 1825.[78] Flint was a prolific writer, producing several novels, and personally composing three-fourths of the material published in the *Western Review*.

Flint's notions of the west reflected his eastern upbringing. Of Cincinnati in particular he remarked, "The prevalent modes of living, of society, of instruction, of associating for any public object, of thinking and enjoying, struck me, generally, to be copies of the New England pattern."[79] This identification of the west with New England made Flint the recognized spokesman of the west for New Englanders. The *North American Review* pointed to Flint's autobiographical *Recollections* as "one of our few genuine national works. It could have been written nowhere but in the Western Valley. It could have been written by no one, whose mind had not been moulded by a constant contact with western scenery and people."[80] And Isaac Appleton Jewett, then a young New Englander in Cincinnati, described Flint as "unquestionably the oracle of the West. I for one am quite pleased with him, but he is far from being popular."[81] It is not surprising that, having established a reputation in the east by publishing in the west, Flint returned east in 1833 as editor of the prestigious *Knickerbocker Magazine* in New York.[82]

Flint dominated the *Review*. Most of the material, coming as it did from his pen, was in the same style, marked by "an indulgence in commas which he carried to an extreme," by a gravity "too heavy to be easily digestible," and occasionally by "a nimble sense of humor, . . . though sometimes careless and verbose," according to Frank Luther Mott.[83] In

---

[78]Venable, *Literary Culture*, pp. 323-48; Timothy Flint, *Recollections of the Last Ten Years*, C. Hartley Grattan, ed., (New York: Knopf, 1932), i-xii.

[79]Flint, *Recollections*, p. 45.

[80]*North American Review*, XLIII (July, 1836), p. 2. Quoted in John E. Kirkpatrick, *Timothy Flint: Pioneer, Missionary, Author, Editor, 1780-1840* (Cleveland: Arthur Clark, 1911), p. 266.

[81]Isaac Appleton Jewett to Joseph Willard, Cincinnati, May 8, 1831, in James Taylor Dunn, ed., "'Cincinnati is a Delightful Place': Letters of a Law Clerk, 1831-4," *Bulletin of the Historical and Philosophical Society of Ohio*, X (July, 1952), p. 260.

[82]Venable, *Literary Culture*, p. 358.

[83]Mott, *American Magazines*, I, 559-61.

addition to Flint's personal contributions, his family also helped out. His son Hubbard was the publisher; another son, Mican, contributed poetry; and a daughter, Emmeline, did translations. A periodical so dominated by a single personality could hardly bring about a renaissance in western letters since it would tend not to promote the involvement of a broad-based literary community. It died, as C. Hartley Grattan remarked, of "chronic literary anaemia, being sustained through its last months by translations. It was a gallant joust with indifference."[84]

Much of the matter in the *Review* consisted of reviews of recent literature. Flint wrote these reviews himself, often using the editorial we, although all original pieces were unsigned. The intent of these reviews, which usually rambled on with no sign of organization beyond synopsis, was to promote literature, especially western literature, and to edify the public at the same time. No Cincinnatian would embody the magazinist as pedagogue more fully than Flint.

The magazine lasted from May, 1827, to June, 1830, then failed because of a lack of patronage. In the final months, Flint toyed with the idea of going to a quarterly format, or of publishing a list of delinquent subscribers, hoping thereby to shame them into paying back some of the $3000 he claimed he was owed.[85] The broad regional audience necessary for financial stability eluded this over-punctuated organ of western literature.

The next notable monthly was James Hall's *Western Monthly Magazine*. Hall, like Flint, came from prominent eastern stock. But his upbringing was in upper-class Philadelphia society. He was also well-connected in the literary world: his mother and brother wrote for the *PortFolio*, and his uncle Samuel Ewing (under whom Hall later studied law) was the founder of the *Analectic Magazine*, which became famous under the editorship of Washington Irving.[86]

After serving in the army during the War of 1812 and living in Pittsburgh and various places in Illinois, political reversals forced Hall to

---

[84]Grattan, ed., Flint, *Recollections*, ix.

[85] *Western Monthly Review*, III (June, 1830), p. 668; "To Our Delinquent Subscribers," (April, 1830), pp. 559-60.

[86]Randall, *Hall*, pp. 3-19.

move again, and he came to Cincinnati in 1833. He brought with him the *Illinois Monthly Magazine* which he had published in Vandalia since 1830. Upon its removal to Cincinnati, it was issued under the new title of the *Western Monthly Magazine*.[87]

Hall, like Flint, gained a reputation as the spokesman for the west through a series of early publications. Most influential were his *Letters from the West*, which were published serially in newspapers throughout the country; and the *Western Souvenir*, a gift book, edited by Hall, and containing five of his short stories, plus contributions from other important early western writers.[88] In 1834 he published a schoolbook called the *Western Reader*. This emphasized selections from western writers, and sold more than 100,000 copies in two years, prefiguring the later success of McGuffey's Readers.[89]

Hall was a secure member of the regional social and political elite. He was a leading freemason, an important member of the Whig Party and a close associate of the powerful John McLean, and a circuit judge. As a promoter of education, he was a member of the important Western Literary Institute and College of Professional Teachers, and was elected to the board of trustees of Catherine and Harriet Beecher's Western Female Institute.[90] He was also a member of the Semi-Colon Club.

The *Western Monthly Magazine* met with instant success in Cincinnati. The subscription list grew from an initial 500 to nearly 3000 names within a single year, "a support greater than has ever been given to any western periodical, and which few of the eastern cities have attained."[91] One reason for this success was the high quality of the material contributed by writers throughout the region (more than half of the contributors to the 1834 volume were from outside Ohio). These included James Handasyd Perkins, Isaac Appleton Jewett, William Davis Gallagher, Ephraim Peabody, Edward Deering Mansfield, Edward Pearse Cranch, Caroline Lee Hentz, and Harriet Beecher. Most of these original pieces

---

[87]Venable, *Literary Culture*, p. 376.
[88]Randall, *Hall*, pp. 147-54.
[89]*Ibid.*, pp. 207-10.
[90]*Ibid.*, pp. 64-5, 123, 94, 129-34, 184-6, 205-6.
[91]James Hall, "The Budget," *Western Monthly Magazine*, I (Sept., 1833), p. 428.

were either signed or initialed. And Hall paid a dollar a page for material accepted and published—the same rate offered by the venerable *North American Review*.[92]

Although Hall and most of his contributors were affiliated with the eastern elite, the *Monthly Magazine* did try to articulate a description of or program for western literature. A prize essay by Jewett in 1833 trotted out a list of "Themes for Western Fiction," which included the frontier life, the deeds of the pioneers, the virtues of western republican simplicity, the Indians, and of course the scenery of the western valley.[93] This was little more than an ecological westernism, however, a case of eastern men writing about the west. Another early article went beyond this, hinting at an independent "Western character," marked by simplicity, republicanism, and raw intelligence.[94] Still, if there was such a western character, it was something to be written about; it was not something which would generate a unique literary style.

The failure of the *Western Monthly Magazine* has been attributed to a number of causes, from arguments with the publishers to ethnocultural tensions between New Englanders and non-New Englanders resulting especially from the controversies over slavery and Catholicism. It is certain that the magazine still had a large regional following and that it had come closer than Flint's *Review* to achieving both popular support and the involvement of talent in the community. The reasons for its failure seem to have been more commercial than literary.

The failure of the *Western Monthly Magazine* coincided with the successful establishment of the *Western Messenger*. This Unitarian monthly, devoted to religion and literature, was far more didactic than the *Monthly Magazine*, and was conducted and primarily read by transplanted New Englanders. At the center of the editorial clique were James Freeman Clarke, Ephraim Peabody, William Henry Channing, Christopher Pearse Cranch, and the talented and sensitive James Handasyd Perkins.

Perkins was born in 1810 in Boston. He was the son of a Perkins and a

---

[92]Randall, *Hall*, pp. 221 *et seq.*; see also Mott, *American Magazines*, I, 597.

[93]Isaac Appleton Jewett, "Themes for Western Fiction," *Western Monthly Magazine*, I (Dec., 1833), pp. 574-88.

[94]"On Western Character," *Western Monthly Magazine*, I (Feb., 1833), pp. 49-55.

Higginson, and was nephew of William Ellery Channing and cousin of William Henry Channing. He was educated at Phillips Academy, Exeter, and other elite New England schools, but at the age of eighteen found himself clerking at the counting-house of Thomas H. Perkins, his uncle and a tremendously well-to-do merchant. Though this position held the promise of a lucrative career, young James found that he lacked the enthusiasm for making money necessary to make that job interesting. So he went west. Arriving in Cincinnati in 1832, he took up the study of law and the courtship of Sarah H. Elliott, sister-in-law of Samuel E. Foote, whose mansion would later be the site of meetings of the Semi-Colon Club. Perkins revelled in western society, which he found "free from trammels of bigotry and conventional prejudice."[95]

Although admitted to the bar in Cincinnati, Perkins abandoned a promising legal career because of a distaste for legal thought and legalistic morality. Instead, he turned to occasional farming and sporadic journalism—in the next decade he edited the *Cincinnati Mirror*, the *Chronicle*, and the *Western Messenger*. In the late 1830s, however, he underwent a sort of conversion experience. After a trip to Boston, he decided to devote all his energies to the achievement of social equality, popular education, Christian brotherhood, and spiritual-mindedness. He took the place of C. P. Cranch as official Unitarian minister at large in Cincinnati, organized a Relief Union, and set about eradicating "Pauperism, Infidelity, Vice, and Crime."[96] He remained a contributor to local journals, however, even after he had resigned his editorial duties.[97]

Perkins' sense of social mission was one of enlightenment. The educated man must instruct the ignorant, and could and should do so through the medium of the public prints:

. . . reverence for what is venerable, respect for what is GOOD, love for what is beautiful, must be spread abroad. And who can do it? The Educated Men; and they only by concert and union. . . . Books have become our pulpits, and newspapers our shrines for daily resort; if at these shrines we worship Mammon or Lucifer, and not

[95]Channing, Perkins, *Perkins*, pp. 1-85 *passim*, 60.
[96]*Ibid.*, pp. 87-8, 108-15, *et passim*.
[97]*Ibid.*, p. 244.

the true God, woe, woe, to us and to our country.[98]

In line with this philosophy, Perkins' contributions were always moralistic, and often appealed to "refined" sentiments. He also became involved in a whole host of benevolent organizations, including the Mercantile Library Association, the Mechanics' Institute, the Cincinnati Lyceum, and the Society for the Promotion of Useful Knowledge.[99]

Perkins articulated an ideal of western literature. At first, his notion was little more than "to storify Kentucky and Kentuck manners."[100] But in essays in the *Western Messenger* he expressed a more radical kind of westernism. He claimed that the west will be "the seat of a new practical philosophy—social, moral, political, religious, and literary." This philosophy was Christian Republicanism—the combination of liberal Christianity and the political doctrines of the American Revolution. Perkins elaborated on this theme:

> The great idea—as Coleridge would call it—the great informing idea of Republicanism, is not that distinctions, and ranks and privileges are to be abolished; but that MERIT shall take the place of BIRTH, WEALTH, and PROWESS, and become the basis of an aristocracy; and Christian Republicanism makes Christ the Judge of Merit.[101]

The west was to be the hen to hatch the egg laid by New England, it seems. Western society would become the society of talent, but that talent meant specifically Unitarian wisdom. Western society would then generate a literature of scientific and literary enlightenment, freed from the shackles of ignorance and bigotry forged by a dead past.

Perkins wrote the essays quoted above before his Ministry to the Poor began. Afterwards his writings became less utopian, more hortatory, more concerned with the reform of a society that already existed than the dreams of one yet to be born. Perkins has the distinction of being the only

---

[98]James Handasyd Perkins, "Association: A Vital Form of Social Action," *Ibid.*, pp. 171-72.

[99]*Ibid.*, p. 254.

[100]Perkins to his father, Cincinnati, May 6, 1832, *Ibid.*, p. 67.

[101]Perkins, "Prospects of the West," *Western Messenger*, I (Nov., 1835), p. 318. See also Perkins, "Agrarianism," *Ibid.*, (April, 1836), pp. 600 *et passim*.

editor of the *Western Messenger* to live out his life in the west—he committed suicide in Cincinnati in 1849.

The *Western Messenger* failed in 1841, when its final editor, William Henry Channing, moved back to New England. The *Messenger* was replaced by the famous Transcendentalist journal, the *Dial*.

The next important "Western" periodical published in Cincinnati was the *Western Literary Journal and Monthly Review*. This lively magazine was edited by E.Z.C. Judson, who, as Ned Buntline, became famous as the author of dime westerns and the "discoverer" of Buffalo Bill; and by Lucius A. Hine, a native western Swedenborgian, who would go on to publish several journals devoted more to philosophy and reform than literature. The *Western Literary Journal*'s circulation climbed sharply from its first issue in November, 1844;[102] but difficulties in management killed it before its first birthday.

These early western periodicals were not commercial. By this, I mean that they were conducted for the most part by amateurs; appealed to the patriotism, regional pride, and sense of community of their readers rather than to their consumer interests; and were distributed by subscription rather than on a cash basis. In the 1840s, cheaper publications appeared, and the local market was flooded by eastern publishers. In 1848, the *Great West* became the first indigenous western periodical to compete successfully with these eastern publications. Beginning at 3000, its circulation climbed to 15,000 by 1856, after merging with the *Columbian*.[103]

The new champion of literary westernism was William Turner Coggeshall. Coming to Cincinnati in 1847, he worked first as a reporter for the *Times* and the *Gazette*, then as editor of the *Daily Columbian* (1854) and the *Genius of the West* (1854–1856). A colorful figure, he traveled with Louis Kossuth in 1851, was a spy during the Civil War, named his daughter Emancipation Proclamation, and died in Quito, Ecuador, after having been appointed United States minister to that country by Abraham Lincoln.[104]

---

[102]*Western Literary Journal and Monthly Review*, I (Dec., 1844), p. 123.

[103]Sutton, *Book Trade*, pp. 191, 197.

[104]William D. Andrews, "William T. Coggeshall: 'Booster' of Western Literature," *Ohio History*, 81 (July, 1972), pp. 210-13; Venable, *Literary Culture*, p. 110.

The new manifesto of literary westernism was Coggeshall's anthology, *Poets and Poetry of the West* (1860). This volume featured selections from scores of western writers, along with biographical sketches. But again, the concentration in this volume was simply on local themes, geographical or historical; the aim was still toward cultural parity with the east.

Serious literary westernism failed, even while commercial westernism succeeded. The reasons are manifold. One was its imitativeness—the appeal always was for western themes, but the literary ideal was always eastern. The literary deities were in Boston, New York, and Philadelphia. Indeed, James Fenimore Cooper fit the prescribed mold of the western writer as well as Cincinnatians like James Hall and William Davis Gallagher, and was a superior craftsman to boot.

Secondly, the west did not achieve cultural parity with the east because the west was in fact culturally immature. There were no professional writers outside of newspaper reporters. There were no established literary institutions—the local colleges were still embryonic, and more emblematic of western pride than of western refinement in education. Most early western writers bore the stamp of an eastern education.

Third, and perhaps most important, was the absence of a large market that was both specifically western and highly literate. Those westerners who were highly literate were largely satisfied with eastern products. Those who were less refined in literary taste still did not care for the pretentious treatment of western themes they could find in the local periodicals. Mass tastes, it would seem, ran more to entertainment than erudition.

Polite Literature

As class distinctions sharpened, social attitudes toward women became polarized. The image of 'the Lady' was elevated to the accepted ideal of femininity toward which all women would strive. In this formulation of values lower-class women were simply ignored. The actual lady was, of course, nothing new on the American scene; she had been present ever since colonial days. What was new in the 1830s was the cult of the lady, her elevation to a status symbol. The advancing prosperity of the early 19th century made it possible for middle class women to aspire to the status formerly reserved for upper class women. The 'cult of true womanhood' of the 1830s became a vehicle of such aspirations. Mass circulation newspapers and magazines made it possible to teach every woman how to elevate the status of her family by setting 'proper' standards of behavior, dress, and literary taste. *Godey's Lady's Book* and innumerable gift books and tracts of the period all preach the same gospel of 'true womanhood'—piety, purity, domesticity. Those who were unable to reach the goal of becoming ladies were to be satisfied with the lesser goal—acceptance of their proper place in the home.

—Gerda Lerner[105]

Women's and family periodicals were exceptional. Their success signaled wide popular acceptance—if only among a group in society—of instruction from social betters. Magazines designed to be read by women and children were highly didactic, very moralistic, and largely written by adult males, often ministers.

Women's periodicals in nineteenth-century America are of great importance. This importance lies in their commercial success rather than in their literary significance. The first magazine devoted to women's interests to last more than five years was founded as late as 1828 by Sarah Josepha Hale in Boston.[106] By 1860, the most important women's magazines—*Graham's*, *Putnam's*, and *Godey's*—had circulations of around 100,000. They had ushered in the age of commercial periodicals through "a telling combination of lachrymose fare and hard economic astuteness: they led the way in the signing of articles, the use of copyright, and the cultivation of advertising on a large scale . . . ."[107]

The active participation of women in these enterprises has been well-documented.[108] Cincinnati's periodical establishment was no exception to this rule. In 1825, the *Cincinnati Literary Gazette* announced that "Our best correspondents have been of the gentler sex . . . ."[109] And as early as 1828, a literary periodical appeared, devoted specifically to women's interests, and edited by a woman, Mrs. J. L. Dumont. This was the *Literary Parterre and*

---

[105]Gerda Lerner, "The Lady and the Mill Girl: Changes in the Status of Women in the Age of Jackson" (1969), reprinted in Lerner, *The Majority Finds its Past: Placing Women in History* (New York: Oxford University Press, 1979), pp. 25-6.

[106]The *Ladies' Magazine* was later to become *Godey's Lady's Book*. Mott, *American Magazines*, I, 348-51.

[107]Ann Douglas, *The Feminization of American Culture* (New York: Knopf, 1977), p. 229.

[108]*Ibid., passim.*

[109]*Cincinnati Literary Gazette*, III (Oct. 29, 1825), p. 278.

Ladies' Magazine.[110]

The *Literary Parterre* was the first ladies' magazine to be published in Cincinnati. It failed quickly, but was succeeded by the *Ladies' Museum and Western Repository of Belles Lettres* in 1830. The *Museum* merged into the *Mirror* in 1831, and the *Mirror* in turn survived until 1836. But neither the *Museum* nor the *Mirror* was edited by a woman, though both appealed to women's interests and printed contributions from women. Male management of female concerns would be the pattern hereafter.

The *Cincinnati Mirror* may be called Cincinnati's first successful women's periodical, although it was not exclusively female in appeal or influence. This eight page paper appeared once every two weeks (at first; in 1833 it became a weekly); a year's subscription was very cheap indeed at $1.50 in 1831. It was edited by William Davis Gallagher, later with the help of Thomas H. Shreve and James H. Perkins, all respectable literary figures. Its original motto was "A Voice in the Wilderness!"

The aim of the *Mirror* was to instruct. It featured historical accounts, character sketches, excerpts from famous works, essays, reviews, literary notices, and occasional short stories and poetry, while also publishing news of local social and cultural events, like weddings and lectures. The intent of all this was to produce a literary periodical "nearly if not quite equal to any issued from the eastern press."[111]

The *Mirror* promoted a specific idea of woman's sphere. This is exemplified in a letter from Miss Beecher (probably Catherine) on "Female Influence," wherein the author argues that women must play a unique role in a world no longer governed by force but by reason: "the voice of reason and affection may ever convince and persuade," and woman in particular "has already received from the hand of her Maker those warm affections and quick susceptibilities, which can most surely gain the empire of the heart." In her moral and affectional capabilities, woman was "a purifying and blessed influence."[112]

Social limits would not restrict but enhance woman's influence. This

---

[110]*Saturday Evening Chronicle of General Literature, Morals, and the Arts*, Feb. 23, 1828.

[111]John H. Wood, "To Patrons and Others," *Cincinnati Mirror*, October 1, 1831.

[112]Miss Beecher, "Female Influence," *Ibid.*, Oct. 27, 1832.

influence would be exerted outside the marketplace and the political forum, in the home, in the church, and now in the press:

> Since it is neither desirable nor practicable for females to enter the learned professions, the only plan to which they can resort for the attainment of mental equality with men, is—to write. The press is open to all, and no branch of knowledge is beyond the vigor of female intellect. . . . Such a cultivation of mind will infallibly create a distaste for frivolous pursuits, banish the love of ornament and flippant affectation.[113]

The *Mirror* promoted the cultivation of women's sensibilities, but eschewed sentimentality. Its combination of general knowledge, brief moral didacticism, and polite literature, with a format more newspaper than magazine proved appealing, and in its first six months of publication its circulation climbed from an initial 800 to over 2000.[114]

The *Mirror* failed in 1836. It was followed by the *Family Magazine* (1836–1841), a stereotyped reissue of a New York publication; the *Western Lady's Book*, which printed just two issues in 1840; and the *Ladies' Repository and Gatherings of the West* (1841–1876), a production of the Western Methodist Book Concern, which combined literary and religious interests with an appeal to women. These all embraced the philosophy of woman's sphere.

This philosophy was pervasive, at least among the middle and upper classes, in Jacksonian America. The indignation with which the Democratic press dismissed attacks on Rachel Jackson's character and reputation, for example, signifies a recognition of the special sphere of women's lives—theirs is not the world of politics, or war, or finance. The following verses by L. J. Cist, son of Charles Cist, the newspaper conductor and census-taker, summarize this sentiment:

> Where lieth woman's sphere? Not there,
> Where strife and fierce contentions are;
> Not in the bloody battle field,
> With sword and helmets, lance and shield;

---

[113]Ex-Mutator, "A Scheme for the Advancement of Female Power," *Ibid.*, Dec. 10, 1831.
[114]*Ibid.*, March 31, 1832.

Not in the wild and angry crowd,
Mid threat'nings high, and clamors loud;
Nor in the halls of rude debate
And legislature, is <u>her</u> seat.
* * * * *
What, then, is "woman's sphere?"—The sweet
and quiet precincts of her home;
Home!—Where the blest affections meet,
Where strife and hatred may not come!
To bless—in every stage of life,
As MOTHER—DAUGHTER—SISTER—WIFE!

Yet this was not to deny woman power: her power was moral, and all-pervasive, rather than political or commercial:

All potent still, for good or ill,
Hath been the force of woman's will.
And mightier, with each added year,
Grows WOMAN's POWER IN WOMAN's SPHERE![115]

The power of woman springs from "a degree of sanctity thrown around the female character that makes the very name of woman a kind of spell, to bring the blushes of shame to the cheeks of the profligate." Her mere presence banishes vulgarity and profanity. And this moral force affects every man of woman born: "Thus, from infancy to manhood, from the cradle to the grave, over the enthusiasm of youth, as well as the sternness of age, woman exerts an almost unbounded influence."[116] Hence it was fitting that the motto of the *Western Lady's Book* should read, "The Stability of our Republic, and the Virtue of her Institutions, is with the Ladies."

The intent of these periodicals was overtly to refine female sensibilities. In the west, these periodicals were particularly moralistic—the Methodist *Ladies' Repository* is a good example—unlike eastern periodicals, which were more belletristic and commercial. This didactic sobriety may be attributed to a provincial imitativeness in relation to the east; it may also have sprung from an intimation of the need for moral stability in a

[115]L. J. Cist, "Woman's Sphere," *Cincinnati Miscellany*, I (April, 1845), p. 235.
[116]D. W., "Woman's Sphere," *Ladies' Repository*, I (Feb., 1841), pp. 38-9.

perceived as crude and volatile.

The mass appeal of these women's periodicals indicates a large body of western women who aspired to the fashionability and respectability associated with the east and the upper class. Hence literature published in these journals would always be referred to as polite. Subscription to a family magazine, or a children's or parlor magazine, would likewise be perceived as a badge of refinement.

As a means of popularization of social status and respectability, women's periodicals succeeded for social and not literary reasons. The longevity of magazines like the *Ladies' Repository* and in the 1850s *Moore's Western Lady's Book* is proof of the persistence of a sense of regional inferiority, and signifies that this mute acknowledgment of inferiority was more realistic than the more numerous and more vocal claims to parity. The polite lady's magazines dealt more effectively with popular western attitudes and aspirations than the more ambitious western literary journals.

General Knowledge

Just as the goal of enforcing moral sentiment through polite literature was invoked by more than exclusively literary periodicals, so was the goal of spreading general knowledge common to virtually all periodicals. Thus the opening address of the *Western Monthly Magazine* promised "to promote the cause of virtue, and elevate public sentiment"; and two paragraphs later declared,

We would promote the cause of science and useful knowledge. We invite the laborers in this wide and noble field, to enrich our pages with the results of their researches. We appeal to the patriotism of all who desire to advance the best interests of their country.[117]

The joint appeal to virtue, science, and patriotism was characteristic of early periodical ventures. The motto of the *Chronicle* was "Knowledge is the Soul of Freedom." The second motto of the *Cincinnati Literary Gazette* read simply, "Knowledge is Power."

[117]James Hall, "To the Reader," *Western Monthly Magazine*, I (Jan., 1833), pp. 1-2.

This spread of knowledge was intended to be serious. The preface to the third volume of the *Hesperian* announced that "We aim to inform, more than to amuse."[118] This belief in the popularization of knowledge may have been a mark of high-minded patriotism, but it was not successful as science, just as it had not been successful as theology; and it was not successful as commercial literature.

More will be said of specifically scientific periodicals in the next chapter. But inasmuch as literary periodicals were devoted to the spread of interesting and useful knowledge, they were failures. Despite claims to serious instructional intent, the brief items presented were in fact more amusing than informative. And, eventually, the attempt, and even the avowal to attempt to instruct in scientific matters ceased to be a feature of the average journalistic venture.

There were two relatively successful "general knowledge" periodicals. These were Charles Cists's *Cincinnati Miscellany* and a monthly entitled the *American Pioneer*, associated with the Logan Historical Society. Cist's *Miscellany* was a compilation of the most interesting articles from his weekly *Western General Advertiser* and ran for a year and a half, from October, 1844, to March, 1846. Mostly written by Cist himself, the *Miscellany* is eminently readable, and a valuable source for historical information. Its chief interest, however, as its title suggests, is as a digest of miscellaneous interesting information, not as an organ of enlightenment. The *American Pioneer*, on the other hand, was written by contributors. It was devoted to chronicles of the early settlement of the old Northwest, and its intent seems more to have been substantiating a claim to a glorious heritage and bolstering the status of the older families in the region than spreading genuinely historical knowledge. It too lasted a year and a half, and also contains some information interesting to the historian.

Conclusion

In terms of stated intentions, most literary periodicals were failures. The more ambitious the ideals advanced, the more sure the journal

[118]William D. Gallagher, "Preface," *Hesperian*, III (1839), iii.

seemed of embarrassment. The most successful ventures were the most commercial—the ones that appealed most to sentiment, and the ones that cost least. That this was so is not surprising.

What is surprising is the persistence with which promoters continued to found magazines. As early as 1824, the *Literary Gazette*'s P. quipped,

> For now each dull poetic dunce,
>   Who thinks his fame eternal
> Because he wrote a sonnet once,
>   Must start a Monthly Journal.[119]

Why were early western magazinists so eager to establish commercial failures?

One answer to the question "Why" is simply "Why not?" The motto of Paul Guthrick's *Cincinnatian* read "Shall we not try? We may as well try. There can be no harm in trying." A literate group of gentlemen with leisure time may as well publish a literary journal. The *Semi-Colon* was such a journal—more of a hobby than a magazine. Likewise were the student journals—the *College Mirror* (1839), the *Western Mirror* (1844), and the *Woodward Miscellany* (1844).

But other than these casual attempts on the part of the early "leisure class," there were more serious attempts. These were of two sorts: the altruistic (or idealistic), and the moralistic. The altruistic strain in periodicals sought to spread enlightenment, to arouse an interest in serious scientific or literary effort, or to generate a profound indigenous literary culture. The moralistic strain sought to reinforce social or religious attitudes in what was perceived to be a context of volatile change.

Both idealistic and moralistic strains of thought were couched in a rhetoric of patriotism—regional or national—and public service, at least initially. But as time passed, commercial viability became more obviously the enemy of these high-minded magazines, which tended to avoid advertising, to print unpaid and unsigned articles, and to rely on a like-minded public-spiritedness on the part of readers and contributors. These magazines were not only non-commercial, they were virtually anti-commercial.

[119]P., "The Age of Magazines," *Cincinnati Literary Gazette*, I (Feb. 28, 1824), p. 72.

Unfortunately, attitudes in Jacksonian America were not non-commercial. There was no mass readership to support such altruistic—and often poorly written and worse managed—ventures. Many people were willing to sign a subscription list, to be sure, but constant complaints of non-payment indicate that few were willing to pay money to be enlightened or refined.

Magazines that were successful found some way of exploiting popular attitudes. Women's magazines appealed to religious sentiment, to a sense of woman's sphere, and to the image of the lady to attract readers. The popular weekly *Great West* offered illustrations and exciting fiction at a low price.

That commercial success determined magazine success does not imply an economic determinism. That certain magazines met with commercial success was due to popular approbation, not to any impersonal "Market." Commercial success was attitudinal.

It is interesting, then, that magazinists tended to go on assuming that the public would support attempts to create a "serious" western literature, or that a mass readership would welcome journals devoted to instruction in interesting and useful knowledge. These expectations were based on the assumption that a rational populace, a free rational populace released from bondage to superstition, would be anxious to devote time and money to scientific and literary endeavors, rather than to mere entertainment. These expectations were also based on uncritical self-confidence in the worthiness of ventures often quite unworthy.

But commercial success greeted the most moralistic and, to contemporary tastes, the most elitist periodicals, namely the ladies' magazines. Why was this? One surmise is that these women's periodicals offered a reassurance to westerners anxious over social legitimacy, and that they also appealed to women's sense of importance as a moral force and their sense of superiority in affectional sensibility.

Ultimately commercialization of the press did not improve literary content. In my opinion, the best of these periodicals were commercial failures—the *Western Monthly Magazine*, the *Western Literary Journal and Monthly Review*, and perhaps the earlier *Cincinnati Literary Gazette*—and certainly not the *Ladies' Repository*, although that periodical did have its charm. Nor did commercialization lead to the rule of the common man—editors of commercial magazines tended to be just as firmly rooted in the social elite as their professedly elitist rivals, who sought to improve popular taste rather than exploit it.

What, then, did the so-called Golden Age of Periodicals achieve in the area of literary publications? Nothing less than a popular culture embedded in a print communications network. This network was characterized by the development of formats and formulae effective in reaching a wide readership, whether of the general public, as in the case of popular literary periodicals, or of a particular religious group. This network was posterior to the shaping of literary tastes and religious institutions. It was more conservative than revolutionary or even progressive, then. It tended to reinforce religious, moral, and social attitudes rather than to reshape them. It tended to be operated by a conscious elite—indeed a clerical elite in the case of religious periodicals—even though it relied on "the people" for financial support.

This communication network was itself a crucial aspect of popular literary culture and popular religion. In a post-traditional nation, where political authority rests on public opinion, and where the metaphor of the political system is applied to religion and culture in general, it is essential that "leaders of public opinion" have access—normal and frequent access—to their public, be it Methodist or western, youth or women. And in nineteenth-century America, the periodical became the regular and frequent channel of access to public opinion.

CHAPTER VI

The Press, Science, and the Professions

If truth is simple and obvious, why are we so ignorant and consequently miserable? . . . we too much desert the book of nature, which is present to our senses, and strive to realize phantoms which only exist in imagination.

—Plain Sense[1]

The sciences and useful arts, which may be ably supported by popular disquisition; and many branches of that knowledge, which are now buried in ponderous volumes, or concealed in the jargon of foreign idioms, may be emphatically made to be, knowledge for the people.

—James Hall[2]

Western Museum—this evening Mr. Dorfeuille will lecture on the 7th order of birds, (GRALLE) or WADERS; after which the NITROUS OXIDE will be administered.

—Advertisement[3]

The years following the American Revolution witnessed an explosion of interest in popularizing scientific knowledge. The number of scientific journals increased rapidly, even though failures were common. Across the nation, throughout this period, a scientific journal's chances of lasting five years were under fifty percent. And editors were aware of the

[1]Letter of Plain Sense, *Liberty Hall*, May 13, 1812.
[2]James Hall, "To the Reader," *Western Monthly Magazine*, I (Jan., 1833), pp. 3-4.
[3]Advertisement in *Cincinnati Literary Gazette*, I (Feb. 28, 1824), p. 71.

likelihood of failure.[4] Why were they so persistent?

One contributing factor was a sense of patriotism. Americans were eager to prove their competence to Europeans. Likewise, westerners were anxious to demonstrate that, even though they were inferior in refinement, their powers of raw observation were equal to any in the world.

But beyond these superficial motives was a faith in reason and in the people. Knowledge that was once arcane because rooted in superstition and social corruption could be rendered intelligible to the common man. In the new Republic, reason had conquered tradition and superstition; blindfolds had been removed, and eyes could now be trained on the book of nature. Nature's truth is simple. All men can understand it.

This faith in popular enlightenment was pervasive. It influenced the foundation of early medical and agricultural journals; it informed early movements for popular education; and it encouraged the establishment of institutions like the Western Museum, dedicated to mobilizing popular interest in nature and natural history. But the Museum eventually resorted to administering laughing gas after lectures to encourage attendance. Popular education became the public school system, justified by reinforcement of moral values, not refinement of intellectual capabilities. And medical and agricultural periodicals withdrew from appeals for a broad readership, and concentrated instead on those sub-groups actively engaged in medical practice or agricultural innovation.

Popularization of enlightenment ended either in professionalization or in quackery. Popular medical knowledge, for example, came to mean little more than familiarity with patent medicines or a passing interest in phrenology. Other forms of knowledge were of interest only as they might assist in improving commerce, manufactures, or agriculture. This interest converged with regional and local boosterism, enhancing descriptions of the "rise of the west."

The rationale behind scientific periodicals was, then, a mixture of faith in enlightenment, commitment to democracy, and a sense of national or regional patriotism, usually linked with material improvements. In other

[4]Donald B. Beaver, "Altruism, Patriotism, and Science: Scientific Journals in the Early Republic," *American Studies*, XXII (Jan., 1971), pp. 6-7.

words, scientific magazinists believed that truth was discoverable by reason, that reason was available to all men, and that scientific truth could be applied to processes like agricultural production or medical treatment to advance the welfare of man, the nation, or the region. But as time went on, the advance of reason and democracy became suspect. This development is quite apparent in agricultural journalism.

Agricultural Journals

Interest in agricultural improvements was traditionally limited to an elite of gentleman farmers. These businessmen and professionals (whose main interests and sources of income were generally outside of agriculture) founded learned societies devoted to agriculture and useful knowledge, and these societies printed "Proceedings" or "Memoirs" that promoted innovations in method and produce of little or no interest to the "dirt farmer."[5] This situation changed around 1820.

In 1819, regular American agricultural journalism began when John S. Skinner established the *American Farmer* in Baltimore. Between that time and the end of the Civil War, over 400 agricultural papers appeared in the United States. In 1840, more than thirty periodicals were in circulation, with maybe 100,000 readers; in 1860, there were between fifty and sixty papers with as many as 250,000 readers.[6] Although individual journals rarely lasted more than three years, agricultural journalism itself flourished in early nineteenth-century America.

The first specifically agricultural journal published in Cincinnati was probably more noteworthy for its devotion to the advancement of radical or agrarian democracy. than for its pursuit of agricultural science. This was the weekly *Western Tiller*, established in 1826 by ex-Congressman James

[5]Albert Lowther Demaree, *The American Agricultural Press, 1819-1860*, Columbia University Studies in the History of Agriculture, Harry J. Carman, ed., (New York: Columbia University Press, 1941), pp. 8-9; Margaret W. Rossiter, "The Organization of Agricultural Improvement in the United States," in Alexandra Oleson and Sanborn C. Brown, ed., *The Pursuit of Knowledge in the Early American Republic: American Scientific and Learned Societies from Colonial Times to the Civil War* (Baltimore: Johns Hopkins University Press, 1976), p. 279.

[6]Demaree, *Agricultural Press*, pp. 13, 17-8.

Gazlay. The *Tiller* was sold in 1828 to William J. Ferris, and survived until 1830.

Gazlay was a lawyer by profession, a politician by habit, and a journalist by way of both. His interest in farming *per se* was remote, but his interest in the farmer as citizen was a matter of immediate ideological importance, for Gazlay was an agrarian of the strict sort, associating true freedom with the independent farmer. Take for example his arguments in favor of agricultural societies: "they bring together citizens in pursuit of one common object, viz. knowledge and liberty . . . . They are the true schools for agriculture, and being such are the true schools for freedom."[7]

The *Tiller* was intended to help western farmers "Keep pace with the improvements of the world. What these improvements are they can learn more effectually by a public journal than any other channel."[8] The press was the ideal means for keeping the farmer, the backbone of republican society, in step with the march of progress of agricultural science. The press was the vital link between science and the common man, between Enlightenment and Democracy.

Gazlay's *Tiller* originally devoted as much time to partisan politics as to agriculture. But, to be sure, the spread of agricultural science remained the key element in its program. As early as 1826, Gazlay offered to give up politics in return for broader support of a strictly agricultural *Tiller*.[9] In 1828, he sold the paper to William J. Ferris, who ignored politics to concentrate on farm information and proceedings of agricultural societies.

Despite its almost utopian image of democracy and the farmer, the *Tiller*'s agricultural material was very tame. It consisted mostly of practical advice on matters like crop rotation,[10] or impractical advice on fanciful projects like silk culture, long a fantasy of the gentleman farmer.[11] The *Tiller* also participated in the campaign for internal improvements, arguing especially for increased navigation in the west, a stance common

[7]*Western Tiller*, Sept. 8, 1826.

[8]"To the Public," *Ibid.*, Aug. 25, 1826.

[9]*Ibid.*, Nov. 24, 1826.

[10]James H. Cooper, "Extract from an Essay on Rotation of Crops," *Ibid.*, March 23-30, 1827.

[11]Archibald Stevenson, "The Culture of the Mulberry and the Silk Worm," *Ibid.*, Dec. 22, 1826-March 16, 1827.

among those hoping to enlarge the market for western produce.[12]

The *Western Tiller* is of little interest in terms of its practical effect on agriculture in the Ohio Valley. This is of course difficult to gauge, but was almost certainly negligible, especially when compared with the grandeur of the paper's ambitions. What is of interest is the *idea* of agricultural journalism it espoused.

That idea was to take a science that had hitherto been arcane and make it available to the common farmer. The privileged domain of the elite agricultural society would be thrown open: every agrarian would rival Jefferson himself. And, as the most democratic society was agrarian, so too would agrarian science become democratic. Science and Democracy would be united.

But the ideal failed. This was not because it lacked believers: the relatively long survival of the *Tiller* invalidates any such simple statement. But the ideal was not practical. Science simply did not have that much to tell the dirt farmer in Jacksonian America. The "common man" did not have the resources to experiment with silk culture or Merino sheep or Berkshire hogs or Justus Liebig's chemical approach.

Besides lacking a basis in science, the ideal of popularizing the science of agriculture lacked an institutional framework. Later periodicals would surpass the *Tiller's* success in part because they were associated with agricultural organizations. The *Farmer and Mechanic* (1832-1836) was issued once every two weeks. It was less a scientific than a self-improvement periodical, more practical in its concerns than the *Tiller*, although officially devoted to the interests of the "artisan and agriculturist." It was edited by the Hamilton County Agricultural Society.

The *Farmer and Mechanic* was succeeded by the *Western Farmer and Gardener* (1839-1845). This monthly was supported by a group of wealthy and prominent citizens, among whom were Nicholas Longworth, Cincinnati's largest property holder, and members of the Taft family. Among its most attractive features were lithographs of flowers and plants. After a brief suspension (1842-1843), it was revived by the Horticultural Society of Cincinnati. Eventually it was merged into the *Indiana Farmer*

---

[12]Wm. J. Ferris, "Commerce of the West," *Ibid.*, II (Feb. 5, 1830), p. 185.

and Gardener, and moved to Indianapolis.[13]

These three journals mark three phases in the evolution of agricultural journalism. The first, associated with the 1820s, was characterized by democratic utopianism, based on great expectations of a social and cultural revolution to match the political one wrought by the heroes of 1776. The second, occurring in the 1830s, was more practical, more conscious of its appeal to members of an occupational group, neither as universalistic nor as utopian as the first, even while sharing an optimism in the spread of knowledge. The third phase, centered in the 1840s, was characterized by the same elitism that informed the earlier agricultural societies, and was not concerned with the social effects of the spread of agricultural science.

These three phases involved an evolution in format, in focus, and in intended readership. The shift in format was from weekly to bi-weekly to monthly. The shift in focus was from "science and democracy" to practical knowledge to leisure interest. And intended readership moved from the common man to the middle class to the upper class.

This kind of evolution was shared by many kinds of periodicals. It implied a shift from Enlightenment to Organization, from social reform to social form. This same shift was evident in the history of educational journals.

Educational Periodicals

Cincinnati was the western center for the publication of educational periodicals. This was because Cincinnati had been the leader in educational innovation in the west and in the movement for public schools. And Cincinnati was to be the regional center for the publication of school textbooks.

The first significant educational experiment in Cincinnati was the establishment of a Lancasterian Seminary. This project had been actively promoted in the local newspapers since at least 1812, when a letter was printed in the *Western Spy* entitled "Lancasterian System of Education"

---

[13]Demaree, *Agricultural Press*, p. 16; Charles Cist, "The Western Farmer and Gardener," *Cincinnati Miscellany*, II (July, 1845), p. 61; prospectus of the fifth volume, *Daily Enquirer*, Dec. 9, 1845.

from a correspondent who chose the significant pseudonym "S.[pirit] of Seventy six."[14] The Lancaster Seminary was a visionary proposal—a radically new and enlightened system of universal public education. It was converted into the Cincinnati College in 1819.

Meanwhile a vigorous newspaper campaign for state-supported common schools had begun. In 1816, the *Western Spy* printed a series of letters from "Bacon" entitled "To the Legislature of Ohio" arguing for public schools.[15] The *Spy* at that time was co-edited by Micajah T. Williams, who would later be one of the most important promoters of public education in the state legislature. Williams and Mason, publishers of the *Spy*, had also begun issuing editions of Albert Picket's line of schoolbooks.[16] From that time on, Cincinnati's newspapers—especially the *Spy, Liberty Hall, Advertiser*, and *National Republican*—would be vigorous supporters of public education.[17]

Next to newspapers, the earliest public means of advocating public education was the almanac. The most important figure here was Nathan Guilford who put out *Freeman's Almanack*, also known as *Solomon Thrifty's Almanack*. Guilford, born in Massachusetts and educated at Yale, would be another important state legislator in the cause of public education.[18]

Cincinnati's public schools date from 1829, when the state legislature granted the city a charter for an organized, tax-supported system of common schools. The city was thereupon divided into ten school districts, administered by officers elected from the five wards, who together made up the Board of Trustees and Visitors of Common Schools.[19] In 1837, the city system was absorbed into a statewide organization when the

[14]*Western Spy*, Feb. 2, 1812.

[15]*Ibid.*, Jan. 24, 31, Feb. 7, 14, 21, 1816.

[16]*Ibid.*, Aug. 6, 1817.

[17]William McAlpine, "The Origins of Public Education in Ohio," *Ohio Archaeological and Historical Society Publications*, XXXVIII (Fall, 1929), pp. 438-40.

[18]Edward Alanson Miller, *The History of Educational Legislation in Ohio from 1803 to 1850*, Supplementary Educational Monographs, (Chicago: University of Chicago Press, 1920), p. 8; Richard C. Wade, *The Urban Frontier: The Rise of Western Cities, 1790-1830* (Cambridge: Harvard University Press, 1959), p. 246.

[19]Miller, *Educational Legislation*, pp. 47-8.

legislature instituted the office of state school superintendent.[20] By the 1840s, Cincinnati's public school system was considered a model for other cities to imitate. Charles Dickens, who was impressed by very little in America, was impressed by Cincinnati's public schools.[21]

If the crucial instruments in advocating the establishment of the school system were newspapers, the main forces behind its early formation were educational periodicals and the organizations they served. Both periodicals and organizations postdated the legislative movement to create the school system. But both were instrumental in shaping that system in its formative years.

I have identified nine periodicals published in Cincinnati between 1831 and 1848 devoted specifically to education or the school system. Many of these were ephemeral; the two longest-lived were the *Common School Advocate* (1837-1841) and the *School Friend* (1846-1851). All shared, to some extent, certain thematic concerns.

The most obvious of the intentions of the educational periodical was to advocate public education and the school system. To do this, most periodicals—especially the earlier ones—strived to reach the public, to justify the school system in terms of the public interest, to inform public opinion as to the designs and virtues of public education. As time passed and educational institutions became more firmly entrenched, this role diminished in importance.

Early educational periodicals also sought to promote the cause of learning and of science in the abstract. They espoused a messianic attitude toward knowledge, and reaffirmed the widespread democratic belief in the universal diffusion of universally understandable knowledge. This attitude was inseparable from a belief in the importance of education to republican institutions.

Republicanism in the educational periodicals was always coupled with the diffusion of sound moral principles. Cincinnati's first educational

[20]Sally Harris Wertheim, "Educational Periodicals: Propaganda Sheets for Ohio Common Schools" (Unpublished doctoral dissertation, Case Western Reserve University, 1970), pp. 9-10.

[21]Charles Dickens, *American Notes for General Circulation*, Works of Charles Dickens, National Library Edition, vol XIV, (New York: Bigelow, Brown, & Co., undated), pp. 213-15.

journal, the *Academic Pioneer*, underscored this perceived connection between knowledge and virtue in its first issue:

No maxim in politics is better established, than that if men are to govern themselves, they must have their minds well-informed. They must be individually capable of controuling [sic] their own turbulent and unreasonable desires, and be capable also of giving and receiving instruction, and of submitting cheerfully to reasonable and lawful authority.[22]

The common schools, then, were designed to spread knowledge and moral order; the two were seen as inseparable. Again, this was the message of the *Common School Advocate*:

What, are you not interested in your country's freedom and prosperity? Care you not whether knowledge and intelligence, virtue and peace spread throughout these United States? Or instead of these, that ignorance, and vice, and superstition prevail? . . . If you are a patriot—if you are a philanthropist, you must, you will feel interested in them [the public schools]. They are your country's safeguard—They are your neighbors' only barrier to ignorance and crime. . . . The safety of your property and life lies in the virtue and intelligence of those around you.[23]

So the popularization of knowledge was essential not only to political but also to social stability. Republicanism and morality would stand and fall together with the public schools. "UNIVERSAL EDUCATION" was an "absolute necessity . . . in this great Republic, in order to give permanency to all its valuable institutions, and enable it continually to make advances in respectability, virtue, and happiness."[24] Knowledge, virtue, and happiness were as firmly interconnected in the educational creed as life, liberty, and the pursuit of happiness or liberty, equality, and fraternity had been in different political creeds.

This goal of promoting moral order through the means of public schools was shared by virtually all educators, despite differences in geographical origin and political allegiance. Moses Dawson, for instance, the Jacksonian stalwart, promoted in his editorials "a system of education

[22]Dr. Bishop, "Address," *Academic Pioneer*, I (July, 1831), p. 8.

[23] Edward Deering Mansfield, "What Have I to do with the Common Schools," *Common School Advocate*, I (June, 1837), p. 41.

[24]Nathaniel Holley, "Prospectus," *Universal Educator*, I (Jan., 1837), p. 2.

by which the morals will be improved, the safety of our community promoted, and our valuable institutions perpetuated." In line with Jacksonian political rhetoric, Dawson further contended that "To the bigotted [sic] and aristocratic we cannot conceive of anything more disagreeable."[25]

It is dangerous, then, to quickly conclude that educational leaders acted in terms of class interest. Educational leaders may have "appeared to advocate a type of education which was oriented toward the needs of only one group in society, that leadership group to which those who supported or wrote the journals aspired or already belonged."[26] But the appeals of these educators always invoked_ the public interest. And the ideal of spreading virtue by spreading knowledge and thereby bolstering republican institutions had its roots in the venerable tradition of Republican rhetoric—of the distinction between knowledge and superstition, ignorance and freedom, and liberty and licentiousness. And the rationale of the early educational periodicals mirrored the general ideology of the press as public servant: it would inform public opinion, and public opinion would see to the rest. An educated, professional elite controlled these journals. But, at least initially, this elite was idealistic and public-spirited.

As time passed, educational periodicals tended to become organs for large publishing houses specializing in school books. The firm of Truman and Smith, publishers of McGuffey's Eclectic Readers, issued the *Common School Advocate* (1837-1841) and the *School Friend* (1846-1851), the two most durable of Cincinnati's educational periodicals. The *Western School Journal* (1847-1849) promoted the Sander's School Series. The *Educational Disseminator* (1838-1839) promoted the Picket schoolbooks.[27] These periodicals were assured of having lucrative advertising, and some of them were circulated free to educators.

Educational periodicals became commercialized then. They were freed

[25]*Advertiser*, June 26, 1833.

[26]Wertheim, "Educational Periodicals," p. 142.

[27]Walter Sutton, *The Western Book Trade: Cincinnati as a Nineteenth-Century Publishing and Book Trade Center* (Columbus: Ohio State University Press, 1961), pp. 180-84; Wertheim, "Educational Periodicals," pp. 49-51.

from bondage to public opinion by the independent support of commercial publishing firms. Therefore they sought out an audience of professional teachers and school administrators rather than the attention of the public at large.

After 1840, with the school system firmly established, educational journalism turned more toward advancing and refining educational methods and organization. Periodicals commonly printed plans for school houses, along with advice on curricula and, of course, school books. Historian Sally Wertheim contends that "They presented to their reading public, composed mainly of teachers, school examiners, and others interested in education, very specific, practical ideas and methods, which, if followed, would result in uniformity of practice."[28]

So educational periodicals, like agricultural periodicals, turned away from an earlier idealistic approach to the public at large in favor of a narrower practical approach to an occupational minority. These periodicals also campaigned for the professionalization of teachers. By this I mean that they sought to make teachers a self-regulated autonomous body of specially trained professionals.[29]

This idea had been present in educational journalism from the start. In 1831, the *Academic Pioneer* argued that "As medical men are the best qualified to judge of medical science, and the treatment of disease; so men engaged in teaching are the best qualified to judge of the most proper system of popular education, and the best modes of community instruction . . . ."[30] In 1837, the *Common School Advocate* contended that "the teacher's employment should be made as honorable and as separate as the physician's, the divine's, or the lawyer's."[31] So popularization of knowledge, it was argued, justified and required professionalization.

The teachers' association was a creature of Jacksonian America. Cincinnati's first teachers' association was founded in 1821. This was the

---

[28]Wertheim, "Educational Periodicals," p. 105.

[29]*Ibid.*, pp. 80-94.

[30]Rev. C. B. McKee, "Address to the First Anniversary Meeting of the Western Academic Institute and Board of Education," *Academic Pioneer*, I (July, 1837), pp. 3-4.

[31]Edward Deering Mansfield, "Teaching Made a Profession," *Common School Advocate*, I (June, 1837), p. 41.

second such organization ever founded in the United States.[32] But this association was short-lived.

In 1829, an Academic Institute was founded in Cincinnati. This held a convention of teachers from throughout the west in 1831, and out of this convention there emerged the Western Literary Institute and College of Professional Teachers. By 1840, this organization included representatives from eighteen states throughout the south and west.[33]

The stated goals of the Literary Institute were as follows:

1st, the production of a proper feeling on the part of the public with regard to education.

2nd, the elevation of the profession of teaching to its proper rank among the professions.

3rd, the connection by acquaintance and friendly intercourse of teachers and all interested in education.

4th, the collection of facts relating to education.

5th, the arrangement and digestion of these facts, so that from them general principles may be drawn, and the true science of education gradually developed.[34]

The goals of the Literary Institute, then, were part political, part professional, and part scientific.

In line with the public nature of its mission, the Literary Institute counted among its members not only prominent educators like John and Albert Picket, William Holmes McGuffey, Nathaniel Holley, and Calvin Stowe, but also leaders of public opinion like Charles Hammond and Edward Deering Mansfield, and religious leaders like Archbishop John Baptist Purcell, Alexander Campbell, and Presbyterian Joshua Lacy Wilson. Mansfield recorded that the involvement of "gentlemen of science and general reputation, who had weight in the community," was essential in promoting the cause of public education itself. After that cause was won, an exclusive association of professional teachers replaced the

---

[32]Henry A. and Kate B. Ford, *History of Cincinnati, Ohio* (Cleveland: L. A. Williams, 1881), p. 198; McAlpine, "Public Education," p. 441.

[33]Allen Oscar Hansen, *Early Educational Leadership in the Ohio Valley*, American Education: Its Men, Ideas, and Institutions, Lawrence Cremin, ed., (1923, reprinted New York: Arno Press and the New York Times, 1969), pp. 13-6, 101-6.

[34]Transactions of the College of Teachers, 1840, quoted in Hansen, *Educational Leadership*, pp. 13-6.

Literary Institute.[35]

This professionalization of teachers' organizations coincided with what I have called the commercialization of school journals—namely their turn from public advocacy to institutional promotion, advertising school books, and other things of little or no interest to even the educated layman. Here it will be useful to run through the chronology of educational journalism.

Educational journalism began in the United States in 1811, when Albert and John W. Picket established the *Juvenile Monitor, or Educational Magazine* in New York. This was a short-lived quarterly. It was succeeded by the *Academician* (1818-1820), also edited by the Pickets.[36] By 1831, they had migrated to Cincinnati. There they founded the first educational periodical in the west, the *Academic Pioneer*.

The *Pioneer*, intended as a monthly, published only two numbers—in July, 1831, and again in December, 1832. In effect it did little more than publish the transactions of the Western Academic Institute, predecessor of the Literary Institute. But its intention was anything but narrowly organizational.

The *Pioneer* appealed to "the intelligence, penetration, and enterprise of our fellow citizens."[37] It hoped to disseminate information on "all that may relate to physical or moral science."[38] And it claimed expectations no less than millennial: "Wars, bloodshed, tyranny and oppression, shall soon be blotted from the catalogue of human evils, and be mentioned only to be detested, or to swell the paean of triumph for a happy deliverance."[39]

The *Academic Pioneer* was enthusiastic in its espousal of the public aspects of education. It appealed to the public at large. It proclaimed public edification as a goal. And it envisioned as the result of education the

[35]Edward Deering Mansfield, *Personal Memories, Social, Political, and Literary, with Sketches of Many Noted People, 1803-1843* (Cincinnati: Robert Clarke & Co., 1879), pp. 267-68.

[36]Frank Luther Mott, *A History of American Magazines, 1741-1905* (Cambridge: Harvard University Press, 1930), I, 148.

[37]"Prospectus," *Academic Pioneer*, I (Dec., 1832), p. 27.

[38]*Ibid.*, p. 26.

[39]*Ibid.*, I (Dec., 1832), p. 27.

perfection of the body politic. Its appeal was to enlightenment and social reform. And it quickly failed.

The *Academic Pioneer* was succeeded by the *Western Academician and Journal of Education*. The *Academician* was also edited by the Pickets and devoted to the interests of the Western Literary Institute. And its goals were also social, but less visionary, more conservative:

> . . . The objects are, to aid in giving tone & character to the public mind; to create a taste for scientific attainments; to build up a strong rampart about our country, by the introduction of a manly and vigorous education diffused among the people, that they may know how to estimate rational liberty, as well as to preserve it.[40]

The underlying assumption was that "a sound education, both intellectual and moral, is the best safeguard of a republican government."[41] The notion of education is as a rampart and a safeguard of rational liberty, a conservative measure.

Not too much should be made of the difference in tone between the *Academic Pioneer* and the *Western Academician*. Both were short-lived journals, and while the *Academician* was more substantial, neither betrayed a radical approach to educational journalism. Both showed a strong tendency toward being house organs of the Western Literary Institute, even while espousing a visionary attitude toward education.

The *Western Academician* ceased publication in February, 1838. But meanwhile a new educational periodical had begun publication. This was the *Common School Advocate*, edited by Edward Deering Mansfield, with the assistance of Lyman Harding of Cincinnati College and Alexander McGuffey of Woodward College.

The *Advocate* marked a departure in educational journalism. It was only eight pages long, and was distributed free to professional educators throughout the south and west. While it was not opposed to organizations like the Literary Institute, its primary affiliation was with a publishing house.

The *Advocate* espoused the same attitude toward the social importance of education as earlier periodicals. Mansfield asserted that the common

---

[40]John Picket, "Editor's Notice," *Western Academician*, I (March, 1837), p. 4.
[41]*Ibid.*, p. 3.

schools "are at once the <u>sources and the guardians of freedom</u>," and that "the good order and happiness of society are secured or lost, according to the character of the common schools."[42] But the format of the *Advocate* betrayed a withdrawal from the forum of public opinion. It was not designed to appeal to the general public.

The readership of the *Advocate* consisted of professional educators. And content was geared toward an audience of specialists. The *Advocate* promised

to show the want and necessity of well-qualified teachers—to point out the defects in the prevailing systems of instruction, and the evils from bad school government—to suggest remedies for these defects in teaching and government—to recommend proper school books—to describe the wrong structure and location of schoolhouses, and to suggest plans for their improvement . . . .[43]

These practical items were intended for an audience of professionals, not the general public. By 1840, the *Advocate* had shrunk to four pages. In substance it was little more than an advertising circular for McGuffey's readers.

After 1840, educational periodicals were almost strictly professional. The layman, the outsider, would find little of interest, and no direct appeal was made to her or his attention. The idea of educational journalism had shifted from public to professional.

I should underscore that it was primarily the *idea* of educational journalism that changed. The *Academic Pioneer* and the *Western Academician* did not have large popular followings, although they did aspire to wide readership. And they did not print material substantially more popular than later periodicals. But they did perceive a need to communicate with and to inform public opinion, and they did affirm the appropriateness of that need. Later journals were more complacent.

One reason for this inattention to public opinion was the success of proponents of public education. In 1837, a statewide public school system was provided for. The legislative battle of 1837 had sparked a tremendous

[42]Edward Deering Mansfield, "Objects of this Paper," *Common School Advocate*, I (Aug., 1837), p. 55.

[43]"Notice," *Ibid.*, I (Jan., 1837), p. 1.

outburst of journalistic activity. In the first three months of that year, three periodicals were launched: the *Universal Educator*, the *Common School Advocate*, and the *Western Academician*. Of these, however, only the *Advocate* survived more than a year, and that was as a specialized journal with a professional readership and the backing of a publishing house.

The success of the *Advocate* implies the second reason for the shift away from public educational journalism. This was the fact that such ventures simply were not commercially viable. Too few citizens were willing to contribute to such ventures.

But educational journalism was in itself atypical of public journalism. For even the most visionary educational periodicals did not propose to enlighten the public themselves; rather they promoted a system of enlightenment beyond themselves. In this, they differed from agricultural periodicals, which were intended to promote science single-handedly, without the aid of educational institutions. The educational press saw itself as a secondary aid, not the primary instrument for attaining the benefits to society it claimed would accrue from education.

But even with this exception in mind, we can still discern an evolution from enlightenment to organization and professionalization. This evolution is also visible in medical journalism, though in a more complex and problematical pattern.

Medical Journalism

The history of medicine in the early nineteenth century is most easily described in religious terms. There were orthodox physicians, with a creed of blood and purgation, led by the great Enlightenment thinker Benjamin Rush. And there were heretics, disciples of Sylvester Graham and Samuel Thomson, or Spurzheim and Gall, or Mesmer, who believed in theories which we are prone to consider exotic, but which were actually quite popular—animal magnetism, phrenology, botanic and eclectic medicine, hydropathy, and homeopathy, to name a few of the most prominent. These medical sectarians claimed superiority to the traditional superstitions of the "bloodletters."

At the root of this heterodoxy was the uncertainty of medical knowledge. Theories easily gained legitimacy in times when established theories often failed. As epidemics of cholera and other diseases recurred, and as the helplessness of orthodox medicine was repeatedly underscored, people were more and more willing to try new, confident medicines and to reject traditional treatments.

But since medical knowledge was so uncertain, the arguments for medical systems tended to be less scientific and more political. Sectarians adopted the rhetoric of democracy, labeled conventional doctors aristocrats, and proposed, through patent medicines and simple theories, to make each man his own doctor. The people would be sovereign in medicine as in politics.

The popularization of medicine did not result in enlightenment of the populace. Medical science did not become common knowledge. And, in the passage of time, sectarian physicians became nearly as institutionalized as their conventional brethren. Both branches of the medical profession established colleges and published texts and journals that were increasingly professional rather than public.

The grand medical phenomenon of the age was the patent medicine. This phenomenon, however, was commercial more than scientific. Health became a purchasable commodity, and patent medicines became a mainstay of advertising revenue for newspapers. In short, in medicine, as in other fields of science and learning, popularization broke down into a dialectic of professionalization and commercialization. As a stark formula, this perhaps seems meaningless or chimerical. A discussion of medical journalism, however, will fully bear it out.

I have identified twelve distinct medical journals published in Cincinnati between 1822 and 1848. These represented all schools of thought: botanic or Thomsonian medicine (the *Botanico-Medical Recorder*); eclectic medicine (the *Western Medical Reformer*, later the *Eclectic Medical Journal*); phrenology and animal magnetism (*Journal of the Phreno-Magnetic Society of Cincinnati*); and a host of more conventional journals. Four medical journals, the *Botanico-Medical Recorder*, the *Eclectic Medical Journal*, the *Western Lancet*, and the *Western Journal of the Medical and Physical Sciences*, survived more than five years.

The dominant figure in the early medical history of Cincinnati was Dr. Daniel Drake. Drake was born in New Jersey in 1785, but spent his early childhood in rural Kentucky. He studied medicine at the University of Pennsylvania, then under the spell of Benjamin Rush, whose medical theories have been described as "an almost perfect transfer to medical theory of the principles of Newtonian mechanics . . . ."[44] But Drake's own bent was toward the empirical, and his mentor was Benjamin Smith Barton.[45] Drake would always be more Baconian than Newtonian.

Drake opened his practice in Cincinnati in 1807. Immediately he displayed a staggering affinity for organizational activities. In the next two decades, he was instrumental in founding the Cincinnati Lyceum; the First District Medical Society; the School of Literature and the Arts; the Cincinnati Lancaster Seminary; the Cincinnati College; the Cincinnati Society for the Promotion of Agriculture, Manufactures, and Domestic Economy; the Western Museum Society; the Medical College of Ohio; the Commercial Hospital and Lunatic Asylum; the Cincinnati Eye Infirmary; and the *Western Medical and Physical Journal* . He became a member of the American Philosophical Society, the American Antiquarian Society, the American Geological Society, the Philadelphia Academy of Natural Sciences, and the National Institute for the Advancement of Science. He authored two important treatises, *Notices of Cincinnati* (1810) and *Natural and Statistical View, or Picture of Cincinnati* (1815), which were widely read in the east, and are credited with spreading both his fame and Cincinnati's.[46] He also became a lion in local social and literary circles, and

[44]Henry D. Shapiro, "Daniel Drake: The Scientist as Citizen," in Daniel Drake, *Physician to the West: Selected Writings of Daniel Drake on Science and Society,* (Lexington: University Press of Kentucky, 1970), xiii.

[45]*Ibid.*, xiii-xv.

[46]Emmett F. Horine, *Daniel Drake (1785-1852): Pioneer Physician of the Midwest* (Philadelphia: University of Pennsylvania Press, 1961), pp. 90-109; Henry D. Shapiro, "Daniel Drake's Sensorium Commune and the Organization of the Second American Enlightenment," *Bulletin of the Cincinnati Historical Society*, 27 (Winter, 1969), p. 46; William Henry Venable, *Beginnings of Literary Culture in the Ohio Valley: Historical and Biographical Sketches* (1891, reprinted New York: Peter Smith, 1949), pp. 304-6; Edward Deering Mansfield, *Memoirs of the Life and Services of Daniel Drake, M. D., Physician, Professor, and Author* . . . . (Cincinnati: Applegate, 1860), pp. 184-86; Shapiro, "Scientist as Citizen," xix; Gorham Worth, "Recollections of Cincinnati,

his Saturday evening salons were for a time the focus of Cincinnati's elite. Drake has understandably been called the Benjamin Franklin of the Ohio Valley.

One of Drake's main interests was the promotion of western medical training. But he was to encounter a great deal of frustration in pursuit of this goal. He was a founder of the Medical College of Ohio in 1819, although personal disputes involved in the founding of the College led to a public challenge to a duel by Dr. Coleman Rogers. Despite opposition, the College managed to open, but dissension among the faculty appeared in the first year of operation, and but two years after its founding, the Medical College presented to the public the curious spectacle of an institution expelling its own founder. Drake fought back, and hostility within the orthodox medical profession continued for a decade and a half. John P. Foote would later suggest that "A History of the Medical College of Ohio may, not inaptly, be styled 'A History of the Thirty Years' War' . . . ." He exaggerated but slightly.[47]

The early local conventional medical profession, then, was volatile. But the volatility was the result of personal, not ideological disputes, and the tendency of the profession at large, and especially of its most powerful representative, Daniel Drake, was toward more complete organization as a profession. It was in this milieu that the first medical journals were established.

As early as 1819 Drake had gathered a list of 200 subscribers for a medical journal.[48] But this first western journal was not actually established until March, 1822, when Dr. John Godman began the *Western Quarterly Reporter*. Godman was born in Annapolis, Maryland, in 1794, and apprenticed to a printer at the age of seven. He worked as a printer until 1814, when he undertook the study of medicine, graduating from

From a Residence of Five Years, 1817 to 1821," (1851) in *Quarterly Publications of the Historical and Philosophical Society of Ohio*, XI (Spring, Summer, 1916), p. 37.

[47]Horine, *Drake*, pp. 153-66, 172; Edward Thomson, *Sketches, Biographical and Incidental* (Cincinnati: Swormstedt & Poe, 1857), p. 111; Otto Juettner, "Rise of Medical Colleges in the Ohio Valley," *Ohio Archaeological and Historical Society Publications*, XXII (Fall, 1913), pp. 487-88; John P. Foote, *The Schools of Cincinnati and its Vicinity* (Cincinnati: F. Bradley & Co., 1855), p. 141.

[48]Horine, *Drake*, p. 167.

the University of Maryland in 1818 and moving west to teach at the Medical College of Ohio. In 1824, he returned east, where his career was cut short by an early death in 1830. He was a close friend of Drake, and was considered to be one of the most talented physicians of his time.[49]

The *Western Quarterly Reporter* was a short-lived experiment. In spring of 1826, a more successful venture began when two physicians, Guy W. Wright and James M. Mason, established the *Ohio Medical Repository*. This periodical was taken over by Drake, and became the important *Western Journal of the Medical and Physical Sciences*.[50]

Drake's *Western Journal* was consciously patterned on Benjamin Smith Barton's *Philadelphia Medical and Physical Journal*. Its bent was empirical; its motto was "E Sylvis Nuncius"—a messenger from the wilderness. The goal was to provide a medium for the skilled observation of medical and physical phenomena. Hence most articles were descriptive, and all were written by physicians. In addition, a great deal of space was devoted to lengthy reviews of medical literature. Although Drake apparently penned a great deal of the material published himself, he did solicit contributions from the country at large, even offering the substantial sum of a dollar a page for articles over four pages long.[51] Subsequent periodicals similar to the *Western Journal* in approach were the *Western Medical Gazette* (1832-1835), the *Western Quarterly Journal of Practical Medicine* (1837), and the *Western Lancet* (1842-1927).

The intent of these journals was professional in a strict sense. As Drake himself resolved in the prospectus to the sixth volume of the *Western Journal*, "We hope, the time has now come when the Profession, disencumbered of adverse influences, will co-operate harmoniously in establishing an independent literature . . . ." Toward this end, Drake encouraged contributions from physicians for a readership composed primarily of physicians.[52]

[49]George H. Daniels, *American Science in the Age of Jackson* (New York: Columbia University Press, 1968), p. 208; Horine, *Drake*, p. 173.

[50]Jonathon Forman, "The Medical Journals of the Period, 1835-1858," *Ohio State Archaeological and Historical Quarterly*, XLIX (Oct.-Dec., 1940), p. 364.

[51]Daniel Drake, "Preface," *Western Journal of the Medical and Physical Sciences*, II (Aug., 1828), i-vi, in *Physician to the West*, pp. 184-87.

[52]Prospectus for vol. VI, appended to *Western Journal*, V (1832).

Drake's "professionalism" was enhanced by his zeal for medical education. He argued for medical school training as a prerequisite to state licensing: "a state should acknowledge none as members of the profession, who have not graduated" from such a medical college, and if the states make provisions for such colleges and licensing procedures, they need never worry about the medical profession: "It will regulate itself."[53] Hence the *Western Journal* campaigned vigorously that the local board of health, established in 1826, be composed solely of physicians.[54]

Conventional medical journals were designed to provide a substitute for and supplement to "professional intercourse and conversation."[55] They were also intended to encourage professional behavior. Dr. Thomas D. Mitchell, for instance, published a series of articles on medical ethics in the *Western Medical Gazette* in 1833; and Drake published a famous lecture series on medical education in the *Journal* in 1832.

In addition to observation and professional exhortation, early medical periodicals in Cincinnati were often devoted to western boosterism. The *Western Medical Gazette* encouraged westerners to attend western medical schools.[56] Daniel Drake proclaimed a belief that in the west, through discourse with nature and openness to natural phenomena, man would be freed from the "empire of prejudice" and achieve a second enlightenment.[57] Hence the prevalence of the adjective "western" in the titles of these journals.

In behavior and in rationale, these journals were devoted to the idea of a medical profession. They were written by doctors, edited by doctors, and read by doctors. They claimed for the medical profession a unique competence in matters medical. Drake himself mocked democratization of the medical profession in these terms:

[53]Daniel Drake, "Essays on Medical Education, and the Medical Profession in the United States," *Western Journal*, V (Winter, 1832), pp. 527, 526.

[54]Wade, *Urban Frontier*, p. 299.

[55]"Prospectus," *Western Medical Gazette*, Dec. 15, 1832.

[56]Medicus, "To the Students of Medicine," *Ibid.*, II (Sept., 1834), pp. 237-38.

[57]Drake, "Discourse on the History, Character, and Prospects of the West" (1834), in *Physician to the West*, pp. 241-44; Shapiro, "Drake," pp. 44-5.

Break down the <u>aristocracy</u> of learning and science: give the people their rights: let the drunken and the lazy among the tailors, and carpenters, and <u>lawyers</u>, and coblers, and <u>clergy</u>, and saddlers, and ostlers, now rise to the summit level, and go forth as ministering angels! . . . newspaper abroad their pretended cures; and handbill away the proofs of their murders![58]

Drake criticized not only democratization of medicine, but also the communication strategies associated with this process. He scorned the newspapers and handbills that sought to present medical "information" to the "people."

As early as 1831, a new type of medical journal had appeared in Cincinnati. This was the short-lived *Western Journal of Health.* Appearing twice a month rather than monthly or quarterly, this paper was designed to be read by the public at large. It claimed to treat matters which everyone should know regarding health. This was a step toward the popularization of medical knowledge which presaged the great medical "heresies" of the nineteenth century. The first notable heresy was Thomsonianism.

Thomsonianism was a botanical medical system proposed by Samuel Thomson. He discovered his system, and his own healing abilities, in 1805, when he was a semi-literate farmer. In 1813, he was granted a patent, the first medical patent ever granted. Thus began the age of patent medicine.

Thomson began publicizing his discoveries with the aid of Elias Smith, the Universalist preacher who had begun the first religious weekly paper in America, the *Herald of Gospel Liberty.* Thomson also set up factories to produce the simple medical preparations his system required. One of the largest of these plants was in Cincinnati.[59]

Thomsonianism was a gentle medical system, not at all as rigorous as conventional medical treatment. Its milder nature, coupled with an appeal to democratic sensibilities and relative success in treating cholera during the epidemics of the early 1830s, made Thomsonianism very

[58]Daniel Drake, "The People's Doctors: A Review by 'The People's Friend,'" (1830), in *Physician to the West,* p. 198.

[59]Frederick C. Waite, "Thomsonianism in Ohio," *Ohio State Archaeological and Historical Quarterly,* XLIX (Oct.-Dec., 1940), pp. 323-27.

popular, especially in Ohio. By 1835 it was estimated that virtually half of all Ohioans subscribed to the botanical system. Ohio had become "the most extensive field for Thomsonians in the country."[60]

But the new medical system was greeted with scorn by the educated. The *Chronicle* granted Thomsonianism one virtue: "By resorting to it, those persons who are tired of life and have not the moral courage to cut their throats, may most speedily doctor themselves out of existence . . . ." The new medicine was branded as simply another abuse of the gullibility of an uneducated populace.[61]

Despite opposition, the new medicine achieved popular acceptance and gradually built an institutional framework in Ohio. A bi-monthly *Thomsonian Recorder* was established in Columbus in 1827. This paper later changed its name to the *Botanico-Medical Recorder* and moved to Cincinnati. In 1839, the Literary and Botanico-Medical Institute of Ohio was chartered at Worthington. This college moved to Cincinnati two years later, where it occupied the building that once had housed Mrs. Trollope's Bazaar. Its guiding spirit was Alva Curtis, editor of the *Recorder*.[62]

Thomsonianism, or botanic medicine, claimed a direct appeal to the people. Through efforts at public enlightenment like the *Recorder*, Thomsonianism encouraged "each and every person to acquaint himself thoroughly with all our simple articles as well as their compounds . . . ."[63] In line with this philosophy, the *Recorder* was a short paper—only sixteen pages long—and was issued frequently—every other Saturday—at a low price—$2.00 per annum. Rather than lengthy articles, which conventional medical journals encouraged, the *Recorder* printed brief letters to the editor. Like religious journals, the *Recorder* delighted in presenting evidence of "conversions in the field," along with news of conventions, addresses, and other organizational and educational activities throughout the United States. As a popular and national paper, the *Recorder* claimed that its circulation "far exceeds the subscription to any other medical

[60]*Ibid.*, p. 327.

[61]*Saturday Evening Chronicle*, Feb. 16, 1828.

[62]Waite, "Thomsonianism," pp. 324-26; Juettner, "Medical Colleges," p. 489.

[63]Alva Curtis, "Preface," *Botanico-Medical Recorder*, VI (1837), v.

journal in the United States."[64]

Botanical medicine invoked the political symbols of the American Republic in its appeal to the minds of the people. Alva Curtis claimed that "our papers are taken by patriots and philanthropists, read by them and their families, and handed over to their neighbors . . . ."[65] Thomsonians stated that their opposition to conventional licensing laws was in the tradition of the American Revolution: "We go with the Constitution for equal privileges to all, and will constantly oppose monopolies of privileges, as well as to professions and trades as to bankers and dealers in money."[66] Invoking the image of the Boston Tea Party, Curtis later claimed that "It will be well for the demagogues of Ohio, (to remember) that the blood of that tea party still lives and runs in their own Botanic constituents . . . ."[67] Again, when students of the Botanic College were illegally prohibited from using the Cincinnati Commercial Hospital as a learning facility, Curtis warned his readers that "If the price of Liberty is eternal vigilance, it is the duty of every citizen to watch the progress of every encroachment upon equal rights, and to nip it in the bud."[68]

And, just as the language was political, so was the idea of an appeal to public intelligence based on the analogy of the working of public opinion in a republican political system. Curtis claimed success through this appeal to the public:

Over a large portion of our country, the true practice of medicine, has produced so salutary an impression on the minds of the people, that the bleeder and the poisoner, even when received into families on account of his superior pretensions to science, and the slowly dying popularity of 'the profession,' is not permitted to bleed, poison, blister, freeze, or starve his patient.[69]

The Thomsonians, he claimed, had successfully challenged "the

[64]Curtis, "Preface," *Ibid.,* VI (1838), iii. He claimed over 1000 paid subscriptions.

[65]*Ibid.*

[66]"Doctor Monopoly," Bedford, Ohio, *Intelligencer,* quoted in *Ibid.,* VI (March 24, 1838), p. 208.

[67]*Ibid.,* VI (August 25, 1838), p. 376.

[68]Curtis, "The Ohio Medical College, and the Commercial Hospital of this City," *Ibid.,* X (Feb. 4, 1842), p. 139.

[69]"Preface," *Ibid.,* X (1841-1842), iii.

profession" by appealing to "the people."

But even so, botanic medicine was undergoing a process of commercial and organizational articulation. As time passed, its practitioners would form a body discrete from the populace. Its journals would be written and read largely by these professionals. And its chief "democratic" appeal would become the commercial practice of selling patent medicines through broad advertising campaigns.

The first step in this process was the emergence of sectarian controversy within Thomsonianism. Basically, the movement broke into three factions: the Eclectics, the Physio-medicals, and the True Thomsonians, or Botanics. Each of these established a college in Cincinnati.

The most important of these reform colleges was the Eclectic Medical Institute. Established as the Reformed Medical School of Cincinnati in 1842, the Eclectic Institute was chartered in 1845 when a petition signed by 1100 citizens was presented to the state legislature. In its first three years of operation, the Institute enrolled 428 students—compared with 404 at the Louisville Medical Institute, 255 at the medical department of Transylvania University, and 73 at the Ohio Medical College.[70] Eclectic medicine was, it seems, quite popular.

The guiding spirit behind the formation of the Institute was T. Vaughn Morrow. Born in Kentucky in 1804, Morrow was the first cousin of a former Governor of Ohio, a confirmed anti-slavery man, and a dedicated organizer. In addition to founding the Eclectic Medical Institute, he edited the *Western Medical Reformer*, and served as president of the newly formed National Eclectic Medical Association in 1848.[71]

The Eclectic movement proclaimed that "the practice of medicine should be entirely free and untrammeled, that no General Body, no Association, combination or conspiracy, should have the power to prescribe a certain standard of faith or Medical Creed . . . "[72] But the language here was that of *religious* freedom.

---

[70]Harvey Wickes Felter, *History of the Eclectic Medical Institute, Cincinnati, Ohio, 1845-1902* (Cincinnati: Eclectic Medical Institute, 1902), p. 27.

[71]*Ibid.*, pp. 86-7; Ralph Taylor, "The Formation of the Eclectic School in Cincinnati," *Ohio State Archaeological and Historical Quarterly*, LI (Oct.- Dec., 1942), pp. 279-80.

[72]"Circular Address to the Medical Profession," in Taylor, "Eclectic School," p. 281.

Medical theories were faiths or creeds. Even while arguing for free and untrammeled investigation, however, Eclectic physicians regarded themselves as members of a learned profession. Thus their claim was to parity with conventional physicians, not to the competence of just any individual: "We recognize every enlightened, educated, and honest physician as standing upon the same platform of professional respectability and enjoying the same rights no matter what doctrine he may deem it his duty to adopt."[73] The opponents of the conventional medical profession sought equal privileges, not an end to privilege.

As time passed, Eclectic physicians came to match their brethren in journalism and institutional framework. The *Western Medical Reformer* was like conventional journals in frequency of publication, format, and rationale more than the *Botanico-Medical Recorder*: it was designed for use by the learned few, not the public at large. All sorts of reformed medicine came to insist on specialized training in medical colleges. And, just after the founding of the American Medical Association in 1847, the National Eclectic Medical Association was established in 1848.

There was an intrinsic reason for this kind of institutional specialization. Medical knowledge is neither simple nor easily taught. Most people are either incapable or unwilling to spend much time acquiring medical expertise. And medical theories are not things which can be voted into effect.

Nevertheless, medical heresies were long-lived. This was due to the uncertainty of medical knowledge in the early Republic. This uncertainty was such that medical systems were compared to religious ones in their claims on faith.

Medical heresiarchs invoked patriotism and democracy. But ultimately it seems that medical knowledge had little to do with equality, nationalism, or regionalism, despite hopeful claims that simple truths would be made available to all men.

Ultimately, the most important role of the press in medicine would not be the popularization of medical knowledge. It would be the service of professional training on the one hand, and the promotion of commercial patent medicines on the other. Medicines had been advertised in the

[73]*Ibid.*

Liberty Hall as early as 1811. By 1840, a single New York company was spending $100,000 a year to advertise its line of patent medicines. And in that same year, Cincinnati claimed four patent medicine manufactories, employing a total of ten hands and producing $68,000 of medical goods per annum.[74] Patent medicines were the chief form of popular medicine, and newspaper advertisements were the chief form of popular medical journalism.

Despite the rebellion of medical sectarians against the medical establishment, then, medicine remained for the most part the province of a learned elite. The years 1800-1840 ultimately saw the removal of medicine and science from the public domain to the closed world of the college and laboratory.

Conclusion

Two more examples will conclude this discussion of the professionalization of knowledge in the early Republic. Both involve a journalistic enterprise. The two fields involved are astronomy and law.

Cincinnati experienced a brief infatuation with pure science during the founding of the Cincinnati Observatory. But the actual founding of the observatory was due largely to the enthusiasm of a single man, Ormsby MacKnight Mitchell. A native of Kentucky, Mitchell was educated at West Point, studied law, and then came to Cincinnati, where he entered the elite as the law partner of Edward Deering Mansfield and as a professor at the Cincinnati College.[75]

In the early 1840s, Mitchell delivered a popular series of lectures for the Society for the Diffusion of Useful Knowledge entitled "The Stability of the Solar System." Out of this lecture series arose a movement to set up an observatory in Cincinnati. Mitchell orchestrated this movement, selling 300 shares of stock at $25 a share to fund the purchase of a telescope.[76]

---

[74]Forman, "Medical Journals," p. 361; Charles Cist, *Cincinnati in 1841: Its Early Annals and Future Prospects* (Cincinnati: Charles Cist, 1841) p. 56.

[75]Mansfield, *Personal Memories*, pp. 277-90.

[76]Stephen Goldfarb, "Science and Democracy: A History of the Cincinnati

Mitchell's hopes, idealistic and democratic, proved unfounded. Although designed to be a popular subscription, the funding of the telescope and observatory turned out to rely on the benevolent interest of a very few wealthy investors, men like Nicholas Longworth.[77] And although the observatory was at first open to the public, Mitchell requested in 1852 that it be closed, and devoted solely to scientific research. As Stephen Goldfarb concludes, "Mitchell's own development from the enthusiastic amateur of 1842, affirming the importance of the study of astronomy for the benefit of mankind, to the professional of 1852, who wanted exclusive use of the telescope for scientific purposes, parallels the currents of emergent professionalism in America."[78] The urge to popularize scientific enlightenment quickly yielded to an ideal of science that had little to do with the public.

As part of his earlier campaign to arouse public interest in astronomy, Mitchell had begun a periodical entitled the *Sidereal Messenger*. This attempt to reach the public through journalism passed out of existence after its second year. It had been of more interest to the self-styled man of science than to the average citizen. Journalism was no longer an intimate part of thinking about science.

A similar journalistic venture was the *Western Law Journal*. This was begun after the establishment of the Cincinnati Law School by John C. Wright and Timothy Walker in 1833.[79] Wright and Walker were both prominent lawyers, and would both be judges. Wright eventually became editor of the *Liberty Hall and Gazette*, and Walker authored a popular textbook, *Introduction to American Law*.[80] In 1843, Walker founded the *Law Journal*. It was to last ten years, a life-span that entitles it to be called a success by the standards of its time. But it was a professional journal, not a popular paper, and it was devoted to the interests of an endogenous legal

Observatory, 1842-1872," *Ohio History*, LXXVIII (1969), pp. 173-4.

[77]Walter Stix Glazer, "Participation and Power: Voluntary Associations: the Functional Organization of Cincinnati in 1840," *Historical Newsletter*, V (Oct., 1972), p. 163.

[78]Goldfarb, "Science and Democracy," p. 178.

[79]Foote, *Schools of Cincinnati*, p. 23.

[80]A.G.W. Carter, *The Old Courthouse: Reminiscences and Anecdotes of the Courts and Bar of Cincinnati*, (Cincinnati: Peter G. Thompson, 1880), pp. 122-23.

profession.

The history of scientific journalism in Cincinnati, then, followed a clear pattern. This consisted of a movement in the idea of journalism from an ideal of popularizing hard knowledge to an altogether different goal of serving a learned profession. In terms of its perceived social effect, scientific journalism became an agent of professional privilege rather than an instrument of democratic enlightenment.

This trend was a breaking away from a powerfully charged confluence of the ideas of science, democracy, and patriotism. Early journalists espoused a belief that all men, freed from the shackles of ignorance by the achievement of political democracy, were now able to exercise their rational capabilities in reading the book of nature. They claimed that all men would be able to understand the simple rules by which nature was governed. They believed that the press would help achieve this understanding.

CHAPTER VII

The Press, Individualism, and Reform

Press ideology in the early Republic was shaped by the memory of the American Revolution. It was natural for the press to be seen as the guardian of the great legacy of the Revolution; the established authority of public opinion in the republic of rational liberty. The idea of the press in politics was based on this perceived role as servant to informed public opinion. And, as we have seen, the initial philosophy of the religious and scientific press was similar in its appeal to a wide readership of independent and intelligent citizens.

In practice, however, the mainstream press failed to serve the needs of an independent intelligent readership. In politics, religion, and the sciences, it became instead the servant of powerful organizations. In literature it succeeded only in exploiting an appetite for sensationalism and the conceits of over-refined sensibilities. In any case, the attraction of the newspaper or periodical was non-rational: its authority resided outside the reader's mind and outside the arguments presented: the authority of these public prints resided in the social fact of organization, profession, or majority sentiment. The mind of the individual had not been "unshackled" from social fact by the establishment of political democracy.

As time passed, the ruling idea of the press ceased to be utopian. It became instead commercial and organizational. Political papers became less interested in providing impersonal and impartial political information as a public service while becoming more interested in advertising revenue and partisan organization. Religious and scientific periodicals became less interested in facilitating a broad popular interchange of knowledge and opinion as they became more involved in denominational and professional organizations. Literary periodicals were less interested in refining and enlightening a broad popular readership as they became more concerned with acquiring a commercially viable readership by promoting polite morality and appealing to crude sensations. The press became more commonly perceived as socially and economically conservative. This was true most particularly of the most innovative forms of public prints: penny papers in Cincinnati were, if anything, more conservative than their conventional rivals.

The history of the press in the early Republic, in theory and in practice, presents the interesting paradox of a revolutionary element becoming itself an establishment. By 1848, through an interaction of market competition, technical innovation, and the seemingly inexorable evolution of the idea of democracy, a press establishment characterized by conservatism, majoritarianism, and allegiance to organization had emerged.

The precise nature of this development requires some explanation. What actually became of the idea of rational liberty? And how did the idea of democracy relate to other ideas of enlightenment and individualism? These questions can best be addressed through a discussion of reform papers.

For my purposes, "reform" will include a wide variety of periodicals. I will discuss not only the traditionally regarded reform movements, like anti-slavery, temperance, and labor, but also radical movements, like anarchism, plus others usually not considered reform-minded, like satirical gossip papers. The single element these all have in common is opposition to established values and attitudes.

This section could logically discuss many of the periodicals already dealt with as religious, literary, or scientific. For the sake of clarity, I have arbitrarily excluded these from the category of reform periodicals. Any conclusions drawn from the following discussion will have to bear equally on those other publications, however.

I have identified twenty-seven distinct periodicals as reform periodicals. These range in format from daily newspapers to regularly published tracts. Most of the ventures—twenty in all—involved weekly and bi-monthly publication, however.

In an age of short-lived periodicals, reform journals were among the most ephemeral. Nineteen of the twenty-seven reform journals failed within a single year. Only six lasted more than two years, and of these only two lasted more than five. These six "successful" reform journals were all devoted to anti-slavery or temperance.

Public reaction to reform journals ranged from violent rejection to apathy or bemused toleration. Two papers were the victims of mob violence: the *True Blue and Castigator* and the *Philanthropist*. Almost all were held in some disrepute.

These reform periodicals are, however, among the most interesting products of the early Cincinnati press. At least three editors were of national prominence: Gamaliel Bailey and James G. Birney of the *Philanthropist*, and Josiah Warren of the anarchist *Peaceful Revolutionist, Equitable Commerce Gazette*, and *Herald of Equity*. In general, strong-minded individuals like Bailey, Birney, and Warren controlled these periodicals. The reform press thus almost inevitably focused on the problem of the individual in conflict with the majority in a democratic polity.

Gossip and Satire

One of the most interesting sorts of reform journalism was the satirical gossip paper. These rare papers specialized in criticizing well-known people and accepted fashions, placing the papers outside of and in opposition to mainstream society, even though their chatty intimacy suggests insider status, and even though their criticisms were usually not associated with concrete reform proposals and did not seem to indicate extreme disaffection with established norms. Reaction to these papers was often hostile. As early as 1820, a paper called the *Western Minerva* was suppressed before distribution because it was too disrespectful in its references to local worthies.[1] An even more controversial paper, the *True Blue and Castigator*, was mobbed in 1832.

The *Castigator* was a lively paper in its time. It was published weekly beginning in January, 1832, at a price of $1.50 a year. Within two months it claimed a circulation of over 800, a sizable readership for that time.[2] Its management was somewhat novel, in that its editor concealed his identity behind the pseudonym Nimrod Wildfire. (The editor was actually a young New Englander named Ladd, it seems.)[3] Its motto was a quotation from Shakespeare: "I claim as large a charter as the wind, to blow on whom I please."

The *Castigator* was unrestrained in its criticisms. It attacked causes and concerns as disparate as anti-Masonry and Owenism, the Water Company, unfair pricing, hypocritical ministers, dandies, and pious but sensuous women.[4] In doing so, it occasionally named names. In March, 1832, it accused a bartender named Johnson and an adventurer, Jackson M. Hulse, of planning to bomb its printing office.[5] In its brief career it found time to print pointed criticisms of such local papers as the *Mirror, Chronicle,* and *Gazette.*[6]

The *Castigator* claimed that its course was in the best interest of public morality. Its program was outlined in a poem printed under the editorial masthead in February:

> With ink, and paper, here take my stand,
> To note the follies of this western land,
> The rogue, the hypocrite, and such like trash,
> Shall a'ye receive the tickle of my lash.
> The task be mine, I ask no richer prize,
> Than leave "to shoot at folly as it flies";
> Clip short its wings, and lay the subject bare,

[1]Emmet F. Horine, *Daniel Drake (1785-1852): Pioneer Physician of the Midwest* (Philadelphia: University of Pennsylvania Press, 1961), pp. 142-43.

[2]*True Blue and Castigator*, March 5, 1832.

[3]See Isaac Appleton Jewett to Joseph Willard, Cincinnati, Aug. 16, 1832, in James Taylor Dunn, ed., "'Cincinnati is a Delightful Place': Letters of a Law Clerk, 1831-4," *Bulletin of the Historical and Philosophical Society of Ohio*, X (July, 1952), p. 270.

[4]*Castigator*, April 23, March 19, 1832.

[5]*Ibid.*, March 5, 1832.

[6]*Ibid.*, April 27, March 19, 1832.

Expose to public view, to public stare.
So shall my muse, my humble task fulfill.
And bend its purpose to the public will,
"For with a charter free as any wind,"
I claim a right to puff on all I find.[7]

Several elements make this statement remarkable. First was its simple moralism: the targets of the *Castigator* would be rogues and hypocrites. Second, the weapon of the *Castigator* would be public opinion: "the public stare." And third, the aim of this paper would be to serve the public will. In its appeal to public moral sensibilities, the *Castigator* placed itself well within the guidelines of traditional press ideology.

In its chatty personality, however, the *Castigator* departed from the traditional ideal of an impersonal press. It indulged subscribers, for example, in such unorthodox ways as advertising for prospective husbands and warning away over-solicitous suitors.[8] Eventually it offended someone so seriously that he rushed to the office and gave Nimrod Wildfire a sound thrashing. That evening a mob attacked the office and destroyed the press. The *Castigator* did not resume publication.[9]

The *Castigator* was mobbed because it offended individuals. But it was never revived, probably from a lack of support in the community. Its advertising income must have been very small—paid advertising usually filled less than one page, whereas in established dailies it filled almost three, and very few ads were repeated. Although its material—quite racy for its time—had a fairly wide following, the paper itself was not commercially viable.

In addition, it is undoubtedly true that the *Castigator* offended many citizens. And it is doubtful that the only folk offended were rogues or hypocrites. The paper attacked many of the most respected civic institutions and journals. The fact that its demise was not only not deplored but even mentioned in the conventional press signifies a considerable level of public disapprobation.

[7]*Ibid.*, Feb. 27, 1832.
[8]*Ibid.*
[9]Jewett to Willard, p. 270.

What the destruction of the *Castigator* signifies is the existence of an accepted standard of press behavior in relation to majority opinion. Free expression, as it were, was tolerable only within certain limits. This sense of propriety involved not only social sensibilities (which the *Castigator* offended) but also political and economic interests, as is apparent in the controversy over the anti-slavery press.

Slavery

Cincinnati found itself hard put on the issue of slavery. As part of the Northwest Territory, the Queen City had never permitted slaveholding. Yet it was separated from the slave states only by the Ohio River. Slaveowners frequently summered in Cincinnati, and customarily brought slaves with them. And a great deal of the traffic on the Ohio River—Cincinnati's main commercial artery—involved the produce of the slave economy. Propinquity and common economic interest bred a certain sympathy.

But Cincinnati was also a haven for free blacks—whether escaped or manumitted—and idealistic New Englanders. This was, after all, the city that shaped the consciousness of Harriet Beecher Stowe, that witnessed the critical controversy over slavery at Lane Seminary, that saw the conversion of Salmon P. Chase to anti-slavery principles. This was the adopted home of Levi Coffin, reputed head of the Underground Railroad.

Cincinnatians were bitterly divided over slavery. This local controversy had deep roots. Ohio had passed laws in the first decade of the nineteenth century requiring all resident blacks to post $500 bond, along with proof of freeman status.[10] These strict requirements had been ignored, however. The slavery controversy was apparent in the press, but only peripherally;[11] and as late as 1826, a daily newspaper could take an anti-slavery stance without arousing any considerable animosity.[12]

[10]Richard C. Wade, *The Urban Frontier: The Rise of Western Cities, 1790-1830* (Cambridge: Harvard University Press, 1959), pp. 225-29.

[11]See, for example, letters from "A Friend to the Oppressed Africans" and "A Hater of Duplicity," *Liberty Hall*, May 8, 1815.

[12]*Mercantile Daily Advertiser*, Sept. 8, 11, 1826, quoted articles on the cruelty of slavery, and a eulogy of key abolitionists

In the later 1820's, several trends combined to enhance local racial tensions. The city was undergoing a commercial boom, featuring increased intercourse with the south. Meanwhile, the black population in the city also boomed, rising from four to ten percent of the local population. And this black community was articulate and self-interested, forming a highly visible discordant element. Blacks in Cincinnati dissented from one of the most cherished national traditions by celebrating the anniversary of American Independence on the Fifth of July.

Outspoken opposition to local blacks resulted in 1829 in a movement to enforce the long-neglected black laws. Blacks were given sixty days to put up the $500 bond or leave the city. Riots broke out, and eventually about half the black community left Cincinnati for Canada or other points north. Curiously, there were no accounts of this rioting in the newspapers.[13]   This racial violence was but a prelude to the anti-abolitionist riots of 1836 and 1841. These outbursts would inflame opinion and arouse citizens throughout the nation. And both involved a reform periodical: the anti-slavery *Philanthropist*, founded in 1836 by James Gillespie Birney.   James Birney was born and raised among the well-to-do. The son of a prominent Kentucky planter, he was educated at Princeton, then studied law in the office of Alexander J. Dallas in Philadelphia. He became a distinguished member of the bar in Kentucky, Alabama, and Ohio, and held public office as Kentucky and Alabama state representative and Mayor of Huntsville, Alabama. He was also active in the Temperance movement, the Bible Society, and the Sunday School

[13]Ohio Anti-Slavery Society, *Narrative of the Late Riotous Proceedings against Liberty of the Press in Cincinnati: With Remarks and Historical Notices, Relating to Emancipation* (Cincinnati: Ohio Anti-Slavery Society, 1836), p. 13; Leonard L. Richards, *Gentlemen of Property and Standing: Anti-Abolition Mobs in Jacksonian America* (New York: Oxford University Press, 1970), pp. 34-5; Frank U. Quillen, *The Color Line in Ohio: A History of Race Relations in a Typical Northern State* (Ann Arbor: George Wahr, 1913), p. 32; Patrick Allen Folk, "'The Queen City of Mobs': Riots and Community Reactions in Cincinnati, 1788-1848" (Unpublished doctoral dissertation, University of Toledo, 1978), pp. 17, 45-6; Edward S Abdy, *Journal of a Residence and Tour in the United States of North America, From April, 1833, to October, 1834, 3* vols., (London: John Murray, 1835), II, 382-83.

[14]Betty Fladeland, *James Gillespie Birney: Slaveholder to Abolitionist* (Ithaca, N.Y.:

Birney gradually became more interested in the slavery question. At first he sided with the colonizationists; he read the *African Repository and Colonial Journal*, organ of the American Colonization Society, and in 1832 he accepted an invitation to be an agent for that society. But the more deeply he became involved in colonization efforts, the more frustrated he grew.[15]

In 1834, Theodore Dwight Weld led a body of students at Lane Theological Seminary in Cincinnati in the formation of a society to promote immediate abolition. Birney followed the ensuing controversy between students, the administration, and the community with great interest. Eventually he came to Cincinnati to visit Weld and left a confirmed abolitionist. He resigned his memberships in the Colonization and Gradual Relief Societies and manumitted his slaves, then wrote a public letter explaining his actions and condemning colonization. This letter was circulated throughout the Mississippi Valley in pamphlet form.[16]

Soon after his conversion to immediate abolition, Birney decided to begin an anti-slavery newspaper. His first intention was to publish it in Danville, Kentucky, but concerted public opposition and threats of violence convinced him that it would be impossible to conduct a campaign against slavery anywhere in the south. He decided instead to set up his paper in Ohio.[17]

Birney intended to begin publication in Cincinnati. Again, concerted public opposition and the warning of Mayor Samuel Davies that the municipal government would be unable to protect the paper from mob violence induced Birney to set up the *Philanthropist* in New Richmond, Ohio, some twenty miles outside of Cincinnati. A few months later, in April, 1836, he moved the paper to Cincinnati proper.[18]

The *Philanthropist* was conventional in format. It was a four-page weekly, costing $2.00 per annum in advance, with advertising at the usual

Cornell University Press, 1955), pp. 1-12, 14-37.

[15]*Ibid.*, pp. 38-9, 51.

[16]*Ibid.*, pp. 80-5.

[17]William Birney, *James G. Birney and his Times* (New York: Appleton, 1890), pp. 180-87; Fladeland, *Birney*, pp. 113-22.

[18]Birney, *Birney*, p. 208; Fladeland, *Birney*, p. 133.

rates, although few Cincinnati commercial concerns actually bought space in the paper. Its motto was biblical: "We are verily guilty concerning our brother * * * therefore, is this distress come upon us."

The *Philanthropist* claimed complete openness in its columns. It was to be an organ for the scientific or rational investigation of the slavery question:

> It is our intention to make the *Philanthropist* a repository of facts and arguments on the subject of Slavery as connected with Emancipation. The discussion we invite, and the aid we desire, we are willing to accept from any quarter that will furnish it. To the south, we have offered in our main editorial article today, the free use of our columns, to defend a system which they seem determined to continue . . . .[19]

Thus Birney claimed to be open to all parties.

But he did not try to hide the fact that he was advocating a cause. This cause, however, was not partial or partisan; it was a national heritage, the birthright of all Americans: the cause of freedom, "the principles of the American Revolution."[20] Although open to communications from any quarter, the *Philanthropist* would always promote emancipation.

The newspaper quickly became the organ of the Ohio Antislavery Society. As an organizational periodical, it printed notices and minutes of meetings, and reprinted lectures, editorials from other papers, and reports from the field, much like denominational religious paper. Editorials by Birney appearing in the *Philanthropist* were often reprinted in pamphlet form and distributed. Birney was active in forming anti-slavery societies throughout Ohio, and the *Philanthropist* office was also a repository for all sorts of abolitionist literature, all available for purchase, as an eighteen-foot-long sign on the office's Main Street entrance announced.[21]

When the paper moved to Cincinnati, absolute silence greeted it. Violent, vocal hostility failed to materialize for three full months. In that period the *Philanthropist*'s subscription grew from 700 to 1700.[22] But rapidly in July, opposition would mobilize, and a chain of events

[19]*Philanthropist*, Jan. 1, 1836.
[20]*Ibid.*
[21]*Ibid.*; Birney, *Birney*, pp. 233, 240, 256-58.
[22]Anti-Slavery Society, *Narrative*, pp. 12-4; Birney, *Birney*, p. 221.

ultimately leading to mob action was set in motion.[23]

On the nights of July 12, 1836, a band of thirty or forty men entered the *Philanthropist* office and dismantled the printing press. The night watch did not interfere, although the activities of such a large group of men on one of the city's main thoroughfares could hardly have been inconspicuous. But the press was repaired the next morning, and the next issue of the *Philanthropist* appeared on schedule.[24]

After the initial attack, the *Philanthropist* became a matter of pressing concern to the community. A public meeting was called to meet in the Market House on July 23. The announcement named a committee of local notables to draft resolutions.[25] When the meeting convened, it numbered about 1000 individuals, but was conducted peacefully, even though it had a clear bias against the *Philanthropist*.

The Market House meeting drafted resolutions condemning the anti-slavery paper. It also appointed a committee to meet with Birney, to attempt to persuade him to close down the *Philanthropist*. This committee consisted of some of Cincinnati's most prominent citizens: Jacob Burnet, former United States Senator and Ohio Supreme Court Justice; Josiah Lawrence, president of Lafayette Bank; Robert Buchanan, former president of the Commercial Bank of Cincinnati; Nicholas Longworth, lawyer, merchant, and the largest property-holder in the city; two important ministers, Oliver M. Spencer and William Burke; two wealthy proprietors of the Cincinnati Water Works, John P. Foote and William Greene, both members of the Semi-Colon Club; businessman and merchant David Loring; David Disney, former speaker of both houses of the Ohio legislature; and Timothy Walker, the lion of Cincinnati's legal profession.[26] The *Daily Gazette* described this meeting as "very large and respectable," stressing the applicability of that venerable formula.[27]

---

[23]The events of the riot have been treated in secondary literature. See Daniel Aaron, "Cincinnati, 1818-1838: A Study of Attitudes" (Unpublished doctoral dissertation, Harvard University, 1945), pp. 454-76; Fladeland, *Birney*, pp. 136-42; Richards, *Gentlemen*, pp. 92-100; Folk, "Mobs," pp. 57-147.

[24]*Narrative*, p. 12; Birney, *Birney*, p. 241.

[25]Birney, *Birney*, pp. 241-44.

[26]*Narrative*, pp. 23-7.

[27]*Daily Gazette*, July 25, 1836.

The respectability of this meeting gave credibility to the opponents of the *Philanthropist*. But when the committee met with Birney, he refused to stop publication. On Saturday, July 30, a mob assembled outside the *Philanthropist* office, destroyed whatever it could lay its hands on there, and then, after visiting the house of Birney and others involved in its publication, and finding no one at home, returned to the office, broke up the printing press, and threw its remnants into the Ohio River. The civil authorities did not try to stop this mob.

A reaction against "mob rule" set in immediately. On Monday a call was issued for a meeting the next day, August 2. This notice, posted by "the Friends of order, of law, and the Constitution, having no connection with the Anti-Slavery Society," was signed by such notables as Salmon P. Chase, William Davis Gallagher, and Charles Hammond. This was a group even in respectability to the promoters of the Market House meeting.[28]

The call for the meeting marked the return to public order. The *Philanthropist* resumed publication on September 23. It would be permitted to publish for another five years before it again encountered violent opposition.

In 1841, the *Philanthropist* press was again destroyed with the acquiescence of the same authorities. Gamaliel Bailey, then editor of the anti-slavery paper, placed special blame on the inactivity of the Morgan Riflemen, a militia company under the command of Charles Brough, editor of the *Enquirer*. But in this case, the *Philanthropist* was not the prime target of the mob, as it had been in 1836. The destruction of its press was peripheral to three days of bloody interracial rioting, the result of long pent-up hostility between whites and blacks.[29]

The *Philanthropist* riot of 1836 was the occasion for a great debate on the press. Birney on the one hand based his arguments not on the worth of abolition but on the American tradition of freedom of the press. His opponents in the regular political press, on the other hand, argued for the saliency of the good of the community in press conduct. These arguments

[28]*Narrative*, p. 42; Birney, *Birney*, p. 248.
[29]*Philanthropist*, Sept. 8, 1841; Folk, "Mobs," pp. 212-26; Richard, *Gentlemen*, pp. 122-25.

are of great significance in terms of the evolution of press ideology. Birney's experience in the south had convinced him that slavery was a threat to freedom everywhere. It threatened not only black freedom but the freedom of investigation of the white citizens of northern states. Slavery demanded that "this common sight of the people be restrained, lest her sacred mysteries be profaned by men of 'unclean lips,' and the secret things of her penetralia be exposed by freemen to the rude gaze of a vulgar world."[30] It is interesting that Birney used the metaphor of religious superstition.

Birney urged the leaders of the masses to refrain from violent attack. He urged "violent men" to listen to the "voice of reason." Yet he feared that people would be manipulated by men of power and influence: "Behold the tyrant: he is in arms, because he guesses if people become enlightened, his gains at the end of the year may fall short a few dollars!" Those with vested interests in ignorance feared enlightenment: "You are apprehensive of a change in the sentiments of others, and therefore would destroy the agent that may work it."[31] This agent was, presumably, the *Philanthropist*.

The *Philanthropist* was designed to be an instrument for rational and scientific enquiry. Birney was a firm believer in the ability of the press to enlighten its readers through impersonal scientific transmission of information and opinions. He cited the traditional press ideology in defending his reform publication as a public servant: "The press must be free: free with an enlightened freedom—which seeks the general good . . . . Demagogues and slaveholders may dread its influence and tremble at at its power, but the friends of rational liberty and public virtue will cherish it as the surest safeguard of a free government."[32] This was the traditional ideology of freedom of the press and rational liberty, and it was in fact a conservative ideology. Birney referred to "the freedom of Speech and of the Press" as "those great conservatives of our government."[33] As he described the free press as a conservative power, he also identified a kind

---

[30]*Philanthropist*, Jan. 1, 1836.
[31]*Ibid.*, Sept. 30, 1836.
[32]*Ibid.*, Oct. 7, 1836.
[33]*Ibid.*, Jan. 1, 1836.

of press behavior that directly threatened America's free institutions.

This anti-Democratic press behavior was the equivalent of demagoguery and tyranny. It excited the passions instead of appealing to reason. It exploited the ignorance of the many for the gain of the Few, opposed free investigation of issues, and encouraged intolerance through a policy of journalistic intolerance. As Birney phrased it, "An intolerant press is a sort of moral mob."[34]

Birney credited the general press with great power, but it was power to do evil. He blamed the conductors of the general press for the outburst of mob violence in 1836. His description of their behavior is laden with the symbols of the traditional press ideology: "The largest nomenclature of abusive epithets was ransacked, for language in which to stigmatize the advocates of constitutional right. The freedom of the press—liberty of speech—the right to discuss—were scoffed at, by that portion of the press that was using with most wanton license the rights they denied to others."[35]

But the main assumption of this press ideology was the honesty and intelligence of the people. This was the precondition for conducting an objective public investigation, for it is the people who rule in a democracy, and it is the minds of the people that must be informed. So Birney claimed, necessarily, that the people were on his side: "The people are anxious to hear on the subject of slavery—they eagerly read the antislavery papers; and if we mistake not, they are in fact beginning to see the utter incompatibility of southern slavery with the continuance of northern liberty." But then what about the mob? Was not the "reign of terror" an exercise of the popular will? Birney claimed not: "Its establishment in the city had been "ordered" by the commercial and slaveholding aristocracy of the south, of their kindred commercial aristocracy of Cincinnati . . . ."[36] The people, supposedly, were mere pawns in this game.

But the people did in fact acquiesce in the destruction of the *Philanthropist's* press, even if they did not take an active part. Those civic

[34]*Ibid.*, Nov. 4, 1836.
[35]*Ibid.*, Aug. 5/Sept. 23, 1836.
[36]*Ibid.*

leaders who refused to interfere with the mob were re-elected, most notably the obviously sympathetic Mayor Davies. And the general press was virtually unanimous in its opposition to the *Philanthropist*.

Why did the press conductors, themselves beneficiaries of constitutional protection of liberty of the press, acquiesce in and even encourage the violent denial of this right to one of their brethren? What rationale did they cite for their conduct? The answer is apparent in the course of their least enthusiastic partner, Charles Hammond.

Hammond's *Gazette* was sympathetic to the right of the *Philanthropist* to publish, and Hammond has been credited by historians with great moral courage for his initial support of Birney's paper and his later involvement in the movement to restore order to the city. He did support liberty of the press: in an editorial of July 22, he argued, "Is the freedom of speech and of the press, to be weighed, in the balance, against pecuniary interest? Such was not the judgment of the founders of our Independence."[37] But this courageous statement was issued before the Market House meeting and the mob action.

These events left Hammond in some confusion. The opposition to the *Philanthropist* was not the work of some illiterate rabble: "It is very plain that the work was not the contrivance of that class of men, with whom mobs are generally associated."[38] Rather the mob action seemed to be the result of concert of opinion in the community at large.

Hammond was thus led to question the propriety of Birney's publication:

The abolition movements were wrong in principle, as is every attempt to assert abstract rights against the interests, the feelings, and the present judgment of a country, or a community. When surrounding circumstances so affect the understandings of men, as to preclude the possibility of their being influenced by argument, sound or unsound, it is always worse than useless to press facts or reasonings upon them.[39]

[37] *Daily Gazette*, July 22, 1836.
[38] *Ibid.*, Aug. 2, 1836.
[39] *Ibid.*

What Birney justified in theory, Hammond denied both in theory and in fact. The individual had no right in theory to conduct public investigation against the clearly perceived interests of the community. And in practise such an investigation would be doomed to backfire anyway, since the public will refuse to be persuaded.

It would seem that the courageous Hammond had waffled in a most cowardly fashion. But his conduct seems liberal indeed in comparison to the course of the other political papers, the *Whig*, *Post*, and *Republican*. These had campaigned vigorously against the *Philanthropist*, and had continued to reprint articles from southern papers urging its forceful discontinuance.[40]

Editors claimed that the *Philanthropist* abused the liberty of the press. In terms of traditional press ideology, its conduct was licentious. Thus James F. Conover argued in the *Whig*:

Abolition papers are licentious and demoralizing, and occupy a ground by no means entitling them to legal protection and . . . it is a profanation, when such papers are destroyed by violence, to say that the glorious prerogative of the liberty of the Press has been assailed.[41]

Conover, Hammond, and the rest of the conventional press also claimed to be moral and conservative.

Both Birney and his opponents invoked the traditional press ideology. But there was a crucial difference. Birney claimed the liberty of a minority to discuss freely an issue and to promote publicly a cause clearly perceived as inimical to the interests of the majority by the majority. His opponents claimed the prerogative of a clearly perceived community interest in denying this liberty of discussion. The question was one of minority rights in a majoritarian state.

The *Philanthropist* riot of 1836 does not fit some accepted notions of rioting in Jacksonian America. Gordon Wood, for instance, ascribes rioting to "social disintegration" aggravated by "the ideology of the Revolution."[42] But the anti-*Philanthropist* mob was, if anything, a sign of

[40]Birney, *Birney*, pp. 205-6.
[41]*Ibid.*, Aug. 13, 1836; quoted in Folk, "Mobs," p. 185.
[42]Gordon S. Wood, "Evangelical America and Early Mormonism," *New York*

the strength of the traditional social fabric. It was led by the most prominent men in the community, and received the implicit support of civil authority. It was not the rioters who signified the forces of social disintegration; rather, the rioters were the forces of social integration.

Nor was the rioting prompted by any methodological innovations introduced by the abolitionists. The *Philanthropist* would not become fully integrated into a reform organization until after the riot, and it was not notable for its "effective use of revivalistic and mass media techniques," factors which historian Leonard Richards has indicated were responsible for anti-abolitionist riots.[43] Rather, the *Philanthropist* was a fairly conventional four-page weekly newspaper, distributed only by subscription, and at that to only about 100 people inside Cincinnati. Local abolitionists did not use mass media techniques with anything near the efficiency of conventional editors, and, as the very fact of the riot testifies, they were far less adept at the use of revivalistic techniques than opposing "gentlemen of property and standing."

The *Philanthropist* riot centered around the press. The issue was the extent to which a paper could print opinions contrary to the interests of the community. More than anything else, the riot centered around the idea of the press in a democracy. It was not so important to Cincinnatians that the *Philanthropist* was read in Cincinnati. Few citizens actually read it, and many more were exposed to anti-slavery ideas through local religious papers like the *Presbyterian Journal* and the *Western Messenger* as well as publications from other cities.[44] Nor did the local leaders react strongly to the paper's publication in New Richmond. It was not important that the paper was read in Cincinnati, but it was important that the paper was seen as a Cincinnati product by people outside the city.

The *Philanthropist* was not a local paper. It was mailed to readers throughout the nation, including the south.[45] When its prospectus appeared, demonstrations against and denunciations were recorded from

History, LXI (Oct., 1980), p. 366.

[43]Richards, *Gentlemen*, p. 150.

[44]*Daily Gazette*, Aug. 5, 1836.

[45]William Sherman Savage, *The Controversy over the Distribution of Abolition Literature, 1830-1860* (Washington: The Association for the Study of Negro Life, Inc., 1938), pp. 99-100.

as far away as Limestone County, Alabama.[46] And after the riot, comment appeared in newspapers throughout the country.

The *Philanthropist* was identified with Cincinnati by outsiders and it was this identification that made Cincinnatians nervous. They did not hide their apprehension over commercial relations with the south, and protested that the city would suffer grave economic harm should it permit an anti-slavery paper to publish within its limits. They especially feared that it would ruin a very hopeful project for building a railroad line from Cincinnati to Charleston, South Carolina. At the time of the riot, a committee of prominent Cincinnatians was touring the south stumping for this project.[47]

The causes of the riot were not fears of internal local social disintegration. Rather the causes were concern for the city's reputation and apprehensions lest commercial success be sacrificed for the whimsical project of a fringe group. Hence it was significant that the Market House meeting passed a resolution comparing the *Philanthropist* to the Tea Act, and invoking the Boston Tea Party as a model for destroying an anti-slavery press: both "illegal" acts of defiance were clearly based on the principle of "the best interests and happiness of our common country."[48] "Public Sentiment," in a letter to the *Whig*, accused abolitionists of being agents "of the Aristocrats and lordlings of Europe,"[49] enemies of democracy and America alike. So the public good was placed in a context of self-interest, civic pride, and patriotism.

That local commercial interests guided the anti-*Philanthropist* riot is obvious from a cursory examination of press reaction. The daily sheets, supported for the most part by the patronage of local businesses and businessmen, especially advertising patronage, all condemned the *Philanthropist* and, with the exception of the *Gazette*, supported the mob. But non-commercial publications, like the *Journal*, the *Cross and Baptist Journal*, and the *Working Man's Friend*, opposed the mob and supported

---

[46]Birney, *Birney*, p. 204.

[47]Savage, *Abolition Literature*, pp. 95-6; Edward Deering Mansfield, *Personal Memories, Social, Political, and Literary, with Sketches of Many Noted People, 1803-1843* (Cincinnati: Robert Clarke & Co., 1879), p. 303.

[48]*Narrative*, p. 25.

[49]*Whig*, July 19, 1836, quoted in *Narrative*, pp. 19-20.

the *Philanthropist*.[50] The division of sentiment was between those more and less interested in the city's commercial success.

But the debate centered on the idea of the press. And here two persuasions clashed. Both were rooted in the traditional press ideology, but each emphasized different aspects of it.

The *Philanthropist* appealed to the independent intelligent reader as the salient social fact of journalism. It was the individual who read and evaluated arguments, and it was the individual mind that Birney sought to convert to his views. Freedom of the press was freedom for individuals.

But Birney's opponents invoked the common good. The press was designed to promote the welfare of the community with which it is associated. The *Philanthropist*, however, would cause irreparable harm to Cincinnati. The individual had no right to promote a cause at the expense of the community.

The fact was that Birney's *Philanthropist* was not a popular periodical. Public opinion did not condone this paper. It would never win wide acceptance in Cincinnati.

The fact was that a mob did shut down the *Philanthropist*. This mob was apparently condoned by the citizens at large. They seemed relieved that the threat of an abolitionist paper in Cincinnati had been removed.

But the fact was that the *Philanthropist* was re-established, and was permitted to publish in Cincinnati for years thereafter. Why was this? I think it was because unpopular ideas were ultimately perceived as harmless. They could thus be permitted to compete freely in the marketplace of ideas, because they would never have the popularity to challenge the more powerful notions of conventional religious groups and political parties.

The social significance of an individual's ideas dwindled before the power of the majority. Dissent would come to be accepted, not because of its own power, but because of its weakness. Were it seen as dangerous, it would not be tolerated. Ideas would have to be certified innocuous before the free flow of ideas was sanctioned by the community.

Reformers in America have always expressed frustration with the free press. Their disappointment is a necessary concomitant of the hyperbolic

[50]*Daily Gazette*, Aug. 5, 1836.

hopes they espouse for the free flow of information. Birney, for instance, thought that the people would be enlightened by his paper. The people declined. The same disappointment greeted Josiah Warren.

Radical Reform

Josiah Warren was born in Massachusetts in 1798. The details of his early life are obscure, but it is known that his primary occupation in early years was as a musician. He came to Cincinnati in 1820 as an orchestra leader and teacher of music.[51] He also possessed remarkable mechanical ingenuity. Some time around 1820, he designed and patented a lamp which burned lard instead of the customary and more expensive oil. Warren built a factory to produce these lamps, and for the next few years enjoyed a healthy income from their sale.[52]

But Warren had become enthralled by schemes for social reform. He sold his factory and joined Robert Owen's New Harmony Community. Thus began a life-long career of involvement in utopian schemes.[53] In 1830 he helped set up a model community named Equity in Clermont County near Cincinnati.[54] In 1831 he worked with a cooperative vocational school for orphans at Spring Hill, Ohio, near Massillon.[55] From 1833 to 1835, he was engaged in another unsuccessful attempt to establish another model community at Tuscarawas, Ohio.[56] In 1847, he returned to Clermont County, where his model community had become a Fourierite phalanx. He reconverted it to his system of "equitable commerce" and renamed it Utopia.[57] Finally he moved to Long Island and joined an

---

[51]William Bailie, *Josiah Warren, the First American Anarchist: A Sociological Study* (Boston: Small, Maynard, & Co., 1906), pp. 1-2; James J. Martin, *Men Against the State: The Expositors of Individualist Anarchism in America, 1827-1908* (DeKalb, IL: Adrian Allen Associates, 1953), p. 13.

[52]Martin, *Against the State*, p. 13.

[53]*Ibid.*, pp. 14-5; Bailie, *Warren*, pp. 3-8.

[54]Kenneth W. McKinley, "A Guide to the Communistic Communities of Ohio," *Ohio State Archaeological and Historical Quarterly*, XLVI (Jan., 1937), p. 15.

[55]Martin, *Against the State*, pp. 36-8.

[56]Bailie, *Warren*, pp. 35-7; Martin, *Against the State*, pp. 42-3.

[57]Bailie, *Warren*, pp. 50-6.

anarchist community named Modern Times.[58] Through these adventures he became an associate of some of the most celebrated radicals of his time, like Robert Owen and his son, Robert Dale Owen, and Frances Wright, who bought Warren's old house when she moved to Cincinnati.[59]

Josiah Warren was disappointed with American society. He described it as a "festering mess," refusing to use "the misnomer of civilization."[60] He referred to the free market economy as "civilized cannibalism."[61]

This mess was the result of society's failure to recognize the true nature of humanity, that ultimately humans are individuals. Society, it seemed, was everywhere in a conspiracy against the individuality of its members. This conspiracy must fail, as it is against the very nature of humans:

A deep-seated, unseen, indestructible, inalienable individuality, ever active, unconquered, and unconquerable, is always directly at war with every demand for uniformity or conformity of thoughts and feelings. We ask again, what is to be done? As we cannot divest ourselves or events of natural individualities, there is but one remedy—this is, to AVOID ALL NECESSITY FOR ARTIFICIAL ORGANIZATIONS . . . .[62]

True civilization could be achieved by dismantling social organization and returning to the primitive fact of human individuality.

The movement toward this great reform had began with the American Revolution. Warren was fond of quoting the Declaration of Independence, especially its affirmation of individual rights. He clearly saw the true legacy of the Revolution as liberty, not majoritarian democracy: "SELF SOVEREIGNTY is the instinct of every living organism; . . . the votes of ten thousand men cannot alienate it from a single individual, nor could the bayonets of twenty thousand."[63]

[58]Martin, *Against the State*, pp. 64-93.

[59]*Ibid.*, pp. 25-36; Alice Jane Gray Perkins and Theresa Wolfson, *Frances Wright, Free Enquirer: The Study of a Temperament* (New York: Harper, 1939), p. 360.

[60]Josiah Warren, *True Civilization, an Immediate Necessity, and the Last Grand Hope for Mankind* . . . (1863, reprinted New York: Burt Franklin, 1967), p. 36.

[61]Quoted in Martin, *Against the State*, p. 45.

[62]Josiah Warren, *Equitable Commerce: A New Development of Principles, as Substitutes for Laws and Governments* . . . *Proposed as Elements of a New Society* (1848; second edition, New York: Fowler & Wells, 1852), p. 89.

[63]Warren, *True Civilization*, p. 10.

But the idea of true democracy, that is of individual rights, although properly identified by the Founding Fathers and enshrined in the official creed of the United States, had never really been applied:

The Democratic idea, theoretically at the base of American institutions, has never been introduced into our military discipline, nor into our courts, nor into our laws, and only in a caricatured and distorted shape into our political system, our education, and public opinion.[64]

It would be Josiah Warren's task to invent the social application of true Democracy.[65]

Warren's invention was the idea of equitable commerce. This meant, simply put, making cost the limit of price. In other words, the price of a product or service would consist solely of the cost of the raw materials and labor consumed. Warren proposed this as an alternative to the value theory of price, namely, that the correct price of a product or service is whatever the market will bear. The gist of equitable commerce was to eliminate unfair pricing and hence the inequitable distribution of wealth. The result that Warren envisioned was an economy where no one could exercise authority, where free individuals would live together in ease and abundance:

That cost being made the limit of price, would necessarily produce all the cooperation, and all the economies aimed at by the most intelligent and devoted friends of humanity; and, by reducing the burthen of labor to a mere pastime or necessary exercise, would probably annihilate its cost; when, like water or amateur music, no price would be set upon it; and the highest aspirations of the best of our race would be naturally realized.[66]

One simple reform—the introduction of equitable commerce—would inevitably bring about this ideal society.[67]

Warren did not sit on his revelation. Rather, he experimented with his ideas. In 1827, he set up an Equity Store or Time Store at Fifth and Elm in

[64]*Ibid.*, p. 24.

[65]Bailie, *Warren*, p. 122.

[66]Warren, *Equitable Commerce*, p. 101.

[67]The labor theory of value is discussed in Martin, *Against the State*, pp. 16-7.

Cincinnati. This store was run on the cost theory: customers paid cash for products, but only the amount that Warren had paid wholesale. On top of that cash sum, customers would give Warren compensation for his labor. This was calculated in terms of the time Warren had spent serving the customer, and could be paid either in cash or in a promise of an equal amount of labor. A carpenter, for instance, would write Warren an I.O.U. for so many minutes of woodworking. This method of commerce eliminated competition and conflict of interests, as neither merchant nor customer could expect to profit from the other's loss. The store in Cincinnati operated successfully for two years, from 1827 to 1829. Then Warren closed it, declaring the experiment concluded.[68]

After closing the Time Store, Warren went about promoting the idea of equitable commerce for general adoption. He went to New York and wrote for the *Free Enquirer* with Robert Dale Owen and Frances Wright. He also published letters in James Gazlay's *Western Tiller*.

Warren believed that his system would be adopted because it was obvious, successful, and simple. All he would have to do would be to present it to the public. They would easily see the advantages of equitable commerce and apply it to everyday transactions.

Warren's beliefs implied an ideology of the press. Warren himself articulated this ideology simply: "Public influence is the real government of the world. Printing makes this governing power . . . ."[69] The press was to be the organ of reform.

The press ideally suited Warren's project in theory. It was a means of communicating ideas and opinions rationally, objectively, and scientifically to intelligent individuals:

I decline all noisy, wordy, confused, and personal controversies. This subject is presented for calm study and honest enquiry; and after having placed it (as I intend to do) fairly before the public, shall leave it to be estimated by each individual according to the particular measure of understanding, and shall offer no violence to his individuality by an attempt to restrain, or to urge him beyond it.[70]

[68]Warren, *True Civilization*, pp. 84 *et seq.*; Bailie, *Warren*, pp. 9-24; Martin, *Against the State*, p. 20.

[69]Warren, *Manifesto* (New Harmony, IN: Warren, 1841), p. 6.

[70]*Ibid.*, pp. 10-11.

This appeal to reason and individuality echoed Birney's press philosophy.

Warren thus decided to set up a newspaper to spread his ideas. But he found that Cincinnati's merchants were so firmly opposed to these ideas that they refused to sell him the needed printing equipment at any price. This was in 1830, two years before the *True Blue and Castigator* was destroyed, and six years before the *Philanthropist* was mobbed.[71]

Undaunted, Warren invented his own printing press, and in 1833 began publication of the weekly *Peaceful Revolutionist*. This paper was similar to other weeklies in format. In production, it resembled the pioneer newspapers, in that Warren single-handedly composed, printed, and distributed his paper. It failed within a year.[72]

The *Peaceful Revolutionist* was more significant in itself than in the material it conveyed. It was an attempt to place the power of the press in the hands of individuals, to take it "out of the exclusive control of merely mercenary managers."[73] Warren stated in the first issue of the *Revolutionist* that "Printing is a power that governs the destinies of mankind. Those who control the Printing Press can control their fellow. creatures."[74] He sought to bring "this mighty power to the fireside and within the capabilities of almost anyone of either sex who may choose to use it . . . ."[75]

Warren's attempt to democratize print took the form of mechanical innovation. He is credited with the invention of a printing press capable of turning out 4000 impressions per hour in 1839. This press, years ahead of its time, was sabotaged continually by its operators for two years, until Warren was forced to remove it from the Evansville newspaper office where it had been installed.[76] In 1844 he invented a method by which "every printer can make his own stereotype plates, as well as plates from

[71]Bailie, *Warren*, pp. 84 *et seq.*

[72]*Ibid.*, pp. 37-8; Martin, *Against the State*, pp. 38 *et seq.*, Frederick D. Buchstein, "The Anarchist Press in American Journalism," *Journalism History*, I (Summer, 1974), pp. 43-4.

[73]Quoted in Bailie, *Warren*, p. 83.

[74]*Revolutionist*, Feb. 5, 1833, quoted in Martin, *Against the State*, p. 38.

[75]Warren, *Manifesto*, p. 6.

[76]Martin, *Against the State*, p. 44.

original designs, at a very trifling expense in his own office."[77] None of Warren's inventions achieved general acceptance, however. His efforts to make the power of print the instrument of the common man failed.

Instead, the power of the press remained in the hands of a narrow class of business-minded men. Warren criticized these press conductors as "too much interested in things as they are, too much under public influence or too superficial in their habits of thinking."[78] Conventional newspapers were rendered worse than useless by political partisanism: "One paper having spoken, others of the same party or Clan copy; the clan repeat and join in the chorus, and confusion follows; and where confusion abounds the ignorant are noisy, the prudent are silent, and imposters triumph."[79] And the extent to which the press was open to ideas and opinions was limited arbitrarily by its interest in its own commercial success and the preservation of an inequitable economic system.[80] Politics and money had prostituted the power of the press:

While the editorship of newspapers is the direct road to office, and while the "cowry" and office are the all-absorbing objects of pursuit, who will expect common newspapers to advocate any principle putting an end to wars? Who will expect them to cease inflaming party against party and nation against nation; or to pay any attention to the responsibility of public counsellers?[81]

Warren showed nothing but scorn for the conventional press. He was distrustful of majoritarian politics. And he considered conventional political economy little more than clever trickery: "I have seen a man dance, blindfolded, among eggs, and wondered how he could avoid breaking them; but I suspect, now, that he learned to do it by studying political economy!"[82]

The truth, on the contrary, was simple. Social reform was simple. All could understand these things, but the majority suffered themselves to be

[77]Letter of Solon Robinson, *Weekly Gazette*, July 24, 1845.
[78]Warren, *Manifesto*, p. 6.
[79]Warren, *True Civilization*, p. 100.
[80]*Ibid.*, pp. 72-3.
[81]*Ibid.*, p. 110.
[82]*Ibid.*, p. 180.

led by self-interested men: "No people can ever rise above this barbarian level as long as they unhesitatingly follow any leaders without thinking where they are going. We want a Luther in the political sphere—and another in the financial sphere—another in the Commercial—another in the educational sphere, to rouse the people to use their own experience."[83]

Warren died a frustrated man. The public never awoke to the realities he tried to convey, self-evident as he held those truths to be. Among his last recorded words were these: "I feel mortified that, having done my best to paint a landscape, I am obliged to label it, *This is a landscape.*"[84]

Although Warren won few converts, his printing ventures were tolerated in and around Cincinnati. At first local merchants tried to thwart his attempts to publish, but eventually these attempts failed because of apathy, not opposition. Anarchism never excited a mob like abolitionism did.

Why was Warren tolerated in Cincinnati? I suspect that the ultimate reason was that his ideas were perceived as innocuous. In the final analysis, Warren was not tolerated but ignored.

Warren's failure also symbolizes the failure of the independent printer, the newspaper conductor as common man. The newspaper had indeed become a corporate enterprise, fully incorporated into an entrepreneurial economic establishment.

The reason for the failure of Warren and the independent printer was a lack of public support. The public preferred the conventional press, and the public was king. The democratic reformer who could not win public support found himself a contradiction in terms, a creature invalidated by its own ideas. The reform press failed because of the people, the same people whose interests it claimed to serve.

What emerged from the ferment of Jacksonian America was a confident majority. Conservative in social and economic terms, satisfied with the American system, and wedded to a matrix of religious, political, and professional organizations, this vast center tolerated all sorts of dissent. Radical ideas could now be expressed freely in the press. What had changed was an attitude—the power of print was no longer feared.

---

[83]*Ibid.*, pp. 42-3.
[84]Josiah Warren, public letter, quoted in Bailie, *Warren*, p. 132.

Cincinnati remained violent in opposition to elements perceived as dangerous. Riots would erupt against banks, blacks, and immigrants in the 1840s and 1850s. Riots would not erupt against newspapers and periodicals.

Conclusion

Reform papers continued to proliferate in the 1840s. These were devoted to such disparate causes as nativism, Swedenborgianism, and temperance. They were usually the organs of reform societies, and they tended to imitate the conventional newspaper in format.

These journals proposed small-scale reforms designed to improve society, not to transform it. Causes like temperance, nativism, and public education, while often not popular, never threatened to disrupt the social fabric. Instead they promised to strengthen it. As such, they were more acceptable to the populace.

The bland acceptance of reform journalism in these later years marked a curious triumph for individual reformers. They had won the right to address the people in a free, rational, and scientific manner. They had won the right to appeal to the independent intellect. But they had won freedom of the press at the expense of the power of the press. They could freely address the people because the people were not listening.

The people were not listening because the ideas did not appeal to them. They had come to view ideas as products to be marketed. They were idea consumers.

This triumph of democracy was also the defeat of that democratic ideology espoused by utopian reformers. How could they expect to convince the people that the society, the majority, is faulty and must be overhauled? The people themselves *were* society, and the customer is always right.

Conclusion

It is my task in this final section to draw together the themes of the preceding discussion, and to try to relate them in some meaningful way to the rhythms of American cultural history in the early national period. This is no simple chore, and I will ask the reader's indulgence if I seem to generalize or speculate too broadly.

Throughout this study I have attempted to outline the implications of Cincinnati's press history in terms of national cultural trends. Up to this point, I have avoided any direct confrontation with the question of whether Cincinnati's press history was representative. I would like to deal with that issue now.

It is my estimation that no locality was "typical" or representative in the early Republic. The U.S. was a mosaic of discrete and distinctive places; we may identify typical midwestern farming counties, or typical eastern ports, but in terms of even so public a feature as a press establishment, no one place could typify the entire nation, or even the major part. And each place changed over time, and not all places changed in the same way.

It is, I think, incorrect to speak about the American press, or American journalism, or the American media in the early Republic as though these terms referred to an actual monolithic entity. Newspaper formats varied widely. Moreover, the social environment that produced newspapers and the cultural environment that gave meanings to them also varied widely. The simple contrast between the *New York Herald* of the 1830s and the countless rural weeklies of the same decade demonstrates that, when one claims to describe "the American newspaper," one is actually describing a creation of the imagination, rather than an actual historical creature. This heterogeneity is compounded when we consider other forms of periodical literature, like literary and scientific journals.

It is necessary to recapture the plenitude and diversity of America's past. Too often historians of the American press have been satisfied to look upon this period as the dark age that preceded objective journalism or, on the other hand, the dawning of the bright age of democracy. In its weakest form, this approach to press history has amounted to a narrative caricature, wherein all of history has contrived to produce the *New York Times*. Our knowledge of what has come to the surface has drawn attention away from the throes and convulsions that produced it.

The decades following the American Revolution saw a proliferation of press products of all kinds. This was an age pregnant with possibility, an age full of random mutations and local particularities.

Cincinnati's experience is fortunate in capturing so many of the different qualities of the early press. In format, the Queen City's press products covered the entire range of common types. Readers of Cincinnati's newspapers and magazines were likewise diverse in occupation, social status, sex, language, generation, and cultural persuasion. This diversity was representative.

In the passage of time, Cincinnati grew from a frontier village to a metropolis. This rapid ontogeny embodied in time many of the variations in place of American society. There were still frontier villages and bustling river towns long after Cincinnati had become a large city. The history of Cincinnati, then, captures in two dimensions a much more complicated national development in three dimensions.

But Cincinnati's history exaggerates the trajectory of American history as a whole, as does the history of any locality. There are some things that are unrepresentative: daily newspapers were still limited to cities; only regional capitals boasted professional journals; not all localities were as evenly balanced politically as Hamilton County; ethnic heterogeneity was not the rule in all localities. But in each case Cincinnati's exceptionality is benign, if not actually beneficial: it widens our perception of early national culture.

The crucial consideration here is not whether Cincinnati's press resembled or typified "the American press," a term which refers to something which may never have existed anyway. Rather, the key point is that the history of Cincinnati's press provides an opportunity to examine the culture of the press. This culture was the significant feature of the early press: it was the ideas and values that surrounded the press, more than the texts or artifacts of early papers, that have been the focus of this study.

Histories of the press have often sought to describe "American Journalism" by concentrating on the newspapers of New York City. This is an important part of U.S. press history, no doubt. But New York is arguably the least representative American city; the fact that New York has usually been in the vanguard of change in the U.S. only serves to reinforce the contention that New York should not be taken as representative of American culture as a whole.

This having been said, what significant features of the culture of the press have appeared in this study?

Perhaps the most commonly-used adjective in this study was "short-lived." Periodicals of every sort were surprisingly ephemeral. This instability had a dual meaning—it was testimony to the power of the idea of the press, but it also implied a real social weakness.

Paper after paper was begun, and failure followed almost all with dull predictability. But Americans persisted in establishing papers. The reason for this eagerness—it almost seems a reflex—lies, I think, in America's idea of herself. Her political institutions—founded by reason to be guided by reason, to be ruled by well-informed public opinion—imply by their very nature a power of the press. The man with the printing press was the priest of reason, as it were—he had the power of the word at his disposal, and among an intelligent and literate electorate, there was no greater power. Early press conductors pondered the duties this power entailed with a self-importance that seems pathetic in light of the ephemerality of their creations. The idea of the press was an implicit feature of American political thought. That this was so is apparent in the behavior of Cincinnati's Germans, who eagerly established papers as part of their embrace of American institutions.

But the men who began papers were a restricted group. It is not surprising that they held this inflated opinion of the Power of the press.

But how widely was this idea shared?

Evidence gives the impression that it was widely shared indeed, at least for a time. The tone of comment about press conduct, both in and out of the press, indicates that high standards of behavior were expected to be enforced, that newspapers were to be high-minded, impersonal, impartial, free but not licentious. The fact that papers seen as licentious were mobbed implies that the idea of the power of the press was at one time strong enough to be a social fact.

But familiarity bred contempt, or at least apathy. The reader could choose between different versions of truth in different periodicals. He or she became a consumer, and became accustomed to having his or her demands met. Commercialization in the press meant more than integration into the market economy in printing commercial information and adopting modern means of production and distribution. Information and opinions became marketable commodities, and were forced to compete for authority.

Then where was the power of the press? Earlier, men had thought that this power lay in the truth—that truth could be communicated, and that the press was powerful only insofar as it could communicate truth. But commercialization meant that truth itself had no power, that power lay solely in the hands—or pockets—of consumers.

While the structure and nature of the press establishment discredited this idea of truth and the Power of the press, it legitimized another. This is the idea inherent in the professions. There is a truth discoverable by scientific inquiry, and the press could facilitate this inquiry; but this truth was not randomly or universally available. To grasp the truth requires talent and effort.

This new idea—and in the social fact of the professionalization of secular knowledge it was new—was a departure from the ideas implied by the American Revolution. "Privilege" survived, not because of superstition, but because of enlightenment. But enlightenment no longer meant what a revolutionary generation had proclaimed. It meant organization, industry, and elite leadership. All men were not created equal, and truth was neither simple nor self-evident.

It is doubtful that the bulk of the Revolutionary generation had believed in an extreme version of Democratic enlightenment. But faith in

Republican institutions, the overwhelming popularity of Bacon and Newton, and the tone of anti-Catholicism are evidence of a powerful confluence of the ideas of democracy, reason, and patriotism. And a rhetoric of popular enlightenment was made available.

There is an inescapable poignancy to the careers of men like Josiah Warren—who took this rhetoric and all it implied seriously. Members of a post-Revolutionary generation, they had witnessed the passing of the heroes who had made this great discovery of rational politics, who had torn away the blinders of superstition and had gazed unashamed on the naked truth of nature—for so the Revolution was remembered. But they confronted a world where inequality and ignorance still ruled. They applied the political rhetoric of the Revolution to society, religion, and science, and collided with the ultimate irony of this rhetoric. As an instrument of gaining political ends, this rhetoric was eminently practical. As a means of understanding society and nature, it was thoroughly utopian.

In a sense, then, belief in the ultimate achievement of enlightenment was an aberration, not a revolution in thought. It came into fashion and passed away. Americans accepted society as it existed as society as the founding fathers had willed it. The rhetoric of the Revolution, so pregnant with hope, had given birth to a changeling—a man of the people whom the people scorned. And the symbol of the Revolution would be employed as a bland seal of approval on the Republic as it was.

The result was a paradoxical democratization. The People were given the power to choose their own truths. But they weren't the real truths, the truths with Power. These truths—religious, medical, educational, and to an extent political—remained in the custody of professional or organizational elites. This triumph of Democracy seemed illusory to those who took seriously the promise of enlightenment. A sense of betrayal has ever since been the birthright of the American utopian.

All the while, the press as a social fact was becoming more pervasive. Newspapers and periodicals multiplied in number, in frequency, and in topic. Growth was explosive.

But growth was not revolutionary. No new economic groups in society were added to the community of the press. There was no social revolution in newspaper readership. Early weekly papers had a remarkably wide readership, and the expansion of the press did not involve a demographic expansion of this readership. But it did imply a change the nature of readership.

This change in nature was the multiplication of the social functions of the press. The early weekly had been justified as a conveyor of information and opinions which had some public significance—some bearing on government and polity. The weekly newspaper was quasi-official in status. Hence the willingness of early federal leaders to legislate privileges for the press.

But the press became an instrument for much besides public information and opinions. It was used to amuse, to instruct, and to persuade; it was used to advertise, and to convey commercial information. These were all functions which appealed to the reader's sense of self-interest, not his or her sense of public service or devotion to the common weal. In a sense, the most public means of communication became private.

What emerged was a popular culture in print. It was popular because it was public—aimed at the anonymous culture consumers, not limited in availability by kinship or occupation or even locality. It emanated outward from urban centers, and emphasized the values of the urban middle class. It was socially and economically conservative. It grew in power, and, I suspect, has continued to grow with but minor reversals to the present day.

What was important about this culture was not its idea of itself but its social fact. Formulas were discovered, techniques of reaching a mass audience, techniques of commercial success, techniques of influencing public opinion by being submissive to public tastes. A formidable national press establishment became a feature of American life.

The development of popular culture in print was not revolutionary. It was a gradual development. It invoked tradition. It invoked morality as its rationale. It called print "the art conservative." It retained the trappings of enlightenment, even while losing its faith in enlightenment. This articulation of the social functions of the press was a smooth development.

The evolution of such a print culture implied an internalization of its critique. To this day, the ideology of enlightenment remains available, and for that reason the instinct to establish newspapers and periodicals as organs of enlightenment remains common, even though such organs have usually been no more successful than their predecessors of the early nineteenth century.

This book has been an attempt at a study of the complex interaction of ideas, idea transmission, the idea of idea transmission, and social fact. I have attempted to weave together developments in local society, regional culture, and national politics with the ongoing discourse on the idea of the press. Such a task is difficult, and the outcome has been complex and sometimes confusing.

What I have outlined here is an alternative to the common Whiggish perspective on journalism history. In my version, objectivity is not a new idea. Instead, its antiquity is acknowledged, its currency in all periods of press thought is granted. In my version, readership does not dramatically expand, "news" is not suddenly discovered, communications technology does not radically change. In my version, the social and intellectual significance of formats which have not survived is acknowledged—the weekly paper, the impersonal political paper, and the popular science magazine are integrated into an account of the evolution of the idea of journalism. In my version, the diversity of the press in the past is accepted.

As a result, I have argued that the press was a creature of the culture and society of its time. The ideas and values generated by the American Revolution spurred the creation of newspapers and periodicals of every sort, while other forces—social, economic, political, technological—acted to direct the development of the press. Ultimately, the press came to occupy a central place in nineteenth-century culture and society.

Evolution of the culture of the press was not the triumphant story of the development of journalism as an independent moral force in society. Rather, it was the story of the integration of print into the prevailing structures of its time.

BIBLIOGRAPHY

Pre–1848 Cincinnati
Newspapers and Periodicals

General and Commercial Newspapers

The following listing is organized alphabetically, according to the first word of the title. For purposes of clarity, the following words have not been considered in determining the alphabetical order: Cincinnati, Daily, Bi-Weekly, Tri-Weekly, Morning, Monthly, Saturday, and Dollar.

Morning Advertiser (daily); June 22-Nov. 21, 1846.

Cincinnati Advertiser and Western Journal (see *Inquisitor*).

Cincinnati Advertizer (weekly); lasted a few months in 1811; edited by Francis Mennessier.

Cincinnati American (weekly and semi-weekly); Feb. 25, 1830–1832?; National Republican, conducted by Isaiah Thomas, Jr., and James F. Conover.

American Republican Bulletin (daily); 1842?–1844?

Daily Cincinnati Atlas; title varies: *Chronicle and Atlas*; Nov. 1, 1843–1854;, Whig, conducted by Nathan Guilford, J. B. Russell, E. D. Mansfield, *et al.*

Centinel of the North-Western Territory (weekly); Nov. 9, 1793–June 11, 1796; conducted by William Maxwell.

Cincinnati Morning Chronicle (daily); Nov. 28, 1839–Sept. 28, 1849; Whig, edited by E. D. Mansfield, published by Pugh, Harlan, & Davis, eventually merged with the *Atlas* to form the *Chronicle and Atlas*. The same office issued the *Dollar Weekly Chronicle* (Sept. 24, 1836–Sept., 1849).

Cist's Daily Advertiser; March 15, 1847–April 15, 1848; and *Cist's Weekly Advertiser*; title varies: *Western General Advertiser*; Feb. 9, 1843–April 29, 1853; conducted by Charles Cist. Articles from these papers were also printed in the monthly *Cincinnati Miscellany*.

Dollar Weekly Columbian; 1846–1856; merged with the *Great West* in 1850 to form the *Columbian and Great West*.

Daily Cincinnati Commercial; title varies: *Cincinnati Commercial Gazette*; Oct. 2, 1843–Dec. 3, 1930; L. Greely Curtiss, original editor. The same office issued the *Dollar Weekly Commercial* (Sept., 1845–Dec., 1882).

Commercial Daily Advertiser; March 2, 1829–Feb., 1834; conducted by E. S. Thomas and O. Farnsworth. Continued by the *Cincinnati Democratic Intelligencer and Commercial Advertiser*.

Cincinnati Commercial Herald (weekly); March 14, 1843–?

Cincinnati Commercial Register (daily); Dec. 30, 1825–1827; conducted by Samuel S. Brooks. Later merged with the *National Republican and Cincinnati Mercantile Advertiser* to form the *Cincinnati Republican and Register*, eventually the *Daily Cincinnati Republican*. The *Commercial Register* was revived briefly in 1828 by Brooks and Edmund Harrison.

Counterfeit Detector (monthly); title varies: *Western or Goodman's Counterfeit Detector*; 1840–? 1853–?; conducted by Goodman & Co.

Day Star (weekly); 1841?–1846.

Cincinnati Democrat (semi–weekly); 1832, conducted by John H. Wood, James J. Faran; and Thomas Henderson.

Democratic Bulletin (daily); 1843–?; printed by R. P. Donough.

Cincinnati Democratic Intelligencer and Commercial Advertiser (daily); March 3, 1834–April 9, 1835; Whig. Continued by the *Commercial Daily Advertiser*, which was in turn continued by the *Whig*.

Dollar Weekly Dispatch and Democratic Union; title varies: *Saturday Evening News and Western Portfolio*; April 8, 1848–Oct. 31, 1850; independent, then Democratic.

Elevator (weekly); Nov. 20, 1841–April, 1842.

Cincinnati Emporium (weekly, semi–weekly); Feb. 12, 1824–1826; merged with the *National Crisis* to form the *National Crisis and Cincinnati Emporium*, edited by Samuel J. Browne; National Republican.

Daily Cincinnati Enquirer; April 10, 1841–survives to the present day; continued the *Advertiser*; conducted by John and Charles Brough *et al.*; Democratic. The same office issued the *Cincinnati Weekly Enquirer*, 1841–1881.

Cincinnati Express (daily); 1837?–1839?; conducted by Isaac Moorhead, Joseph Reese Fry, and John H. Wood; concentrated on commercial information; might have been a penny paper.

Freeman's Journal (weekly); June 18, 1796–Feb., 1800; conducted by Samuel and Edmund Freeman.

Cincinnati Gazette (weekly); June 15–Sept. 2, 1815. Later merged with the *Liberty Hall* to form the *Liberty Hall and Cincinnati Gazette.*

Cincinnati Weekly Globe; Sept. 28, 1848–1849?; Democratic; continued the *Herald and Philanthropist.*

Cincinnati Herald (weekly); April 13, 1833–?

Cincinnati Morning Herald; Aug. 29, 1843–Sept., 1848; continued the *Philanthropist,* listed as a reform paper.

Independent Press and Freedom's Advocate (weekly); July 4, 1822–Nov. 13, 1823; conducted by Solomon Smith. The *Independent Press* was revived for a time by Smith's brother in 1826.

Inquisitor and Cincinnati Advertiser (weekly, June 23, 1818–Dec. 31, 1822); ater the printing office was destroyed by fire, the paper was re-issued as the *Cincinnati Advertiser and Ohio Phoenix* (bi-weekly, tri-weekly, Jan. 6., 1823–Sept. 28, 1838); the name was then changed to the *Cincinnati Advertiser and Western Journal* (daily and tri-weekly); Oct. 4, 1838–April 1, 1841. Conducted by Benjamin H. Powers, George F. Hopkins, and especially Moses Dawson. Succeeded by the *Daily Enquirer.* Democratic.

Kentucky and Ohio Journal (weekly); Aug. 3, 1837–?; Democratic.

Liberty Hall; title varies: *Liberty Hall and Cincinnati Mercury* (weekly), Dec. 4, 1804–April 6, 1809; *Liberty Hall* (weekly), April 13, 1809–Dec. 4, 1815; *Liberty Hall and Cincinnati Gazette* (weekly), Dec. 11, 1815–1857; *Tri–Weekly Cincinnati Gazette* (1831–1857); *Cincinnati Daily Gazette* (June 5, 1827–1883). Its most notable conductors were John W. Browne, Isaac G. Burnet, Charles Hammond, and John C. Wright. Political affiliation varied: Republican, then National Republican, then Whig.

Literary Cadet and Cheap City Advertiser (weekly); Nov. 22, 1819–April 27, 1820; edited by Joseph R. Buchanan, published by Looker & Reynolds; merged with the *Western Spy* to form the *Western Spy and Literary Cadet.*

Mercantile Daily Advertiser; Sept. 4, 1826–?; conducted by Samuel J. Browne and Hooper J. Warren; switched to bi-weekly publication after a few months, and became the *National Crisis and Cincinnati Emporium.*

Merchant's Exchange Reporter and Peabody's Commercial Atlas (weekly); 1844–?; A. Peabody, editor.

Daily Morning Message; 1841–Nov. 25, 1843; conducted by William Davis Gallagher and George S. Bennett, merged with the *Enquirer* to form the *Enquirer and Message* in 1843. The same office also issued the *Dollar Weekly Message*; 1841–1843.

National Crisis (weekly, semi-weekly); May 24, 1824–1829. After a brief involvement in the publication of the *Mercantile Daily Advertiser,* the *Crisis* merged with the *Cincinnati Emporium* to form the *National Crisis and Cincinnati Emporium,* a pro-Adams paper, whose primary editor was Samuel J. Browne.

National Republican and Ohio Political Register (semi-weekly); Jan.1, 1823–Dec., 1830; Democratic; initially conducted by Elijah Hayward. The *National Republican* succeeded the *Western Spy* and was continued by the *Daily Republican.*

Saturday Evening News and Western Portfolio (weekly); see *Dollar Weekly Dispatch.*

The Saturday Morning News (weekly); May–Oct.?, 1838.

Cincinnati Daily Nonpareil; 1848–1853; a co-operative paper, primarily edited by Lucius A. Hine; might be considered a penny paper.

Ohio Union (daily); Sept. 13, 1845–June, 1846; Democratic.

People's Advocate (weekly); 1834–1835; edited by John H. Wood and Benj. Drake.

Daily Evening Post; May, 1835–Dec. 21, 1839; Whig, conducted by E. S. and L. F. Thomas.

Cincinnati Prices Current; 1835; edited by John H. Wood, published by Lodge, L'Hommedieu, & Co.

Cincinnati Prices Current; 1844–1845; J. B. Russell, editor.

Cincinnati Prices Current; edited by A. Peabody: see *Merchant's Exchange Reporter.*

Cincinnati Price Current and Commercial Advertiser (weekly); 1843–1913; conducted primarily by Richard Smith, edited for a time by Edward Deering Mansfield, after 1913 it survived as the *Grain and Feed Journals Consolidated* of Chicago.

Cincinnati Price Current and State of the Market (weekly); June 25, 1831–July 7, 1832; a letter-sheet prices current issued by the office of the *Commercial Daily Advertiser.*

Daily Cincinnati Republican; Jan. 1, 1831–1842; title varies: *National Republican and Daily Mercantile Advertiser, Daily Cincinnati Republican and Commerical Register*; Democratic 1831–1838; Whig 1838–1842; the same office issued the *Weekly Cincinnati Republican*; July, 1833–1842.

Cincinnati Signal (daily, weekly); 1846–1848; edited by James Wickes Taylor; Barnburner, then Free-Soil.

Monthly Southern and Western Bank-Note Table and Counterfeit Detector; 1838; conducted by D. T. Monsarrot.

Spirit of the West (weekly); July 26, 1814–May 29, 1815; edited by David Morris.

Evening Transcript (daily); Nov. 23, 1834–?

United States Register (monthly); 1844–?; a non-partisan political digest, edited by John H. Wood and published by R. P. Brooks.

Western General Advertiser, see *Cist's Advertiser*.

Western Journal (weekly); ?–Sept. 28, 1838; merged with the *Cincinnati Advertiser and Ohio Phoenix* to form the *Cinciinati Advertiser and Western Journal*. See *Inquisitor*.

Western Spy and (Hamilton, Miami) Gazette (title and frequency vary); May 28, 1799–April 6, 1809, 1810–1823; merged with the *Literary Cadet* in 1820 to form the *Western Spy and Literary Cadet*, which was in turn superseded by the *National Republican and Ohio Political Register*.

Western Statesman (weekly); July 23, 1842–Feb. 25, 1843.

Western Token; 1848?

Western Transcript (daily); 1844–April, 1845?; might have been a penny paper.

Cincinnati Daily Whig and Commercial Intelligencer; April 16, 1845–April 23, 1839; Whig, edited most prominently by James F. Conover; continued the *Commercial Daily Advertiser*, which had been merged into the *Cincinnati Democratic Intelligencer and Commercial Advertiser*.

Penny Papers

The following list includes only those papers which can certainly be called penny papers. General newspapers which may have been penny papers are listed above, with an indication of their questionable status as penny papers.

American Patriot; 1843: short-lived.

American Plebeian; 1843: short-lived; issued by D. Rodabaugh & Co.

The Archer; 1844: short-lived.

The Buckeye; 1839: lasted for about four months; edited by John D. Logan, then C. H. Layton.

Cincinnati Morning Bulletin; Aug., 1844–1845; nativist in sympathies; at first edited by J. V. Loomis and U. Tracy Howe, in 1845 it was issued by the firm of Loomis, Browne, and Young.

The Cincinnatian; 1837: lasted about six months; edited by David Martin; the *Cincinnatian* was a partisan Democratic penny paper.

Cincinnati Daily Dispatch and Democratic Union; June 5, 1848–Nov. 3, 1850; at first issued as the politically independent *Daily Dispatch*, this paper adopted partisan Democratic politics and expanded its title in 1850. The same office also issued the *Dollar Weekly Dispatch and Democratic Union*.

Evening Emporium; Jan. 17,–1845?; issued by A. H. Saunders.

English Tattler; 1839:lasted three weeks; edited by Alexander Stimson.

Daily Focus; March 1, 1841: lasted two weeks; published by Col. Edward Stiff.

Hamilton County Democrat; 1837: lasted only one issue; Democratic, edited by David Martin.

Mechanic; 1844: short–lived.

Daily Microscope; 1840–1842; edited in part by L. Greely Curtiss; continued by the *Sun* in 1842.

Daily News; Jan. 3, 1838–Jan. 15, 1839; edited by G. W. Bradbury, E. R. Campbell.

Daily News; Feb., 1839–June?, 1840; issued by Zinn, Clark, and Almon.

Daily Evening News; March–June?, 1845.

Olive Branch; 1839: lasted two weeks; published by Col. Edward Stiff.

Penny Ledger; 1836: lasted two weeks; edited and published by S. Bangs.

People's Paper; Aug., 1843–1846?; established by C. H. Layton, in 1845 this paper was published by Swim & Pickering; after 1843, the *People's Paper* was issued mostly as a morning supplement to the evening *Times*.

Cincinnati Post (and Anti-Abolitionist); January–Sept., 1842; edited and published by L. Greely Curtiss of the *Microscope, Sun*, and *Commercial*.

Public Ledger; 1840: lasted for five months; edited by C. H. Layton.

Queen City; 1843: short-lived.

Queen City; 1844: short-lived.

Daily Queen City; 1847–Sept., 1848.

Morning Star; 1839: lasted three weeks; published by Col. Edward Stiff.

Spirit of the Times. See *Times*.

The Sun; 1838–May, 1839; edited by E. W. Peck, published by John Campbell, merged with the *Republican*.

Daily Sun; 1842–1844?; established by L. Greely Curtiss; originally independent, the *Sun* was sold to Samuel Lewis and Elwood Fisher, who turned it into a hard-money partisan Democratic paper. The same office also issued a weekly.

Cincinnati Daily Times; April 25, 1840–; originally issued as the *Spirit of the Times*, edited by E. R. Campbell, after its first year the title was abbreviated to the *Times*, and the paper was owned by Calvin Starbuck and edited by James D. Taylor. The same office also issued the *Weekly Times* (1844–1901). The *Times* survived as the *Cincinnati Times-Star* until 1958, when it was bought out by the *Post* to form the *Post and Times Star*, which is still active as the *Cincinnati Post*.

True Sun; Oct, 1843: short-lived.

Visiter [*sic*]; May 3, 1841: short-lived.

Western Steamer; Aug. 10, 1840: lasted two weeks; published by Col. Edward Stiff.

The Western World; 1836: lasted twenty-five issues; this was Cincinnati's first penny paper, founded by William A. Harper, formerly of the *Republican.*

Campaign Papers

Campaign and Tariff Advocate (weekly); May 11, 1844–?; Henry Clay.

Cincinnati Campaigner (weekly); June 24–Nov. 18, 1848; Free-Soil.

Daily Clay Champion; Sept. 3, 1844 ?.

Coon-Skinner (tri-weekly); Sept. 7–Aug., 1842; Democratic.

Friend of Reform and Corruption's Adversary (monthly); March 22–Oct. 22, 1828; Jacksonian; edited by Moses Dawson and run in cooperation with the *Advertiser.*

Giraffe (daily); Aug.–Oct. 8, 1842; Whig.

Hamilton County Democrat (weekly); May–Nov., 1840; Democratic. Note: this campaign paper was distinct from the penny paper of the same name.

Log Cabin Advocate (weekly); 1840; Whig.

Log Cabin Herald (weekly), 1840; Whig.

People's Echo (weekly); May–Nov. 3, 1836; Whig.

Rough and Ready; 1848; Whig.

The Spirit of '76 (weekly); 1840; Democratic?

Daily Straightout; Aug–Nov. 1, 1844, Whig.

Truth's Advocate and Monthly Anti-Jackson Expositor; Jan–Oct., 1828; edited by Charles Hammond, in co-operation with the *Liberty Hall and Cincinnati Gazette.*

Wagon Boy (weekly); 1840.

Young Hickory (tri-weekly); Aug. 19–Nov., 1844; Democratic.

German Papers

The following list includes all German-language newspapers and periodicals. German religious, literary, and reform periodicals are also listed in their various categories.

Christliche Apologete (weekly); 1839–; the *Apologete* was the main organ of German Methodism in the United States. It was published by the Western Methodist Book Concern, and was edited by Wilhelm Nast until 1892.

Christliche Hausfreund (bi-weekly); established in June, 1848; the *Hausfreund* was the organ of the Deutsche Vereinigt-Evangelische Synode in Nord Amerika, and was moved to Chicago shortly after its founding.

Der Cincinnati Demokrat; Nov. 18, 1845–Feb., 1846; edited by Dr. Wilhelm Albers.

Der Deutsche Amerikaner (weekly); 1839–1840?; short-lived; edited by Georg Walker, published by August Renz.

Der Deutsche Franklin (weekly); 1835–?; originally Democratic, the *Franklin* became a Whig paper when its editor, Benjamin Boffinger, accepted a cash gift from the local Whig party. It was succeeded by the *Westliche Merkur*.

Deutsche im Westen (weekly); 1839–1841?; Whig; edited by Rudolph von Maltiz, C. Burkhalter, Burkhalter and Hefley, proprietors; succeeded by the *Westliche Merkur*, which was in turn succeeded by the *Ohio Volksfreund*.

Der Deutsche Patriot (weekly); Sept. 14, 1832–?; basically a Henry Clay campaign paper; conducted by Henry Brachmann, Dr. Ritter, and Albert Lange.

Der Deutsche Republicaner (daily, weekly); Sept. 28, 1842–March 23, 1861; Whig; edited by J. H. Schroeder, 1842–1845, then Charles F. Schmidt. Continues the *Ohio Volksfreund*.

Evangelische Kirchenfreund or *Kirchenbote*; 1846?; organ of the Evangelische Protestantische Kirche von Nord Amerika, edited and published by Martin Schaad.

Die Cincinnati Fliegende Blätter (weekly); Aug. 17, 1846–Oct. 2, 1847; a literary paper issue by Emil Klauprecht and Adolf Menzel.

Der Freisinnige (weekly, tri-weekly, daily); Oct., 1841–1845; combined abolitionism, anti-nativism, and Democratic politics; edited by Joseph Schoberlechner, with assistance from Freiherr Richard von Meysenburg.

Der Hochwächter (weekly); published in Cincinnati July 3, 1845–1846, in Louisville 1846–1847 (with a brief lapse), then Cincinnati again, 1848–1849; an anti-Catholic, rationalist paper edited by Georg Walker, the *Hachwächter* was revived by Friedrich Hassaurek, the most famous of Cincinnati's Forty-Eighters.

Licht Freund (semi-monthly); March 31, 1840–April 16, 1842; Universalist; edited by Edward Mühl; published by Stephan Molitor; it was moved to Hermann, Mo., where it became the conventional weekly *Hermann Wochenblatt.*

Der Locofoco (semi-weekly); May, 1845–June, 1845; Democratic; edited by Dr. Wilhelm Albers, with assistance from Georg Walker.

Ohio Adler and Volksbühne, see *Volksbühne.*

Ohio Chronik (weekly); 1826.

Der Ohio Volksfreund (semi-weekly, weekly); brought from Dayton, April 7, 1841, defunct within the year; replaced the *Deutsche im Westen.*

Der Protestant; brought to Cincinnati from Miamisburg in 1838, failed quickly; a rationalist paper edited by Georg Walker.

Unabhaengige Presse (tri-weekly); 1840?; Democratic; Benjamin Boffinger, editor and publisher.

Volksblatt (weekly, May 7, 1836–1919; daily, Nov. 1838–1919); Cincinnati's leading German Democratic paper, its personnel included Heinrich Rödter, Karl Rümelin, and Stephan Molitor.

Volksbote (weekly).

Die Volksbuhne (weekly); 1843: short-lived; Democratic; its personnel included Georg Walker, Friedrich Fieser, and Dr. Bene.

Volksfreund, see *Ohio Volksfreund.*

Wahrheitsfreund (weekly), July 20, 1837–; Catholic, edited by Johann Martin Henni, J. Max Ortel, Published by the St. Aloysius Society.

Der Weltbürger (weekly); Oct. 7, 1834–?: short-lived; "Whiggish"; Karl Hartmann, editor, succeeded by the *Deutsche Franklin.*

Westliche Merkur (weekly); 1836–1839; published by Burghalter & Hefley; Whig; succeeds the *Deutsche Franklin,* succeeded by *Der Deutsche im Westen.*

Westlich Staatszeitung (weekly); 1835?; Democratic, then Whig.

Religious Periodicals

The Baptist Advocate (weekly); 1835–1836?

Baptist Weekly Journal of the Mississippi Valley; 1831–1832; issued by Robbins and Johnston.

Both Sides of Religious Ceremonies: a Monthly Periodical, Devoted to the Investigation of Every Variety of Rituals in Religion (monthly); 1839–1840: a single volume of twelve issues, edited by Robert Smith, printed by Looker & Graham.

Catholic Telegraph (weekly);.1831–the present; Rev. Edward Purcell, brother of Bishop John Baptist Purcell, edited the *Telegraph* in the 1840s.

Children's Magazine (monthly); 1839; a Catholic juvenile periodical.

The Child's Newspaper (semi-monthly); Jan. 7–Sept. 16, 1834; edited by Thomas Brainerd and B. P. Aydelott under the aegis of the Cincinnati Sunday School Union.

Christian's Magazine (weekly); 1824; edited by Isaac G. Burnet; proposed as a non-sectarian religious paper, it is uncertain whether it was ever published.

Christian Politician (weekly); Oct. 26, 1844–1845; Baptist; edited by Dr. William H. Brisbane, displayed a tendency toward abolitionism and other reforms.

Christian Preacher (monthly); 1836–1841; Disciples of Christ; edited by D. S. Burnet, published by R. P. Brooks.

Christliche Apologete, see listing under German papers.

Christliche Hausfreund, see listing under German papers.

The Cross and Baptist Journal (weekly); 1836–1838?

Evangelische Kirchenfreund or *Kirchenbote*, see listing under German papers.

Evangelist (monthly); 1832–1840?; Disciples of Christ; Elder Walter Scott, editor, J. Hefley, publisher.

Der Hochwächter, see listing under German papers

Cincinnati Journal (weekly); Sept. 22, 1829–1839; Presbyterian; title varies: *Cincinnati Christian Journal, Cincinnati Christian Journal and Intelligencer, Cincinnati Journal, Cincinnati Journal and Western Luminary*; edited by Thomas Brainerd; continues the *Pandect*.

Licht Freund, see listing under German papers.

Luther's Plain Dealer (weekly); 1840: short-lived; non-denominational?

The Methodist Correspondent (weekly); 1831: short-lived; conducted by John H. Wood and M. M. Henkle.

Missionary Herald (monthly); an organ of the American Board of Commissioners for Foreign Missions, begun in 1804; a sereotyped re-issue was printed in Cincinnati, apparently from the 1820s through the 1840s.

Cincinnati Observer (weekly); June 4, 1840–Feb. 25, 1841; edited by Rev. J. Walker, published by Sam Alley; New School Presbyterian.

Cincinnati Pandect (weekly); 1828–Sept. 15, 1829; Presbyterian, later became the *Cincinnati Journal*.

Precursor (monthly); 1837–1842; New Jerusalem (Swedenborgian); edited by Milo G. Williams, M. M. Carll, published by Kendall and Henry.

The Presbyterian; 1836.

Der Protestant, see listing under German papers.

Rational Bible Reformer (monthly, irregular); 1825–1827; Universalist; title varies: *Lamp of Liberty*; edited and published by Abel Morgan Sargent.

Cincinnati Remembrancer (weekly?); 1822–1823; non-denominational; edited by William Arthur.

The Sentinel, and Star in the West, see *Star in the West*.

Standard (weekly); Baptist; 1831–1832?

The Standard; Presbyterian; 1836.

Star in the West (monthly); 1827–1880; originally published in Eaton, Ohio, the *Star* moved to Cincinnati and added *Sentinel* to the title in 1829; it was also published in Philomath, Indiana, a Universalist community, for some time in the 1830s, then under the primary editorship of Jonathon Kidwell; the chief editor and publisher in the 1840s was Rev. J. A. Gurley. In 1880, the *Sentinel* merged with the *New Covenant* to form the *Star and Covenant* of Chicago.

Wahrheitsfreund, see listing under German papers.

Watchman of the Valley (weekly); March 4, 1841–March 22, 1849; Presbyterian; edited by Epaphras Goodman, A. Benton; published by J. and R. P. Donough, Caleb Clark.

Wesleyan of the West (weekly); Sept. 21, 1844–?; Methodist.

Western Christian Advocate (weekly); 1834–1934; a publication of the Western Methodist Book Concern; edited by Revs. Charles Elliott and L.L. Hamline; published by Rev. J. F. Wright and Leroy Swormstedt.

Western Episcopal Observer (weekly); 1830?–1908?; founded in Gambier as the *Gambier Observer and Western Church Journal*, moved to Cincinnati in 1836? as the *Western Episcopal Observer*, published simultaneously in Louisville, Ky.; by 1858 it had become the *Western Episcopalian*, and, after several more changes, it merged into the *Churchman* in 1908.

The Western Midnight Cry (weekly); 1844–1845; Millerite; conducted by E. Jacobs and Joshua V. Himes.

The Western Religious Magazine (monthly?); 1826–1829?; Baptist; edited by George C. Sedwick; published by Morgan, Lodge, & Fisher; only the first issue was published in Cincinnati, then the magazine moved to Zanesville.

Youth's Friend (weekly); March 6, 1846–Nov., 1857; Universalist; a Sunday school paper, edited by Friend Abel (Abel Morgan Sargent?).

Youth's Magazine (semi-monthly); 1834–1838; published by Chester and Barnes; also publishers of the Presbyterian *Cincinnati Journal*.

Cincinnati Zion's Advocate and Wesleyan Register (weekly); Jan. 1, 1825–July 30, 1825; Methodist; published by John H. Wood.

Zion's Herald; Methodist.

Literary Periodicals

American Pioneer: A Monthly Periodical, Devoted to the Objects of the Logan Historical Society; 1841–1842; historical; published in Cincinnati and Chillicothe by John S. Williams.

The Casket (monthly); April 15, 1846–Oct. 7, 1846; conducted by J. H. Green ("the reformed gambler") and Emerson Bennet.

Cincinnati Chronicle and Literary Gazette (weekly); Dec. 30, 1826–April 11, 1835; title varies: *Saturday Evening Chronicle of General Literature, Morals, and the Arts*, 1828; edited most prominently by Benjamin Drake and Edward D. Mansfield; in 1835 the *Chronicle* went into publication as a general newspaper, and in 1839 went into daily publication. See listing under general and commercial newspapers.

Courier (of Liberty?) (weekly); conducted by R. C. Langdon; may have been a reform publication.

Cincinnatian: A Tri-Monthly Journal and Review; Dec, 1944– Jan. 10, 1845; edited by Paul Guthrick.

The College Mirror; 1839; edited and published by John C. Schooley.

The Family Magazine, or Monthly Abstract of General Knowledge; 1836–1841; a sereotype re-issue of J. S. Redfield's New York publication; there also seems to have been a local periodical of the same name, edited by James H. Perkins and published by Eli Taylor and J. H. and U. P. James in 1841.

Fliegende Blätter, see listing under German papers.

Great West (weekly); May 6, 1848–March 23, 1850; merged with the *Columbian* in 1850 to form the *Columbian and Great West*; conducted by E. Penrose Jones.

Hesperian, or Western Monthly Magazine (monthly); Jan. 1838–June, 1839; edited by William Davis Gallagher and Otway Curry; vols. I–II published in Columbus, vol. III in Cincinnati.

The Ladies' Museum and Western Repository of Belles-Lettres (weekly); 1830–Nov., 1831; conducted by Joel T. Case and John Whetstone; merged with the *Mirror* in 1831.

The Ladies' Repository and Gatherings of the West (monthly); 1841–1876; edited by Rev. L. L. Hamline; a publication of the Western Methodist Book Concern.

Cincinnati Literary Gazette (weekly); Jan., 1824–Aug., 1825; conducted by John P. Foote, A. N. Deming, and Moses Brooks; published by Looker & Reynolds.

Literary Parterre and Ladies' Magazine (weekly); April 12, 1828–?; superseded *Columbian Parthenon*.

The Magnet (and Cincinnati Literary Gazette) (weekly); March 12, 1827–until at least August.

Cincinnati Mirror and Ladies' Parterre Devoted to Polite Literature (semi-monthly, weekly); Oct. 1, 1831–1836; involved in the publication of the *Mirror* were William Davis Gallagher, John H. Wood, Thomas H. Shreve, and James H. Perkins; title varies: *Ibid.*, 1831–1833; *Cincinnati Mirror and Western Gazette*, 1833–1834; *Cincinnati Mirror and Chronicle Devoted to Literature and Science*, 1834–1835; *The Buckeye and Cincinnati Mirror*, 1835–1836; and finally the *Cincinnati Mirror and Western Gazette of Literature, Science, and the Arts.*

The Cincinnati Miscellany, or Antiquities of the West (monthly); Oct., 1844– April, 1846; historical and miscellaneous, edited and published by Charles Cist.

The Monthly Chronicle of Interesting and Useful Knowledge, Embracing Education, Internal Improvements, and the Arts, with Notices of General Literature and Passing Events; Dec., 1838–Nov., 1839; edited by Edward Deering Mansfield, published by Achilles Pugh.

Monthly Magazine and Review, Feb.–June, 1837; edited by William D. Gallagher.

The Olio (semi-monthly); 1821: short-lived; issued by Samuel S. Brooks and John H. Wood.

The (Columbian) Parthenon (weekly); 1826–Nov. 3. 1827; edited by A. F. Carpenter; continued by the *Literary Parterre and Ladies' Magazine.*

The Quarterly Journal and Review; Jan.–Oct., 1846; edited and published by Lucius A. Hine.

The Querist (monthly); 1844: short-lived; edited by Mrs. R. S. Nichols.

The Rose of the Valley: A Flower that Blooms to Enrich the Mind. Devoted to Literature and Instruction, Amusement, and Interesting Biography (monthly); Jan. 1839–July 1840.

Sackett's Model Parlor Paper (monthly?); begun Dec., 1848, lasted only a few months; conducted by Egbert Sackett and F. Colton.

The Semi-Colon (monthly); Jan. 1–Feb. 1, 1845; the organ of the Semi-Colon Club, published by Robinson and Jones.

Thistle, see listing under reform periodicals.

True Blue and Castigator, see listing under reform periodicals.

The Western Lady's Book (monthly); Aug.,1840: only issue published; edited by "an association of ladies and gentlemen," published by H. P. Brooks.

The Western Literary Journal and Monthly Review; June–Nov., 1836; edited by Willian Davis Gallagher, published by Smith & Day; merged with the *Western Monthly Magazine*.

The Western Literary Journal and Monthly Review; 1844–1845; lasted less than a year; edited by E. Z. C. Judson (Ned Buntline) and Lucius A. Hine; published by Robinson & Jones.

The Western Messenger, Devoted to Religion and Literature (monthly); June, 1835–April, 1841; its editors included Ephraim Peabody, James Freeman Clarke, James H. Perkins, William H. Channing, and J. B. Russell.

The Western Minerva (monthly?); 1827?; Francis and William D. Gallagher.

Western Mirror (semi-monthly); 1844; edited and published by George W. Copelen and George W. Phillips; apparently a student publication at Woodward College.

The Western Monthly Magazine (and Literary Journal) (monthly); Jan., 1833–Feb., 1837; continues the *Illinois Monthly Magazine*; edited by James Hall.

Western People's Magazine (semi-monthly); March 1, 1834–Jan. 3, 1835; H. S. Barnum.

The Western (Quarterly, Monthly) Review; May 1827–June 1830; edited by Timothy Flint.

The Western Rambler (monthly); Sept. 14, 1844: lasted a few months; conducted by Austin T. Earle and Benjamin S. Fry.

Western Shield and Literary Messenger (weekly); Feb. 2, 1833–July, 1834; Richard C. Langdon; continues the *Working Man's Shield*, listed under reform periodicals.

The Woodward Miscellany (semi-monthly); 1844?; J. R. Wright, publisher; a student magazine.

Young Ladies' Museum (monthly); 1841?; published by J. P. and R. P. Donough.

Youth's Monthly Visitor, 1844–1847; edited by Margaret L. Bailey, wife of Dr. Gamaliel Bailey of the *Philanthropist*; the *Visitor* moved to Washington, D. C., with the Baileys in 1847.

Agricultural, Scientific, and Professional Journals

Farmer and Mechanic (bi-monthly); Sept. 25, 1832–Jan. 13, 1836; edited by the Secretary of the Hamilton County Agricultural Society, D. C. Wallace; "devoted to the interests of artisan and agriculturist."

Sidereal Messenger (monthly); July, 1846–Oct., 1848; "devoted to astronomical science," edited by Ormsby MacKnight Mitchell.

Western Farmer and Gardener (monthly); Sept., 1839–July, 1845, suspended Oct., 1842–June, 1843; edited by E. J. Hooper, R. P. Brooks, J. A. and U. P. James; merged with the *Indiana Farmer and Gardener* in 1845 to form the *Western Farmer and Gardener* of Indianapolis.

Western Law Journal (monthly); 1843–1853; edited by Timothy Walker, C. D. Coffin.

Western Tiller (weekly, bi-monthly); Aug. 25, 1826–1830; originally a combined agricultural and general newspaper edited by James Gazlay, the *Tiller* was sold in 1828 to William J. Ferris, who conducted it primarily as an agricultural journal.

Educational Periodicals

The Academic Pioneer (and Guardian of Education) (monthly); July, 1831–Dec., 1832—only two numbers were actually issued; the journal was edited by Albert Picket, and was associated with the Western Literary Institute and College of Professional Teachers.

The Common School Advocate (monthly, bi-monthly); 1837–1841; edited by Edward D. Mansfield, Lyman Harding, and Alexander McGuffey; distributed free to professional educators, published by Truman and Smith.

The Common School Journal; 1838; lasted only two issues; circulated free to educators.

The Educational Disseminator (monthly); July, 1838–July, 1839; circulated free to educators by the publishing house of U. P. James; edited by Albert and John Picket.

The Reformer and High School Messenger, Devoted to the Elevation of the Colored People (monthly); 1845; edited by H. S. Gilmore and J. W. Walker; published by A. G. Sparhawk.

School Friend: Devoted to Educational Purposes; Oct. 1, 1846–March, 1851;, edited by Hazen White; in 1850 the *School Friend* merged with the *Ohio School Journal* to form the *School Friend and Ohio School Journal*.

Universal Educator (monthly); Jan., 1837: only one issue published; edited by Nathaniel Holley.

The Western Academician and Journal of Education and Science (monthly); March, 1837–Feb., 1838; edited by John W. Picket.

Western School Journal (monthly); March, 1847–1849; published by W. H. Moore & Co.; for a time was circulated free to educational professionals.

Medical Journals

Botanico-Medical Recorder (bi–monthly); 1827–1852?; the *Recorder* was established in Columbus, and moved to Cincinnati in 1837; it was edited and published by Alva Curtis from 1837 to 1852, and was devoted to Thomsonian medicine.

Eclectic Medical Journal (monthly); 1837–1937?; begun in Worthington as an organ of the medical department of Worthington College, the *Journal* moved to Cincinnati in 1842; until 1845 it was published under the title of the *Western Medical Reformer*; it was primarily edited by Thomas Vaughn Morrow and Dr. Joseph R. Buchanan, Jr.

Journal of the Phreno-Magnetic Society of Cincinnati (monthly); 1842: only one issue was published.

Ohio Medical Reformer (bi-monthly); Dec. 1–Dec. 15, 1832; eclectic medicine.

Ohio Medical Repository (semi-monthly, monthly); Spring, 1826–1828; conventional medicine; edited by Guy W. Wright, M. D., and James M. Mason, M. D.; in 1828, Daniel Drake obtained complete control of the *Repository* and changed its name to the *Western Journal of the Medical and Physical Sciences*. The *Repository* was briefly revived in 1835 by Mason.

Western Journal of Health (bi-monthly); June 1–Nov. 1, 1831; popular conventional medicine and hygiene.

The Western Journal of Health; 1844–1846; conventional; edited by C. M. Lawson, M. D.

Western Lancet (monthly); 1842–1916; conventional, C. M. Lawson, editor.

Western Medical Gazette (monthly); 1832–1835; conventional, edited by John Eberle, M. D.; merged with Drake's *Western Journal* in 1835.

Western Medical and Physical Journal (monthly, quarterly); title varies: *Western Journal of the Medical and Physical Sciences*; edited by Daniel Drake.

Western Medical Reformer, see *Eclectic Medical Journal*.

Western Quarterly Journal of Practical Medicine; June, 1837: only issue published; conventional; edited by John Eberle, M. D.

The Western Quarterly Reporter of Medical, Surgical, and Natural Science; 1822: short-lived; conventional; edited by John D. Godman, M.D., published by John P. Foote.

Reform and Non-Mainstream Journals

Daily American Citizen; 1845–June, 1846; nativist; the same office issued the *Weekly American Citizen,* Feb. 5–June, 1845.

Cincinnati American Republic (daily and weekly); nativist; edited by E. D. Campbell; 1845?

The Anti-Conspirator, or, Infidelity Unmasked; Being a Development of the Principles of Free Masonry; to Which is Added Strictures on Slavery, as Existing in the Church (weekly); June 5, 1831–April 22, 1832; edited by Dyer Burgess.

Anti-Papist (weekly); Oct. 3, 1846–1847; nativist, conducted by Epaphras Goodman and Homer Ward.

Artist and Artisan Daily; Oct. 7, 1845: short-lived; may have been a penny paper.

Democratic Standard and Whig of '76 (weekly); March 20–Nov. 10, 1846; abolitionist; published by the Ohio State Liberty Committee.

The Disfranchised American (weekly); 1845?; A. M. Sumner, editor; a black newspaper.

The Equitable Commerce Gazette (weekly); 1841?: no certain record of actual publication; anarchist; edited by Josiah Warren.

Facts for the People (monthly, sporadic); 1837–1845; edited by Gamaliel Bailey and associated with the Liberty Party.

Wecli Fonetic Advocat; 1848: short-lived.

Der Freisinnige, see listing under German papers.

The Herald of Truth (monthly); 1847; a general reform periodical with a marked tendency toward Swedenborgianism, edited by Lucius A. Hine.

The Herald of Equity (weekly); 1841; anarchist; edited by Josiah Warren.

Cincinnati Weekly Herald and Philanthropist; see *Philanthropist.*

March of Mind: Devoted to the Great Objects of Theology and Politics (bi-monthly); May 10–Sept, 13, 1828; continues Gazlay's *Western Tiller;* Owenite reform.

The Mechanic's Advocate (weekly); 1831–1832; edited by Isaiah Thomas, Jr., published by Hale & Dougherty.

Morning Star (and Western Temperance Journal) (weekly); Jan., 1841–1843? temperance, edited and published by Luther G. Bingham, and affiliated with the Washingtonian Temperance Society.

National Press and Cincinnati Weekly Herald, see *Philanthropist.*

Ohio Washingtonian Organ (and Sons of Temperance Record) (weekly); Aug. 9, 1845–1848?; edited and published by Walter Smith & Co.; affiliated with the Washingtonian Temperance Society.

Peaceful Revolutionist (weekly); Jan., 1833: did not survive the year; anarchist; edited and published by Josian Warren.

Philanthropist (weekly, daily); 1836–1848; title varies: *Cincinnati Weekly Herald and Philanthropist*, 1843–1846; *Cincinnati Weekly Herald*, 1846–1847; *National Press and Cincinnati Weekly Herald*, 1847–1848; *Cincinnati Weekly Herald*, 1848; *Cincinnati Weekly Globe*, 1848–?; abolitionist, established and initially edited by James G. Birney, followed by Dr. Gamaliel Bailey.

Cincinnati Post, and Anti-Abolitionist, see listing under penny papers.

Daily Sunbeam; Nov. 27, 1848–1849: short-lived; land reform; may have been a penny paper.

The Thistle (irregular); Nov. 18, Dec. 23, 1822: only two issues published; an anonymous gossip sheet, aimed at political figures and local conventional newspapers.

Tracts for the Million (monthly); Jan.–June, 1847; basically a series of pamphlets on various reform topics; issued by Lucius A. Hine.

True Blue and Castigator (weekly); Jan. 16–April, 1832; a gossip sheet, aimed at local citizens and institutions.

Western Fountain (weekly), 1846–1852; temperance.

Western Temperance Journal (monthly); Jan., 1838–1842? official organ of the Cincinnati Total Abstinence Society; merged with the *Morning Star* in 1842.

Working Man's Friend (weekly?); 1836; Thomas Henson, editor; devoted "to the interests and information of working classes of society."

Working Man's Shield (weekly); Aug. 8, 1832–Feb. 2, 1833; continued by the *Western Shield*.